The Remarkable

Education of

JOHN
QUINCY
ADAMS

The Remarkable

Education of

JOHN QUINCY ADAMS

Phyllis Lee Levin

palgrave
macmillan

THE REMARKABLE EDUCATION OF JOHN QUINCY ADAMS
Copyright © Phyllis Lee Levin, 2015.
All rights reserved.

First published in 2015 by PALGRAVE MACMILLAN ® TRADE
in the United States—a division of St. Martin's Press LLC, 175 Fifth
Avenue, New York, NY 10010.

Palgrave® and Macmillan® are registered trademarks in the United
States, the United Kingdom, Europe and other countries.

ISBN 978-1-137-27962-0

Library of Congress Cataloging-in-Publication Data is available from
the Library of Congress.

Design by Letra Libre, Inc.

First edition: January 2015

10 9 8 7 6 5 4 3 2 1

Printed in the United States of America.

As always,

for Bill,

and for our family

The early age at which you went abroad gave you not an opportunity of becoming acquainted with your own country. Yet the revolution, in which we were engaged, held it up in so striking and important a light, that you could not avoid being in some measure irradiated with the view. The characters with which you were connected, and the conversation you continually heard, must have impressed your mind with a sense of the laws, the liberties, and the glorious privileges, which distinguish the free, sovereign, independent States of America.

—Abigail Adams to John Quincy Adams,
December 26, 1783

CONTENTS

PART II

PART III

PART IV

INTRODUCTION

When President George Washington named John Quincy Adams "Minister Resident for the United States of America with their High Mightinesses the States General of the United Netherlands" on May 30, 1794, the nominee, both surprised and humbled, was uneasy about his credentials. "Neither my years, my experience, my reputation, nor my talents," he fretted to his father, "could entitle me to an office of so much responsibility."[1]

Actually, George Washington's choice was inspired. At 27, John Quincy was a world traveler and remarkable linguist—he spoke not only French and Dutch, but at one time or another studied Italian, Spanish, German and Russian, apart from reading and translating Latin and Greek. He was a graduate of Harvard College with Phi Beta Kappa honors, a lawyer and noted essayist of vibrant controversy in significant political circles. He knew from early youth onward Europe's and America's renowned emissaries, including Benjamin Franklin and the Marquis de Lafayette, and he counted Thomas Jefferson a dear family friend.[2]

He even looked the part. The American artist John Singleton Copley paints him in flowing cravat, his dark hair grazing the collar of his fine, caped coat, as the quintessential young Gainsborough nobleman, though in truth he was instinctively and habitually careless about his dress. At five foot seven inches and inconveniently inclined to be stout, he resembled his mother, Abigail Adams. His face had her clarity, her lean, defined nose, her wide, lofty brow, fair complexion, resolute chin and "black eyes of such keenness" that they pierced the beholder.[3]

In personality, character and interests, however, John Quincy was astonishingly like his father. Not only a born-and-bred patriot of spotless integrity, brilliant, fiercely independent, intensely introspective, he was, on occasion, impatiently undiplomatic and pitiably sensitive. As was his father's way, he questioned his own yearning ambition, agonized over his passionate nature, was suspicious of praise but wounded by criticism and suffered a near-fatal flair for denigrating his own accomplishments. His family never doubted his talent. But "the warmth of his temper" was a concern. His beloved sister Nabby told him he was too impulsive, too positive, a little inclined to judge rather prematurely and "to condemn without sufficiently considering the for and against."[4]

With the announcement of his new post, his uncle Richard Cranch predicted his nephew would be "the greatest American Traveller of his Age." He did not exaggerate. John Quincy first sailed for Europe, not quite 11, in 1778, as companion and eventually secretary to his father, one of the three United States Commissioners in Paris. After a brief return home to Braintree, Massachusetts, he and his father headed back to Paris when Congress named John Adams to negotiate peace and commercial treaties with Great Britain. His father's next assignment, to negotiate a loan for the United States from the Netherlands, took John Quincy to Amsterdam and Leyden. In three years he had attended two schools in Passy, where he became fluent in French, and studied in both Amsterdam and Leyden.[5]

Cultivated in the arts far beyond his years, he was a perceptive and confident critic of painting, sculpture, architecture, music and theater. At age 11, he wrote from Europe to his sister Nabby that Italian comedy was "sprightly and agreeable enough" but "the language the wit the passions the sentiments the oratory the poetry the manners and morals are at the French Comedy."[6]

In July 1781, 14-year-old John Quincy left Amsterdam for Russia to be secretary and interpreter for Francis Dana, America's newly appointed minister, who knew little if any French, the language of the Russian court. While still a teenager, he crossed and recrossed the Atlantic Ocean and the English Channel, journeyed thousands of miles in raging storm and blinding snow, by leaky ship, slippery ferry, perilous iceboat, mule, carriage and horseback from Spain to France, Holland, Belgium, Denmark, Sweden, the German states, Russia and Great Britain.

Later, with his father as the nation's first vice president, John Quincy's abilities became well known to President Washington. The two families thrived on "terms of much Friendship," visiting each other often in New York, the nation's first capital, where the Adamses lived near MacDougal Street. Washington undoubtedly appreciated the young man's published essays eloquently reinforcing the president's position of neutrality in the war between France and England.[7]

John Quincy's commission as minister to the Netherlands followed in 1794. Washington's confidence in John Quincy only deepened as he tracked his protégé's career. It was the president's "decided opinion, that Mr. Adams is the most valuable public character we have abroad, and that he will prove himself to be the ablest of all our diplomatic corps."[8]

As the first president of the United States understood the genius of John Quincy Adams, so did the thirty-fifth. John F. Kennedy wrote of his fellow Bostonian that he "held more important offices and participated in more important events than anyone in the history of our nation." During his long lifetime—encompassing the American Revolution, the War of 1812, the early and late Napoleonic Age—John Quincy would serve as minister to The Hague, Prussia, Russia and England, and would head the American mission at Ghent to negotiate peace with England and conclude the War of 1812. In the period between his early diplomatic service and ministerial appointments, he was a professor at Harvard, a Massachusetts state senator, and then a United States senator. He turned down an offer to serve on the Supreme Court and made his final journey home upon his appointment as secretary of state for both terms of President James Monroe. Chosen to be the sixth president of the United States in 1824 by the House of Representatives after a contested election, he served only one term. He returned to elected office as a member of the House from November 1831 until his death in February 1848. During his late political career, he became the stirring defender of the slaves of the notorious Amistad rebellion.[9]

Despite this superlative career, John Quincy, like his father, was haunted by a sense of failure. Having never met the impossibly Olympian standards of his puritan conscience and his demanding intellect, he would conclude at the age of 70 that his "whole life has been a succession of disappointments. I can scarcely recollect a single instance of success in anything that I ever undertook."[10]

Kennedy wrote in *Profiles in Courage* that "the lifetime which was so bitterly deprecated by its own principal has never been paralleled in American history." With sympathy, Kennedy recognized "the fascination and nobility" of this man, "unbending, narrow and intractable," who judged himself more severely than his enemies did and possessed an integrity unsurpassed by major political figures. He "gave meaning, consistency and character to the early days of the American Republic."[11]

Kennedy applauded the man who loved liberty and the law for standing up for his convictions as a minority of one, for his nonpartisan approach, and for his tireless energies in the struggle against slavery. Had John Quincy served in the contemporary Senate, Kennedy said, "we would have admired his courage and determination," but Kennedy was not so certain "that we would like him as a person; as it is apparent that many of his colleagues, on both sides of the aisle, did not."[12]

This, in essence, is the dilemma of John Quincy's life. Respecting him as a statesman, as "Old Man Eloquent" was one thing. Liking him was another. John Quincy's self-portrait was no more forgiving. He saw the awesome, towering figure he had become as a cold, austere and forbidding character. Sadly, in age and fame, his memory of the small boy's pressured wartime life and of the dedicated, brave and adventurous diplomat with tender concern for family, friends and country was forgotten or, worse, made to seem irrelevant.

In the judgment of his son, Charles Francis, John Quincy, with rare exception, never had a private life after his entry into public service. A patriot by ancestry, birth, duty (that word again and again) and parental expectation, his destiny was foreordained, almost as tangible as a pewter spoon in his mother Abigail's cupboard. At times insufferably lonely, his faraway travels made him feel like "a limb lopt off" from home, family and friends. As he tired of his "wandering, strolling kind of life," he grew acutely sensitive to any and every thought of separation. Life was painfully peripatetic. He wasn't with people long enough to trust them, and if he did make friends, they came and went probably never to be seen again. Those few he called friends, he fervently wished he might "Grapple to my heart with hooks of steel."[13]

This is what drew me to John Quincy. I met him while writing about the lives of his mother and his father, came to admire him as a classics scholar, scientist, linguist, diplomat, bibliophile, but also as a son, husband and father, and as a great, flawed and vulnerable humanitarian. More recently, as a result of a close reading of his diary in his own hand, I have also discovered the extraordinary historian, reporter and memoirist—the panorama his pages unfold of Napoleonic and post-Napoleonic Europe are "probably unsurpassed." John Quincy considered "as the business and duty of my life to write" and kept a journal of his thoughts because on occasion he wished to record the "fleeting reflection which originates in some transient occurrence."[14]

He wrote about what he knew, what he saw and how he felt over a period of 65 years. As a result, "No other American diarist," the historian Allan Nevins has said, "touched life at quite so many points, over quite so long a period, as John Quincy Adams." To his contemporaries "he was a frigid and icy New Englander; but we who have seen his diary can perceive that at heart he was really of a hot and passionate nature, volcanic in his hates, intense in his loves . . . the emotionalism of the diary is indeed one of its most appealing qualities."[15]

"We who have seen his diary"—that's the hitch. Unless you have read the unexpurgated version you cannot possibly know, understand or appreciate John Quincy Adams in full. One is grateful to the Massachusetts Historical Society for the first two volumes of the diary, published in the original, which cover his life up to his twenty-first year. More recently, the Society has made it possible to read the diary in John Quincy's own hand online, a fascinating and demanding experience. By far the most influential source prior to this time had been the 15,000-page, 51-volume diary compressed by his son Charles Francis into the 12 volumes of *Memoirs* published between 1874 and 1877. Edited under stringent self-imposed guidelines, it was clear to Charles Francis—given the superabundance of materials, including public and private correspondence, that he feared would equal the hundred volumes of Voltaire—that abridgment was indispensable. It became necessary "to fix upon a rule of selection" with the diary, "to eliminate the details of common life and events of no interest to the public. . . ." Faithful to this rule, Charles Francis trusted he had supplied pretty much "all in these volumes which the most curious reader would be desirous to know."[16]

In fact, he managed just the reverse—draining the works of intimate feelings, tender, conflicted or painfully candid. In the 12 volumes, John Quincy's wife, Louisa Catherine, is barely present, mentioned only 22 times in 6,576 pages. Charles Francis skips almost all references to births and illnesses, to some of the most challenging and moving moments of John Quincy's life. John Quincy's response, for instance, to the death of his infant daughter leaves the reader of his unabridged diary feeling like an apologetic intruder. One fears for him and for Louisa Catherine, both so wounded.

Nor, unfortunately, do the seven volumes of John Quincy's correspondence, titled *Writings,* bring you any closer. Worthington Chauncey Ford, editor of the Massachusetts Historical Society at the establishment of the family trust in 1905, set out to include in those volumes "what is of permanent historical value, and what is essential to a comprehension of the man in all the private and public relations. Nothing is suppressed which can contribute to this purpose and the text is printed as it was written." Accordingly, salutations and entire passages are eliminated, as in the case of John Quincy's detailed, stirring reports from Ghent, wherein the reader would never know he addressed the letters to his wife and expressed his concerns for her well-being. As a result, the John Quincy Adams of Ford's *Writings* "is a bloodless creature, a mere writing machine, and his wife, though a highly articulate woman, is . . . a wraith," commented Lyman H. Butterfield, editor in chief of *The Adams Papers*.[17]

Nor did John Quincy's wife, the tantalizing, tragic Louisa Catherine Johnson Adams, help to improve her husband's public image. She had a cosmopolitan upbringing—she spoke English with a British lilt and French as a native, having been born and reared in England and France. Her father was from Maryland, her mother was British, yet people spoke improbably of her Southern charm. Louisa was "charming, like a Romney portrait," with cherubic cheeks, pleading eyes and dark cascading curls, a woman of immeasurable private wounds and astonishing complexities, mercurial, depressive and gifted, and, at least to her admirers, her gracious manner and fondness for romantic poetry and novels were said to have "compensated for her husband's angular northeast manner." At 50 and again at 65, in punishing depression, pathetically aware of a "constitutional irritability" that was trying to her friends and painful to herself, she wrote two memoirs: first the incorrigibly inventive *Record of a Life* (1825) about her childhood and parents, and second, the embittered, corrosive *Adventures of a Nobody* (1840) in which she aired her disdain for mere worldly honors shared with her husband—honors, she said, purchased at a most bitter expense of duty to her children and personal suffering to herself. Most tragically, these memoirs have won her a host of sympathetic followers at the terrible cost of inscribing her husband's harsh reputation.[18]

One is hard pressed to think of a more unsuitable partnership, this marriage between the romantic and the puritan, yet Louisa Catherine was a faithful and beloved wife to John Quincy through the half century of their troubling marriage. Despite her complaints to the contrary, the surprise in reading John Quincy's unpublished diary and letters is the discovery of a sympathetic, attentive, concerned husband, at his wife's bedside in times of illness, at his desk, when far away, in the fullness of his confidence in her, confiding the stormy negotiations at Ghent that would mark the end of the War of 1812. Heartening as well is the warmth, constancy and intimacy of his affectionate relationship with his proud parents and with his loyal brothers and sister.

John Quincy expressed reservations about his papers. He had found his father's journals deeply interesting but altogether unfit for public inspection. As he predicted that his own journal would "be of the same character," he seemed to think it ought to be confined to an intimate readership, unsuspecting that he might one day attract a far larger audience. To the contrary, he might have been amazed and possibly amused to find that his name and writings live on, and with great flair in contemporary society. "JQA, Twitter Celebrity," the headline of the Massachusetts Historical Society's in-house publication proclaimed five years ago in recognition of the minimalist format of his line-a-day alternate diary.[19]

Brief or dense, as I discovered in reading the diary pages, the very humanity that John Quincy and his editors felt inappropriate to share with readers is precisely what enormously enhanced my appreciation of the statesman and his insights into his tumultuous times, meaningful these centuries later. The valiant traveler and devoted husband and father won my affection as well as my admiration. It is my hope that this memoir of the education of John Quincy Adams shows that the man at the center of so much that formed our young nation had much to say beyond the filtered public utterances of "Old Man Eloquent."

Part I

Chapter 1

"A LEGACY MORE VALUABLE THAN GOLD OR SILVER"

*O*n the lilac-scented evening of June 3, 1794, John Quincy Adams, then 27, left his Boston law office, at Franklin and the corner of Court Street, stopped at the post office in the Daily Mail building on State Street, and retrieved a letter from his father, John Adams, vice president of the United States, postmarked Philadelphia. He mounted his horse once more and wound his way over the hilly terrain, the narrow, crooked cobblestone paths and dirt lanes, mercifully quiet at day's end when the "Rattle Gabble" (his father's words) of sights and sounds had dispersed. He hadn't an inkling of the "very unexpected and indeed surprising" contents of the letter in his pocket.[1]

Home at last—he was boarding with a favorite cousin and namesake of his mother Abigail and her husband, Dr. Thomas Welsh at 39 Hanover Street—he could open the letter that would mark the beginning of his public career and the end of the only "absolute private life he ever had an opportunity to enjoy."[2]

John Quincy read and reread his father's news with some wonder, doubt and hope all at once. His father wrote that he had received an important visit that morning. The purpose of Secretary of State Edmund Randolph's call was to give John Adams a personal report of President George Washington's plan to nominate his son to go to The Hague as minister resident of the United States of America to their High Mightinesses the States General of the United Netherlands. "The President desired to know if I thought you would accept," his father continued. "I answered that I had no authority from you, but it was my opinion that you would accept, and that it would be my advice that you should."[3]

John Quincy's knowledge of Dutch, his education in France and his acquaintance with his father's old friends and colleagues in Europe would give him advantages beyond many others. It would, however, "require all your prudence and all your other virtues as well as all your talents." The tone turned conspiratorial as father warned son: "Be secret. Don't open your mouth to any human being on the subject except your mother. Go and see with how little wisdom this world is governed."[4]

Four days later, overflowing with pride, the eager father assured his son that the nomination, the result of the president's own observations and reflections, was as politic as it was unexpected, proof that "sound principles in morals and government are cherished by the executive of the United States." Further, his appointment ought to be reassuring to England and Holland—in his judgment, it was a pledge given by the American cabinet that they were not enemies to a rational form of government, and that they were not carried away with wild enthusiasm for every unmeaning (that is, Francophile) "cry of Liberty, Republicanism and Equality."[5]

More fatherly advice followed. John Adams had never kept secret from his son his ambitions for him. John Quincy must get to work. He must pursue research in international law and diplomacy; observe the opinions and actions of the belligerent powers; master all of his country's disputes with England, Spain and France; study the lines and boundaries of the United States; and watch the English ambassador and all the rest of the "Anglomaniacs." And this wasn't the whole of it. He must attend to his dress and person, as no man alive was more attentive to these things than the president himself. Taken altogether, he counseled his son: "let no little weakness escape you, and devote yourself to the service of your country."[6]

In his next letter, the proud father reported to John Quincy that the speed of his confirmation—the Senate passed it without a dissenting voice one day after his nomination on May 29—was proof of the president's esteem. As John Quincy studied this letter, he was torn, nagged with questions. He wished he had been consulted before his appointment was irrevocable and, in another way, he wished it had not been made at all. He needed to reassure himself, and to be reassured, that his father's prominence hadn't influenced his appointment.

Father and son met on June 10 at Quincy, where members of the Adams family had already lived for six generations—among pine-steeped woods and massive granite quarries, a mile or two from the intense blue of the salty sea, an 11-mile, two-hour walk from Boston—reconciled to New England's moody weather, its blazing summer sun, cold gray November evenings, January stark white blizzards, the thick, muddy thaws of winter. They met at the family home, variously called Peacefield (in honor of the Treaty of 1783) or Stony Field or Montezillo, or, most often, the Old House, purchased when John Adams served as United States minister plenipotentiary in London in 1787.[7]

There was an aura of affluence about its design—six rooms with graceful additions under Abigail's supervision—and a certain poignancy about its history, reflecting a clash of loyalties that necessitated its original owner's abandonment. Built as a summer house in 1781, poised in the midst of a gentle field, two stories with tall windows, a covered veranda and a Honduras mahogany-paneled interior, it was less the farmhouse of a patriot (according to John Adams) and more an aspiring plantation house originally built by Leonard Vassal, grandson of a sugar planter, nostalgic for his birthplace in Jamaica, the West Indies.

After the grandeur of Europe's palaces, churches, museums, embassies, and their private dwelling places—the gay and really beautiful chateau, the Hôtel de Rouault in Auteuil, just four miles from the heart of Paris, and the doughty brick mansion on the northeast corner of London's Grosvenor Square—John Quincy's father and mother had outgrown their former saltbox house in

Braintree on the coast road that ran from Boston to Plymouth. That "humble cottage" had been both John Adams's law office and the birthplace of his children, brothers John Quincy, Thomas and Charles, and sister Abigail, "Nabby." A prim, white, two-story house of brick and clay sheathed in wood, it had five small rooms with massive fireplaces and cavernous ovens that looked like "fortifications." An addition called a lean-to (sometimes spelled "leanter") included a fireplace and a tiny staircase that reached an airy bedroom whose floorboards, judging from their thick widths and great length, had been claimed from a vast and venerable tree.[8]

This Old House, which Abigail Adams knew and admired from visits in pre-Revolution days, was now better suited to their needs, taste and status. Abandoned by its loyalist owners, the Borlands, who reclaimed it only after the war, the house was bought by John Adams through an intermediary, Dr. Cotton Tufts.

Adams's instructions reveal a passion for his homeland that far exceeds mere real estate. Tufts was to purchase not only the Vassal-Borland place but "every other, that adjoins upon me. . . . My view is to lay fast hold of the Town of Braintree and embrace it, with both my arms and all my might. There to live, there to die—there to lay my bones—and there to plant one of my sons, in the profession of the law and the practice of agriculture like his father." However sincerely meant, his dreams for his son would burst beyond all such boundaries.[9]

On this ravishing day, as John Quincy opened the front gate, the sky was cerulean, a canopy of deep lavender wisteria crowned the front path and, looking left, he could see Abigail's great rectangular garden, her red and white roses ("York and Lancaster united"), framed with a wide border of amethyst-flowering myrtle. Somewhat appeased, he had been gratified that his nomination had been as unexpected to his father as to himself.

John Adams had again advised his son to accept the appointment. The Hague, he said, would provide a stepping-stone to higher and larger spheres, an opportunity to see Europe "at a most interesting period of its history."[10]

His father and mother never doubted that their first-born was destined for greatness. A historian years later confirmed their optimism: "Two streams of as good blood as flowed in the colony mingled in the veins of the infant born on the 11th of July, the summer of 1767, named for his esteemed grandfather John Quincy." Given his patriot parents, visionaries with revolutionary zeal, faith, perseverance, thriving intellect and ramrod integrity, John Quincy Adams had truly started life with an excellent chance of becoming famous. John Quincy recounted the family saga years later in response to the historian Skelton Jones's inquiries.[11]

John Quincy's autobiographical sketch begins in England in about 1609 when Edith Squire, of the little village Charlton Mackrell on the river Cary in Somersetshire, married Henry Adams, of the neighboring village of Barton St. David. He became a congregational dissenter from the Church of England during the reign of King Charles I. The couple sailed to America with seven sons and a daughter, all married; all but one remained in America and left descendants who multiplied, making their name one of those most frequently met with in almost every part of the commonwealth.[12]

Henry and his son Joseph settled in Mount Wollaston, which was incorporated in 1639 in Braintree, about ten miles from Boston, in the province of Massachusetts Bay. It was later called Quincy. Joseph Adams, great-great-grandfather of John Quincy, inherited his father's property and trade in Braintree, where he served as selectman, constable and surveyor of highways.

"They were originally farmers and tradesmen, and, until the controversies with Great Britain and the colonies arose, scarcely any of them had emerged from the obscurity in which those stations were held," one historian wrote. But two who then emerged stood out to John Quincy as mentors and leaders. One was his father; the other was his father's second cousin, Samuel Adams. Samuel Adams and John Adams were both descended from the first Henry by two different sons. There was a very early incident in the life of each one of them which seemed to indicate "that the *Spirit of Independence,* which is so strongly marked in the history of the

New England colonies from their first settlement, had been largely shared by the family from which they came, and instilled with all its efficacy in their own minds." (And especially his own, he might have added with due pride.)[13]

Their education at Harvard College had played a role in encouraging discussion on the relevant issues of the day. "Samuel Adams was many years older than my father," John Quincy continued. "He received his degree of Master of Arts at Harvard College in 1743. It was then the custom of that college, that the candidates for this degree should each of them propose a question related to any of the sciences, in which they had been instructed and, assuming the affirmative or negative side of the proposition, profess to be prepared to defend the principle contained in it at the public Commencement against all opponents. The question proposed by Samuel Adams was 'whether the people have a just right of resistance, when oppressed by their rulers,' and the side that he asserted was the affirmative."[14]

John Adams shared his cousin's opinions. Graduating from Harvard with a bachelor of arts degree in 1755 (the first in his immediate family to attend college), he had written in a letter to his classmate Nathan Webb of the "probability of the severance of the colonies from the mother-country, the causes from which that event would naturally proceed, and the policy by which Britain might prevent it, with the precision of prophecy. The date of this letter, the age at which it was written, and the standing in society of the writer at the time, are circumstances," John Quincy concluded, "which render it remarkable."[15]

When it came to describing his mother's origin, John Quincy made some distinction between the aspiring Adams yeomanry and the Quincy gentry. Abigail Adams too was of English extraction, but her family for three preceding generations had been natives of this country, all with diplomas from Harvard. Her father and grandfather were clergymen, and her mother was a daughter of John Quincy, who had been for many years a member of the provincial legislature, several times Speaker of the House, and afterward a member of the council.[16]

Young John Quincy's parents loved one another deeply, with respect and passion. His father was his mother's "dearest friend" and "beloved partner"; Abigail, who always "softened and warmed his heart," would be the "ballast" he sought on his long and heroic journey. They married on Thursday, October 25, 1764, the fourth anniversary of George III's accession to the throne of England. The couple's life fell swiftly into place, in the tidy white farmhouse built almost catercorner to John's birthplace along the road from Plymouth to Boston, framed by field and farmland. In the front room, remodeled into an office by replacing a side window with a door, John went about expanding his law practice.

Still, this was no ordinary lawyer's household. John Adams could barely conceal his growing disillusionment, immensely influenced by the irascible James Otis Jr., Harvard graduate and lawyer, zealous student and guardian of constitutional rights, and by his cousin Samuel Adams, ardent founder of the rousing Committees of Correspondence. He and Abigail were increasingly preoccupied with the evolving contest between America and England. The schism deepened as Great Britain's pragmatic secretary of the treasury, Charles Grenville, sought to bolster the finances of the ever-spreading empire with colonists' tax dollars.

There was great opposition to one revenue-raising law, the Sugar Act, but it was the consequences of another, the Stamp Act, that gave John much to brood about. The Stamp Act had been perpetrated the precise month he was chosen as one of the surveyors of highways in Braintree, as well as a member of the committee to lay out the North Commons in lots for sale that required the stamping of 15 classes of court documents. There were also college diplomas, real estate certificates, newspapers, even playing cards to be stamped. The resulting chaos brought his law office to a standstill. The future seemed bleak to the man who had achieved a "small degree of reputation" after years of groping in "dark obscurity," he wrote in his diary on December 18, 1765.[17]

John was a charter member of radical groups such as the Sons of Liberty, founded to oppose the Stamp Act, and of the Committees of Correspondence, the town meetings organized by Samuel

Adams to publicize colonists' rights and Parliament's infringement on them. As a political writer John signed himself "Clarendon" and "Misanthrop" and "Humphrey Ploughjogger." The couple's daughter Abigail, called Nabby, was born on July 14, 1765. Twelve days before the birth of John Quincy Adams and just 14 months after the repeal of the Stamp Act, Parliament passed a set of duties alerting the colonists to the presence of a new political villain. Charles Townshend, the loathsome chancellor of the exchequer, was also known as the Weathercock because of his fickle politics. Duties on glass, painter's oils and colors, tea and wine, known as the Townshend Acts, followed by the establishment of a board of customs and the legalization of general writs of assistance (nothing more than disguised search warrants), plunged the colonists into a new round of soul-searching.

A *poignant view* of Abigail on a Sunday evening in Weymouth, September 1767, during a two-day visit with her parents, foretold times ahead. Nabby is rocking the cradle of her two-month-old brother, John Quincy. She is singing, "Come papa come home to brother Johnny." The song reinforces Abigail's sense that Sunday seems a more lonesome day than any other day on which John Adams is absent. He has been traveling, in heat and cold, from town to town and court to court in order to support his family.[18]

One year later, on October 1, 1768, in obedience to His Majesty's commands, seemingly numberless redcoats disembarked at the Long Wharf and at Wheelwright's Wharf, which jutted out into Boston's vulnerable harbor, to march their way uphill to King Street and over to the grassy Common. By December, their artillery focused on the Massachusetts Town House (today's red brick Old State House). With additional troops at Castle William in Boston Harbor and British men-of-war moored just beyond the wharves, the patriots pronounced their beloved city "a perfect garrison."[19]

John Quincy's sister Susanna was born December 28, 1768, and baptized on New Year's Day at the Brattle Street Church. Abigail was pregnant again by early 1770, and the couple mourned the death on February 4 of 14-month-old Susanna, cherished as Suky.

Life was uncertain enough without having to bear personal tragedy, and the events of this time had a marked effect on the young John Quincy.

On February 22, the tense relationship between the British and the colonists blistered into tragedy. A group of boys demonstrated against a merchant who violated the nonimportation agreement not to carry British goods until taxes were rescinded. Next, they marched on the home of Ebenezer Richardson, ridiculing the customs employee, who retaliated by shooting one of the demonstrators, an 11-year-old boy. Reaction to the child's death triggered further bloodshed two weeks later and proved to be a prelude to what would be known as the Boston Massacre.

On March 5, 1770, the British captain Thomas Preston had been taunted by a barber's apprentice for not paying for the dressing of his hair, and a redcoat answered with a crushing blow that made the apprentice cry out. Suddenly five were dead, six more wounded. By morning, the involvement of the British was no longer a matter of rumor, and word of the massacre spread to other colonies. Asked to defend the Englishman, John Adams had accepted the case, risking his popularity in the belief that "Council ought to be the very last thing that an accused person should want in a free country."[20]

On June 6, 1770, John was elected as Boston's representative to the Massachusetts General Court (a colonial legislative body), a responsibility that would entail sacrifice of personal ambition and fortune. Abigail, aware of the danger to him, to her, to their family, was "very willing to share in all that was to come" and placed her trust in Providence.[21]

The *Boston Gazette* reported on November 29, 1773, the arrival of the ship *Dartmouth,* which had traveled eight weeks from London bearing, it was said, 114 chests of the East India Company's tea. Members of the Committees of Correspondence resolved to prevent their landing because of the monopoly and tax imposed on tea and to pitch all the chests overboard if necessary. Some hoped that the ship's owner would obtain permission from the customs collector to return his goods to Britain. Negotiations were unsuccessful, and on the evening of December 16, committee members hoisted to the deck the chests of tea and tossed them overboard. Bells tolled day and night. John Adams wrote to James Warren, "The die is cast. The people have passed the river and cut away the bridge. . . . The sublimity of it charms me."[22]

"The Project of the Tea" (later called the Boston Tea Party) engendered great punishments from England's Parliament. The Boston Port Bill closed the city's port to all commerce until the East India Company was repaid for the destruction of the tea. An army was on its way. British ships would soon blockade the town.

Other measures followed. Town meetings were abolished; another measure legalized the quartering of troops within the town of Boston. A third abolished the writ of habeas corpus. On June 17, 1774, John Adams and three other men were elected by the General Court to be delegates to America's first Continental Congress meeting in Philadelphia.

Horrified as Abigail was to think of the possibility of bloodshed, she told John "I long impatiently to have you upon the stage of action. The first of the month of September perhaps may be of as much importance to Great Britain as the Ides of March were to Caesar."[23]

On Wednesday, August 10, a hot, dry, dusty day in Braintree, Abigail and her four children—Nabby, now nine, Johnny, seven, Charles, four, Thomas (born 1772), two—waved good-bye to John.

Though his father tried to prepare all the family for the "storm that was coming on," the turmoil of the wartime years—memories of ominous drums and screeching fife, of enemy troops exercising directly in front of his family's house—remained vivid in John Quincy's old age, as did the anxiety of his parents and the death of a dear friend. His mother's tears on the day of the battle of Bunker Hill haunted him throughout his life. When he was near 60, John Quincy told cousin Eliza Quincy he remembered "living in the house where I was born, at the foot of Penn's Hill. The day after the battle of Lexington, men came and took the pewter spoons out of our kitchen to melt them up into bullets. On the day of the battle of Bunker Hill, I heard the cannon, and, with my mother, saw the smoke of Charlestown from Penn's Hill. . . . During the siege of Boston, I used to go up that hill every evening to see the shells thrown by the American and British forces; which, at night," he said, "had the brilliancy of fireworks."[24]

When he was president, he remembered one incident as distinctly as if it had been last week, though he was seven or eight at the time of the battle of Lexington. A company of militia had passed the night at his father's house and barn at the foot of Penn's Hill, and he had practiced using a musket as commanded by one of the militia. He also recalled that Sam Adams, his father's cousin, made sure that he saw for himself the presence of the British troops on the Boston Common. His boyhood home was a refuge for the weary, for minutemen, for soldiers needing lodging, breakfast, supper, drink, and for refugees from Boston who sought asylum for a day, a night, a week. An epidemic of dysentery took the lives of the servant Patty, his grandmother Smith, Uncle Elihu and Elihu's six-week-old infant daughter. It was impossible to sleep, what with rattling windows, bursting shells, incessant cannon roar. "I sometimes think I cannot stand it," his mother said.[25]

Two years before his death in 1848, the anxieties of his early years remained indelible, John Quincy recalled: "I saw with my eyes those fires, and heard Britannia's thunders in the Battle of Bunker's Hill, and witnessed the tears of my mother and mingled with them my own, at the fall of Warren a dear friend of my father. . . . He had been our family physician and surgeon, and had saved my fore finger from amputation under a very bad fracture. . . . Yet in that same spring and summer of 1775 [my mother] taught me to repeat daily after the Lord's prayer, before rising from bed, the Ode of Collins—'How sleep the brave who sink to rest / By all their country's wishes blest!'" With one error only ("watch" is substituted for "blest"), John Quincy, 71 years later, could repeat the ode's eight lines by memory. And though on principle his abhorrence of war was never shaken, he wrote the English Quaker Joseph Sturge in 1846, "But it is to war waged by tyrants and oppressors, against the rights of human nature and the liberties and rightful interests of my country, that my abhorrence is confined. *War* in defense of these . . . is, in my deliberate belief, a religious and sacred duty."[26]

For all his brave words, John Quincy commented with increasing disapproval on successive anniversary celebrations of the battle, which grew more elaborate during his lifetime. In 1786, he refused to participate with his fellow students and the faculty of Harvard College to commemorate the opening of the Charles River Bridge on the eleventh anniversary of the Battle of Bunker Hill. Instead, he spent the day in the solitude of his study and dined almost alone in the hall. He was deeply offended. At the dinner on the hill, served to 600 people, he supposed "there was as much wine drank now as there was blood spilt then." To crown the whole, the head of the table, he had heard, was placed on the very spot where Warren had fallen.[27]

Thankfully, not all early memories were steeped in melancholy. At an extraordinarily tense moment, personally and politically—the family was recovering from inoculation against smallpox, and General Washington was in critical combat with General Howe—John Quincy had cheered his parents by assuming a responsibility that took both stamina and courage for a nine-year-old. "Master John has become post rider from Boston to Braintree," Abigail announced to John in her postscript to her letter of September 29, 1776. A week later, John wrote an affectionate response, obviously intended to be shared with their son, "glad," he said, that "Master John has an office so useful to his Mamma and Papa, as that of post rider."[28]

Master John was obviously delighted in his role, riding his horse 11 miles each way from Braintree to Boston and back to collect mail or other intelligence. As post rider, he might well have delivered the fateful letter from his father in Philadelphia to his mother, with longed-for news of July 3, 1776: "Yesterday the greatest question was decided, which ever was debated in America, and a greater perhaps, never was or will be decided among men. A resolution was passed without one dissenting colony 'that these united colonies, are, and of right ought to be free and independent States, and as such, they have, and of right ought to have full power to make war, conclude peace, establish commerce, and to do all the other acts and things, which the states might rightfully do.'"[29]

Chapter 2

"A GREAT DEAL OF ROOM FOR ME TO GROW BETTER"

*T*houghtful and anxious about "our Johnny," not quite seven years of age, his father asked his equally concerned mother, "What school to send him to—what measures to take with him? He must go on learning his Latin, [go] to his grandfather or to you, or somewhere. And he must write." At ten, Johnny's education still presented a challenge. His father wished him to turn his thoughts early to studies that would afford him "the most solid instruction and improvement for the part which may be allotted you to act on the stage of life."[1]

John Adams's obsessive admiration of learning had its origins with his grandmother, Hannah Bass, whose love of literature and documented advice to her children prompted his father, Deacon John, to give his eldest son "a liberal education." As a result of his grandmother's ancestral bequest, John Adams embraced education as the key to his children's grand and promising futures, their economic survival, intellectual pleasures, service to their country and general well-being.[2]

Working in York, Maine, July 1, 1774, John Adams was lonely and missed his children and their mother and found "nothing in any of my rambles to supply their place." He wondered if his time might be better spent at home, farming or, better still, "employed in schooling my children, in teaching them to write, cipher, Latin, French, English and Greek."[3]

Wishful thinking, of course, given his unsurpassed devotion to the new country he was in the process of founding. But if he could not take on the post of schoolmaster, as he had just prior to studying the law, having taught Latin in Worcester directly out of Harvard, he could appoint a surrogate in his stead, and who better than his wife. Enlisting Abigail as headmistress, he assured her: "The highest pinnacle of glory to which a woman can in modesty aspire," was to produce "an hero or a legislator, a great statesman or divine or some other great character that may do honor to the world."[4]

Luckily, Johnny's mother prized learning only a shade, if that much, less than morality. A worldly Puritan, reared in her father's ministry and in the so-called age of reason and enlightenment, one of the first to conceive and to champion the historic notion of women's rights, she was certain that women played as great a role as men in the "great theater" of life, given their responsibility for the care and early instruction of their children. And though she thought herself unequal to the task, she was "sensible" to the "important trust" committed to her.[5]

Having already charged Abigail with management of their farm, John also intended that she supervise the formidable curriculum he had conjured up in the best interests of their children's future, and their son John Quincy's eminent destiny in particular. Together, John and Abigail would found a virtual academy, rigorous like none other.

John Quincy's father had reason to be concerned about his children's education. There were few schools and those were shut during wartime. Instead, in his absence, his law clerks—Jonathan Mason and John Thaxter, who was also Abigail's cousin—recent graduates of Harvard, shared meals with the family and helped out as tutors. In retrospect, given John Quincy's monumental erudition despite his lack of formal schooling—his classroom studies barely exceeded three years before his entrance to Harvard—it wasn't surprising that he would be judged "eminently a self-made man in the broadest sense of the term." There was even some speculation that his irregular life advanced an apt scholar far more than systematic instruction would have done.[6]

Both parents played their parts: The words exalt and excel might have been emblazoned over the archway to their academy. John's ardent pedagogical ambitions are evoked in his letter of October 29, 1775. "The Saracens, the Knights of Malta, the army and navy in the service of the English republic, among many others, are instances to show, to what an exalted height valor or bravery or courage may be raised, by artificial means," that is, by education. "It should be [our] care," he instructed Abigail, "to elevate the minds of our children and exalt their courage to accelerate and animate their industry and activity; to excite in them an habitual contempt of meanness, abhorrence of injustice and inhumanity, and an ambition to excel in every capacity, faculty, and virtue. If we suffer their minds to grovel and creep in infancy, they will grovel all their lives."[7]

But there was more. "Their bodies," he continued, "must be hardened, as well as their souls exalted. Without strength and activity and vigor of body, the brightest mental excellencies will be eclipsed and obscured. Above all things my dear, let us inculcate these great virtues and bright excellencies upon our children."[8]

John Adams had rather specific plans for their three sons. Thomas Boylston Adams—named for his maternal great-grandfather, the surgeon and apothecary who emigrated from London in 1656—was to be a physician. "Would it not please you to study nature, in all her wonderful operations, and to relieve your fellow creatures under the severest pains, and distresses to which human nature is liable," he asked Tommy. The five-year-old must have talked about his aspirations to be a soldier because, if he agreed with his father, he would change his title from general to doctor. Either pursuit, his father advised, "requires the character of rugged and tough, to go through the hardships of riding and walking night and day to visit the sick, as well as to take care of any army."[9]

As for Charles, a thoughtful, sensitive child "always meditating upon some deep thing or other," what course of life did he intend to pursue once the war was over? "Something very good and useful,"

John guessed, "because you have a good capacity and a good disposition. Don't lose a moment," he added, "in improving these to the best advantage, which will be an inexpressible satisfaction to your Mamma, as well as to me."[10]

Nor had he forgotten 12-year-old Nabby in tendering advice to his children. But he was unable to forecast her career or advanced studies. He thought her prudent and steady beyond her years, complimented her "remarkable modesty, discretion, and reserve," traits by which she would be defined and constrained her entire lifetime, sadly inadequate, given the intellectually ambitious and vivid young woman who emerged from her correspondence with her brother Johnny.[11]

Because of her sex she required a different education, and her mother would be the best judge, her father believed, of its components. Though uncertain of the content of her education, he was not without expectations. Informed that she was studying *The Accidence,* subtitled the "First rudiments of English grammar, designed for the use of young ladies," he assured his daughter that learning English grammar would not hurt her, though she mustn't tell many people of it, for it was scarcely reputable for young ladies to understand Latin and Greek, although he hoped her Mamma would teach her French.[12]

Writing in the exhausting heat of Philadelphia in the summer of 1775, John called his "school" to order, suggesting to Abigail a curriculum of spectacular breadth: "I have seen the utility of geometry, geography, and the art of drawing so much of late, that I must intreat you, my dear, to teach the elements of those sciences to my little girl and boys. It is as pretty an amusement as dancing or skating, or fencing, after they have once acquired a taste for them." It was especially important to learn to draw plans of cities, provinces, kingdoms, and countries—especially of America. He "found great inconvenience for want of this art."[13]

As he had mentioned to Nabby, it was also essential that his children learn French. Increasingly a necessary accomplishment of an American gentleman and lady, he wished he knew French as well as Abigail did. He prayed she would not suffer their children to feel a pain of inferiority similar to his.

But it was Johnny who was the anointed star of the family. Johnny had genius. Almost as an afterthought, Charles was included in this elite category. It was up to their mother to safeguard these two. "Fix their attention upon great and glorious objects, root out every little thing, weed out every meanness, make them great and manly." As an authentic Puritan and patriot, he added, "Let them revere nothing but religion, morality and liberty." Concerning Johnny, Abigail was in total agreement. The future hero and statesman in his mother's judgment lacked only diligence and application, since "Nature has not been deficient."[14]

Looking ahead now, John Adams, as his son's advisor, was proving himself to be a pragmatist. Though he repeatedly tended to emphasize his favorite themes—that a taste for literature included the love of science and the fine arts—he also saw the advantages of a "turn for business." This would encompass industry and application as well as a faculty of "conversing with men, and managing affairs." As Johnny would not have income to enable him to pursue his learning alone, he must apply himself to business to procure the means of subsistence.[15]

There were further recommendations to the diplomat-in-training. As the future of America might require other wars as well as councils and negotiations, he wished Johnny to read up on past histories, and none would be more useful, he advised, than Thucydides's *The History of the Peloponnesian War.* He hoped John Quincy would master Greek, "the most perfect of all human languages." But in order to fully comprehend this author, he recommended an elegant translation by Thomas Hobbes readily available on a shelf in his own library. Along with daily exercises in Greek as well as Latin, he also advised John Quincy to read some pieces on algebra, which would be "as entertaining as an Arabian tale."[16]

There was, of course, their country's own immediate past to consider. And to further Johnny's grasp of the causes of the recent revolution of their government, no study would be more worthy than that of the characters who had figured on the stage of civil, political or military life. The most full and complete history that he had seen was the English translation of *The History of the Wars of Flanders,* written in Italian by the learned and famous Cardinal

Bentivoglio. John Quincy at his tender age might wonder at his father's recommendation of such dry things; however, if he kept this letter, he might thank his father at some future date.[17]

But Johnny had already been initiated into the challenges of history. With his father away, his mother had persuaded Johnny to read her a page or two every day of *The Ancient History* by the French historian Charles Rollin, who wrote in his seven-volume series of the Egyptians, Carthaginians, Persians and Greeks.

His father also urged him not to forget his mother tongue. "Read somewhat in English poets every day. You will find them elegant, entertaining and instructive companions through your whole life. To one who has a taste, the poets serve to fill up time which would otherwise pass in idleness, languor, or vice. You will never be alone, with a poet in your pocket," he told John Quincy a few years later.[18]

Organization of one's day was critical. Johnny was advised to measure out his hours for study, meals, amusement, exercise, sleep "and suffer nothing to divert you, at least from those devoted to study."[19]

Fortunately, Johnny was an ideal pupil. His letters are a self-portrait, as prescient as they are appealing. Earnest, sincere, conscientious, dutiful, he was almost heartbreaking in his need and will to please. At six, he was already a perfectionist, fretful about failed expectations and spendthrift hours. He had had it in his mind for a long time to write, he apologized to his cousin Elizabeth Cranch, but affairs of much less importance had prevented him from doing so. "[Too] much time to play," besides which, he confided, he had made "very little proficiency in reading." There was "a great deal of room for me to grow better."[20]

Three years later, the humble nine-year-old feared he would make poor work of writing a letter "but, Sir," he told his father, "Mamma says you will accept my endeavours, and that my duty to you may be expressed in poor writing as well as good."[21]

He told his father that he loved to receive letters much better than he loved to write them, because he wrote poorly. "My head is much too fickle, my thoughts are running after birds eggs, play and trifles, till I get vexed with my self. Mamma had a trouble-some task to keep me steady." As proof of his inadequacy, he is just starting the third of the 16 volumes of Tobias Smollett's *A Complete History of England,* though he had hoped to be midway by this time.[22]

In March 1777, John Quincy wrote his father a critique of Bamp-fylde Moore Carew, the "king of the beggars." Though this dissolute runaway son of a Devonshire clergyman had a great deal of money, he did not live either credibly or honestly, in the ten-year-old's opin-ion. "Surely it was better to work than to beg and better to beg than to lie, for having addicted himself to so many falsehoods . . . his char-acter is odious to all, and a disgrace to human nature." At the end, Abigail added "PS: This is a letter of Mr. John's own composition."[23]

His father acknowledged the letter with pleasure. It was a "pretty composition." That the father meant to be a sympathetic and encouraging teacher was never in doubt, but it was always clear that there was a moral component to the lofty intellectual bar he set for his son. More was wanted. In order to keep up with cur-rent events, did he read the newspapers? his father queried Abigail. Further, did he and his brothers and sister understand the great events they were living through? He hoped too that his children understood how many "losses, dangers, and inconveniences" had been borne on their behalf by their parents and inhabitants of Bos-ton in general. It was his hope that his children would follow this virtuous example, and that if in any future time their country's lib-erties were in danger, they would "suffer every human evil, rather than give them up."[24]

The pressure to teach his children to write, he claimed, stemmed from his work on the Declaration of Independence. "It is worth the while of a person, obliged to write as much as I do, to consider the varieties of style" he had written Abigail on July 7, 1776. He had elaborated on specific exercises:

> [Children] should be set to compose descriptions of scenes and ob-jects, and narrations of facts and events, declamations upon topics, and other exercises of various sorts.

> Set a child to form a description of a battle, a storm, a siege, a cloud, a mountain, a lake, a city, an harbour, a country seat, a meadow, a forest, or almost any thing, that may occur to your thoughts.
>
> Set him to compose a narration of all the little incidents and events of a day, a journey, a ride, or a walk. In this way, a taste will be formed, and a facility of writing acquired.[25]

Judging from John Quincy's earliest diary entries, his mother taught his father's course on writing faithfully and with momentous success, and their academy fulfilled the Adams family's nearly genetic passion for education.

John Adams returned to Braintree on November 27, 1777. His homecoming was a prelude to still another wrenching departure, just two months later. The distance of 300 miles between his father and his family was about to stretch to 3,000. By a vote of the Continental Congress, John Adams was appointed joint commissioner with Arthur Lee and Benjamin Franklin as plenipotentiaries to the king of France. "After much agitation of mind and a thousand reveries" over separation from his wife and children, over his finances, his career as a lawyer, even "his want of qualifications," John gave his formal acceptance on December 23.[26]

Initially, Abigail thought the whole family might go but soon was convinced it was "too hazardous and imprudent." She would have willingly run all hazards to accompany her husband, but he would not consent. The dangers from enemies were so great and their treatment of prisoners so inhumane and brutal that, if she were captured, her sufferings would enhance his misery. These arguments prevailed. It was with great difficulty that they decided to have John Quincy keep his father company. Abigail had already expressed concern for their three sons, "practically fatherless" at a time when they were most in need of his example and precepts. She consoled herself now with the hope that at least one son would reap advantages under the careful eye of a tender parent that were not in her power to bestow.[27]

Abigail also suffered a thousand fears and anxieties for the snares and temptations that might "stain his morals" and hoped for his escape from them. On the other hand, she rationalized, quite magnanimously, to exclude him from temptation would be to exclude him from the world in which he was to live. She concluded the only method that could be pursued with advantage—to spare her Johnny from ruinous temptations—"is to fix the padlock upon the mind."[28]

The use and sense of the word padlock, steely and repressive, suggests Abigail's trauma at parting with her not-yet-11-year-old son. In their stark clarity, her instructions to John Quincy might have been chiseled in granite: "Improve your understanding for acquiring useful knowledge and virtue, such as will render you an ornament to society, an honor to your country, and a blessing to your parents. Great learning and superior abilities, should you ever possess them, will be of little value and small estimation, unless virtue, honor, truth and integrity are added to them. Adhere to those religious sentiments and principals which were early instilled into your mind and remember that you are accountable to your Maker for all your words and actions."[29]

That she meant to enforce these precepts on her own terms there was no doubt: "Dear as you are to me, I had much rather you should have found your grave in the ocean you have crossed, or any untimely death crop you in your infant years, rather than see you an immoral profligate or a graceless child."[30]

Had she been asked, at that time, to justify her harsh sentiments, she might have defended herself. She was, after all, asking no more of others than she and John were willing to sacrifice and endure in their roles as founders of their new country. In truth, letting go of Johnny was an enormous personal deprivation. It was bad enough to be without her "better half"; to part with her son was like having a limb "lopt off to heighten the anguish" she wrote to the boy's tutor John Thaxter. "A mother's heart will feel a thousand fears and anxieties upon the occasion."[31]

"The world might talk of honor, and the ignorant multitude of profit," but what really influenced her decision, she explained to Thaxter, was the belief that the abilities and integrity of her husband might be "more extensively useful in this department at this particular time, than in any other." She would therefore "resign my own personal felicity and look for my satisfaction in the consciousness of having discharged my duty to the public." And at the last, she told her friend Hannah Storer, "I asked not my heart what it could, but what it ought to do."[32]

Chapter 3

"SOME COMPENSATION FOR MY NOT BEING WITH MY FRIENDS AT BRAINTREE"

About his youthful travels in Europe from 1778 to 1785, John Quincy said there was "a character of romantic wildness. . . . Life was new, everything was surprising, everything carried with it a deep interest." He admitted in later years he was surprised he had escaped the fascination of a permanent life abroad. He hadn't, of course, though perhaps he never realized it.[1]

On Friday, February 13, 1778, John Quincy—age 10 years, 7 months—and his father had dinner with Uncle Norton Quincy at his farm on Quincy Bay. Afterward, father and son, the servant and former soldier and seaman Joseph Stephens, a midshipman named Griffin, ship's physician Dr. Benjamin Brown, and Captain Samuel Tucker, commander of the 24-gun Continental frigate *Boston,* walked across Hough's Neck to a barge that would take them to the ship anchored at Nantasket Roads in Marblehead Bay.

The wind was high and the sea was very rough at five o'clock that afternoon, but hunched in their hay-steeped barge and fortified by heavy coats kindly supplied by Captain Tucker, they negotiated the turbulent water to board the ship. Baggage sent ahead included two fat sheep, two hogs, a barrel of apples, five bushels of corn, chocolates, rum, sugar, eggs, a cot with a double mattress, a bolster, sheets and blankets, two quires of paper, quills, ink and Louis Chambaud's French grammar *Nouveau Dictionnaire Français-Anglais.* Of the 172 people aboard ship, including a young college graduate, William Vernon Jr., and the 11-or-12-year-old Jesse Deane of Weathersfield, Connecticut, John Adams was most complimentary about his introduction to Nicholas Noel, a well-bred surgeon and a major in the French army. Accordingly, only four days out, on February 17, Chambaud's grammar in hand, he asked Noel to teach John Quincy the precise critical pronunciation of all French words, syllables and letters.

The horror of the *Boston*'s journey would have been hard to foresee. Initially, the snow was so thick that the captain thought they could not go to sea. By the fourth evening, the constant rolling and rocking of the ship made them all sick—including half the sailors. But mal de mer was a temporary assault. More revolting was the smoke and smell of sea coal, of stagnant, putrid water where the sailors berthed. And then there was the cruel weather, constantly encroaching enemy and, most tragically, death and burial at sea.

Lightning split the main mast and struck one of the seamen, who lived three days and died raving mad. A storm made havoc of all parts of the ship—such a wreck of chests, casks, bottles, tables and chairs that everyone and everything was soaked. One turbulent night father and son managed to stay in bed only by holding on with both hands, bracing themselves against the boards, planks and timbers with both feet.

On Tuesday, March 10, they gave chase, were fired on and won the prize of the English ship *Martha,* loaded with valuable cargo. But their next encounter, with a French brig from Marseilles heading to Nantes, "cost us very dear," John Adams wrote: the tragic death of the *Boston*'s admired First Lieutenant William Barron. In his attempt to fire a gun as a signal to the brig, the cannon burst and shattered his right leg to pieces. Amputation below the knee followed; John Adams held Barron in his arms while the doctor applied the tourniquet. He died on March 25 and was committed to the waters in the presence of all the ship's crew after a burial service.[2]

In those moments when John regretted uprooting John Quincy, he cheered himself somewhat by knowing that his little son was "very proud of his knowledge of all the sails," and that the captain had taught him how to read the mariner's compass. More than anything, John was proud. "Mr. Johnny's behavior gave me a satisfaction, that I cannot express—fully sensible of our danger, he was constantly endeavoring to bear it with a manly patience, very attentive to me and his thoughts constantly running in a serious strain."[3]

Over six weeks from home, on a cloudy Monday, March 30, the harrowing voyage came to an end. John Adams and John Quincy left the frigate in Bordeaux on April 1 and found lodgings in the company of Dr. Noel and young Jesse Deane, who hoped to join his father, the controversial diplomat Silas Deane. Father and son toured the town and saw a performance of *Les deux Avares* at the Comédie, but it was the opera they found most intriguing, "Having never seen any thing of the kind before."[4]

Thirteen pieces of cannon honored John Adams's departure from Bordeaux. The party of five left for Paris on April 4 traveling by chaise, quite riveted by the old houses and narrow streets, the fields of grain and flocks of sheep, the castles, parks, gardens, vineyards, churches and convents along the way. Everything was beautiful, especially the meadows and river banks along the Loire River, yet every place was swarming with beggars. Arriving in Paris at nine o'clock Wednesday evening, April 8, they found rooms at the Hôtel de Valois on Rue de Richelieu. Early Thursday morning, amid the street cries, bells, and clattering carriages, they traveled by coach to join Benjamin Franklin.[5]

Franklin and his entourage lived rent-free on the spacious grounds of Hôtel de Valentinois, on the heights of Passy overlooking the Seine, close to the Bois de Boulogne, owing to the generosity of its owner, the entrepreneur and enthusiastic Americanist Jacques Donatien Le Ray de Chaumont. Franklin showed the Adamses to the apartments and furniture left by Silas Deane, which were more elegant than John desired but, he admitted, as comfortable and convenient as he could wish. Noting the motto over the door *"Si sta bene, non se move,"* which he translated as, "If you stand well, do not move; or stand still," he thought it "a good rule" for his own conduct, though one he would shortly forget to follow.[6]

By April 19 John Adams was able to reassure Abigail: "My Johnny is well fixed in a school and his behavior does honor to his Mamma." John Quincy was, indeed, quite cheerfully boarding at Monsieur Le Coeur's respected private school nearby in Passy. His American schoolmates included his shipboard friend Jesse Deane; Benjamin Franklin's grandson and namesake, 12-year-old "Benny" Bache (who at a future date, as editor of the *Aurora,* would be an implacable enemy of the Adams family); and Charles B. Cochran from Charlestown, South Carolina.[7]

John Quincy's letters were also reassuring. "I am now at a (good) school which I like very well," he told his "kind and tender . . . Mamma. . . . I will now give you an account how we live here . . . at 6 o'clock in the morning we get up and go in to school and stay till half after 8 when we breakfast and play till 9 when we go in & stay till 12 when we dine after dinner we play till 2 when we go in and stay till half after 4 when we come out and play till five when we go in and stay till half after 7 when we sup after supper we go up and stay about an hour and go to bed."[8]

In remarkably adult fashion, he added that he supposed "before this reaches you you will hear of the treaty concluded between France and America which I believe will rouse the hearts of the Americans exceedingly and also of the desire of the English to make peace with us and of the commissioners dispatched from England for that purpose."[9]

On May 25, he wrote his first letter in French to his mother, hoping she would receive it with the same pleasure as if it were better written. The letter ended with a flourish. *"Je suis Ma chere Maman votre obeisant fils,* Jean Quincy Adams," his signature accurately reflecting the way the French pronounced his first name.[10]

But for all his brilliance and bravado, John Quincy was lonesome for home. Dutifully he reported on his special adventures.

On a glorious May day, he had dined with Doctor Franklin and his grandson and secretary William Temple Franklin at a "Place called Montmartre. . . . from which place there is a most beautiful prospect of the city," he wrote his cousin William Cranch. In his first mention of keeping a journal or a diary, these excursions "afford me some pleasure & give me some consolation for my not being with my friends at Braintree. . . ."[11]

In a similar, wistful vein, though separated from his brother Tommy, there was yet an important consolation left: "we are not deprived of the liberty of writing to one another which we must do as often as we can."[12]

His letter to his brother Charles was more overt. "I envy you the pleasure you enjoy in being at a place where you with pleasure look around you upon the rugged rocks & homely pastures & what is of more consequence you can converse with Mamma, sister & brother." These were pleasures not exceeded "by all the gaiety & riches of Europe." He was convinced from experience, that his brother Charles's opportunities for contributing to society were as good as his, having as he did the advice of "a most excellent mother and the use of a valuable library."[13]

By autumn John Quincy seemed more comfortable, even self-assured. Having found the French language so agreeable—his father reported home that he "reads and chatters French like a French boy"—he believed he could be helpful to his brothers.[14]

He thought it might be useful to sketch a plan for "easy & effectual acquisition of so elegant & useful accomplishment" of reading, speaking, and writing French. "There were great number of excellent books written in this language in all sorts of arts, sciences & literature and there were more conversation and correspondence in this language than in any other throughout Europe, for which reason it is worth while for children of your age & mine, to take a great deal of pains to acquire it."[15]

An astonishing bibliography of French textbooks followed: a detailed treatise on grammar, orthography, rhetoric, prosody, lexicography and the philosophy of the French language. He especially recommended Abbé Gabriel Girard, "a most elegant and beautiful performance the style, so beautiful and the researches into the principles of the language . . . so rational, ingenious and curious that the book is as entertaining as a romance though the subject is so dry."[16]

Luckily, "Jean" had not entirely lost his sense of humor. Recalling that his brothers Tommy and Charles were six and eight, "Methinks," he wrote, "I hear you ask 'why does my brother trouble himself to write and [tell] me to read this long role of title pages which has so much appearance of pedantry?['] I answer that you may have the means in your possession of furnishing yourself sometime or other of a complete collection of books for learning the French tongue."[17]

Though the son was reasonably content, his father was extremely troubled. The more he was exposed to Benjamin Franklin, the more frustrated he grew. In his diary, just 13 days after his arrival in Paris, John wrote of encountering a "rope of sand." Having been warned, he was instantly alert to the disputes between the other American commissioners, of the "bitter animosities" between Silas Deane, Arthur Lee, and Ben Franklin. Shortly, he would not only complain of Franklin's inefficiency—days passed before the statesman signed the documents prepared for him—but of the arbitrary manner in which he had hired his own grandson, William Temple, as his private secretary, without consulting a single soul.[18]

It was one thing for all of Europe to regard Franklin as "the most important character in American affairs." It was another, in John's opinion, to recognize that he was, in reality, a poor executive, extravagant and wasteful. As for his French: He was "wholly inattentive" to grammar and, worse, his accent was "very far from exact."[19]

On May 21, John took steps bluntly—myopically, in hindsight—that would account for a "revolution" in his life, and therefore in John Quincy's. He wrote from Passy to Samuel Adams on a subject that was heavy on his mind, and which he proceeded to detail with total abandon. The expense of the commissioners was vast. The system was all wrong. Instead of three, one public minister, at a single expenditure, would be quite sufficient for all the business.

The "revolution" took effect the following September 14 when Franklin was elected the sole minister to France. New instructions drawn up on October 26 that dissolved the Franklin-Lee-Adams commission would be delivered by the Marquis de Lafayette. John was already aware of the impending change, having heard hints of some new congressional regulations, of his being sent to the Viennese court, and was obviously dismayed at that prospect. To be kept abroad, to be idle or even to travel to countries in which he would not be formally received was the most painful situation he could imagine. He was at a loss as to whether he ought to head for home immediately or stay.

He had written Congress of his intention to return unless he received other orders. Though he assured Abigail that he would not take any step that would offend Congress or the people, he could not eat "pensions and sinecures," as "they would stick in my throat." Unfortunately, as Abigail had not heard from John since the past August—she had received only five letters in their 11-month separation—she was unaware of his predicament, however self-provoked. For the first time in their 14 years of marriage, her own confidence lagged.[20]

Overwhelmed by her solitary existence, she wrote of her need for reassurance. In response, on December 2, a melancholy John meant to soothe, but the next day, with the arrival of Abigail's letters of September 29 and October 10, his tone was far less conciliatory. Her letters, in fact, gave him more concern than he could express: "I will not say a fit of the spleen," but something close. He was embarrassed, impatient, even angered. "Let me alone, and have my own way," John begged. "For mercy sake don't exact of me that I should be a boy, till I am seventy years of age."[21]

Abigail's sharp tone must have provoked John to share his tribulations with their son, who now entered the fray, quite fearlessly for an 11-year-old. Johnny was pitifully protective of the father, who considered himself treated roughly by the world and especially by his wife, the person he counted on most. He wrote on February 20, 1779: "I last night had the honor of reading a letter from you to my Papa dated Jany. 4th. in which you complain much of my Papa's not writing. He cannot write but very little because he has so many other things to think of, but he can not let slip one opportunity without writing a few lines and when you receive them you complain as bad or worse than if he had not wrote at all and it really hurts him to receive such letters."[22]

Only if she were by his side would she have understood just what agonies John endured abroad, his crisis of self-confidence and even of purpose in the latter days of February 1779. Congress's choice of Franklin had left him in a deep depression. He felt ignored, unappreciated. He, John Adams, was simply a man nobody had ever heard of before, and therefore a man of no consequence. The French and English newspapers celebrated Samuel Adams as "*le fameux Adams*" and dismissed him as a "perfect cypher, a man who did not understand a word of French—awkward in his figure—awkward in his dress—no abilities—a perfect bigot—and fanatic."[23]

John's main regret at leaving France was that he had finally "happily succeeded, *très heureusement reussi* in learning French." He understood it perfectly and could talk as fast as he pleased. His son Johnny harbored no such misgivings about going home. He considered the "charming prospect" a "feast" to his mind. The joy of being reunited with his mother, sister and brothers would be greater than all the pain he had suffered when he left them. But possibly, he added bleakly, "this pleasing dream may be all disappointed by a battle at sea, by captivity or by shipwreck. All I can say is god's will be done."[24]

Father and son left Passy on Monday, March 8, and arrived in the thriving port of Nantes five days later. They expected to sail to America on the Continental frigate *Alliance* in April but, detained for political reasons, they would leave for home on another frigate, the *Sensible,* on June 17. Even under these unusual circumstances, John Quincy's studies continued—though with slightly altered focus. His father helped him to translate, among other papers, Cicero's first Philippic against Cataline, and Horace's *Carmen Saeculare.* He also asked the ship's engineer to teach his son the fundamentals of architecture.

Despite innumerable disappointments due to their postponed travels, father and son enjoyed the beauty of Nantes, on the banks of the Loire River, 35 miles from the Atlantic Ocean. Going everywhere together, "My son," John proudly told Abigail, is "treated with more attention than his father. . . ." Among the many Americans in Nantes, John Adams met a number of times with Joshua Johnson, whom he had seen briefly months before in Paris. Johnson lived with his British-born wife Catherine and their eight children in a rather grand complex of apartments in Baroque Nantais style, justly called Le Temple du Gout, where they entertained John and presumably John Quincy at tea and dinner.[25]

Johnson, age 39, had been born in Calvert County, Maryland, the brother of the esteemed Thomas Johnson with whom Adams had served in the Continental Congress. He had worked in London as a successful, affluent factor of an Annapolis shipping firm until the Revolution—with which he was in complete sympathy—had necessitated his departure. Intending to return home, en route he had crossed into France. But dreading the dangers of an ocean voyage to his family, he was able to find refuge and work in Nantes, to undertake various commissions for both Congress and the state of Maryland.

During John's stay and their several visits, the two men discussed the subject of a free port. But at no time could either possibly have been prescient enough to discuss the subject most critical to the future of their families, to Johnson's daughter Louisa Catherine, and to John Quincy. When told of the couple's marriage in 1797, Adams congratulated his son Thomas on his "new acquisition of a sister," supposing "this match grew out of a spark that was kindled at Nantes in 1779 when your brother was with me frequently in the family of Mr. Johnson." John Adams most likely had forgotten that Louisa Catherine was, at that time, a four-year-old child, and John Quincy not quite 12.[26]

If crossing the seas to Europe had been a hazardous experience, maneuvering home was a totally frustrating venture. First, father and son made their way to Brest, where the *Alliance* was waylaid, "embarrassed" with 40 unruly British prisoners who refused to leave ship until a workable exchange was made.

No sooner had Adams arranged for the prisoners' departure when Benjamin Franklin, on behalf of the king, requested that the *Alliance,* which father and son had boarded on April 22, remain on duty in France. The alternate plan to travel on the *Sensible* had to be held up until the arrival of the new French minister to the United States, Le Chevalier Anne-César de La Luzerne and his secretary, the French diplomat François Barbé-Marbois.[27]

With the party complete at last, on Thursday, June 17, father and son boarded the *Sensible* in the company of the minister and the tall, genteel and pleasant secretary of the mission, Barbé-Marbois. At sea only a few days the French diplomats were "in raptures" with John Quincy. They had gotten him to teach them English. On Sunday morning, June 20, John found the two diplomats in their stateroom, the ambassador seated between the two cots, one occupied by Barbé-Marbois, the other by Johnny. The ambassador was reading out loud from Blackstone's *Discourse* on his start as a law professor, and Johnny was correcting his pronunciation of every word and syllable and letter. The ambassador said he was astonished at John Quincy's knowledge. "Your son teaches us more than you do. . . . He shows us no mercy, and makes us no compliments. We must have Mr. John."[28]

Father and son had been home in Braintree a scant four months when a letter dated October 20, 1779, signed and sealed by the president of Congress, Samuel Huntington, informed John of his nomination as minister plenipotentiary to "confer, treat, agree and conclude" with representatives of His Most Christian Majesty, George III, in the negotiations of a peace.[29]

Once again there was flattering recognition from Barbé-Marbois. Respectful of the father, he wrote in glowing praise and sympathy of John Quincy on September 29, 1779: "I desire very much, Sir, that you would carry with you again to Europe, the young gentleman your son, notwithstanding the aversion he has to navigation. He will learn of you the means of being, one day, useful to his country; and your precepts and your sentiments will teach him to cherish my nation, who perceive more and more from day to day, how much her union with you is natural and reciprocally advantageous."[30]

Intense family discussions about John Quincy's staying or going along on his father's mission had preceded their departure on a forlorn Saturday, November 12. This time, however, Johnny was joined by his brother Charles, by John Thaxter Jr., their 24-year-old cousin, trusted friend, tutor and his father's private secretary, as well as the servant Joseph Stevens. Francis Dana, the 36-year-old Harvard graduate and former delegate to the Continental Congress, also accompanied John Adams as secretary to his mission and chargé d'affaires.

In truth, John Quincy had not wanted to leave home. He aspired instead to study at Phillips Academy at Andover to prepare for Harvard College. But one Sunday evening after church his mother took him aside and convinced him to go. With "resolution and . . . Roman matronlike affection," she had urged him onward.[31]

As for nine-year-old Charles, his tears, Abigail admitted, melted her heart a thousand times. But, she insisted, in his case, being the sweet favorite of the neighbors, bound to a golden destiny, it was well that he had gone. Both boys were at an age, in her opinion, when a mother's care was less important. In Charles's case, he would have the opportunity to see a foreign country, learn a foreign language that might be useful to him, and form, at this early period, friends who would do him honor in the future.[32]

Never shaken in her conviction about the urgency of current events, Abigail nonetheless suffered great loneliness in Braintree, and perhaps out of fright when she had no word from them for weeks after their departure, she felt the need to explain her motives to John Quincy. "If I had thought your reluctance arose from proper deliberation, or that you [were] capable of judging what was most of your own benefit, I should not have urged you to have accompanied your father and brother when you appeared so averse to the voyage."[33]

But she would further inspire him. "Great necessities call out great virtues. When a mind is raised, and animated by scenes that engage the heart, then those qualities, which would otherways lay dormant, wake into life, and form the character of the hero and the statesman."[34]

Chapter 4

A JOURNAL

In 1784 John Adams would advise his son that "there is no accomplishment more useful or reputable, or which conduces more to the happiness of life to a man of business or of leisure, than the art of writing letters. . . . The habit you now form will go with you through life. Spare no pains then to begin well. Never write in haste. Suffer no careless scroll ever to go out of your hand. Take time to think, even upon the most trifling card."[1]

Certainly by 1779, John Quincy had already received the message that the effort of writing and writing well was important, and so he began his early journal with this title page inscription:

A
Journal By Me
JQA
Vol:
1st.

But the title page was revised, the contents made more specific on the inside cover:

A Journal by J Q A
to

Spain Vol. 1st.
begun Friday
12th of November
1779.

That day on one of 11 sheets of paper he had ruled and bound into a booklet, 7 x 4¾ inches, John Quincy, age 12, wrote: "This morning at about 11 o'clock I took leave of my Mamma, my sister, and brother Tommy and went to Boston with Mr. Thaxter, in order to go on board the frigate the *Sensible* of 28 twelve pounders." He would see his mother and sister again five years later on July 30, 1784, and his brother on his return to America one year after that.[2]

This was the beginning of John Quincy's earnest attempt to honor his father's wishes. But easy as this practice of journaling appeared to be, he wrote later, it required one quality "not very common among men, and yet scarcer among boys—perseverance. I had it not." His journal soon became "irksome." He ceased writing a journal and would do so several times before resuming it faithfully in 1795 for the rest of his life.[3]

Still, despite his protestation, he at once proved himself to have the ear and eye of an instinctive diarist and a born historian, his thriving curiosity leavened by a skeptic's humor (perhaps unintentional at times) and a keen and honest pen that sharpened with maturity. Intrigued by details, he was enthralled by numbers, nurturing an affinity for lists and charts with compelling patience. On board the *Sensible*, he decided to list the names of the officers and principal passengers in categories. He placed American gentlemen in a separate category; another, boys, included himself and his new friend Samuel Cooper Johonnot. In retrospect, it seems unsurprising that as an adult he would initiate a unified system for the United States in his milestone *Report on Weights and Measures* that was to be regarded as "a classic in the historiograph of modern science."[4]

On Saturday, November 13, he was joined by his Papa and his brother Charles. Together they boarded the ship at about four that afternoon and took their lodgings, Charles to room with Papa and

John Quincy with Thaxter. The ship filled up over the next two days, about 350 passengers in all. Francis Dana, who was accompanying John Adams as his mission secretary and chargé d'affaires, came aboard, followed by Captain Tucker, with whom they had made their first voyage on the *Boston*. Tucker warned about the presence of two British ships and a brig off Cape Ann. "We were very glad he told us of it," John Quincy wrote, "so that now we can take proper measure for shunning them."[5]

They set sail on Monday, November 15, accompanied by the chasse marée, the brig *Courier de L'Europe,* returning to Europe. No question but that John Quincy anticipated the hazards implicit in this ocean voyage. Just 200 leagues out, on November 20, he addressed a letter: "Mrs. John Adams Braintree near Boston, To Be Sunk in Case of Danger." Then, as though to reassure his mother in case she imagined the worst, he spoke of his new young friend Sammy Cooper, "a very agreeable young gentleman who makes me more happy on the voyage than I should have been without him; as to his language I have not heard him say any thing amiss till now."[6]

Sounding very much like the seasoned traveler, he bravely and repeatedly attempted to dismiss the vagaries of the wind that gave way to a continued gale and the subsequent quiet as "nothing remarkable." "Sailors," he noted, "say that when there is a bad wind drink a bowl of punch upon the capstan and the wind will come right. Mr. Dana, Mr. Allen (a Boston merchant) and Mr. Thaxter try'd the experiment and the wind changed and came fair; there's superstition for you," he concluded.[7]

The weather grew rougher and on Thursday, November 25, John Quincy had the first sign that the *Courier* was in trouble. She lost her foremast, the *Sensible* lay by; hours later she recovered it and they set sail again. The next day, early on, "every face [was] fill'd with contentment," but only for a short while. In raging wind and sea the *Courier* lost her foremast for a second time "and we were obliged to leave her." John Quincy had recounted the tragedy with reticence, but still—"O! I had like to have forgot that . . . night." Francis Dana's journal elaborated somewhat: the tempest carried their own ship at such a speed, at a turbulent 76 leagues, that they could be of no help and sadly, "There were about thirty souls on board . . . one a woman. Heaven protect them from further harm."[8]

"The ship is very leaky," John Quincy noted on Monday. As the ship rolled back and forth, amid continued squalls, thunder and lightning, passengers were called to the pump four times a day, at 8 a.m., 12 noon, and 4 and 8 p.m. At noon the next day working the pump, the beam struck his head and hurt him. On Friday, the captain announced his decision to head for Spain to search the ship to see if he could find the source of the leak—they were 180 leagues from Cape Finisterre.[9]

By Sunday, December 5, hoping to see land, John Quincy and Charles took turns at their father's porthole. At night John Quincy was not sure if he saw dolphins or porpoises; it was too dark to make the distinction. He could only write in his journal during the day because the captain forbade light at night for fear of British frigates. When the next night some sailors cried "land, land," the fog was deep, and it was only early the next morning that they could see plainly and clearly that they had arrived at the coast of Spain at Ferrol.[10]

John Quincy only hinted at the bleakness, never mind the danger of these last weeks: "One thing which is remarkable is that all our voyage," he wrote "we have not had once the sun set clear."[11]

The port entrance to the city of Ferrol was narrow, only a mile wide; the city was small but the houses seemed to be well built; the large building in the middle appeared to be a monastery. With at least this first effort behind him, the diarist was relieved to claim "Thus have I given a small description of this place." His father, however, allowed himself not a moment's respite. He needed to focus on getting to their intended destination: Paris.[12]

All of this uncertainty, especially when his family was involved, was an "embarrassment" to John Adams. He worried about whether to travel to Paris by land with the dangers of crossing the Pyrenees or to wait for the frigate, a two-month prospect. There was also the question of suitable accommodations and, as always, expenses, and he was all too aware that the entire party faced a "very difficult" time. At least he could comfort himself on how much greater his problem would have been if the rest of his family had been traveling with him.[13]

Yet he remained true to form. On this "unexpected journey," he was honestly concerned about his children's welfare, but he could never, under any circumstances, allow physical hardship to excuse or interfere with their intellectual growth. As he and the children had to be in Spain for some weeks, he was determined to acquire the language of the country "as fast as possible." Almost immediately he headed for a bookseller, and soon the children as well as the rest of the group were studying the language. He had flattered himself, he later admitted, that in a month he should be able to read, make himself understood, as well as understand the Spanish, but found instead that a language was very difficult to acquire "especially by persons in middle life."[14]

John Quincy began his second set of notes on the tenth and meant to keep them throughout December. He was 12 years, 5 months old, at his most earnest, capable beyond his years of perceptive anecdote and subtle portraiture. The young French consul, for instance, who came to help them in La Coruña was, according to John Quincy, "about 35 years of age. He is pitted with the smallpox without which he would be handsome. He is a little tall but not overgrown. He is very sociable and very polite."[15]

But clearly John Quincy would never be content in the role of mere observer or reporter. In the privacy of his diary, his unique and premature brand of intellectual skepticism fostered irreverent musing on a spectrum of subjects, including patriotism, religion and Christmas observance.

On Tuesday, December 14, the muleteers came and carried the travelers' things down to a boat, in preparation for their departure the next morning to cross the bay to La Coruña, five leagues away and 30 miles north of the religious shrine of Santiago de Compostela, the first leg of their overland journey to Paris. The officers of the ship were French and Spanish, and wore cockades of red and white honoring the alliance between France and Spain. But Captain Chavagnes wished all his officers to add black to the color scheme; as France was now allied to the 13 United States of

America, "it was only what was due for the politeness that he had been used with in Boston. There's an example of French compliments," John Quincy commented with wry humor in the privacy of his diary.[16]

On Wednesday, December 15, at 5 a.m., the party of 13 dressed and, warmed with cups of Spanish chocolate, set out "like so many Don Quixote's and Sancho Panza's or Hudibras's and Ralpho's" for La Coruña. John Quincy relished the imagery: Samuel Butler's farce come to life, their three mule-drawn carriages trundling through corn and turnip fields, in the month of December verdant and plentiful as though it were May.[17]

From his room in the tavern at La Coruña, he had a view of rocks and mountains, sea and town; the breaking waves were as beautiful a sight as he had ever seen in his life. But he was curious about the three monasteries and two convents. Disappointed that he did not witness a nun take her orders, he was puzzled by the young women who would choose to be "shut up in convents and never see any men except the friars." As to their reasons for embracing such a restrictive life, he concluded, "Sometimes the thing is this. In these European countries a girl must marry the person that her parents . . . choose for her. If they are ever so obstinate as to absolutely refuse to marry a person. . . ."[18]

"This is a great day with the Roman Catholics," he wrote on Saturday, "Fête de Nousailles," Christmas. "However I find they don't mind it much. They dress up and go to mass but after that's over, all is . . . But stop. I must not say any thing against their religion while I am in their country."[19]

On Sunday John Quincy began his third journal. By now he was growing impatient. "One look at the chaises and any body would think that they were as old as Noah's ark made in the year one." Their itinerary was arduous: John Quincy wrote of bad and muddy roads, of "prodigious mountains" that caused the axle of one of their carriages to break, and of a "miserable cottage" where they stayed in a room filled with straw, grain, chests, barrels and chestnuts—but for once not among the mules, although he believed "we sha'nt have that to boast of long."[20]

By January 3, when they had at last reached Astorga, he could say they had not once had to lodge with the mules "but not much better." They had been shown chambers in which "any body would think a half a dozen hogs had lived for six months." But as angered as John Quincy was by their living conditions, he was not without sympathy for the inhabitants. "I do not wonder at it. Poor creatures, they are eat up by their priests. Near three quarters of what they earn goes to the priests and with the other quarter they must live as they can. Thus is the whole of this kingdom deceived and deluded by their religion. I thank Almighty God that I was born in a country where any body may get a good living if they please."[21]

Through the journey he noted the convents and monasteries, places of worship, a cathedral in Astorga that was said to be very magnificent and elegant, and he indeed found it "so exceeding rich and magnificent that it is beyond the reach of my pen to describe it." Nurtured in the simplicity of the family church in Braintree, he was uncomfortable and even suspicious of the grandeur of the ancient churches of Spain. "All this show cannot come from the heart but is all out side appearance." Of his morning's visit with his father to the cathedral in Leon, he wrote of seeing the procession. "The bishop passed. Our guide told us to kneel. I did. He gave me his benediction but I did not feel the better for it."[22]

When they reached Bayonne on January 23, John Adams paid the Spanish guide and bought and rented several port chaises for travel over frozen roads to reach Bordeaux. From there, it was familiar territory, a repeat of their earlier journey. They arrived in Paris late in the afternoon of February 9.

A letter from Abigail was waiting for John Adams. It gave him, he wrote back, "more pain than I can express to see your anxiety, but I hope your fears will be happily disappointed." In earlier letters dated January 16, John had sought to reassure her that "those at home are best off," while John Quincy had written from Bilbao that they had arrived safely for "one more storm would very probably carried us to the bottom of the sea."[23]

So she was undoubtedly reassured to hear from him a month later, that after a terrible journey of about 1,000 miles from Ferrol they had at last reached Paris, and that the day after their arrival:

"Papa put me to one of the pensions where I was before, and I am very content with my situation." Brother Charles, he added "begins to make himself understood in French and being as he is he will learn that language very soon."[24]

John Quincy was very content in Passy, returning to the school, sometimes known as the Ecole de Mathematiques, run by M. Pechigny and his wife. "My Work For a day," was the title of John Quincy's letter to his father on March 16, 1780.

Make Latin

Explain Cicero, Erasmus

Pierce Phaedrus

Learn Greek racines, Greek grammar

Geography

Geometry

Fractions

Writing

Drawing

"As a young boy can not apply himself to all those things and keep a remembrance of them all I should desire that you would let me know what of those I must begin upon at first."[25]

His father responded the next day and left no doubt about his preferred curriculum. "Making Latin, construing Cicero, Erasmus, the Appendix de iis et Heroibus ethnicis, and Phaedrus, are all exercises proper for the acquisition of the Latin tongue." He would not have his son omit, on any consideration, the Greek grammar and racines (roots) because the most perfect models of fine writing in history, oratory and poetry are to be found in that language. "Writing and Drawing," he continued, "are but amusements and may serve as relaxations from your studies. . . ." Finally, he hoped to hear "that you are in Virgil and Tully's orations, or Ovid or Horace or all of them." And, in a postscript: "The next time you write to me, I hope you will take more care to write well. Can't you keep a steadier hand?"[26]

The cost of his children's education, 1,200 livres a year, was of critical concern to John Adams. The bills added up, seemed very high to him, especially regarding clothing. Perhaps the outlay for equipment or clothing influenced his request to Pechigny that the children no longer spend time on fencing or dancing.

Increasingly, every facet of John's work appeared to be a paradox, and America's complicated relationship with France especially upsetting. In December 1775 the French had informally assured America of its backing, that it would welcome American ships, and seemed already to be thinking in terms of financial aid. Bonded by the threat of their mutual foe, Great Britain, and with Spain's consent, Louis XVI had, by orders signed on May 2, 1776, decisively come to America's help. By stealth and intrigue the supply of one million livres worth of munitions administered by the French secret agent Beaumarchais through a fictitious company, Roderigue Hortalez et Cie, and a like amount from Spain's Charles III would account for 80 percent of America's gunpowder in 1776 and the following year.[27]

The Franco-American alliance of February 6, 1778 had affirmed the countries' ties—with the Treaty of Amity and Commerce, the countries granted one another most favored nation status; the Treaty of Alliance stipulated America would aid France if war broke out between France and Great Britain, and that neither country would conclude peace with England without assurance of the independence of the United States. Furthermore, the two nations had combined forces in July 1778 to attack the British on American shores.

John's doubts about the sincerity of the French had only surfaced when he had come to Paris to negotiate the peace treaty with Great Britain when military and political conditions were ripe for talks. It was then that he had begun to question not only the honesty, integrity, and efficiency of the Americans' representatives, but also the loyalty and intent of the French. One could be grateful to the French for their financial aid but quite accurately perceive, as John did, that the foreign minister, Count Charles Gravier de

Vergennes, meant "to keep his hand under our chin to prevent us from drowning, but not to lift our heads out of the water."[28]

Uneasy with the intricacies of the situation in Paris, John was hardly at his best: To be patient, to be "so idle and inactive" did not suit his temperament. He therefore decided to visit Brussels, The Hague, and Amsterdam to serve his country "by transcribing intelligence and in every other way." He left Paris on July 27, 1780, with John Quincy and Charles. The brief trip turned into a year's stay, the start of what was, perhaps, the most unhappy period of his life personally and the proudest diplomatically.[29]

By September, before their mother had even learned of their whereabouts, Johnny and Charles were enrolled in the Latin school on the Singel canal in Amsterdam, across from the Bloemenmarkt, the flower market. But for the first time John Quincy was unequal to his work. Because of his deficiency in Dutch, the school authorities had held him back. John was of the opinion that John Quincy, 13 years of age, would be discouraged if kept in the lower forms. The letter of November 10 from the rector and preceptor of the Latin school, H. Verheyk, indicated no such confidence. The schoolmaster found John Quincy far from advanced or in any way praiseworthy: "The disobedience and impertinence of your older son, who does his best to corrupt his well-behaved brother . . . can no longer be tolerated, as he endeavors by his bad behavior to bring upon himself the punishment he deserves, in the hope of leaving school, as a result."[30]

John Adams's cherished Johnny had been, in fact, expelled. On the back of H. Verheyk's note, that same day, John wrote: "I have this moment received, with surprise and grief, your billet. I pray you, Sir, to send my children to me this evening and your account, together with their chests and effects tomorrow. I have the honor to be, with great respect, Sir, your humble servant."[31]

As John Quincy's diary shut down from September 30 until the following June, his reaction to this difficult moment was not recorded but for one bleak passage. On September 6, John Quincy noted: "Brother Charles and myself study in a little chamber apart because we don't understand the Dutch."[32]

On December 18 John Thaxter moved John Quincy and Charles to Leyden, to pursue Latin and Greek and attend lectures with the celebrated professors of Leyden University. It was cheaper there, the air infinitely purer, and the company and conversation better, John Adams informed Abigail. Without directly commenting on the humiliating experience with the Latin School in Amsterdam, John wrote he did not wish to have his children educated in the common schools of the Dutch "where a littleness of soul is notorious, where masters are mean spirited witches, pinching, kicking, and boxing the children upon every turn. There is besides a general littleness arising from the incessant contemplation of stivers and doits, which pervades the whole people. Frugality and industry are virtues every where, but avarice, and stingyness are not frugality."[33]

Five months later, in mid-July 1781, the children's lives changed again, as their father resigned himself to parting with both sons. As John informed Abigail—on John Quincy's fourteenth birthday—Charles, who was, as always, the amiable child who won the hearts of everybody, especially the ladies, had suffered a fever and was unwell. He had his heart set on going home. "Put him to school," he advised Abigail, "and keep him steady—He is a delightful child, but has too exquisite sensibility for Europe."[34]

John Quincy was to accompany Francis Dana, the Boston lawyer who had been serving John Adams as secretary to the peace commission, on his new post in Russia. Congress appointed Francis Dana the first American minister to Russia on December 19, 1780, and ordered him to go to St. Petersburg with instructions to conclude a treaty of friendship and commerce with the empress. John Quincy was to serve as his interpreter and secretary. "He will be satiated with travel in his childhood," his father predicted, "and care nothing about it, I hope in his riper years."[35]

Chapter 5

"ALMOST AT THE WORLD'S END"

The move from Amsterdam to St. Petersburg in the company of Francis Dana, begun July 7 and completed August 29, had been extremely abrupt. In fact, John Quincy had not a week's warning of the 2,400 mile journey, across Germany, Poland, Lithuania, Latvia and Estonia, that landed him at the edge of the Gulf of Kronstadt. Though Dana's appointment was months brewing and officially confirmed in Washington on December 19, 1780, he learned only in March that he was to "engage Her Imperial Majesty to favor and support sovereignty and independence of these United States and to lay a foundation of a good understanding and friendly intercourse between the subjects of her Imperial Majesty and the citizens of these United States to the mutual advantage of both nations."[1]

In short, Dana was sent to convince the Empress Catherine that it would be to Russia's advantage to establish commercial trade with the newly founded country. Or put more formally: "to refute the assertion of the British that the independence of the United States will be injurious to the commercial interests of the Northern Nations, and of Russia in particular."[2]

Facing formidable prospects, an immense journey and an awesome mission—and unable to speak a word of French, the "traveling language" of Europe and of the Russian court in particular—Dana had sought assistance and company. Refused by several candidates fearful of "Siberian exile," Dana asked for John Quincy's services as interpreter, secretary and companion. Though John Adams had initially disapproved of the idea, he recognized with a great deal of pride the validity of the suggestion. Out of respect for Dana, he had agreed, and was even willing to pay John Quincy's expenses.[3]

The elder Adams had great confidence in Dana, the notably ethical, 38-year-old Puritan lawyer, Bostonian, Harvard graduate and member of the Continental Congress. Both men acknowledged the risk involved in this new venture.

But John Adams took heart at the new turn of events. Ambitious, adventurous, visionary, yet a shade naive, he assumed that Russia's recent Declaration of Armed Neutrality, also known as the League of Armed Neutrality, signified Empress Catherine's opposition to British naval practices, and that her support for free trade presaged the rise of a flourishing American mercantile empire. His enthusiasm was wholly shared by Benjamin Franklin, who declared, "The great public event in Europe of this year is the proposal by Russia of an armed neutrality for protecting the liberty of commerce." It was with the comforting premise that America's "cause is that of all nations and all men; and it needs nothing but to be explained, to be approved" that Adams had reassured Francis Dana before his departure.[4]

Dana, at his most optimistic, now indulged in the notion that the maritime powers wanted nothing "but good information"—presumably he would be the bearer of such—"to convince them that it was for their substantial interest to form the most intimate connections with our country, and that speedily." Both men were encouraged by visions of brisk trade: Russian iron, hemp and sailcloth, tallow, wood and salted meat, in exchange for American tobacco and tobacco seed, rice, indigo, masts, flax, tar, pitch and iron. In the case of hemp, in competition with the Russians, the Americans aspired to increase their production and volume of export.[5]

A *three-hour boat ride* along the River Wahl brought John Quincy to Utrecht to meet Francis Dana on Saturday evening, July 7, 1781. In the days before his departure, busy as he was with packing and a round of farewells, he copied Edmund Waller's poem, "Of the Fear of God: In Two Cantos" and the first 70 lines of Joseph Addison's translation of Horace's Ode III, Book III. On the day of his ride to Utrecht he added four pages from William Guthrie's *Geographi-cal Grammar* on the Dutch constitution and government and five pages the next day on the history of the 17 provinces, also troubling to list the towns and provinces in the Netherlands retained by the French in the Peace of Aix-la-Chapelle.[6]

That Monday Dana bought a new coach and by ten the next morning the two, accompanied by Dana's servant, began their arduous journey. They crossed the Rhine by means of a unique rope ferry, a moving bridge inventively constructed from a series of small vessels connected together and overlaid with a platform of planks. From Nijmegen to Moers-Hochstrass they passed through Kleve, Xanten, Rheinberg, three small unfortified towns, all the king of Prussia's territories. John Quincy noted that at the end of the trip there was "a pretty good inn there, but the road that day was not good, and all that the ground produces is wheat, buck wheat, and spelts." He did not mention that the date, July 11, was his fourteenth birthday.[7]

John Quincy wrote about the church in Cologne where the bodies of the three wise men of the east were said to be interred and of a brick tower a little way up the river where Julius Caesar had supposedly built his bridge spanning the Rhine. A village opposite Cologne, inhabited by Jews, was "A nasty, dirty place indeed, and fit only for Jews to live in." Put more emphatically by Francis Dana: "the little dirty village which is chiefly peopled by Jews, and like all other places they inhabit (none more striking than *their* quarter of the City of Amsterdam) is most shockingly offensive to every person who hath a nose."[8]

Reading their separate journals with their overlapping notes, and from references in John Quincy's letters, it is quite clear that Dana was his trusted mentor and friend. Both man and boy were puzzled by the spectrum of religious prejudice they encountered on their travels—with the blatant exception of the case of the Jewish people. In Cologne, John Quincy observed that about 50 Protestant families who were denied worship in the city gathered on Sundays at a church three miles away, in the small village of Mulheim on the other side of the Rhine. Forbidden to own houses or farms in their own names, Protestants could, however, buy property under a Catholic's name. To his surprise, Jews were also permitted to have a synagogue in Mulheim.

Reaching Frankfurt on Main via Coblentz some days later, John Quincy noted that Lutheranism was the dominant religion in this city, that Catholics and Jews were tolerated, but that Calvinists were not and had to worship on Sundays in neighboring Bockenheim. "There are 600 Jew families here who live all in one street," he wrote on July 16, "which is shut up every night, and all day on Sundays, when the gates are shut they can only come out upon occasions of necessity, but the Jews can keep their shops in any part of the city."[9]

Hanau, Hünfeld, Gotha: the roads past these towns leveled to a very large plain. Naumburg led to Leipzig, which they left on Monday, July 23. About half past eleven at night, in the middle of a forest, their carriage sank into a hillside mud puddle, one pair of wheels under and the other pair up. They tied ropes to the wheels, the horses pulled hard, and they rode onward to arrive in Berlin on Wednesday, July 25. Berlin, he wrote to his father, was the first place of any consequence they had stopped. The capital of Fredrick the Great's dominions was a very pretty town, with its beautiful palaces, churches and green squares, much prettier than Paris or London according to Mr. Dana. The teenager favored the king's ambitious housing plans, replacing low, small houses with large, elegant ones and permitting their owners, no matter how humble, to return to their property.

Still, the king was not beloved in Berlin "for he certainly treats [the people] like slaves." It was the manner in which he recruited his army that most particularly offended John Quincy. "Among other things, if a farmer has two or more sons, the eldest inherits all the land and the others (when of age) are soldiers for life at a gros[chen] and a half which is about two pence sterling per day." Everybody tall enough, he added, was subject to recruitment and service for life, and in peacetime, the native troops were disbanded nine months in a year without pay, to seek their living as they can.[10]

Riga, the capital of Livonia, struck him as more Russian than Polish. And here, in shocking detail, he told his father that all the farmers lived in the most abject slavery, "bought and sold like so many beasts, and sometimes even chang'd for dogs or horses. Their masters have even the right of life and death over them, and if they kill one of them they are only obliged to pay a trifling fine . . . their masters in general take care not to let them grow rich . . . if anybody buys land there he must buy all the slaves that are *upon* it."[11]

John Quincy's diary does justice to his amazingly adventurous 14-year-old life. Disarmingly boyish, he liked to measure and to count, recording with fastidious precision mileage and temperatures. He also compared the German and English currencies and the French guinea to the Dutch ducat.

But the subject that roused his great sympathy and interest was the cause of the downtrodden. Subjugation or repression of any person was immediately equated with slavery. Taught by family, history and experience that freedom was every man's right, his abomination of slavery was almost genetic. His mother had written her husband two years before the Declaration of Independence wishing "most sincerely there was not a slave in the province. It always appeared a most iniquitous scheme to me—to fight ourselves for what we are daily robbing and plundering from those who have as good a right to freedom as we have." Generations onward, John Quincy's grandson Henry Adams claimed that Abigail's descendants were "anti-slavery by birth, as their name was Adams and their home was Quincy."[12]

In sight of the steely Baltic Sea, Dana and John Quincy reached their final destination in Russia on Monday morning, August 27, 1781. They had traveled 2,400 English miles, according to John Quincy's mathematics, to lodge temporarily in an inn rather grandly called L'Hôtel de Paris, not far from the imperial Winter Palace. Two days later they moved in with M. Artaud, a gentleman with obscure credentials in whose company the lonely John Quincy would spend a great deal of his time.

St. Petersburg was a stirring sight, "the finest" John Quincy had ever seen. Though "not yet half finish'd" and "requir[ing] another century to be render'd compleat," it was "far superior to Paris, both for the breadth of its streets, and the elegance of the private buildings, for the most part made of brick, and plastered over in imitation of stone." This was his first and lasting impression. Twenty-seven years later, on his return as the American minister to Russia, he told Emperor Alexander that "to the eye of a stranger," St. Petersburg appeared "like a city of princes . . . the most magnificent city of Europe, or of the world."[13]

John Quincy had spent some time studying the city. Somewhere between Cologne and Coblentz, he had fortified himself with Voltaire's two-volume *Histoire de l'Empire de Russie sous Pierre le Grand*—a laudatory guide, paid for by the Empress Catherine the Great—written between 1759 and 1763 without an actual visit to the country. John Quincy had painstakingly translated the first chapter from French to English thinking it would enable his mother, more than 6,000 miles away on her farm in Braintree, to "form an opinion of the place where we are," to envision the nine branches of rivers, five imperial palaces, admiralty, dockyard, marketplace, public squares. The city's 35 churches, of which five were for foreigners, including Roman Catholics, Calvinists and Lutherans, were, according to Voltaire, "monuments of the spirit of toleration, and an example to other nations."[14]

No less than 400,000 souls occupied the city. Rimming the town, villas or country houses were "surprisingly magnificent," some having "*jet d'eaus* or water-works, far superior to those of Versailles. . . . There was nothing of all this in 1702, it being then an impassable morass."[15]

In fact, Peter the Great had created St. Petersburg out of the formerly marshy delta of the Neva River. Declared the capital of Russia in 1712, it was a triumphal collage of baroque exuberance and neo-antiquity thanks to a revolving team of famed French, Italian and Scottish architects and their patrons, Peter's daughter Elizabeth and Catherine the Great. The formidable Empress Catherine had achieved her famed destiny by a circuitous route, marrying Elizabeth's despised and eventually deposed nephew, to rule alone. With blue eyes and chestnut hair, famed for her wit and her love affairs, she was brilliant and ambitious beyond anything the Americans, naive emissaries from abroad, might have gleaned from reading Voltaire.

Catherine, the so-called benevolent despot whom the Americans so ardently and sincerely intended to convert to their country's cause, had been born in Stettin, Pomerania, on April 21, 1729. Christened Princess Sophia Frederike August von Anhalt-Zerbst, she converted to the Russian Orthodox faith and was baptized Catherine Alexeyevna (after Peter's mother) in 1744, the year before her marriage to Peter III on August 21, 1745. An intellectual, a writer who loved French culture and Russian history, she collected European painting, sculpture and books, coveted scientific knowledge and new territories. A bold expansionist, she fought Poland, Turkey, Greece, and the Balkan Nations, founded new states in Moldavia and Wallachia, and conquered the holy city of Constantine, cradle of the Orthodox church. At the time of the arrival of the American diplomatic mission, she was willing to settle for a slippery sort of peace with both Great Britain and France rather than forge the most meager accommodation with the barely established United States.

Twelve days after their arrival, Dana realized their mission was doomed. It was all too clear that the empress would not be persuaded to grant an audience. Her formal recognition of the newly created republic must be preceded by that of the Dutch before the Americans could be received into the League of Armed Neutrality.

The diplomat and his teenaged secretary had learned almost immediately that "favoritism and blackmail played an important part in the routine of Russian official life—while bribery offered a golden key to every negotiation." The British minister, Sir James Harris (the future Lord Salisbury), had protested immediately to the Russians against recognition of the American agent "in any capacity."[16]

When Dana asked the French ambassador, Charles Olivier de Saint George, Marquis de Verac, about the appropriate time to present his letters of credence to Catherine the Great's court, he was advised that he was in St. Petersburg "too soon, that the proper time is not yet come." Obviously, the marquis had been instructed to be less than cooperative, "to hold himself apart . . . unless the Russian government should desire such an issue." Blame for the diplomatic fiasco was laid to lack of communication. Dana knew no French; the marquis, no English. The first was dependent on the teenaged Adams; the other, on his son-in-law. But clearly, language alone did not explain the frustrated mission. Rather, the timing was off, the rivalries and personalities incomprehensible to the purposeful, courageous but untried Americans.[17]

During the nearly four-month hiatus between communications, John Adams had stored up a great deal of advice for his son. When at last John Quincy's note of August 21 arrived, he was pleased to see his that son's handwriting had improved and that his judgment had ripened as he traveled. And, above all, he was happy to find his son's behavior had been such that Dana employed him as a copyist, which required a great degree of patience and steadiness as well as care. In an expansive mood, John Adams was also comfortable about his son's education and certainly about his son's mentor.

But that was December 14, 1781, 24 hours before John Quincy's letter of a snowy October day was hand-delivered to his father. While his son revealed qualms about his studies in St. Petersburg, he carefully omitted any hint of inner desolation. If he stayed, he told his father, he needed his copy of Littleton's *Latin and English Dictionary,* which he had left behind in Amsterdam. He could not buy either a good dictionary in French and Latin or English and Latin. "Indeed this is not a very good place for learning the Latin and Greek languages." There was no academy or school in the city, and the very few private teachers available demanded 90 pounds sterling a year for an hour and a half each day. At that extravagant rate, Mr. Dana did not choose to employ a tutor without his father's permission. Rather cheerlessly, John Quincy added that he hoped to go it alone.[18]

The tone and content of his father's follow-up letter was understandably confused and troubled, as John Adams had been thrown off course in his own plans and expectations. In contrast to his previous day's opinion, he did not perceive, he told John Quincy, "that you take pains enough with your handwriting." Nor was he satisfied with his son's "sketch" of his travels in the August letter: "You have not informed me whether the houses are brick, stone or wood, whether they are seven stories high or only one. How they are glazed, whether they have chimneys as in Spain. What public buildings, what maison de ville or state house"—and what about churches, palaces, statuary, paintings, music, spectacles, he asked, and whether there is a toleration of various religions.[19]

About schooling, his father wrote, "The price for a master is intolerable. If there is no academy, nor school, nor a master to be had," he really didn't know what to say to his son's staying in Russia. "You had better be at Leyden where you might be in a regular course of education. You might come in the spring in a Russian, Swedish or Prussian vessel, to Embden perhaps or Hamborough," and go on to Amsterdam. He was also afraid of John Quincy being too much trouble to Mr. Dana.[20]

"You make me a great number of questions at a time," John Quincy responded in January, and he would answer them as well as he could. He had come to question Voltaire. Seven of these nine branches of rivers described by the philosopher statesman "are nothing more than creeks made into canals about as wide as the Singel at Amsterdam." As for his claim to 35 churches: "I believe if anybody had set him about finding them out he would have found it very difficult."[21]

The main church was modeled after St. Peter's in Rome, but only half finished after 25 years. There were two palaces, "in one of which her Majesty resides in the winter. . . . The Empress stays all summer at a palace called Czarskozelo [Tsarskoe Selo] about 25 English miles from the city." The religion was neither Roman Catholic nor Protestant, but as Voltaire had in his history of Peter the Great dealt with that subject, he would quote him a full seven paragraphs in French. As for the absence of a dictionary, "there is nobody here but princes and slaves, the slaves cannot have their children instructed, and the nobility that chose to have theirs [educated] send them into foreign countries. There is not one school to be found in the whole city."[22]

Dana himself confirmed John Quincy's difficulties. "My ward is not troublesome to me. I shou'd be unhappy to be deprived of him, and yet I am very anxious about his education. Here there are neither schools, instructors, or books."[23]

John Quincy had abandoned his diary on his arrival in St. Petersburg at the end of August and resumed keeping it on January 27, 1782. That Sunday he wrote one line only: "Began to read Hume's history of England." Luckily Francis Dana belonged to a subscription library of English books and, though John Quincy had not made many acquaintances, he had begun late in January to read intensely about England. He finished the eighth volume of David Hume's *History of England, from the Invasion of Julius Caesar to the Revolution in 1688,* 327 pages worth, on Sunday, February 24. This was followed by another eight-volume series, Catherine Macaulay's *The History of England from the Accession of James I to that of the Brunswick line.* William Robertson's three volumes came next: *The History of the Reign of the Emperor Charles V.*[24]

He also borrowed Samuel Foote's plays and took out two of an eight-volume series on the new English theater: plays of Congreve, Fletcher and Jonson, Thomas Davies's *Memories of the Life of David Garrick,* and Robert Watson's *History of the Reign of Philip the Second, King of Spain.* He studied the poetry of Dryden, Pope and Addison and the Third Oration of Cicero against Catiline. He bought a Russian and a French grammar. He read Samuel Richardson's *Clarissa.* He had private lessons in German every Tuesday, Thursday and Saturday.[25]

Just as John Quincy instinctively understood and appreciated St. Petersburg's beauty, grace, splendor and stateliness, he soon learned the eccentricities and hardships of this dramatic city. Though his visual pleasure never faded, living in St. Petersburg posed harsh challenges. The noise bothered him, and almost every night some robbery or murder was committed, he complained to John Thaxter. There was not a week without a fire.[26]

As for the improbable weather, it was cold for seven months and the chimneys were too few; it rained continually for four months; and for one month the heat was excessive during the day and so

cold at night one needed a frock coat. He grew weary of the damp-
ness, that the sun never fully rose in winter nor set in high summer,
that snowflakes fell in July and that it sometimes froze in August
or even as early as June. The ordinary heat in rooms was 14 or 15
degrees above freezing, but could dip to 28 degrees below. Indoors,
people depended on wood stoves. Outside, people wore coats of
beaver, sable, bear, fox, wolf, dog or sheep, the last very common.
They also wore boots with doubled wool into which one slid one's
shoes. In summer, the Russian men with long beards changed to
cloth gowns. With sunshine almost as rare as in Holland, John
Quincy declared himself in favor of the Dutch climate, about which
he had been less than complimentary before experiencing Russia.[27]

In early spring John Quincy seemed slightly cheered, possibly because the weather was improving. After some exceedingly cold
days, it was thawing and likely not to be as severely cold again. A
window was opened every morning for about half an hour, he assured his father, so that they always had fresh air in their chambers.

But something deeper was revealed in his diary. According to
this forlorn record he was demoralized, so much so that he spent
many days at home: an entire weekend one time, nearly a week
another. Some of the time he did not feel well, nor did Dana. Logi-
cally, he stayed home in bad weather, but at times also in good
weather. Going about his young life, John Quincy must have spent
some time copying and translating official correspondence, but
the record is spare. Apart from picking up a newspaper or delivering mail and his own elaborate reading projects, he often walked
along the quay with Dana, and he frequented booksellers as often
as possible.

He also noted recurrent visits with several diplomats, Swedish,
French, German, Dutch—all the nobility spoke French and German. His sightseeing ventures were numerous, his accounts dutiful,
responsible but, for the most part, joyless. He saw Her Majesty's
artworks, the heart of the fabulous Hermitage collection bought
from Sir Robert Walpole at auction in Paris. With a party in three
sleighs, he crossed the icebound Gulf of Kronstadt from St. Petersburg to Kotlin Island to see Oranienbaum, the country palace on

the Gulf of Finland, and continued by land to the Peterhof. On July 9, 1782, he borrowed a domino (a loose cloak with an attached half mask) to wear to a ball the next night at the Peterhof. He mentioned a walk in the gardens but wrote nothing of the famous brilliant illuminations and flowing fountains that created a marine entry to the palace grounds. As a typical teenager he did note that he "slept till noon, Stay'd at home all day. Fine weather."[28]

So proud, so disciplined, John Quincy did not once complain to his parents of his sense of deep isolation. But in March, to his cousin Elizabeth Cranch, he elaborated a little further on his troubles. He had not written to her since he had been in Europe, he said, because he thought she expected that his letters would be very entertaining, and he did not wish to disappoint her by writing letters that would give her no pleasure. But he could no longer excuse himself, and must do as well as he could. A poignant confession followed: He was "at present distant 2,000 of our miles from my father, but my being with Mr. D[ana] compensates, if anything can, for my loss."[29]

But then, feeling himself obligated after all to entertain his cousin, he thought perhaps she would be glad to hear something about Russia and the formidable six-foot-seven-inch late emperor and offered to tell her briefly what he knew after seven months in Russia. To conclude, John Quincy offered his cousin 38 lines from "a eulogy of this prince" by Thomson, in his *Winter,* which began:

> What cannot active government perform,
> New moulding man? wide stretching from these shores
> A people savage from remotest time,
> A huge, neglected empire, ONE VAST MIND
> By heaven inspired Gothic darkness call'd.

He also recommended that she read Voltaire's history of Russia under Peter the Great.[30]

Months later, in July, news that John Thaxter had been ill and was returning to America prompted John Quincy's admission, all in French but for the key word (for which, perhaps, there was no adequate translation): "*Je voudrais bien être en train de suivre la même route, car je suis tout à fait* home-sick."[31]

Thaxter, though tender in his response, also tried to be firm and positive. "You tell me you are home-sick. I can easily conceive of it, and that you are very anxious about your future education." But, he continued, John Quincy must not consider his "Boreal Tour" as lost time. Rather, it was an opportunity few young gentlemen enjoy. Thaxter also reminded John Quincy of his privileged association with Francis Dana.[32]

John Quincy was deeply appreciative of Dana, and it was not only respect but abiding affection that bonded these two. Some years later, when John Quincy was a student at Harvard and heard that Dana had suffered a stroke, he wrote: "To me, he has been a second father." After a slow recovery Dana resumed his distinguished career as judge and later as chief justice of the Massachusetts Supreme Judicial Court. John Quincy would christen his third son Charles Francis Adams, in honor of his deceased brother Charles and "as a token of honor to my old friend and patron Judge Dana."[33]

John Adams, though disappointed, did respond with sympathy to his son's plight. On May 13, 1782, he addressed the problem decisively. "I want you with me. Mr. Thaxter will probably leave me soon, and I shall be alone. I want you to pursue your studies too at Leyden." But he still could not resist lecturing John Quincy. "Your studies I doubt not, you pursue, because I know you to be a studious youth: but above all preserve a sacred regard to your honor and reputation. Your morals are worth all the sciences. Your conscience is the minister plenipotentiary of God almighty in your breast. See to it, that this minister never negotiates in vain."[34]

His father's May letter was delivered on September 4. By Saturday, September 7, 1782, John Quincy, who had turned 15 in July, was at work planning his departure. Fortified with letters of introduction to people of power and consequence, to ambassadors, prominent merchants, manufacturers, he was already a responsible if youthful diplomat.

In his report months later to his "Honored Mamma," July 23, 1783, he gave some account of his travels since leaving Mr. Dana. In a sense he was apologizing to her indirectly for being so incommunicative the past 14 months when he wrote that he hoped his friends understood that he was "a little behind hand" in his correspondence with them because he had been "all that time almost at the world's end . . . in such an out of the way place, that it was inconvenient to write."[35]

He had left St. Petersburg on October 3; he wouldn't reach The Hague until April 21, 1783. Due to bad roads, weather and a great number of water passages that had begun to freeze over, a journey of about 800 miles in all, he first arrived in Stockholm on November 25. After about six weeks there, he reported to his mother that Sweden pleased him the most, "that is, of those I have seen, because their manners resemble more those of my own country than any I have seen." The king was a man of great ability, "extremely popular," who had persuaded his people that they were "free, and that he has only restored them their ancient constitution. . . ."[36]

Sweden had held other attractions, which the lighter-hearted 15-year-old would confide to his sister Nabby while they were together in Paris. She would tease him with a story of her encounter with a lady who knew him in Stockholm. "Now what think you young man. Does not your heart go pitepat, now bounce, as if it would break your rib. Nor do you know how many of your adventures she confided to me. No matter what they were, I well remembered with how much pleasure you used to speak of Sweden, and how many encomiums you passed upon *some* ladies there." Twenty-eight years later, John Quincy recalled the Swedish people as "the kindest hearted, friendliest and most hospitable people in Europe. . . . To me, it was truly the 'land of lovely dames,' and to this hour I have not forgotten the palpitations of heart which some of them cost me."[37]

John Quincy left Stockholm December 31, stayed about three weeks at Gothenburg and arrived at Copenhagen on February 15. Denmark, in his opinion, treated strangers with a great deal of politeness and civility, but not with the same openheartedness as Sweden. Hamburg was next—he stayed for a month—a large city, quite commercial, and, in the future, he thought, would carry on a great deal of trade with America. By way of Bremen, where he drank some Rhenish wine said to be about 160 years old, he arrived at The Hague on April 21. It would not be until July that he would meet up with his father on his return from Paris, ending a separation of more than two years.

His mother had been far less fortunate in the number of letters from John Quincy during this period; in fact, she had received only one letter since he had left Amsterdam for St. Petersburg. It was too hard to be deprived of the company of her husband and to be forgotten by her son; she was desolate. "Has the Northern region frozen up that quick and lively imagination which used to give pleasure to your friends, chilled your affections," she wrote. Pleading, she urged him to give his own reflections in his own language of his experience in Russia. "I do not expect the elegance of a Voltaire nor the eloquence and precision of a Robinson."[38]

Her letters of November 13 and 20 of the previous year reached John Quincy at The Hague in July, and he now attempted to redeem himself from her reproach: "the idea of which I cannot bear . . . I must," he continued, "beg your pardon for having scratch'd out of your letter these words, to be forgotten by my son, for I could not bear to think that such an idea should ever have entered the mind of my ever honored Mamma."[39]

He should have written more often, he continued, but no vessels sailed directly for America; there were few private opportunities and post was very expensive. Besides, seals were broken and not a letter passed whose contents were not known at the post office. Complaints were useless; officials suggested it was the letters rubbing together that had broken the seals.

In September, in response to his mother's plea for his observations on the countries through which he had traveled, he chose to write his thoughts on Russia. During these past travels he had bitterly condemned slavery a number of times, but never before with such depth or intensity. Tracing the chronology of the monarchy, its relationship to nobles and serfs, the 15-year-old historian had obviously left Voltaire's empress-subsidized work far behind, broadening his research to include the presumably more critical *Memoirs of Russia* by Prussian general Christoph Hermann von Manstein.

In this letter he wrote, "The government of Russia is entirely despotical; the sovereign is absolute in all the extent of the word. The persons, the estates, the fortunes of the nobility depend entirely upon his caprice. And the nobility have the same power over the people that the sovereign has over them. The nation is wholly composed of nobles and serfs, or, in other words, of masters and slaves. The countryman is attached to the land in which he is born; if the land is sold he is sold with it; and he is obliged to give to his landlord the portion of his time which he chooses to demand."[40]

The Russian form of government, John Quincy concluded, "is disadvantageous to the sovereign, to the nobles and to the people . . . it exposes the sovereign every moment to revolutions, of which there have been already four in the course of this century." And nobody, he believed, "will assert that a people can be happy who are subjected to personal slavery."[41]

In response, Abigail wrote the day after Christmas that she was "not a little pleased." If he did not write with the precision of a Robinson, nor the elegance of a Voltaire, "it is evident," she wrote, "you have profited by the perusal of them. The account of your northern journey, and your observation upon the Russian government, would do credit to an older pen."[42]

Acknowledging both his privileges and his deprivations, she continued: "The early age at which you went abroad gave you not an opportunity of becoming acquainted with your own country. Yet the Revolution in which we were engaged, held it up to so striking and important a light, that you could not avoid being in some measure irradiated with the view. The characters with which you were connected, and the conversation you continually heard must have impressed your mind with a sense of the laws, the liberties, and the glorious privileges, which distinguish the free sovereign independent States of America."[43]

And then too, his mother reminded him most firmly of the lesson to be learned from his experience: "Let your observations and comparisons produce in your mind an abhorrence, of domination and power, the parent of slavery, ignorance, and barbarism, which places man upon a level with his fellow tenants of the woods."[44]

Abigail recognized the force of her son's intellect but also his temperament. In regard to his education, she wrote in March, she hoped that he would finish at "our university," meaning Harvard. "And I please myself with the prospect of your growing into life a wise and good man. In your early days you had a great flow of spirits and quick passions. I hope you have acquired reason to govern the one and judgment to guide the other, never suffer the natural flow of your spirits to degenerate into noisy mirth. True contentment is never extremely gay or noisy."[45]

Chapter 6

"PROMISE TO PRODUCE A WORTHY CHARACTER"

The Dutch artist Isaak Schmidt's beguiling pastel of the 16-year-old John Quincy Adams depicts a charming innocent. According to an 1887 issue of *The Studio* magazine, his head was "powdered, but a lock of the dark hair is indistinctly seen falling down the boy's back in a queue, and tied with a black ribbon. The complexion is a fine blond, charmingly accented by the dark eyes and irregular arched eye-brows, while a slight cast in the left eye, with the faint roguish smile that plays about the mouth, add a certain piquancy, making the face very pleasant to look at. The coat is of pale blue silk, with a jabot of lace."[1]

Despite his contented, almost placid, demeanor in the portrait, John Quincy remembered that period at The Hague as one of heartfelt transition, "the precise time of my change from boy to man." But all times in this city were to be meaningful and cherished. He had first come to The Hague in July 1780, journeying from Paris to Holland with his father and his brother Charles. This second time, since his return from Russia, he lived with the family of Charles W. F. Dumas. He would leave in July, but return the next year, from January to May, and leave again in June and return once more in July. Residing at The Hague at what he calls "several of the most interesting periods of my life," the city "left indelible impressions upon my memory."[2]

"It was here that the social passion"—for Mr. Dumas's daughter, undoubtedly—"first disclosed itself with all its impetuosity in my breast. It was here, ten years later, I made my entrance on the political theatre as a public man." In 1814, approaching The Hague on a peace mission, a configuration of recollections would surge, "so various, so tender, so melancholy, so delicious, so painful, a mixture so heterogeneous, and yet altogether so sweet, that, if I had been alone, I am sure I should have melted into tears."[3]

Only when he had reached Stockholm on his way back from Russia did John Quincy learn that his father would be absent from The Hague, at work instead in Paris. In an early version of shuttle diplomacy, this was John Adams's third go-round in quest of a definitive treaty of peace between Great Britain and America since he had parted with his sons at The Hague in July 1781. But, as always, despite his pressing concern for his country's future, the father's regard for John Quincy's education was hardly a secondary issue.

Though John Quincy was offered a choice—he might also have gone to Leyden to his former tutor with whom he studied Latin and Greek for six months—he had, immediately on arrival at The Hague the night of April 21, joined the Dumas family living in the "large, roomy and handsome" house that his father had rented the previous April in anticipation of official recognition of the United States by the Dutch. Located on the Fluwelen Burgwal (the Street of Velvet Makers), the mansion that was to serve as the country's first foreign embassy would be known as the Hôtel des Etats Unis, "or if you will 'L'Hôtel de nouveau Monde,'" John Adams said.[4]

The Dumas family was greatly admired. Charles William Frederic Dumas, unofficial chargé d'affaires of the embassy, was "a walking library, and so great a master of languages ancient and modern [which] is rarely seen." Dumas's prudent wife took "exceeding good care of the house" and their daughter Nancy, "a very pretty young lady of about 16 or 17 years old, had a talent for composing patriotic verses."[5]

Dumas, then 62, was an enigmatic hero of the American Revolution—"the Committee of Secret Correspondence of the Continental Congress had retained this interesting friend of America to whom the United States owe a debt of gratitude never adequately recognized," the historian Samuel Flagg Bemis wrote. German-born and educated in Switzerland, Dumas was a spy and secret agent for the United States in Holland, as well as a man of letters. To John Quincy's later dismay, there would be vast political differences between them when Dumas, perhaps owing to his French parentage, subsequently turned passionate partisan of the French Revolution. But now, "The advantage you have in Mr. Dumas's attention to you," the father assured his son, "is a very precious one."[6]

Under Dumas's tutelage, John Quincy worked on extraordinarily complicated translations in Greek, Latin and French, including ten *Eclogues* of Virgil, Horace's *Odes* and Suetonius's *Life of Caligula,* and later he began to read the works of Plautus and Terence. For "amusement" he turned to Virgil, read a hundred verses of the *Aeneid,* about which Dumas "explained to me every thing which regards the ancient rites; and ceremonies." With the Dumas's daughter, he "whiled away the time" singing duets and playing the flute. He also took walks every day and rode horseback twice a week.[7]

But Dumas wasn't John Quincy's only tutor. As always, John Quincy's father offered rigorous instruction from Paris. Though he found his son's handwriting distinct and legible, it failed to be remarkably neat. "I should advise you to be very careful of it: never to write in a hurry and never to let a slovenly word or letter go from you. If one begins at your age, it is easier to learn to write well than ill, both in characters and style."[8]

A week later John Adams was glad, he said, to learn that John Quincy had actually begun to translate Suetonius. This was a very proper book to teach him to love his country and her laws, but did he translate it into French or English? Then again, he should always have a book of amusement to read, along with his severe studies and laborious exercises. John did not advise his son taking these books from a shelf of plays and romances, or history. Instead he would recommend books of morals as the most constant companions, "of your hours of relaxation, through the whole course of your life." Specifically, he had in mind Jean Barbeyrac's *An Historical and Critical Account of the Science of Morality,* which he would have him read with care early in life. He also advised the writings of Samuel Clarke, Ralph Cudworth, Francis Hutchinson, Joseph Butler, William Woolaston and "many sermons, upon morals subjects will be worth your attention, as well as Cicero Seneca &c."[9]

On further consideration, John Adams was pleased with John Quincy's studies. "An abler instructor than Mr. Dumas is not to be found," and yet, somewhat protective, he wondered if 100 verses at a time made for too long a lesson. And whether he was familiar enough with the Latin to understand so many verses at once? He presumed he had Robert Ainsworth's *Dictionary, English and Latin,* "Let no word escape you, without being understood." He also noted different translations of Virgil, some better than others, and, among other thoughts, advised him to make a complete translation of Suetonius, in order to make the student "master of the work."[10]

Heralding his father's return, John Quincy noted succinctly in his diary on July 22: "*A 11 heures du soir mon Père arriva de Paris.*" His father was equally elated at their reunion and proud, understandably, to find his offspring "grown to be a man, and the world says they should take him for my younger brother if they did not know him to be my son."[11]

As of late November 1781, John Adams had been given a new assignment. By vote of Congress on August 18, he was to form a treaty of alliance between France, the United Provinces, and the United States, contingent on Dutch recognition of American independence. As British General Charles Cornwallis had surrendered at Yorktown, Virginia, on October 18, John thought himself in a strong position to press for recognition at The Hague.

Reinforced with the title and position of minister plenipotentiary to the Netherlands, acclaimed rather than ignored and "lately grown much into fashion," by March 1782 he was convinced that he would be received at The Hague in "awful pomp in a few weeks."[12]

His lofty aspirations were shortly confirmed. On March 28 "the Lords of the States of Holland and Westfriesland" resolved "that Mr. Adams be admitted and acknowledged, as soon as possible, by their High Mightinesses [the States General], in quality of Ambassador of the United States of America." On June 11 he signed five bonds in the amount of one million guilders each, for a loan to be raised by a syndicate of Dutch banking houses, at 5 percent interest—allowing for a 4½ percent commission to the bankers, repayment to begin in 10 years and to be completed in 15. Congress ratified the contract on September 14, 1782. This was the first of four loans John maneuvered in the Netherlands, totaling 9 million guilders, or more than $3,500,000, "a crucial sum," and the sole effective support to languishing American credit, Samuel Flagg Bemis wrote, "which barely enabled the government of the Confederation to survive the peace, to function until recognition of Washington's new national government under the Constitution of 1787."[13]

The next month, after "innumerable vexations" yet buoyed by the full success of his negotiations with the Dutch, which included a signed treaty of amity and commerce between the two powers, John left The Hague once again to return to Paris. There he joined Benjamin Franklin and John Jay in completing the negotiation of provisional articles of peace between Great Britain and the United States, culminating two months later in the signing of the provisional treaty on November 30, 1782. Two months later, on Monday, January 20, 1783, preliminary articles of peace between Great Britain and Spain, and between Great Britain and France, were signed as well, which promised the longed-for official declaration of the end of hostilities between the old nations and the new. "Thus was this mighty system terminated," John said, "with as little ceremony, and in as short a time as a marriage settlement."[14]

But then, as late as June, the definitive treaty, the Treaty of Paris, formally ending the war, was still unsigned (and would remain so until September 3, 1783). With formal ratification as uncertain as it had been six months earlier, John was abysmally frustrated on so many counts: He was skeptical about the role of the French, doubtful that Franklin was aggressive or suspicious enough, and "weary beyond all expression of waiting in this state of uncertainty about every thing." He was also fearful that the Dutch, in this unwelcome interval, would be quick to take advantage of British restrictions on American trade. He decided to visit the Netherlands to boost the loan process and "to turn the speculations of the Dutch merchants, capitalists and statesmen, toward America." He would pay his respects to the Stadtholder and write lengthy reports back home to Congress on the sugar trade, on American commercial opportunities and on European politics. Fortunately, this self-appointed mission coincided with his July reunion with his beloved son.[15]

After two weeks of discussions with friends at The Hague, merchants, and bankers, and a detour to Amsterdam with John Quincy now by his side, father and son departed for Paris on Wednesday, August 6, at 4 a.m. Judging from John Quincy's diary, he and his father made an intensive study of art in both private collections and public displays on their way back to Paris. On arrival in Antwerp they had breakfast before going to the cathedral, about which the 16-year-old reported his impressions of its treasures in detail and with firm authority.

Next they viewed several private collections with a great many very fine pictures. There was one at Mr. Beckman's, he wrote, "representing Rembrandt's mother; painted by Rembrandt; which surpasses all description. The art of portrait painting was perhaps, never carried to so great a perfection as in this picture. She is represented with an old bible in her lap; with a paper in it, her spectacles in one hand, and the other upon her breast, reflecting upon what she is supposed to have just been reading. Every step you take the bible shows itself in a different position. It is nature itself."[16]

Departing Antwerp, en route to Paris via Mechlin, Brussels and Halle, John remained constantly alert to the practical as well as aesthetic aspects of the countryside. They arrived in Paris at the Grand Hôtel du Roi in the Place du Carrousel on Saturday evening, August 9, 1783, at seven o'clock, unsure of John's next assignment. Word of a joint commission to make a treaty of commerce with Great Britain had not yet been received. He was lonely for his family, but Congress had not given him leave to return home. He wrote

Abigail, John Quincy was "a great comfort" to him, "every thing you could wish him." Steadiness and sobriety, "with all his spirits are much to his honor. I will make him my secretary."[17]

He wrote at greater length to Nabby. Uncertain of his future abroad yet longing for his family's company, he told his beloved daughter that "nothing in this life would contribute so much to my happiness, next to the company of your mother, as yours. I have reason to say this," he explained, "by the experience I have had of the society of your brother. . . ."[18]

From this first day back in Paris, John Quincy's diary reveals a who's-who as well as a what's-what of the political, social, cultural and even scientific world and concerns of European and American diplomacy.

In the next weeks he talked with the British minister David Hartley about the hopes for peace. He dined with the Dutch minister plenipotentiary to Paris, Gerard Brantsen, and with the French ambassador to The Hague, Duke de La Vauguyon; walked in the Tuilleries with the Abbé Arnoux, the educated gentleman who taught French to his father; and caught up one Saturday morning with the minister of France at the court of Denmark, the Baron de la Houze, whom he had last seen in Copenhagen. He also renewed his acquaintance with his old schoolmate Ben Bache, Benjamin Franklin's grandson.

The budding diplomat carefully recorded his conversation with the Abbé Gabriel Bonnot de Mably, historian, philosopher and family friend, who talked a good deal at dinner about his recent travels in Poland, ranging from the severity of the weather to the constitution of Poland, the slavery of the people, the tyranny of the nobles and the kingship, which oddly was an elective office though the king was usually chosen from the family of the preceding ruler. But perhaps most challenging was that of the new light the abbé cast on the Jews, whom the 16-year-old John Quincy viewed most harshly—"that they could not live in Poland without the Jews. T'was they who carried on all the commerce. The nobility were too proud to engage in commerce, the slaves could not; everything that was done there in that way, was done by the Jews."[19]

Apart from semi-official activities, the heady world of John Quincy in Paris in 1783 involved many evenings of music and theater, about which he was not shy of opinions. He pronounced *Le Français à Londres,* demonstrating the difference between the French and English, "very laudable," its author, Louis de Boissy having "carried both to a pleasing extravagance." Crebillon, one of the best dramatic poets of France, wrote tragedies that were "very deep, indeed." And though the French in general were not lovers of tragedy, "this [August 16] audience of his play" most remarkably rose in "universal applause; which lasted for some minutes."[20]

But by far his most fascinating experience of the summer took place Wednesday, August 27, in the Champ-de-Mars. John Quincy had somewhat diffidently yet truthfully dismissed his morning's venture at the Louvre: "There are some good paintings there among a great number of indifferent ones." After dinner, the first public viewing in Paris of "the experiment of the flying globe" was an altogether different and wholly riveting venture.[21]

He quite marveled at the Montgolfier brothers, Joseph Michel and Jacques Etienne, and their discovery that a 14-foot sphere of taffeta, glued together with gum and lined with parchment, when filled with heated air could ascend to immense heights. Their first successful unmanned flight had taken place two months before, on June 5. This night, at 5 p.m. the Ecole Militaire's booming cannon signaled the globe's immediate rise, perpendicular, then slanted, then vanishing out of sight into the very cloudy sky as two more cannons fired in celebration. John Quincy was awed by the event.

In subsequent days, engrossed by news of the momentous invention of the flying globe, he copied word for French word the near breathless reports published in Thursday's *Journal de Paris,* including 62 lines of a poem titled "Sur le Globe Ascendant." John Quincy was bemused by the enthusiasm for the flying globe and that people would vie for the honor of being the first travelers to go up in them and "run ten risques to one of breaking their necks."[22]

But his own interest did not flag. Convinced that "this discovery is a very important one, and if it succeeds it may become very useful to mankind," he thought it worthwhile to collect every good thing that had any relation to it. This included a tracing from a sketch in the *Journal de Paris* of a winged horse and rider, which he pasted in his diary. But while appreciative of the magic, he understood the dangers—the flying balloons had so far met with several accidents and he noted that the process of superheating air was such a dangerous operation "that governments have prohibited them."[23]

John Quincy's fierce interest in the flying globes and his visionary appreciation of their portent for the future were perhaps the earliest hint of his lifelong study of various aspects of science that led to critical accomplishments. Ten years later, home in Boston, he would attend seminars based on "Lectures on Natural and Experimental Philosophy" by George Adams, the British author and maker of precision instruments, microscopes and telescopes that were a significant part of King George III's collection. Studies begun on John Quincy's return to Russia would result many years later in his milestone "Report on Weights and Measures." His passion for "lighthouses of the skies" would initiate the formal study of astronomy and the building of observatories across the United States. His support as a congressman of the legacy of British scientist and philanthropist James Smithson would lead to the establishment of the namesake institution, the Smithsonian. And John Quincy was committed to helping the engineer and inventor Robert Fulton promote his steam-powered boat, the first commercially successful craft of its kind.

In his diary entry for September 3, 1783, John Quincy wrote one line: "Signature of the Definitive Treaty" signed in the Hôtel d'York on the Rue Jacob. (The Continental Congress would officially ratify the Treaty of Paris on January 14, 1784.)[24]

On September 7, he wrote of attending the theater but skipped the truly momentous news of that day in Passy, historic in terms of the fate of his family as well as his country. On that day Benjamin Franklin put into John Adams's hands official notice of Congress's resolution dated back to May 1, authorizing both men and John Jay, any of them "in the absence of the others, to enter into a Treaty of Commerce, between the United States of America, and Great Britain," and in the meantime, "to enter into a commercial Convention, to continue in force, one year."[25]

The appointment, though official orders would not arrive until May 1784, was enough to renew John Adams's faith in his pursuit and to refurbish his ambition. That same morning, as he explained to Abigail, the waiting had made him anxious; he was still uncertain as to how to proceed. But there was much to be done. "It is of great importance that such a treaty should be well made." The loan in Holland required attention; when the present one was fully implemented, another must be opened, which only he or his successor could accomplish. And there were "still other things too to be done in Europe of great importance."[26]

At last, possibilities he had explored for hundreds of hours past crystallized, and his letters to Abigail were full of optimism and purpose. "Will you come to me this fall and go home with me this spring," he asked. And would she bring Nabby and leave the boys with her brother-in-law, Mr. Shaw, the schoolmaster. As to his work, in order to save Congress expense, "I shall have no other secretary than my son. He however is a very good one."[27]

John Adams's expectant note to Abigail belied his own intense problems. Suffering from a debilitating fever, he felt himself in deplorable physical condition. In general he was unhappy at the Hôtel du Roi. He minded the location, at the confluence of so many streets that it was a kind of thoroughfare. Moreover, he minded the noise, the constant roar, like incessant rolls of thunder, of the stream of carriages that rolled by—only from two to five in the morning was there something like stillness and silence. Sometimes he thought it would kill him.

In this critical state and on the advice of his physician James Jay, "the country air being thought necessary for him, we removed from Paris to Auteuil," John Quincy noted in his diary on Monday, September 22, to lodgings Thomas Barclay had leased from the Count de Rouault, where his father might enjoy the gardens, one full of vegetables and fruit, grapes, pears and peaches, the other, of flowers. There John Quincy would take up his duties as replacement for the beloved John Thaxter, who had served his father as "nurse, physician and a comforter at Amsterdam" as well as secretary. He also managed to continue his studies, some probably begun under Dumas's tutelage, including translation of Horace's

Odes and Caesar's *Commentaries*. Auteuil was the seat of the revered poet Nicolas Boileau. Benjamin Franklin's friend Madame Helvetius lived a few doors away. But neither medicine nor diet, the tranquil views of the village of Issy, of the Castle Royal of Meudon, of St. Cloud and of Mont Calvare, nor walks in the Bois de Boulogne, nor rides on horseback provided a cure. Not even the garden, which John Adams acknowledged was of excellent quality, despite his complaint that "every thing suffers for want of manure." Though he had recovered from his fever, he was still "extremely emaciated and weak."[28]

Urged by friends to take the waters at Bath, John planned for a six-week visit. But first there was to be a stay in London, which he had contemplated for several months before his present illness. Prior to learning of his new commission, John's anger with his government was clear in a letter to Abigail: "if I cannot obtain leave, I must take it." But that anger was tempered by eloquent praise of John Quincy. John planned to "take my son with me, whose company is the greatest pleasure of my life."[29]

Father and son and one servant, Leveque, left Auteuil on Monday, boarded a packet boat at Calais at 9 a.m. Thursday morning, October 23, 1783; 18 hours later, a pilot boat put them on Dover's shore at 3 a.m. They had suffered a horrendous voyage, "never before so sea sick, nor was my son," the father wrote. One day and 72 miles later, having asked to stay at the best inn in London, they were carried off to Osborne's Hotel in the Adelphi Buildings. To their surprise they found themselves in a street marked "John's-street"; the postilion turned a corner, and they were in "Adams-Street" and "I thought surely we are arrived in fairy land. How can all this be?" John Adams had wondered.[30]

This was to be the first of many visits that would culminate in John Quincy's appointment as his country's minister to Great Britain a distant 22 years later. More tantalizing was John Quincy's father's notation in his diary of an afternoon call on Joshua Johnson, merchant, future United States consul and his son's eventual father-in-law, whom they had met in Nantes. Johnson had moved back to London and now lived with his family in Cooper's Row, in view of the great hill crowned with the forbidding Tower of London. The

Johnsons' home served the Adams men as a mailing address during this visit to England. They would dine at the Johnson home later in their stay, on November 13, before their departure for Bath. If John Quincy's future wife, Louisa Catherine Johnson, was present, she was then eight years old.

Chapter 7

"A SON WHO IS THE GREATEST TRAVELLER OF HIS AGE"

Settling in on October 27, 1783, they might have permitted themselves time to recover from the punishing Channel boat trip, loss of sleep and tedious hours on horseback. But father and son were indomitable and, beginning the next morning, "curiosity," as John Adams put it, "prompted me to trot about London as fast as good horses in a decent carriage could carry me."[1]

The challenging itinerary was ideally designed for the thoughtful and sometimes pensive 16-year-old diplomat-in-waiting who was also a confident critic. Highlights of London included its famed churches, libraries, museums, Parliament, Mr. Wedgwood's manufactory, and even the popular waxworks of an entrepreneurial American-born Quaker, the sculptor Mrs. Patience Lovel Wright.

Initially, John Quincy wrote seldom about his travels for fear, he explained to his cousin Elizabeth, that he fell short of the improvements expected of him ("from the advantages I enjoyed"). But he was now ready to "confide entirely in the indulgence of my friends."[2]

Going on the fifth year since he had left home, having visited almost all the nations of Europe, the farther he went, he assured his cousin, the more he loved and cherished the place of his birth, and he knew of no punishment that would give him more pain than to be condemned to pass life abroad. Still, he did admit that of all the European nations, he believed he should prefer England because it had best preserved its liberty, and because, understandably, in many things its manners and customs were "the least unlike, those of my own country." Still there were differences to which he responded with robust candor.[3]

London was also the largest city he had ever seen and, both for convenience and beauty, far superior to Paris. Among the most remarkable things was his visit to the monuments in Westminster Abbey. He was struck with "awe and veneration, at finding myself on the spot, where lay the remains of the greatest part of the sages, and heroes, which Great Britain has produced." His admiration, however, was tempered by "a painful sensation at seeing a superb monument erected to the infamous traitor of the American Revolution," Major John Andre. "How much degenerated a nation must be," he thought, "which can find no fitter objects for so great an honor than a spy, than a man whose sad catastrophe, was owing to his unbounded ambition and whose only excuse for his conduct was his youth, as if youth gave a man the right to commit wicked and contemptible actions."[4]

Nor did the Tower of London win entire approval. He was taken by the admirable display of the weaponry, by the many old things, including the axe "with which the famous Earl of Essex (they say,) was beheaded." But he took exception to the royal treasury. On learning that the crown the kings wore at their coronation was said to be worth "a million," he thought that "the money might have been better employed."[5]

Two visits to St. Paul's Church, which was so much talked of, did not meet his expectations. Its dome was very high and "you might have a very fine view of all the city from it, if the smoke was not too thick to be able to see far."[6]

He was far more responsive to the immense and unique collection at Sir Ashton Lever's museum on Leicester Square, also known as the Holophusicon, which contained "the completest collection of natural history (such as stuff'd birds and beasts, insects, minerals) of any in Europe." Still more curious was a whole room ornamented with instruments and articles discovered in the last voyage of the unfortunate Captain Cook, murdered by Hawaiians in the Sandwich Islands in 1779, including a dress entirely made of birds' feathers and a kind of coat of mail made of dogs' teeth.[7]

That same day he also found a number of curious things at the British Museum, especially the letters of all the kings and queens of England dating back to Henry VIII and particularly those of Queen Elizabeth. He almost sounded guilty, confessing to the pleasure he took, "which I could not well account for, at seeing the original productions of persons so illustrious." Among other very curious manuscripts that interested him was an original of the Magna Carta.[8]

When John Quincy told his cousin that his visit "to the Queens Palace, called Buckingham House," on November 8 was arranged by "particular favor," he referred to the American-born painter Benjamin West, who obtained permission from the royal residents. The visitors also saw a great number of beautiful paintings by the greatest masters, including those of Vandyke, Rubens and West himself (including one called "The Death of General Wolfe"). The cartoons of Raphael were looked upon as "the master pieces of the art" which would be sent to Brussels to be worked in tapestry.[9]

John Adams also prevailed on his friend John Singleton Copley to secure places at the opening of Parliament on November 11. They witnessed the introduction of the Prince of Wales—recently turned 21 and then titled Duke of Cornwall—as the future King George IV in purple velvet took his seat among the scarlet-and-white-robed peers.

John Quincy did not mention to his cousin innumerable evenings at the theater—Drury Lane and Covent Garden—including a performance of *Hamlet,* of which he was quite critical. Initially, he did not think the British acted tragedy as well as the French in Paris. He had a particular problem with the precision and gait of British diction. The tragedy was not acted as he expected; there was "I think something like affectation; throughout the actors lay an emphasis upon almost every word."[10]

But exposure to Sarah Siddons evoked an ebullient reappraisal, judging from his letter to his friend Peter Jay Munro:

"Dear *Moron*" at Chaillot:

On Friday evening, I went in company with your uncle, Mr. & Mrs. Bingham and some other gentlemen to see that wonderful, wonderful, wonder of wonders Mrs. Siddons. The most capital performer upon the stage; not only of Europe, at present, but that ever was seen. (N.B. While I am in England, I must talk like an Englishman.)

She out Garrick's Garrick, Sir, cent per cent she play'd that evening Isabella in *The Fatal Marriage* [by Thomas Southern]: you probably know nothing of this piece: it is the deepest tragedy I ever saw or read: and I must confess I never saw any player, so possessed of the pathetic, as this said Mrs. Siddons. All the audience were in tears and there was a young lady in the next box to us, who was so near falling into fits that she was obliged to be taken away. . . .

Adieu, my dear fellow

porte toi bien.[11]

All this London activity began in October and now, in late December, despite London's gratifying sights, and because John Adams felt himself still "feeble, low and drooping," John Quincy accompanied his father to Bath with guarded hope that its legendary waters might restore his health. Twenty minutes after their arrival on Christmas eve, their cousin John Bolton came to dine with them and to guide them about Bath's glorious crescent—its public buildings, its card, assembly and dancing rooms. But regretfully, accommodations for the baths themselves reserved for another day were never to be experienced. Dispatches from America, London and Amsterdam informed John Adams of his country's potential financial crisis. The Dutch loan he had painstakingly negotiated the past summer was overdrawn; he must work out a new one immediately.[12]

Back in London on December 28 and at Harwich on January 3, father and son were set to board a packet for Hellevoetsluis, the Dutch port about 20 miles south of The Hague. Owing to the turbulent and treacherous Channel waters, they landed on Goeree and OverFlackee, the southernmost delta island of South Holland, trudged four miles through ice and snow, bumped along the roughest roads in a horse-drawn wagon, and early one morning boarded an ice boat (a large ferry boat fastened on runners). They reached Briel on January 10, and two days later The Hague and the Hôtel des Etats Unis. Frequently wet, chilled to the heart, John Adams had suffered mightily on this punishing journey, but he was philosophical about the experience. As had been said before, he realized, "Human nature never knows what it can endure before it tries the experiment," And though he thought he looked like he felt, "like a withered old worn out carcass," his son had been touchingly solicitous. "My young companion was in fine spirits; his gaiety, activity, and attention to me increased as difficulties multiplied, and I was determined not to despair."[13]

At The Hague throughout winter and spring, their son was again "everything you would wish him to be," John wrote Abigail. John Quincy labored over a number of translations: 237 pages of the *Aeneid* into English; 462 pages of Suetonius's *Lives of the Twelve Caesars* and 60 pages of Tacitus's *Life of Gnaeus Julius Agricola* into French.[14]

This concentration on the classics pleased both his father and his mother. Back in Braintree, the trunkful of books and papers he had sent home convinced her that he had not been idle, that he was storing his mind with "useful historic knowledge." And his large pile of "poetical" transcripts also reassured her that his taste "in poetry was delicate chaste well chosen and made with great judgment."[15]

In May John Quincy's studies were again interrupted. His mother and sister were expected to take passage to England on Captain John Callahan's ship, scheduled to sail in April 1784, and his father sent him back to London to greet them on their arrival. But the trip was to serve a double purpose for John Quincy: to pay "principal attention" to Parliament and to the bar as he would only be in London for a short time and not apt to return soon. John Adams expected all three to join him at The Hague. When

John Quincy did attend Parliament, his father wanted him to think about the oratory of the great speakers in the house, for "if you begin to judge now you will be skillful in time."[16]

But all of this was not simple. Back in London John Quincy was at first in low spirits, frustrated by both aspects of his mission. He was continually trying to get acquainted with someone who would introduce him into the House of Commons. Furthermore, Callahan, in lieu of his mother and sister, had brought only some letters. "So that I have not been able as yet to put in execution the two principal reasons, for which you sent me here. It gives me real pain, to find that I am so unsuccessful an ambassador," he wrote his father on June 1.[17]

Abigail and Nabby were now expected toward the end of July, if not August. His father's initial response to his son's disappointments was to have him return to The Hague, but he changed his mind. Resolute as ever about broadening and perfecting his son's education, he couldn't bear for him to miss out on the "seminar" on debating offered by the most brilliant orators of the day, including William Pitt the younger and Charles James Fox, at what he thought of as the "great and illustrious school" of the British Parliament's House of Commons. Instinctively, perhaps, priming his son for his future role as public speaker (and future professor of rhetoric and oratory at Harvard), he suggested that Mr. Copley, Mr. West, or one or two other friends might ask a member to assist him. Or for a guinea, John supposed, the doorkeeper to the House of Commons would admit him.[18]

To his father's pleasure and relief, John Quincy did find his way to the massive medieval Palace of Westminster, where the two houses of Parliament, the House of Lords and the House of Commons, met. The last week of May, Benjamin Vaughan, a family confidante, introduced him into the House of Commons and there he stayed from about 2 p.m. one Wednesday afternoon until 1 a.m. the next morning. He thought the subject of debate—about an election and evidence of the involvement of several hundred illegal voters at the poll—very dry. But the participants in the debate were immediately fascinating—principally the 24-year-old William Pitt, elected the previous year as Britain's youngest prime minister, and his arch-enemy Charles James Fox, ten years his senior. "And if I may be allowed to give my opinion," he wrote to his father,

> Mr. Pitt is upon the whole the best, and most pleasing speaker of them all. He has much grace in speaking, and has an admirable choice of words; he speaks very fluently, so distinctly that I did not lose a word of what he said, and he was not once embarrassed to express his ideas. Mr. Fox on the contrary speaks with such an amazing heat and rapidity, that he often gets embarrassed, and stammers sometime before he can express himself; his ideas are all striking, but they flow upon him, in such numbers, that he cannot communicate them without difficulty. . . .[19]

An intent observer for the next two weeks—his father had urged daily attendance—on June 15 John Quincy heard the renowned Edmund Burke's passionate challenge to King George IV in defense of the House of Commons as the protector of the people's liberties. The next session, June 18, he felt himself "a witness to something very extraordinary" when Fox spoke with Pitt in support of a committee to enquire into the state of parliamentary representation.[20]

John Quincy allowed that he couldn't pretend to say Pitt surpassed Fox in argumentation, yet he thought "no body will deny that he does in the delivery." Fox, he also noted, "has a small impediment in his speech, and one would think his nose was stopped by a cold when he speaks, whereas Mr. Pitt has the clearest voice and most distinct pronunciation of any person I ever remember to have heard." But conclude as he would that "they are both very great men," he felt, "It was a real misfortune for this country that those talents which were made to promote the honor and the power of the nation should be prostituted to views of interest and ambition."[21]

Intrinsically, of course, as an American born-and-bred patriot, he remained the country's relentless critic. "It might be a most happy country," he wrote his cousin Elizabeth, "for nature seems to have been really partial in their favor; but the general corruption and vice, which possesses them all, high and low, effectually prevents them from being happy, as it is impossible as well for a whole nation, as for particular persons, to be vicious and happy."[22]

In general, his father was content that his son had spent so much time and taken so much pleasure in the chancery and Parliament, or so he wrote. But perhaps fearing that his son found his days in Parliament more seductive than his studies, he urged him to return to The Hague. "You have had a taste of the eloquence of the bar and of Parliament: but you will find Livy and Tacitus more elegant, more profound and sublime instructors, as well as Quintilian Cicero and Demosthenes." Besides, he would ask that John Quincy remember, "I have no secretary or companion, and I cannot do without you."[23]

John Quincy left London about June 26 and remained at The Hague until his father received news of Abigail and Nabby's prospective arrival in London. After a 30-day passage on the *Active* (appropriately named), the women had landed safely at Deal on July 20, traveled to London and stayed one night at Low's Hotel in Covent Garden before moving with the help of their cousin William Smith to Osborne's New Family Hotel. Here, Abigail waited "in the joyful hope of soon holding to my bosom the dearest best of friends."[24]

John had responded immediately. Her letter of July 23 had made him "the happiest man upon Earth. I am twenty years younger than I was yesterday." It was a cruel mortification to him that he could not go to meet her in London. Meanwhile, he was sending her "a son who is the greatest traveller of his age."[25]

While they waited for John Quincy, a week passed most sociably for the women. Acquaintances from Virginia, Maryland and Connecticut left cards, and old Tory friends came to call. Agreeable as all this was, there was tension. Nabby was in a state of suspense that she found most painful. Her Papa or brother were expected at every hour. Much as she loved her brother, he was somewhat of a stranger to her, and she was apprehensive of the person she was about to meet. Friends spoke very pleasantly about him. It would be a relief to find him equal to her wishes, "and happy will he be to equal my expectations."[26]

On Friday, July 30, Abigail, tired out by her visits to the Foundling Hospital and the Magdalen Hospital, and by her long walks in green squares, was determined to stay at home. She had a headache, and Nabby, too, was down with what everyone called the London cold. Nabby was writing to her cousin Elizabeth, "when a servant runs puffing in to announce: 'Young Mr. Adams is come.' And that he has stopped at the next house to dress." She must stop writing, she told Eliza: "Let me enjoy the present moment and anticipate future satisfaction." But she promised that after she had seen her brother, she would at least tell her cousin how he looked: "if he is any thing short of a monster I shall be disappointed, from the accounts I have had of him."[27]

Initially, Abigail thought, she would know her "dear and long absent son," that she "could not be mistaken in him," though she had seen him only in a brief, three-month interval during the past six years and five months. But when he did appear, she drew back, not really believing her eyes till he cried out, "O, my mamma, and my dear sister!"—all that was needed to quiet her worries. Later she would admit that at first sight, only his eyes appeared familiar, and she might have "set with him for some time without knowing him. His appearance is that of a man, and in his countenance the most perfect good humor; his conversation by no means denies his stature. I think you do not approve the word *feelings*," she wrote Mary Cranch, "but I know not what to substitute in lieu, or even to describe mine. His sister he says he should have known in any part of the world."[28]

One day later she was happy to tell her niece that she also found in "his manners behavior and countenance, strong resemblance of his Papa. He is the same good humor'd lad he formerly was. I look upon him scarcely realizing that he belongs to me. Yet I should be very loath any one else should lay claim to him." And no, Nabby had the pleasure to inform Eliza, she did not find her brother a monster. He was not larger and not so tall as mutual friend Harry Otis. He looked like a sober lad. She was indeed gratified, and hoped to inform her cousin that she was satisfied when she became acquainted with him.[29]

As for John Quincy, he would not attempt to describe his feelings at meeting two persons so dear to him after so long an absence. "I will only say," he told his father, "I was completely happy."[30]

One week and a day later, another reunion took place. Nabby returned to her family's apartment at noon to find things mysteriously changed with the additions of an unfamiliar hat, a sword, a cane and two books. Her own room was rearranged as though someone had been sorting its contents. Suddenly, Nabby understood. Her father had arrived. She did not hesitate for a moment, but flew upstairs to his room where he was resting, knocked softly at his door, and was received "with all the tenderness of an affectionate parent after so long an absence. Sure I am, I never felt more agitation of spirits in my life; it will not do to describe."[31]

The family of four stayed the night in London, but plans had changed. Word of Thomas Jefferson's unexpectedly prompt arrival in Europe, following Abigail's by six days, influenced John to forgo a trip to The Hague in favor of their immediate departure for Paris.

The prospect of the family being together did not make Abigail feel 20 years younger, as it did her husband, but rather "exceedingly matronly with a grown up son on one hand, and daughter upon the other." Still, unsurpassingly proud, "were I not their mother," she told her sister, "I would say a likelier pair you will seldom see in a summer's day."[32]

Chapter 8

"A SISTER WHO FULFILLS MY MOST SANGUINE EXPECTATIONS"

The reunion long in coming was heartfelt but lasted only nine months. Abigail wrote her sister Mary Cranch, "Poets and painters wisely draw a veil over those scenes, which surpass the pen of the one, and the pencil of the other." They were, "indeed, a very, very happy family, once more met together, after a separation of four years."[1]

They rode into Paris on Saturday, August 13, and settled by Tuesday in the suburb of Auteuil. The vast and picturesque stone dwelling with 40 beds at 43–47 Rue d'Auteuil belonged to the Comte de Rouault and bordered the Bois de Boulogne, the park John Adams proudly claimed as his own "without any expense." Passy and Montmarte were silhouetted in the distance; closer by, turreted chateaus with elaborate cutwork fences sat on vast and rolling lawns, their chestnut-lined driveways resolved into secret, ivy-mottled courtyards. Above the river Seine and distant from the putrid streets of Paris, John said, it "is the best I could wish for."[2]

Abigail was both fascinated and frustrated by the challenge of affording and regulating the "gay and really beautiful" house and fabled gardens with a staff of seven, especially when the young man in charge of scrubbing floors looked like a Merry Andrew, dancing as he drove foot brushes over the red tile in the first-floor salon. She also was intrigued by the décor of the mansion, particularly the opulent display of mirrors. Rather charmed to see the beautiful sofa with pillows and cushions in abundance reflected in these mirrored ceilings and flower-festooned side panels, she felt differently on a personal level. "Why my dear," she told her niece Elizabeth, "you cannot turn yourself in it without being multiplied 20 times and being rather clumsy and by no means an elegant figure, I hate to have it so often repeated to me."[3]

As for John Quincy, the Hôtel de Rouault was familiar ground. He had lived there the year before at the invitation of its previous tenant, Thomas Barclay, the United States consul general in France, during his father's convalescence. Happily, he now spoke French as if he were a native. He knew precisely the location of his favorite bookseller as well as a number of his father's colleagues and friends, the elite of the diplomatic world, including Mr. Jefferson and Mr. Franklin.

Nabby, 19, who had so longed for the change, now found the adjustment most difficult. Confused and conflicted about her separation from a problematic romance with a young lawyer named Royall Tyler, she missed her tight circle of friends ("who is married and who is dead, the two important periods you know"). Besides, the language was difficult and some aspects of the culture wholly unfathomable. Just two weeks after her arrival in the little village a few miles from Paris, she felt herself "unknowing and unknown" to every person around her except her own family, without a friend, a companion or an acquaintance of her own sex, studiously endeavoring to gain a knowledge of the French language which, she assured her cousin Elizabeth, "was not a very easy matter."[4]

As for Paris, if she gave her real opinion or a just description of this city or country, her cousin would not believe her: "The people were the dirtiest creatures in the human race." Paris was known as a beautiful city and perhaps it could be judged so by the strict rules of architecture and proportion, but to her eye it was very far from

beautiful. The streets in general were very narrow and the buildings amazingly high, all built of stone, and what was once white
had turned very disagreeable with smoke and dirt. At least the public buildings, she did admit, were more elegant than in London. All
in all, she was suspicious of this new environment and defensive of
her own. In her brief exposure, she did not see an American who
did not ardently wish to return to his country, which would be the
very first wish of her heart, she was certain, after a 12-month stay.[5]

But even as Nabby wrote so negatively about her challenging
new circumstances, she allowed, with rare candor, insight and a
foreboding sense of resignation, that there might be another interpretation in contrast to her own bleak view by someone with
greater gifts and of more poetic sensibility. Indeed, she allowed
that there was ample scope for an observing, sentimental mind to
see things differently, for a person of sprightly imagination to find
a thousand sources of amusement and entertainment about her life
in Paris which, regretfully, she passed over "without even knowing that they exist." For instance, from her window she could see
a beautiful flower garden and hear the voice of a pretty lass in the
adjoining garden that, she thought, could inspire a mutual friend's
imagination with poetical images sufficient to compose ten pages
of poetry, while she could only view things as they are. A more
poetic view, she admitted, was beyond her capabilities.[6]

Unfortunately and unfairly, given her dismal response to her early
days in Paris, these letters home have tended to confirm history's
view of her as a "pallid figure of mediocre intellectual gifts." Her
sense of her own limitations seems most disturbing in light of her
young dreams confided to the "dearest of brothers" of an education, of adventures in a wider world that might be on par with his
but for being born female. It was not in envy—she surely did not
believe herself his equal intellectually—but out of a bitter sense of
deprivation that she spoke so longingly of lost opportunity shared
with so many of her own generation and those to come.[7]

Not that her parents did not love, even admire and respect her.
Her mother was "Happy in a daughter who was both a companion

and an assistant in her family affairs, who had a prudence and steadiness beyond her years." Both father and mother spoke repeatedly of her generous tenderness and good sense. But for all their admiration and affection, and appreciation of her statuesque beauty, there were concerns about her silence and what her mother spoke of as her formidable reserve, "as much apparent coldness and indifference as ever you saw in one character." Nabby herself wished she could find some way to avoid the appearance of this "detested disposition" and even asked for her Cousin Elizabeth's help. Her father wrote that he liked her the better for her reserve because "she thinks and feels the more." Which she undoubtedly did, more profoundly than even he realized. As a shy and dutiful young woman, overtly troubled by her long separation from her beloved father and brother and by her thwarted aspirations, she tended to cope in silence. Unlike her mother, with her "early, wild and giddy days," Nabby's childhood was a casualty of wartime, a country in revolution, a family shuttling between Boston and Braintree, and ocean-wide separations.[8]

Apart from her beleaguered family life, Nabby felt her education extremely wanting. A letter refers to her going to Boston and to school at the invitation of the sister of Jonathan Mason, their former lodger, law student and tutor, to tarry with them "as long as inclination and improvement can make it agreeable." Also, her mother refers to a winter's visit with Mercy Warren that the family friend and historian might "advise, admonish and direct, with the same freedom she would one of her own." As for arts and accomplishments which were merely ornamental, they should not be avoided or neglected especially by her sex, her father noted; but "they ought to be slighted when in comparison or competition with those which are useful and essential." He hoped instead that his daughter's "attention will be fixed chiefly upon those virtues and accomplishments, which contribute the most to qualify women to act their parts well in the various relations of life, those of daughter, sister, wife, mother, friend."[9]

Nabby was frustrated by the lack of knowledge of a particular language or subject but even more so by her life in general and its narrow confines. She had longed to make the original voyage with Johnny and her mother had said that if she had been of the other sex, she would have encouraged her to do so. Conscious of her brother moving on daily, having new and pleasing objects continually engaging his attention, Nabby found the contrast stark. Instead, it was her lot to pass time "in a very contracted sphere." "Sensible of her own unworthiness," she had scarcely visited, she wrote Johnny in 1781, "as many towns as you have kingdoms." And she would remind her brother of his luck in being with their father.[10]

A year later, with Johnny in St. Petersburg, Nabby's boredom had deepened into melancholia. Their home in Braintree was more solitary than ever. As her mother thought it best to put Nabby's brothers under the care of Reverend John Shaw, her schoolmaster brother-in-law at Haverhill, they were, in Nabby's opinion, deprived of a very agreeable part of their family, especially Charles, who was just becoming a companion and enlivened many a solitary moment.[11]

Wistful, seemingly helpless in her submission, her sense of deprivation grew more intense, as she identified the contrasting nuances of their increasingly separate lives. As she told her brother Johnny,

> It is not the person that goes abroad in quest of any object whether knowledge, business or pleasure that is pained by the separation, but the one who remains at home. For the travelers, every object they meet imprints new ideas on their minds; new scenes soon engage their attention. Having much to look forward to, they have but little time to reflect on their past, the pleasure they receive is so much more than a balance for the pain that their time passes in almost an uninterrupted course of happiness. On the contrary the friends they leave at home are still dwelling on the painful event that deprived them of much happiness, the imagination pained with a repetition of past pleasures and present pains.[12]

But even as Nabby elaborated on the glories of Johnny's life, she cautioned him that privilege was tantamount to responsibility and, echoing the insistently moral teachings of her parents, reminded him of the peculiar advantages he was receiving.[13]

Her mother was well aware of Nabby's troubled state, and on July 17, 1782, she wrote John to ask what he thought of his daughter coming to keep house for him. "She proposes it. Could you make a bridge she would certainly present herself to you, nor would she make an ungraceful appearance at the head of your table. She is rather too silent. She would please you the better. She frequently mourns the long absence of her father, but she knows not all she suffers in consequence of it. He would prudently introduce her to the world, which her mamma thinks proper in a great measure to seclude herself from, and the daughter is too attentive to the happiness of her mamma to leave her much alone."[14]

Three weeks later her father acknowledged that her proposal of coming to Europe to keep her papa's house and take care of his health "is in a high strain of filial duty and affection." The idea pleased him much in speculation, but not at all in practice. "I have too much tenderness for you, my dear child, to permit you to cross the Atlantic. You know not what it is." If God spared him and her brother to return home, which he hoped would be next spring, "I never desire to know of any of my family crossing the seas again."

He was also, he continued, glad she had received his small present of a book, but it was painful, he said, to decline her more recent request. He had not approved of her choice of author, and would have been happier if she had asked him for Bell's *British Poets*."[15]

Nabby was devastated. In the glare of her father's disapproval of her reading choice, she suffered a shattering loss of the self-confidence of which she had a negligible share to begin with. As though on bent knees, she apologized and begged forgiveness, all but promising never to think for herself again. "I assure you my Dear Sir," she wrote that May 10, 1783, "that I have suffered, not a little mortification, whenever I reflect that I have requested a favor of you that your heart and judgment did not readily assent to grant. T'was not that your refusal pained me, but the consciousness that there was an impropriety, in my soliciting whatever you should consider incompatible to comply with. It has rendered me so thoroughly dissatisfied with my own opinion and judgment."[16]

From here on it was to be "whatever books my Dear Sir" thought proper to recommend to her. Those of her father's choice could not fail "to gratify your daughter. I have not that taste for history which I wish and which might be greatly advantageous, but I hope it is yet to be acquired."[17]

Thirteen months later, given his most recent ministerial appointment, John Adams reversed his position and earnestly requested that Abigail come to him with their daughter as soon as possible.

By this time, Nabby had a suitor, Royall Tyler, a tall, darkly handsome lawyer with a musical voice, a chaise, a mansion, a ship and a store. Heir to 4,100 pounds, he had graduated from Harvard in 1776 as valedictorian of his class, earned a master's degree, read law, and was admitted to the bar in 1779. Abigail sensed a growing attachment between this charismatic gentleman and their daughter. Uncertain of her role, she knew John's sentiments so well, she wrote, that the merit of a gentleman would be his first consideration, and she had made every inquiry that she could "with decency, and without disclosing my motives."[18]

At Christmastime 1782 Abigail reported that she had welcomed Tyler, who had opened an office in town in the past nine months and boarded with the Cranches, to the family circle. "Losing his father young and having a very pretty patrimony left him, possessing a sprightly fancy, a warm imagination and an agreeable person, he was rather negligent in pursuing his business in the way of his profession; and dissipated two or three years of his life and too much of his fortune . . . all of which he now laments but cannot recall."[19]

At 23 he had resolved to come to Boston to pursue his studies and save his remaining fortune, which had suffered from devaluation in connection with paper currency "so that out of 17 thousand pounds, he could no longer realize more than half the sum," he had told Abigail. But Tyler was also a favorite child of a mother in possession of a large estate, and Abigail thought of Tyler's plan to purchase the substantial Vassal-Borland property (which, oddly enough, became the future Adams home) as significant evidence of his meaningful intentions.[20]

Admittedly, there was a darker side. Gossip had tainted Tyler with "great disorders" of drinking, profanity, noisy binges, even of shattering the glass of dormitory windows. Far graver, and never entirely refuted, he was charged as the father of Royal Morse, the son of a charwoman at Harvard.

Now, however, from Abigail's vantage point, despite Tyler's questionable past, his behavior was "unexceptionable," and she was sure he would not fail to make a distinguished figure in his profession if he pursued it steadily.[21]

In fact, she had added, she was not acquainted with any young gentleman "whose attainments in literature are equal to his, who judges with greater accuracy or discovers a more delicate and refined taste." She did not know a young fellow whose language was so pure, or whose natural disposition was more agreeable: "his days are devoted to his office, but evenings of late to my fire side. His attachment is too obvious to escape notice." And, she did not think their daughter wholly indifferent, though it was difficult to understand her position and in a sense, perhaps, even her appeal.[22]

The enigmatic Nabby, in her father's absence, Abigail would remind him, had grown "tall, large and majestic," was handsome but not beautiful, had a good figure and stately manners that some mistook for pride and haughtiness. But no air of levity ever accompanied either her words or actions, and in her mother's opinion, should she be "caught by a tender passion, sufficient to remove a little of her natural reserve and soften her form and manners, she will be a still more pleasing character."[23]

Given her own fretful concerns about her daughter, she was certain Nabby's "reserve and apparent coldness" put Tyler in miserable doubt. At which point, harboring more sympathy for Tyler than for Nabby, she intruded, undoubtedly with the best of intentions, on her daughter's presumed love interest.[24]

One evening, a conversation had taken place that led her to write Tyler a note to tell him of the possibility that she might leave the country in the spring and, if so, with her daughter, whom she would wish to carry with her unattached. Tyler's response had deeply moved her—"I shall be happy when I *deserve;* and it shall be my every exertion to augment my merit, and this you may be assured of"—which made her strongly sympathetic to his cause. Re-calling her own early love, she wrote to her husband that she could not forbid Tyler some hope. While early on, she admitted, she had been confused as to whether to think of Tyler in "the character of a gay, tho not a criminal youth," she saw now that he would win Nabby's affections as he seemed to have won her own. Frantically in need of advice, "What ought I to say," she asked John. "Suffer me to draw you from the depths of politics to endearing family scenes."[25]

One month later in Paris, on January 22, John read Abigail's let-ter about the presumed match, now referred to as "the family af-fair," and was unsparing in venting his displeasure. He did not like the subject at all. His child was too young for such thoughts and not under any circumstances did he relish the word "dissipation." His child was a model and was not to be the prize of any, even reformed, rake. A lawyer would be his choice, but it must be a law-yer who spent his midnights as well as evenings at his age over his books, not at any lady's fireside.

He also thought Abigail would have been enough on her guard not to write notes to such a youth. And in "the name of all that is tender," he continued, Abigail wasn't to criticize their daugh-ter for those qualities which are her greatest glory—her reserve and her prudence, which he was amazed to hear her call "want of sensibility. The more silent she is in company, the better for me in exact proportion," and he would have this observed as a rule by the mother as well as the daughter.[26]

Moreover, he grumbled onward, with regard to finances, Abi-gail ought to know how long it took for a young lawyer of even the most promising talents and obstinate industry to make his way and of his own inability to offer financial support. "My children" he re-minded his wife, "will have nothing but their liberty and the right to catch fish on the Banks of Newfoundland. This is all the fortune that I have been able to make for myself or them."[27]

While vigorously protesting to Abigail any thought of a mar-riage between Nabby and Tyler, he had even included a paragraph to Nabby in his letter of January 29, 1783: "If I mistake not your character it is not gaiety and superficial accomplishments alone that will make you happy. It must be a thinking being, and one who thinks for others good and feels another's woe. It must be one who can ride 500 miles upon a trotting horse and cross the Gulf Stream with a steady heart. One may dance or sing, play or ride, without being good for much."[28]

Toward the end of January, as though exhausted by the subject, John signaled signs of capitulation. He had admitted earlier that, after all, he did not know enough of the subject to decide anything and after checking with friends and colleagues on Tyler's moral character, future as a lawyer and literary talents, John concluded that he must leave all to Abigail's judgment. If Nabby wished to marry him, her father could no longer object. Besides, as Abigail had written, Tyler's purchase of the Vassall-Borland house and land was impressive and could not be overlooked, along with favorable references from esteemed friends of whom they had both inquired.

John was now not only resigned but quite pleased. "Miss Nabby is attached to Braintree and you think upon advising with your friends, her object worthy, marry her if you will and leave her with her companion in your own house. Office, furniture, farm and all. His profession is the very one I wish. His connections are respectable, and if he has sown his wild oats and will study, and mind his business, he is all I want."[29]

Ultimately, the thought of being reunited with Abigail made him feel for the younger pair. "If my consent only is wanting they shall be asunder no longer than they choose. But we must consult upon plans about this. They have discovered a prudence. Let this prudence continue and all will be right by and by."[30]

Ultimately, "from necessity than choice" Nabby decided to leave Tyler to accompany her mother abroad. Abigail understood the sacrifice: the parting of two persons strongly attached to each other "is only to be felt . . . description fails." She also was surprised by her daughter's discipline aboard ship. She appeared to be calm and cheerful, though only one passenger during the crossing had been able to elicit a smile from her, even a sad one.[31]

John's formal letter of consent had arrived after Nabby's departure. Tyler's response was exquisitely polite. Marriage was indeed a "serious affair" and, he assured his prospective father-in-law, the parties involved had not proceeded without suitable reflections on its significance to the happiness of their friends and relations, as well as themselves. Tyler also discussed financial entanglements regarding his 83-acre property and promised to make use of John's library "which is becoming a man who wishes to be serviceable to his friends and country." He was speaking for Nabby as well as himself when he ended his letter with the hope that their union would afford John and "his lady" the satisfaction which parents experience when they perceive their children "useful, worthy, respectable and happy."[32]

Three months in France made a vast difference. "I find myself more reconciled," Nabby told her cousin Elizabeth. For even as she protested the differences, she found herself by December comfortably settled in the grand chateau in Auteuil. "Poor Braintree seems to fall away strangely," she wrote in response to news from home about friends marrying and moving onward. Both literally and figuratively, she might have added.[33]

Observing the dauphin in the palace gardens, which were open to the public on Sundays, she found the three-year-old pretty and sprightly but thought it ridiculous that people should pay so much homage, either from necessity or choice, to a being who might rule them with a scepter of iron. The centennial celebration of the playwright Pierre Corneille was to occur in October; a piece by Handel was considered *"un chose curieuse,"* of its time but modern; "A Sentimental Journey" by Laurence Sterne had just been published.[34]

There was a pattern to these days Nabby shared contentedly with her brother and parents. She was 9 years of age when they last lived together and was now 19. Johnny's record was even slighter—3 months out of the past 10 of his 17 years. Family life involved momentous change. First of all, both she and her mother slept later than they had when there were turkeys and geese to care for back in Braintree. Then, between eight and nine o'clock, as soon as Abigail's fire was made and her room cleaned, she roused Nabby and knocked on Johnny's door, which he always opened with a book in his hand.[35]

At breakfast Papa, Nabby said, always took chocolate, while the others had tea. Afterward, Abigail tended to her housekeeping, Johnny retired to his room to his translations of Horace and Tacitus, Nabby to her translations of Fenelon's *Les Aventures de Telemaque* into English—she had gotten as far as Book 4—or to read Molière in French, or to work on her sewing. At noon her father took his cane and hat to walk for four miles—if he missed the morning, he took Johnny with him in the afternoon—while the women repaired to their rooms to have Pauline, Abigail's chambermaid, dress their hair.

They met again to dine at two. The table was laid for four persons; they had soup and a piece of bread daily, and as many other things as their cook pleased to give them, "Papa and Mamma with a servant behind their chairs, the custom of this country," as Nabby explained to Elizabeth. Afterward, she and Johnny read to their mother or played a game of romps, vigorously pursuing one another in the salon to one side of the center hall; glass doors at one end of the room opened into the garden, to the courtyard at the other end.[36]

The afternoon was short. As soon as tea was finished the table was covered with mathematical instruments and books and not a word was heard until nine at night other than that of theorem and problems bisecting and dissecting tangents and sequences which John Adams was teaching his son. Sometimes there were games of whist "to relieve their brains," and other times they had or went to company or to Paris for dinner, theater, the opera.[37]

Ten o'clock was the usual curfew, except on nights Nabby and Johnny rode into Paris on their own. Then, Abigail would fret: "Ten o'clock and these young folks not returned, a dark stormy night too." But she would remind herself that lamps did light the road from Paris and what a very pretty ride it was in agreeable weather with the River Seine on your right-hand side. When she heard Caesar's welcoming bark and the gate bell rang and knew her children were safely home, she could go peacefully to bed. Judging from John Quincy's diary, Abigail was up far more frequently than she chose to mention to her sister Mary Cranch, not only waiting for her children but joining them on occasion.[38]

John Quincy was in Paris almost daily. He persistently bought books at Froulle on the Quai des Grand Augustins. He joined his mother and sister for visits to Mr. Graff's lace shop on the Rue des Deux Portes Saint-Sauveur and to the celebrated Mademoiselle Rose Bertin, the queen's milliner on the Rue St. Honoré, who in mid-March was occupied making dresses at vast cost for the 10-year-old infanta of Spain, shortly to marry a 12-year-old prince of Portugal.

One Saturday John Quincy dined with perhaps his most favorite people of all, Thomas Jefferson and his daughter Martha, recently arrived in Paris, and the next day with the Paris banker Ferdinand Grand; other times with the Abbés Arnoux, Chalut and Mably; with the painter Benjamin West; the Marquis de Lafayette and John Paul Jones. On January 29, he wrote, "Paris afternoon, alone. Mr. Jefferson's. He looks much afflicted. The last letters brought him news of the death of one of his daughters [Lucy Elizabeth] . . . he has a great deal of sensibility." Another evening in Paris found him again with Mr. Jefferson: "whom I love to be with, because he is a man of very extensive learning, and pleasing manners."[39]

On another evening, May 4, Jefferson spoke about his native Virginia, where the blacks "are very well treated, increase in population, more in proportion than the whites," where before the war, "the negroes were to the whites, in the proportion of 3 to 4. Now they are as 10 to 11, which is a very material difference. He supposes about 500,000 souls in the state." He also said that Jefferson "Disapproves very much the cultivation of tobacco, and wishes it may be laid entirely aside." Wheat, he thought, "would be much more advantageous, and profitable, much less laborious and less hurtful to the ground." After respectfully recording Jefferson's observations, John Quincy concluded that his host was "a man of great judgment."[40]

Frequently, along with his family, he was in the company of Benjamin Franklin. During Holy Week, his mother and sister joined Franklin's son Temple and Mary (Polly) Hewson, daughter of Benjamin Franklin's London landlady, Margaret Stevenson, at a concert. The "old gentleman" was found to be perfectly well, "except

the stone, which prevents him from riding in a coach, and even
from walking," but he said he was determined to return to America
in the spring; the motion of a vessel would not, he thought, be painful to him. John Quincy believed that Franklin had been so long
in France that he was "more a Frenchman than an American" and
doubted whether he would enjoy himself perfectly if he returned to
America.[41]

Many Paris evenings or afternoons involved theater, opera and
viewings of painting and sculpture, about which John Quincy wrote
searching, detailed, informed and candid, if not blunt, critiques.

In regard to the Duke of Chartres's art collection, one of the
most famous in Europe: It held more Raphaels than he had seen
anywhere else; a remarkable painting by Rubens, and an admirable
Rembrandt, as indeed were almost but not quite all the pictures.
John Quincy was astonished that some were so bad, and others
he felt quite absurd and ridiculous—especially one in which the
washed linen is passed from the Virgin Mary to Christ and on to
Joseph, and at the last hung by a parcel of angels to dry on the
branches of a tree. Though he did not consider himself a connoisseur, he knew, he said, when ideas were groveling, despicable and
impious. Or when both Italian and French companies put on "poor
stuff" just calculated to please the mob.[42]

By mid-March, he was puzzling over the news that the fabled
Monsieur Augustin Caron de Beaumarchais—author of the "too
famous comedy," *La Folle Journée ou Le Marriage de Figaro*, the
notorious satire on the aristocracy—had been picked up immediately after supper a day or so ago and carried to St. Lazare, where
he was imprisoned. Inquiries as to the reasons for the measure
provoked as many questions as answers. "That is the beauty of
the French government," an acquaintance responded, "to lock up
a man without saying why nor wherefore." Supposedly, it was because Beaumarchais had written a song about a pastoral letter by
the archbishop of Paris that warned his faithful against seeing the
comedy or buying the works of Voltaire (a number of which were
banned in France) that Beaumarchais had printed.[43]

Another reason might have been Beaumarchais's recent letter
to the *Journal de Paris* in which he boasted of having "*surmonte*

tigres et lions pour fair jouer sa pièce." Despite the efforts of the king to scuttle the production, the queen, in extreme favor of the work and coupled with a court order, had prevailed. Wonderfully successful—especially effective in its attack on the *ancien régime* and press censorship—through 74 performances over the previous two years, many more were anticipated, unless the playwright's imprisonment brought an end to the production. Whatever the outcome, Beaumarchais, John Quincy concluded, "is not in an agreeable situation now. It is not an easy thing to get out of those prisons." Three days later, on learning of Beaumarchais's release from St. Lazare due to public intervention, he wrote, "I imagine he will be pretty humble, after this lesson."[44]

John Quincy began writing more consistently of French customs and royal rituals, his acute eye and nuanced pen tending more by inference than bold proclamation to categorize his distaste for royal or religious ritual and customs as pretentious, useless, or possibly amoral. On a cold disagreeable Good Friday, March 24, with his father and "the ladies" as he referred quite often to his mother and sister, John Quincy attended the Church of St. Sulpice; went afterward to Longchamps, where everybody "that has got a splendid carriage, a fine set of horses, or an elegant mistress, sends them out on these days to make a show"; and then to tea with Dr. Franklin. Holy Thursday was the day, he noted in his diary, that "the king washes the feet of 12 poor children in imitation of our Saviour's washing those of the apostles. The king's brothers serve those children at dinner, and they have some peculiar privileges; such as being pardoned twice for crimes for which any other persons would be hang'd etc."[45]

With the news the next Sunday, March 27, that the queen, about seven o'clock in the evening, "was delivered of a son, who is *Monseigneur le duc de Normandie*," John Quincy commemorated the event in his diary:

This is one of the most important events that can happen in this kingdom, and every Frenchman has been expecting it as if the fate of his life depended upon it. One would think that after having a dauphin they would be easy and quiet; but, say they, the Dauphin is young and may die; and, tho' the King has two brothers, one of whom has several children, yet the capital point is, that the crown should pass down eternally from Father to Son; insomuch that they would prefer being governed by a fool or a tyrant that should be the son of his predecessor, than by a sensible and good prince who should only be a brother.

The Queen was taken ill only an hour before her delivery, a circumstance which must have been very agreeable to her; for, a few minutes before she is delivered, the doors of her apartments are always opened, and everybody that pleases is admitted to see the child come into the world, and if there had been time enough, all Paris would have gone *pour voir accoucher la Reine.*[46]

The next day, the Marquis de Lafayette, after a visit to Versailles, had reported "a curious circumstance. The queen was so large, that it was suspected she might have twins, and the controller general had prepared two blue ribbons, in case two princes should be born, for the king's children must be decorated with those badges, immediately after they come into the world." Later in the day, when John Quincy walked in the Palais Royal gardens, he said it was pleasing to see how joyful, how contented the *badauds* (strollers) looked. "All take the title given to the prince as a doubtless presage of his future conquests and are firmly persuaded that it was expressly given him, that England may be a second time subdued by a duke of Normandy. If they dared," he added, "they would mention another point in which the pretended conqueror may resemble the real one." John Quincy's not-so-subtle reference was to rumors that the newborn child might be the illegitimate child of a liaison between Marie Antoinette and a lover, a colonel commandant of the Royal Swedish Regiment in the French army.[47]

On March 31, Madame de Lafayette sent a card to offer them places for the Te Deum, which was to be sung the next day at Notre Dame when the king was to be present. Her husband had recently returned to Paris after a short, sentimental and successful tour of the United States, having been made a citizen of the state of Connecticut. The father of three had named one child after George Washington and the youngest daughter was Virginia. As did his mother, John Quincy found Madame (Marie Adrienne François de

Noailles de Lafayette) a very agreeable woman with a very pleasing countenance, "extremely fond of her husband and children, which is a most uncommon circumstance: especially as when they were married, neither of them was more than 12 years old."[48]

Their party included Thomas Jefferson and Benjamin West. By the time they reached the Pont Royal at about half-past-three, both sides of the quay "were so amazingly crowded with people, that there was just space sufficient for the carriages to pass along; without strategically placed guards, there would have been no passage at all for the coaches. As it was, the troops had the utmost difficulty to restrain the mob."[49]

On their arrival, Parliament was found to be sitting in the choir on the right side,

> in scarlet and black robes; the Chambre des Comptes were seated in the same manner on the left sides, in black and white robes. The foreign ambassadors were in an enclosure at the right of the altar, and between them and the Parliament was a small throne, upon which the archbishop of Paris officiated. Soon . . . the bishops arrived, two by two. There were about twenty-five of them. They had black robes on, with a white muslin skirt which descended from the waist down two-thirds of the way to the ground, and a purple kind of a mantle over their shoulder. As soon as his majesty had got to his place and fallen upon his knees, they began to sing the Te Deum, which lasted half an hour, in which time we heard some exceedingly fine music.[50]

But John Quincy had not finished his notes for that day, unsparing in his distaste for the religious as well as political significance: "What a charming sight—an absolute King of one of the most powerful empires on earth, and perhaps a thousand of the first personages in that empire, adoring the Divinity who created them, and acknowledging that he can in a moment reduce them to the dust from which they sprung!"[51]

Perhaps the most unsettling testimony to the burgeoning unrest heard by John Quincy was that of the Marquis de Lafayette. On the evening of April 9, the marquis talked on various subjects, and among others about the dukes and peers. He said he did not believe that "upon the face of the Earth, an order of men could be found, so numerous, in which there were so few men of sense." In fact, "they are a parcel of fools."[52]

Furthermore, the only privilege of any consequence attached to their title was the right to take a seat in Parliament where, "if they had any ambition and abilities, they might serve to counterpoise in some manner the power of the king" who, instead, gave them to understand that he wished they would not go to Parliament. And in true courtier style, they gave up this precious right. "I am continually sparring them up," the marquis said, telling them that it was fully in them to assert their rights, but, to his grave disappointment, "all without effect. . . ."[53]

In retrospect, reviewing Lafayette's statement and copying it carefully into his diary, John Quincy wondered uncomfortably, that "the marquis spoke somewhat openly and freely for a French nobleman; especially for one so nearly allied as he was to two or three dukes. Perhaps," he concluded, "he thought that among Americans he could freely speak his mind without any danger."[54]

Only two weeks later John Quincy's concerns shifted immeasurably. On April 26, 1785, a few minutes after dinner, Thomas Jefferson told John Quincy that the packet *Le Courier de L'Orient* had arrived with the news of February 24: His father had been appointed minister to the Court of St. James's in London. He knew he must face a decision he had worried over for many months now. Because his father's fortune had suffered for his lifetime of public service, his children must therefore provide for themselves, which he would never be able to do if he continued to "loiter away" his precious time in Europe.[55]

Whether or not John Quincy knew there was opposition to his father's appointment—some southerners objected on grounds that John Adams was "totally averse to the slave trade" and would not exert himself "to obtain restitution of the Negroes taken and detained from them"—he was concerned for his father's well-being. He feared that his father's sense of duty would induce him "to make exertions which might be detrimental to his health."[56]

Writing by candlelight later that evening, he also took time to explore his own somewhat tantalizing position, past and future, both of which he had been mulling over for months. "Having been traveling for these seven years, almost all over Europe," he did not doubt that going to London with his father would afford him more immediate satisfaction than returning to America to embark on a program of study.[57]

He did not minimize the difficulties of returning to two years of college, subjected to all the rules which he had so long been freed from, followed by the "dry and tedious study of the law" and, subsequently, three or four years more to achieve, if ever, any prominence. Altogether, it was, he admitted, a discouraging prospect for a youth of his ambition: "for I have Ambition, though I hope its object is laudable." But still: "Oh! how wretched / Is that poor man, that hangs on princes' favors." As long as he was able to get his own living in an honorable manner, "I will depend upon no one."[58]

He did not have to look far to see a striking example of the perilous situation a person was reduced to by adopting a different line of conduct. He was determined not to fall into the same error as William Temple Franklin, whom he termed "a hybrid citizen" who claimed two countries and identified with neither.[59]

There was no question that his father's appointment to the Court of St. James's opened a new phase in America's quest for recognition, a new era for American diplomacy. On March 7 Congress gave leave to Benjamin Franklin "to return to America as soon as convenient," and on March 10 Thomas Jefferson "was unanimously elected to succeed Franklin at the Court of Versailles"—but the new assignments made for a most immediate wrench within the Adams family.[60]

For John Quincy it seemed as though his future was at stake, and he was prepared, in some mysterious way even compelled, to make the sacrifice. "You can imagine what an addition has been made to my happiness by the arrival of a kind, and tender mother, and of a sister who fulfills my most sanguine expectations," he had written his cousin William Cranch the past December. "Yet the desire of returning to America still possesses me. My country has over me an attractive power which I do not understand." He did have one specific reason for wanting to return to his native country. He wished very much to have a degree from Harvard. After those peripatetic seven years without any regular course of study, he would likely need substantial preparation before attending college. Therefore, he had serious thoughts of going home in the spring to stay with his schoolmaster uncle, Mr. Shaw, for a year and then entering college for the last year of required study.[61]

Four months and his father's appointment had made all the difference. Both parents agreed that America was the theater for a young fellow who sought to distinguish himself. And while his mother thought no young man of his age was superior in accomplishments, she acknowledged that her son was deficient in many branches of knowledge which he would be best able to acquire in his own country.[62]

As for his father, John had long hoped that John Quincy might attend Harvard College. Possibly one of the first parents to attempt to ease the way for a cherished child, he eagerly sought the help of Dr. Benjamin Waterhouse, Harvard's first Hersey Professor of the Theory and Practice of Physic at the recently founded Harvard Medical School. John thought of his 31-year-old friend as "a sprightly genius, very studious and inquisitive" as well as sociable.[63]

The two had met through Benjamin Franklin in Paris, and John "did not . . . hesitate to consider him, in some respects as one of my family." Waterhouse had kept a watchful eye on John Quincy and Charles at the University of Leyden, and John needed his help once again. In doing so, John was a typical loving, proud and ambitious father. Being John Adams, his letter, eloquent, candid and deferential, not only affirms the unusual, affectionate bond between father and son, but also offers a unique portrait of John Quincy, age 18, and his astonishing education, loopholes and all. "Dear Sir," John Adams addressed Dr. Waterhouse on April 23, 1785[64]:

> This letter will be delivered you, by your old acquaintance John
> Quincy Adams, whom I beg leave to recommend to your attention
> and favour. He is anxious to study sometime, at your university before

he begins the study of the law which appears at present to be the profession of his choice.

He must undergo an examination, in which I suspect he will not appear exactly what he is; in truth there are few who take their degrees at college who have so much knowledge; but his studies having been pursued by himself, on his travels without any steady tutor, he will be found awkward in speaking Latin, . . . and . . . in that accuracy of pronunciation in reading orations or poems in that language, which is often chiefly attended to in such examinations.

It seems to be necessary therefore that I make this apology for him to you, and request you to communicate it in confidence to the gentlemen who are to examine him, and such others as you think prudent. If you were to examine him in English and French poetry, I know not where you would find any body his superior, in Roman and English history, few persons of his age; it is rare to find a youth possessed of so much knowledge. Although you will find . . . [his Latin] translations . . . inaccurate in point of style . . . it is impossible to make . . . [them] without understanding his authors and their language very well.

In Greek his progress has not been equal. Yet he has studied Morcells in Aristotle's Poetticks [sic], in Plutarch's Lives, and Lucian's Dialogues, the Choice of Hercules in Xenophon, and lately he has gone through several books in Homer's Iliad.

In mathematicks I hope he will pass muster. In the course of the last year, instead of playing cards like the fashionable world, I have spent my evenings with him. We went with some accuracy through the geometry in the Praeceptor, the eight books of Simpson's Euclid, in Latin and compared it problem by problem and theorem by theorem with Le Père Dechalles in French, We went through plain trigonometry, . . . algebra, and the decimal fractions, arithmetical and geometrical proportions, and the conic sections in Ward's Mathematicks. I then attempted a sublime flight and endeavored to give him some idea of the differential method of calculation of the Marquis de L'Hospital, and the method of fluxions and infinite series of Sir Isaac Newton. But alas, it is thirty years since I thought of mathematicks, and I found I had lost the little I once knew, especially of these higher branches of geometry, so that he is as yet but a smatterer like his father.

However he has a foundation laid which will enable him with a year's attendance on the mathematical professor, to make the necessary proficiency for a degree. He is studious enough and emulous enough, and when he comes to mix with his new friends and young companions he will make his way well enough. I hope he will be on his guard against those airs of superiority among the scholars, which his larger acquaintance with the world, and his manifest superiority in the knowledge of some things, may but too naturally inspire into a young mind, and I beg of you, sir, to be his friendly monitor, in this respect and in all others.

With great esteem I have the honour to be sir, your most obedient and most humble servant.[65]

John also wrote on John Quincy's behalf to relatives and friends, hoping to make the transition easier for the son who had not been home in seven years, who felt himself a stranger to his American family, who was worried that his English might sound a little odd.

Abigail was not only concerned about John Quincy but also how she herself might fare in the transition. She admitted that she dared not trust herself to think about his departure. She had grown used to sitting in his room and talking over his future plans, to writing by his fireside and having him copy over her letters, which seemed to improve with the benefit of his penmanship. "In proportion as a person becomes necessary to us we feel their loss; and in every way I shall," she confided to her sister Mary. She would miss him more than she could express.[66]

Abigail also wrote to ask that her sister take care of him in the same way she would her own children "in like circumstances." This was to include the matter of her sons' "female attachments," about which she held very firm, if not autocratic, notions.[67]

"Thoughts flew quick" when Abigail learned that Charles, in the care of her sister Elizabeth, had fallen in love: "I would not, that a son of mine, should form any sentiments with respect to any female, but those of due decorum, and a general complaisance, which every youth acquainted with good manners, and civility will practice towards them, until years have matured their judgment, and learning has made them wise." And further, "no passion but for science, and no mistress but literature."[68]

Nabby had tried to think as little as possible of John Quincy's imminent departure. He was, after all, not only her brother— she did not possibly see how his place "should be supplyd"—but also her companion and friend. She did find some consolation in knowing that, at least, he was going home to all their friends and relations.[69]

Even so, she alerted her cousin Lucy, he felt himself almost a stranger to them, having been absent so long and at a period of life when a few years makes more alteration in people than any other. "You will all tell him perhaps as the Chevalier de la Luzerne did the other day . . . —he speaks English but pronounces it as most people who learn a language at so advanced an age—'You was little *boa* when you went to America last but now you are great man.'" Both thoughtful and protective, Nabby counted on her cousin Elizabeth's promise to admit him as another brother.[70]

Speaking of her brother's "alteration" over his years abroad, Nabby recognized her own transformation as well. In just a matter of months in Paris, she could now joyfully share and understand the pleasures of the garden with her cousin Elizabeth: "At the bottom of it there is a thicket of lilacs and jasmines, planted to attract the birds in the spring. They will in a few days be out in blossom, and there is already a number of nightingales who have taken their residence in the bushes and every morning and evening when the weather is warm enough to admit, they sing to us most beautifully. The scenes I am sure would enchant my dear cousin. I never go into the garden without thinking of her. My fancy often places her by my side and I sometimes listen to her raptures upon the surrounding scenes."[71]

But she also wished to call her cousin's imagination from this rural and romantic picture to a description that would afford ample scope for her fancy, to the opera titled *Panurge dans l'Isle des Lanternes,* which she had attended with her brother in February. "The plan of this piece and the situations are very *comique:* It had been received with great applause and has had a great success." But she had found the scenery and dresses very curious.[72]

And Nabby was very sure the dancing upon the stage here would not please her cousin, because, though skillful, it lacked every idea of female delicacy and modesty. As an American lady had told her when she first went to the opera and saw the dancing, she wanted to conceal herself. "But in a very little time she could see it with the rest of the world and admire it as they did."[73]

Still, she was humbled by the difficulty of learning to speak French fluently, though she had taught herself to read it perfectly by translating a page a day from French to English, and looking up each word in the dictionary. She and her mother welcomed the move from France to England because they knew the language and looked forward to seeing some very agreeable American acquaintances living in London.

This would be an improvement over life in Paris, where everything among the people of rank must be sacrificed to pleasure, amusement, dress and etiquette. About this, Mr. Jefferson had said, she reported to Lucy, "no Gentleman or Lady should ever come to Europe under five and thirty years old, unless they are under very good guardianship—and," she added, "he is a man of great judgement."[74]

The night before his departure, John Quincy walked in the Palais Royal gardens for half an hour, went to Froulle, his bookseller, and paid his account. He also took leave of Mr. Jefferson and his family, and on his way home, he stopped at Dr. Franklin's (who had signed his passport).[75]

On May 12 John Quincy wrote in his diary: "I took leave of my parents and my sister, and got into my carriage at 12:30, with such feelings, as no one that has not been separated from persons so dear, can conceive." Eight hours and about 56 miles later he had arrived in Dreux, from which he wrote to Nabby: On the whole he did not know of any journey he had ever made that pleased him more than this would have done, had not all his enjoyments "been poisoned by recollection. You know by experience, what it is to leave, for a long, we know not how long, a time those we love. I shall not therefore describe you my feelings upon this occasion."[76]

Chapter 9

"YOUR EVER AFFECTIONATE BROTHER"

"We were then strangers almost and we are nearly so again I fear," Nabby wrote her brother a few days after his departure. Perhaps no words more poignantly capture the urgency underlying the pact between brother and sister, in John Quincy's words, "never to let a day pass without adding something to the letter which we were to be continually writing." On a more positive note, "by constant and unreserved communications" Nabby hoped "we shall not lose the knowledge we mutually gained in the last twelve months of each other's sentiments and dispositions. It is a very unpleasing idea to me, that a whole family, should grow up, strangers to each other, as ours have done, yet it has been unavoidable, and will tis probable still continue so."[1]

In their agreement when they parted, they also promised to be punctual and to "let no circumstance however trivial escape" their pens, and to discuss the various characters they met in their differing pursuits.[2]

John Quincy arrived at 4 a.m. Monday morning, May 16, at L'Orient. That night he paid 500 livres for the passage he had reserved. He then bought bedding, including a mattress, a pair of sheets, a pillow and two pillow cases; he had brought along from Paris a coverlet and half a dozen napkins. The ship was expected to furnish him with everything else.

He boarded the *Courier de l'Amérique* at L'Orient with his two trunks on May 17, 1785, planning to sail on Wednesday afternoon, May 18. He was pleased to have by far the best apartment on board, except those of the captain and officers. His quarters had a large window and two small ones that opened on the deck. This made for far fresher air than in the cramped, windowless rooms below, so dark it was impossible to read without a candle, which was forbidden for fear of fire. There were few passengers, and those he had seen did not impress him. But, he counseled himself, "the first rule of a person, who has any thing to do with the world, should adopt, should be never to judge from appearances."[3]

On the morning of May 18 he hurried to the post office. He was expecting mail from Paris, including the Marquis de Lafayette's correspondence, four letters of introduction and, most keenly anticipated, a letter from his sister. Nothing had arrived. "I am sure, you will conceive, what were my feelings," he confessed to his sister. Only one thing could excuse her; her letters were sent too late to come by Saturday's post and would not arrive till Friday, when he feared that he would have sailed. The reprimand continued: "I shall not forget, going to the Post Office without effect. You know my vanity is wounded at any appearance of neglect from any of my friends: how much must it then be mortified, when, the person is so dear to me."[4]

The boat, becalmed by lack of wind, was still in harbor when mail from Paris arrived two days later, on May 20. John Quincy begged Nabby's pardon for having accused her of neglecting him, and he had kept her letter for last. "I will not attempt to express my sensations in reading it. Was I to tell you that a tear involuntarily started from my eye, you would think I carry sentiment too far, and that I am weak."[5]

Having set the rules for their correspondence, he was embarrassed to dwell in depth on his feeling for his sister. She, too, was not unmindful of his "prohibitions" to her. Sentiments he could get from books and therefore she was to avoid them. He wanted only a "plain relation of facts as they should take place in the family."[6]

Though distances were formidable, loss inevitable, and delays in routing their correspondence almost as interminable as they were frustrating—a lapse of three months between writing and receipt of letters was the norm—brother and sister kept their parting promise "to be continually writing" sometimes 25 pages in length over a month's effort. Between July and December 1785, a span of 184 days, Nabby wrote about 57 letters to her brother and he, between his departure from Auteuil on May 12 to his end of October arrival in Haverhill, wrote 107 out of 173 days, a pace that was tempered thereafter by his studies for admission to Harvard. As of August 11, Nabby had not heard of her brother's arrival in New York; by August 26, John Quincy had received from Nabby only four short pages and these early on, before sailing. But they were both gracious. Ultimately, he was certain that she had been as punctual as he. If all he had written afforded her half the pleasure one of her letters gave to him, "I shall never regret my time."[7]

In the summer of 1785 Nabby awaited news from her brother with trepidation. Her letters during this epic interval in her life are a moving affirmation of her unsurpassing love of family and for her brother especially. They are heartfelt in their revelation of her own character, her longing for adventure, her appreciation of horizons beyond her circumstance, her humility in regard to her lesser education. Her description of her life in London reveals her compassionate nature, wisdom beyond her 19 years and, most tellingly, her wit, candor and style.

The reciprocal correspondence testifies to his loving concern for his sister. Though more guarded, less overtly emotional, John Quincy hungrily anticipated her letters, tenderly soothed her doubts about their interest and content, and kindly welcomed her advice. "Do not think, my sister, that any thing coming from you, can ever be by me considered as ridiculous or trifling." Putting her at ease, he tells her he had feared his own letters were so detailed as to be tiresome "but I now hope otherwise, and am certain it cannot be so, if I judge of your feelings from my own. . . ."[8]

Writing on July 4, 1785, Nabby had settled into the "peace and quietness" of Grosvenor Square on the corner of Duke Street only two days earlier. Though she found the situation pleasant, she was disoriented by the journey, her new home and the "whole suit of adventures enough to puzzle the brain of a philosopher."[9]

"Every day, hour, and minute, your absence *mon cher frère*, pains me more and more. I have got settled . . . in our own house in this place." But then, she continues, "I would walk, my Brother is gone. I would ride, my Brother is gone. I would retire to my chamber. Alas, I meet him not there. I would meet him in his apartment—but where is it? I would set to my work, and he would read to me—but alas, this is passed—and I am to draw the comparison between Auteuil and Grosvenor Square and sigh, and—and, wish to recall, the former."[10]

But "No." She did not wish to live in the past; she only wished that they both might be happy. And she already found herself better pleased to live in London, where "We shall live more as if we were a part of the world" than in France.[11]

Then too, always admiring, if not envious, of her brother's travels, she wondered whether his "disposition for rambling" had left him. If it had, she believed he had bequeathed it to her, not as a blessing, she feared. For her part, she would like "above all things to make one of a party to go round the world," and should this ever happen, she promised to take him along.[12]

"But to be serious," she could not see why people who have the "inclination and [*ability*] which to be sure is the most essential of the two, should not gratify themselves" by seeing as many parts of the world as possible.

If they are possessed of proper principles, it will not injure them, but make them wiser and better and happier. Pray don't you feel a great deal wiser, than if you had never been outside the limits of the State of Massachusetts Bay, which though a very respectable place, one may gain a little knowledge in other parts.

And then you know with a little policy, one may be thought nearly more respectable, for the people of our country have a wonderful liking to those who can say, "I have been in St. Paul's Church. I

have seen the lions, tigers, etc. in the Tower. I have seen the King, and
what is more have had the extreme honor of being saluted by him."

What the King!

Yes by George, the King of Great Britain France and Ireland,
defender of the Faith etc.[13]

In mid-July, Nabby worked on decoding two paragraphs of a
letter to her father from Jefferson, who noted her ascendancy to the
commission of secretary on her brother's departure for America.
She had also grown quite comfortable in her parents' house on
Grosvenor Square. Her detailed report—illustrated with a minute diagram at one juncture—toured her brother through family,
guest and dining rooms, her mother's parlor, in which they took
breakfast and drank tea, her father's library and the long room that
served him for public business, and her own room. Her furniture
included a bed on one side, three chairs covered in green velvet, a
bureau, a dressing glass, a rolltop desk and bookcases that held a
cherished gift from her father, *Bell's Edition: The Poets of Great
Britain Complete from Chaucer to Church.*[14]

Over the bookcase she had hung her brother's portrait—the
one probably painted in Holland in 1783 by Isaak Schmidt. She
was pleased to take care of it while he was away, though at the
same time wished it were better. Given her thorough description,
she thought were he to be set down blindfolded at the corner of
Duke Street and Grosvenor Square, he would be at no loss to find
her chamber.

Amused by and skeptical of London's royalty and aristocracy,
of her neighbors and their food, she was intrigued by current politics and relished a bit of gossip. "We have some respectable neighbors, at least they inherit every title to which the world affix the
ideas of *respectability,*" and some were, Nabby assumed, "perhaps
entitled to the epithet from their own merit." The man who supplied some of their furniture was "a singular kind of a body," who
had some knowledge of these great folks, his business being what
was called upholsterer and undertaker. "We made some few inquiries of him by whom we were surrounded and I must give it as he
told it":

> Upon the right hand side she is Lady Tacher and on the left Lady Lucy
> Lincoln sister to the Famous Conway [General Henry Seymour Con-
> way, described in the *Dictionary of National Biography* as a "steady
> and outspoken opponent of Britain's treatment of America"] and there
> is my Lord North's and there a house formerly belongs to the Duke
> of Dorset, but he has sold it. Such a house belongs to the Duchess of
> Bedford who ran over to France the last winter and in such a one,
> lives, Lady *what do you call* her whose husband ran a pen through her
> nose the other day, etc. etc. etc.[15]

Furthermore, she noted that "Lady Lincoln's parlor window
makes one side of the square and, our drawing room windows the
other thus, so you see we have a chance of looking at each other, an
opportunity we each have already taken advantage of. She peeps at
us, and we can not do less you know than return the compliment."
The English, she continued, might call the French starers but she
never saw so little civility and politeness in a stare in France as she
had in England."[16]

Nabby also informed her brother "what a rage for painting has
taken possession of the whole family," that a painter had lived with
them for more than a week, and they now had "the extreme felicity
of looking at ourselves upon canvas." She quoted a July 25 newspaper: "Sir J. Reynolds is employed in taking a portrait of Lady
Dungannon. Copely and Brown are exerting their skill upon their
illustrious countryman Mr. Adams, the American Ambassador."
Nabby fully expected it would soon be reported that the Boston-
born Mather Brown "is painter to the American Ambassador's family." He was very solicitous to have a likeness of Papa, thinking it
would be an advantage to him, and Papa consented. Mamma has
set for hers, and I, followed the example. It is said that "he has taken
[an] admirable likeness of my Ladyship, the Hon'ble Miss Adams."[17]

The painting portrayed her as a noblewoman of the day, lavished with ribbons, feathers and lace. Nabby assured her brother
that it was "a very tasty picture . . . whether a likeness or not." Her
father was very pleased with it, saying it had captured her character, "a mixture of drolery and modesty. I wish we could have the

other three, yourself and Charles and Thomas. I think we should make a respectable group."[18]

A visit from Ann Torkington Jebb and her husband, Dr. John Jebb, strong supporters of the American cause, delighted Nabby and her mother. Mrs. Jebb was "a great politician," and talked readily about the American war. But ever self-conscious and apologetic, Nabby cautioned her brother, "Now do not laugh at me, for, writing politicks to you, and tell me I am a *dunce*."[19]

And last, he could not complain about her not having written enough, although she feared he might find little of interest. (To her Aunt Mary Cranch she confessed that she never closed a packet of letters without wishing after they were gone that it was in her power "to recall and burn them)." However, encouraged by friends who derived pleasure from her "scribbling," and with no word of objection from her brother, the diplomat's daughter found herself "induced to continue" and to bravely voice her withering views of King George, his queen and their family, royalty in general and British policies in regard to Americans in particular.[20]

"I thank fortune we are not dependent," she wrote on September 13, "upon the favors nor smiles of majesty, nor think ourselves servilely dependent upon their customs, so we will act as we like, and bid them defiance not fearing [the] mob or anything else." This postscript was obviously her response to her father's observation that all the foreign ministers feared being mobbed if they befriended him. Faced with that danger, she added, she "should willingly put herself at the mercy of so many savages as to the nobility of this country. But all this is high treason," she added, "so keep it to yourself."[21]

One week later, the family witnessed the anniversary of the king's coronation in a palace drawing room with the Prince of Wales and the Princesses Royal, Augusta and Elizabeth. "Such a ridiculous ceremony," commented Nabby, wondering at all the people hoping to be spoken to by the royal family and eager for their smiles. "I'll tell you what," she wrote John Quincy, "I like the king better than the queen, or at least he dissembles better than the queen. . . . She is a haughty proud imperious dame—and I believe feels excessively mortified to see our family at her drawing room," for which reason Nabby would choose to go often for spiteful pleasure. "Her countenance is as hard and unfeeling as if carved out of an oak knot. It nevertheless expresses her sentiments with respect to us."[22]

Though she disparaged Britain's royalty and politics, its theater had gained an ardent fan when Nabby witnessed Sarah Siddons's performance as Desdemona. Although seen under the disadvantages of being pregnant, Siddons nonetheless exceeded Nabby's expectations.

As of August 11 there was still no word from John Quincy. Nabby envisioned her brother in Boston. "And now," she asked, "tell me all that I am entitled to know, of what passes within your own mind, from what sources you derive pleasure, and from what you receive pain. No one can more sincerely rejoice in the one, regret the other and participate in both than a sister."[23]

August 11 is also the date of a decisive letter from Nabby to Royall Tyler. She returned his letters and miniature, and requested that he would return hers to her Uncle Cranch, with her hopes that he was well satisfied.

The same day, Abigail wrote John Quincy of Nabby's decision, warning him about the contents of some mail he would be receiving, but urging approval of the writer's wise and prudent conduct. "Be Silent! We are all rejoiced because it came to her own accord free and unsolicited from her, and was the result I believe of many months anxiety as you were witness."[24]

Nabby's letters to her brother made constant reference to Colonel William Stephens Smith, who had taken lodgings with them. The tall, 30-year-old soldier, with a good figure and a ruddy complexion, a graduate of the College of New Jersey (later called Princeton University), class of 1774, had proven himself a most dashing character.

As Nabby told her brother, they had gone to call on a friend. "Just as we were in the carriage, Col. Smith rode up in his carriage with a General Stewart from America. Mamma told the colonel that she intended to have asked him to accompany her, but he had company. Next moment, he ordered the door opened and jumped into our carriage, telling his companion that he would find papa at home. Perhaps you will say that Col. sacrificed politeness to gallantry," but Nabby was obviously impressed. And so were her parents.[25]

As his mother later confided to John Quincy, they were not long at Grosvenor Square before she saw that "the gentleman who made a part of the family" was happier reading to the ladies and walking, riding and going to the theater with them, than in any other company or pastime. While she was anxious about his being a "stranger" to Nabby's situation, Abigail felt awkward saying anything to the colonel, not sure that he was aware of his own feelings. But finally, she had felt compelled to intervene, as she had with Tyler, this time, to "hint" to the colonel about Nabby's engagement in America. This led to a discussion of "utmost frankness," followed by the colonel's request for a leave of absence to attend Frederick II's last major military review in Prussia. While Smith was away, Nabby made her decision and released Tyler from his commitment.[26]

But even as his mother angled for John Quincy's approval—"I like him much, but I do not rely wholly upon my own opinion"— Abigail included a copy of her husband's near fawning recommendation to Richard Henry Lee, the president of Congress. Sadly, John Adams would come to question and regret his early enthusiasm following the colonel's disastrous business ventures. "Col. Smith has been very active and attentive to business, and is much respected. He has as much honour and spirit as any man I ever knew. His principles are those of his country, and his abilities are worthy of them."[27]

One omission is prescient in hindsight; in the copy she made of her husband's recommendation of Smith, Abigail left out: "I suspect, however, that a dull diplomatic life, especially in a department so subordinate, will not long fulfill all the wishes of his generous heart."[28]

In early September, the colonel still away, Nabby longed for word from her brother. But with none since they had parted in May, their mother was admittedly *"triste"* and Nabby, in truth, nearly despondent. She wished he was with them, that he had not gone home; they were "so inanimate and stupid" without him that she expected he would hear of her "from Bedlam next, as a melancholy mad one."[29]

She had counted on the July boat to bring her news of his arrival in the United States but heard nothing. Spirits soared only at breakfast on September 5, as Abigail described with vivid pleasure to John Quincy:

> enter Mr. Spiller the butler, who by the way is a very spruce body, and after very respectfully bowing with his hands full "Mr. Church's compliments to you Sir, and has brought you this pacquet, but could not wait upon you today as he was obliged to go out of town." Up we all jumpt, your sister seized hold of a letter [of July 17] and cry'd my Brother, my Brother. . . . We were not long opening and perusing, and I am so glad, and I am so glad, was repeated from one to another. . . . The Chocolate grew cold, the top of the tea pot was forgotten . . . yet nobody felt the loss of breakfast, so near akin to joy and grief that the effect is often similar.[30]

Nabby, at the sight of her brother's handwriting, had rushed—"a nimble footed Daphne" her mother later said—to break the seal of the envelope and was actually rewarded with two letters of May 25 and July 17.[31]

And now that Nabby had perused them "and got a little over the agreeable flutterations and heart beatings," she could thank him for his punctuality and chide him for not having been more particular, for not having told her more about his new acquaintances than their names. She wanted to hear his remarks on every one, "in short I wished you only to have thought aloud, to me."[32]

But she forgave him; she knew about the "insipid sameness" of life on shipboard, and given her intuitive understanding of her brother's temperament, sympathized that "an impatient disposition must suffer more than I can have an idea of." She might have been looking over his shoulder as he wrote on his first morning at sea on May 25: "We had nothing but the sea, and the azure vault bespangled with stars, within our sight." And four days later: "Sea sickness has already prevented me for several days from putting pen to paper."[33]

But if he could not write to Nabby, he could imagine what she might be doing at different times—now at the door of the post house with half a dozen beggars around her, now stopping at a public house, now on the road, then at Monsieur Dessin's waiting at Calais for a wind to cross the channel, and now at last safe in London, better situated than at Auteuil. "There is a real pleasure in thinking of our friends when absent, and the greater the illusion is, the more satisfaction we enjoy," he wrote on June 1. Two weeks later, on June 14, he remembered her birthday, "consequently a *jour de fête* for me."[34]

On Sunday, July 17, at one o'clock in the morning, *Le Courier de l'Amérique,* after an eight-week passage, sailed up Manhattan's Hudson River. About to anchor, John Quincy told his sister that "one of the numerous reasons for which I am rejoiced at arriving, is that for the future I shall not be obliged incessantly to speak of myself. I shall immediately begin another letter, and I hope it will not be so insipid as this." New York's *Independent Journal* took note of the arrival of "the son of the Honorable John Adams, Esq., Minister Plenipotentiary from the United States of America to the United Netherlands."[35]

Chapter 10

"THE SENTIMENTS OF MY HEART AS THEY RISE"

ith the tedious eight-week journey behind him, John Quincy accepted the invitation of Richard Henry Lee, the president of Congress, to stay with him. He had at first excused himself but with repeated offers—he "press'd it on me, with so much politeness, that I did not know how to refuse." Such attentions embarrassed him, "yet they give me more pleasure, than they would, if I was myself the object of them," he wrote Nabby on July 19.[1]

John Quincy had no illusions about his popularity. Since his arrival every moment of his time had been taken up. He had a great number of letters to deliver—to Mr. Jay at Number 8, Broadway, and to Governor Clinton among others—and an even greater number of visits to make. He had been introduced at different times to almost all the members of Congress; he had walked, talked or dined with a great spectrum of leaders of the day, including with François Barbé-Marbois, the French diplomat (whom he had tutored in English during their voyage together in 1779 on *La Sensible*); with Diego de Gardoqui, the Spanish chargé d'affaires; with Pieter Johan van Berckel, the Dutch minister (whom he had known in Rotterdam); with the Reverend John Witherspoon, president of the College of New Jersey (later Princeton); with Elbridge Gerry and Rufus King, the Massachusetts delegates to Congress. He had also attended the city's largest church, St. Paul's, just off Broadway between Partition and Vesey Streets, which he found quite unlike its namesake in London—akin to comparing Alexander the Great and the virtually unknown apostle Alexander the Coppersmith.

And then there was his encounter with the "most curious" General Robert Howe, commander of the southern department of the Continental Army. On August 5, General Howe attended one of President of Congress Lee's weekly dinners, after which guests were invited to sing songs. That evening after the general failed to find his voice, he had cried out, "give me that madeira to revive me, for I have been flattening my voice by drinking burgundy." And sure enough, after his glass, John Quincy told Nabby he sang "Once the gods of the Greeks" very well.[2]

To his father he wrote about the crisis of the day, which concerned trade and disagreement over "An Act for the Regulation of Navigation and Commerce," prohibiting all exportation from Massachusetts to British vessels and restricting all British vessels to three ports, Boston, Falmouth (later Portland, Maine) and Dartmouth. Although generally considered a necessary measure, John would be hearing from the president of Congress who was much against it. On rereading his letter he added, "you will perhaps think I had better be at my studies, and give you an account of their progress, than say so much upon politics. But while I am in this place I hear of nothing but politics. When I get home I shall trouble my head very little about them," he promised.[3]

Soon it was time to think of how he would travel to Boston, by boat or stage, and money, of course, was a consideration. He finally decided—friends told him it was the best way to see the country and meet people who might be of use to him afterward—on horseback. Carriages were dangerous, and if he could find a proper horse, on good terms, he could buy one and sell it in Boston for close to his purchase price.

He ended up bargaining with the Dutch minister, who wanted 50 pounds. He offered 40 and settled with Mr. van Berckel for 45, a bad buy as it turned out, as the horse threw a servant early on in the trip, and, wrote John Quincy, "stumbles considerably." Ten miles out of New York, on August 14, he wrote Nabby fearing his parents would think this venture by horseback "an imprudent, headless scheme." But he insisted his parents should know every-thing he had done—"I may commit faults, but I will not add to them, by concealing them."[4]

His companion on the journey was the son and namesake of Jacques-Donatien Le Ray de Chaumont, the French aristocrat, supporter of the American Revolution, and John Adams's recent landlord in Auteuil. The two young men—Chaumont traveling by carriage—were slowed frequently by powerful heat but also en-countered pleasant surprises. Middleton, Connecticut, situated on the banks of the Connecticut River, deserved the poet's songs as much as ever the Rhine, the Danube, or the Tiber did; heading toward Hartford there were some of the most beautiful prospects he had ever seen.

On delivering a letter to Dr. Ezra Stiles, the president of Yale College, John Quincy recalled Mr. Jefferson's assessment of him as "an uncommon instance of the deepest learning without a spark of genius." Nevertheless, John Quincy found him "very civil," al-though the university library was neither as large nor as elegant as his Papa's.[5]

Past Springfield, the mistress of the tavern at which they dined called him by name because of his resemblance to his father, who had stopped there many times. At Worcester, where his Papa had studied law, the appearance of the town pleased him very much. Arriving in Boston on August 25, 1785, the young men found a room to share at Mrs. Kilby's in State Street.

Of course, he realized that "the absence of two of the best parents in the world and of a sister on whose happiness my own depends, can certainly be compensated by nothing." But he also wrote: "No person who has not experienced it can conceive how much pleasure there is in returning to our country after an absence of 6 years especially when it was left at the time of life, that I did, when I went last to Europe. The most trifling objects now appear interesting to me."[6]

John Quincy immediately went in search of brothers, uncles, aunts, cousins, his grandmother, friends, colleagues, acquaintances and, so it seemed, his earlier life. At day's end, he wrote most movingly: "I shall not attempt to describe the different sensations I experienced in meeting after so long an absence, the friends of my childhood, and a number of my nearest and dearest relations. This day will be forever too deeply rooted in my memory, to require any written account of it. It has been one of the happiest I ever knew."[7]

And yet, alongside his great pleasure, John Quincy also found reentry bewildering and sometimes sad. His first visit was to his mother's Uncle and Aunt Smith. Their 15-year-old daughter came to the door and though John Quincy knew her, she did not recognize him. He then tracked his uncle to his store and to his pleasure was immediately recognized. Dinner with his Uncle Cranch and cousins was strained but not unhappy. "We sat, and look'd at one another; I could not speak, and they could only ask now and then a question concerning you." And yet he was quite content: "How much more expressive this silence, than any thing we could have said." He trusted Nabby would not think him too sentimental for going to Cambridge to see his brother Charles, now a student at Harvard. His aged, honored Grandmamma Adams gave him the most heartfelt welcome of all. But her repeated question, "When will they return?" in reference to his family, was one he could only answer with a sigh.[8]

Sunday at church he was surprised that the Reverend Anthony Wibird's voice, looks and manner seemed so familiar to him, as though he had heard him every week during his long absence from Braintree. Looking around the meeting house, he knew every face over 30 but scarcely anyone under 20. The same was true of his relatives. He might have been in the company of his cousin Billy Cranch a hundred times without having even the most distant suspicion of who he was, though he would have known his aunt and uncle at first sight anywhere.

That afternoon, after church, his courage faltered. "No object ever brought to my mind such a variety of different sensations" than visiting his family's home and his birthplace. He did not stay two minutes, "nor would it give me the least pain, was I forbidden to enter it again," he told Nabby, "before your return." He did look over his father's library, found the books in good condition,

only somewhat musty and dusty "which shows that their owner
is not with them." It reminded him of the days of his childhood,
most of which were passed there, "but it look'd so lonely, and
melancholy without its inhabitants, as to draw a deep sigh from
my breast." A month later he again visited the house, spent three
hours there, and told Nabby: "There is something to me, awful
in the look of it now. All within is gloomy, and sad, and when it
will look more pleasant—oh! I must not think of that." In truth,
he very much feared it will be "a long, long time before, I shall see
you again. I dare not tell our friends here, my real thoughts on the
subject."⁹

On Wednesday, August 31, he rode on to Cambridge, looked
around Harvard, admired several exceedingly fine portraits done
by Mr. Copley, and found the library "good, without being magnificent." He then paid a visit to the president of Harvard, Joseph
Willard, who advised, as anticipated, further studies in Greek and
Latin in preparation for his entrance the next spring. A week later
he was on his way to Haverhill to the home of the Shaws for a
three-month tutorial.¹⁰

Just before sunset, he reached Haverhill, a town of about 33.3
square miles, and a population of about 2,400, thriving on farming, fishing, shipping and shipbuilding, and a number of tanner-
ies. The Shaw family's white-columned house, the parsonage of
the First Parish Church of Haverhill, lay near the top of the hill on
Main Street. He detailed for Nabby his reunion with their 13-year-
old brother Tommy, last seen at age 6. Reverend Shaw had taken
John Quincy around to Tommy's room and called out, "Here's
somebody wants to see you." His announcement had been greeted
with silence. Three minutes passed without a word until at last Mr.
Shaw had prodded Tommy: "Don't you know this person?" "I believe I do," said Tom, "I guess it's brother John." So you see, John
Quincy told Nabby, rather cheerfully, "I could not remain long
incog." His good friend John Thaxter was also in attendance, but
"of course [he] knew me."¹¹

Nor did recognition of her esteemed nephew pose a problem
for his Aunt Elizabeth, who wrote to her sister Abigail: "The long

looked for, the modest, the manly, the well accomplished youth, is come at last. And had he needed any thing to have made him doubly welcome to our house, but his own agreeable behaviour, the evident credentials he bears in his eyes, about his mouth, and in the shape of his face of being the son of my excellent, and much loved brother and sister, would alone have gained him a most hearty reception."[12]

And further, she told his mother, "Never was there a youth that bore a greater resemblance to both parents," given his "father's lus- ter and the mother's bloom." His mannerisms—"his head inclined on his left shoulder, one eye half shut, and his right hand in his breeches pocket"—strongly recalled the happy days she had spent with them early in their marriage.[13]

By October 1 John Quincy felt settled but found his studies far more arduous than he had counted on. Greek was to be "the grand object" that claimed his greatest attention. He was to master nearly all of the New Testament and between three and four of the eight volumes of Xenophon's *Cyropaedia,* plus five or six books of Homer's *Iliad.* More secure in Latin, he had already done part of *Horace*'s four books of lyric poetry. In English, he had to study Watts's *Logic: Or, The Right Use of Reason in the Enquiry After Truth* and John Locke's *Human Understanding,* and something in astronomy.

Given the formidable task ahead, he felt obliged to ask Nabby for a temporary suspension of their agreement to write frequently, at least until he got to Cambridge. He planned to do little social- izing in Haverhill, and he anticipated a continual sameness in the days ahead, which meant that he should have little of interest to write her. Still, he would set apart half an hour two days a week to write at least something.

Studying through the winter, progress was painfully slow at times. Getting through 100 verses in the Old Testament was rela- tively easy, though it was time-consuming to look up the vocab- ulary. But the more he read in both Greek and Latin, the more deeply he admired both the classic and the lyrical poets. He felt rewarded for all his pains in making the acquaintance of Virgil and in Horace he found many "noble sentiments." The Latin lines copied into his diary may have had deep personal resonance for him; in translation, they read, "Cease to ask what the morrow will bring forth, and set down as gain each day that fortune grants!"[14]

Initially, on arriving at the Shaw home, John Quincy had been glad his trunks were delayed: the lack of decent clothes provided him with an excuse to refuse invitations. He was not eager to make new acquaintances given his experience of the last eight years: no sooner had he made friends, he had been obliged to leave them, probably never to see them again. As a result, his heart, "instead of growing callous by a frequent repetition of the same pain, seem'd to feel every separation more than any of the former ones." Not for the first time he declared himself "really weary of this wandering, strolling kind of life" and vowed to "form few new acquaintances, have few friends," but such as he might—quoting Hamlet—"Grapple to my heart with hooks of steel."[15]

In spite of his intense resolve, he did make new friends with members of a prosperous Haverhill family, the Whites; he enjoyed his first Thanksgiving celebration, a recently established custom determined by the governor of Massachusetts on December 15, and seemed a bit disappointed that Christmas, "a great and important day among Roman Catholics and the followers of the Church of England," was not observed in this country, nor anywhere, he believed, by the dissenters.[16]

Nevertheless his preparation for Harvard was his first priority. Unforeseen interruptions were inevitable, but where he could help it, he remained focused. His Aunts Mary and Elizabeth were keenly aware of their nephew's motivation and commitment. Both women were sympathetic, but only to a point. They frankly disapproved of his sleeping habits. Elizabeth wrote that her nephew was not quite so fleshy—she had written "fat" in the initial draft—and wasn't prey to distractions; to the contrary, "he was too much *engaged* to suffer any thing but sickness or death to impede his course." Mary, in the same sentence that she assured Abigail that Cousin John, as she called her nephew, had not lost his studious disposition by coming to America, also told her sister that she was almost afraid to let her children visit Haverhill this last vacation lest they interrupt him. And because he never retired before one o'clock in the morning, she feared "he would wear out both body and mind."[17]

Had Aunt Mary been privy to her nephew's diary, she would have learned that he could not study in the morning because the household was so busy, "but that when every body else in the house was in bed, I have nothing to interrupt me"—hence the late hours.[18]

Predictably, given the realities of his life in Haverhill, John Quincy admitted to an "impatient state of mind." Early on he had fretted about how to continue with his journal, facing as he did a continual repetition of one day like another. But then he decided that his approach would be different: "Little narrative, and the most part of what I write will be observations." It was to be the same with his letters, in which with disarming, if not reckless, candor, he would dramatize not only his "family values," but his moral, emotional and philosophical struggles to bridge the transition from a worldly life abroad to the confines of "so small and retired a town as this."[19]

From the start, he confided to his cousin William Cranch that he could appear content in person or in print when "I have it not at heart." Haverhill was not the place for politics or local public affairs. Nor was the climate helpful. Wintry weather began within a month of his arrival, cheerless gray days of pouring rain and chilling cold reminiscent of St. Petersburg. On a snowy, stormy day in November, he recalled "The cherish'd fields / Put on their winter robe of purest white"—lines from James Thomson's poem called "Winter"—"I am not fond of seeing this robe."[20]

As for the locals, they were really persuaded they should incur divine displeasure as much by dancing—violently opposed as a heinous sin by the Baptist minister Mr. Smith—as by stealing or committing murder. John Quincy despaired over this mysterious tendency to take exception to rational amusements by minds "disposed to strain at a gnat and swallow a camel."[21]

His world had shrunk. The family he lived with presented as perfect an example of happiness as he had ever seen, but their demeanor differed from his. "Variety is my theme, and life to me is

like a journey, in which an unbounded plain looks dull and insipid."
Left far behind across the ocean were conversations with diplomats
and princes about state affairs. In Haverhill "The way we have here
of killing time, in large companies, appears to me, most absurd and
ridiculous. All must be fixed down in chairs, looking at one another, like a puppet show, and talking some commonplace phrases
to one another."[22]

And "talk of the follies and fopperies of Europe"—there even
young ladies of fortune were given an excellent education before
they were introduced into the world. In Haverhill, young ladies
without fortunes or titles thought it beneath them to know anything but to dance and were taught that if they could "talk non-
sense very fluently, and sit very straight and upright five hours
together in one chair, they will be most accomplished women."
For the most part, "our damsels are like portraits in crayons,
which at a distance look well, but if you approach near them, are
vile daubings." He hesitated to continue: "you will think I am too
severe," he told Nabby, "but it is certainly too often the case with
our young women."[23]

Even more challenging than small-town life was his tantalizing
infatuation with another of his Aunt and Uncle Shaw's boarders,
the 17-year-old Nancy Hazen. Nancy had an eye that seemed "to
have a magic in it," and a "fine natural genius . . . so long employed
upon trifles" that they almost were a part of her, he wrote his sister.
Rather short but well-proportioned, with a very fair complexion,
she was not a beauty but had in her countenance something uncommonly interesting. As to her character, he had not seen enough
of it in October 1785 to define it precisely, but after further acquaintance he would know more.[24]

Meanwhile, he could say that she lost her father when she was
very young, which had been her great misfortune. She had boarded
for a considerable time in Boston and was drawn very young
into a mindless social whirl. He did not doubt that she would be
much more universally admired than she was, had she been well-
educated. Lacking that benefit, she was instead celebrated by a
parcel of fops. He was nevertheless obsessed by Nancy Hazen,

granting that "Nature has been liberal to her in mind, and person, though her foibles were probably owing to education."[25]

Even as days passed, he persisted in his argument: "Oh! that our young Ladies were as distinguish'd for the beauty of their minds, as they are for the charms, of their persons! But alas! too many of them are like a beautiful apple, that is insipid, or disgusting to the taste." At this point he admitted he might sound too extreme and supposed he heard his sister cautioning him to "Stop, stop, young man. . . . It ill becomes you, at your age, to set up, as censor of the conduct of the ladies . . ."[26]

Which was "True my Sister," he conceded. "I will own I am wrong, and had I not made a resolution, to give you my most secret thoughts, I would restrain the indignation, which I cannot prevent from rising in my breast, when I see the best gifts of Nature neglected or abused."[27]

Still, in the privacy of his diary he showed no such restraint, at once jealous and protective: "Afternoon and evening out, as indeed she always does . . . She seems to have engrossed the attention of almost every youth in Haverhill . . . the girl has surely something bewitching in her for she treats them all very ill." When she was unwell after having had one of her teeth drawn, John Quincy wished she could be persuaded to take care of them: "the want of proper attention to the teeth, is an universal failing in this country, very hurtful both to the beauty and the health of our ladies."[28]

On an afternoon in the company of both cousin Lucy Cranch and Nancy, he was struck by their essential differences: "You know how serious, how prudent, how thinking your cousin is," he told Nabby. Nancy, by contrast, "is as gay, as flighty, and as happy as you could wish to see a person." He added, two days later: "Miss H(azen) I have mentioned before; her form is very pretty, her wit agreeable, her ruling passion vanity."[29]

By November, John Quincy admitted his impatience, discontent, and bleak spirits. At first he supposed that his demanding schedule of study—some days he did not even get outside—might explain his melancholy state. But, truthfully, he had to recognize another cause of his suffering. He was hopelessly in love and knew that

"When our reason is at variance with our heart, the mind cannot be in a pleasing state." He recognized the symptoms, regretted the inconvenience. An ardent young man, and a lonely one, he knew he had to "exert all my resolution to keep myself free from a passion, which I could not indulge, and which would have made me miserable had I not overcome it."[30]

Obviously schooled on his mother's precepts on the subject of choosing the right mate, this issue was uppermost in his mind. Having known men, undoubtedly those he had met abroad—"of great sense and experience who fell into fatal errors, when discretion should have guided their actions"—he feared with passions high and the blood warm that it was impossible to make a prudent choice.[31]

He hoped for at least another decade "never to have my heart exclusively possessed by an individual of the other sex." Passions, he declared, were "the jaundice of the mind." Finishing his letter to Nabby at two in the morning, he noted in his diary that he then burned his fingers on the lighted candle and bruised his toes in the darkness. Worst of all, he had affronted Miss Nancy earlier by speaking somewhat too abruptly.[32]

With two months to endure before his departure for Cambridge and Harvard, his plight over Nancy Hazen ended rather abruptly. On February 9, according to his diary: "Miss Nancy finally left us, this afternoon; and is going to board at Mr. Israel Bartlett's. Her going away has given me pleasure, with respect to myself; as she was the cause of many disagreeable little circumstances to me."[33]

His attraction to Nancy can hardly have sat well with a young man who had described his priorities to his sister as follows: "Study for years and years to come, is to be my only mistress, and my only courtship that of the Muses. These sentiments, which my parents and dearest friends have always inculcated in me, and which my own reason and inclination confirm, will, I have no doubt, be lasting."[34]

John Quincy did not mention—he may not have known—that Nancy had left at his aunt's request. As Elizabeth Shaw explained in answer to Nabby's inquiry about the young woman her brother had referred to at some length: "The frequent Assemblys occasioned her being out at so late hours as made it very inconvenient."

In America, late hours were considered "as greatly prejudicial to health, and as incompatible with the peace and good order of families. . . . Any deviation from those good and wholesome rules, would be viewed as more criminal in our family than in others. This with some other things made me feel very desirous that she should remove her lodgings."[35]

"Nature had indeed been very bountiful to this young lady," she continued, "and lavished her favors almost with too liberal a hand." At the first acquaintance she seemed made "to engage all Hearts, and charm all Eyes. . . . She had a qui[c]k wit, a fine flow of spirits, and good humor, a lively imagination and an excellent natural capacity." Yet with all these endowments, at least in Elizabeth Shaw's estimation, Nancy found it utterly impossible to establish "those sentiments of sincerity, delicacy, and dignity of manners, which I consider as so essential to the female character." The banishment of Nancy Hazen was undoubtedly motivated by his aunt's urge to protect her nephew from any romantic attachments. She had great hopes for her nephew but felt "His time is not yet come. . . ."[36]

On the last day of January, John Quincy made this terse notation: "about two months longer, will put an end to my residence here, and I shall then rejoice, for more than one reason." Almost from the start he had minded living in the clergyman's strictly regimented establishment: breakfast at 8, dinner at 1, prayers at 9 and retirement a short time after. The severity of such a schedule, he thought, would discourage people inclined to the study of divinity in America from following that profession and, he predicted, "will lessen the number very greatly in a little time."[37]

But there was more to his disillusion with the Shaw household. He discovered that his aunt had read his diary, and concluded he "could not be induced to live long in such a situation, to be suspected and spied, and guarded" no matter how good his relatives' motives and wishes for his welfare.[38]

His aunt was equally alarmed by what she found in the course of invading her nephew's privacy. Aunt Elizabeth wrote to Nabby of finding extensive records of the sensitive discussions taking place in the household: "These journal[s] of [h]is are a continual spy upon our action." And the spy's offense at being spied on was keener because of the judgments rendered. Aunt Elizabeth "was never half so afraid of any young man in my life," because John Quincy was "so exceedingly severe upon the foibles of mankind."[39]

He was certainly merciless about the foibles of women. One day she had mentioned to him some lines of Matthew Prior about the female sex, "Be to their Virtues very kind, be to their Faults a little Blind," and "do you believe it," she asked Nabby, he had placed them in his journal "in a most satyrical point of view." When called on this point, John Quincy innocently claimed "my aunt thinks as I do." And so, she had concluded, "he finds a fine shelter for himself, under my wing."[40]

In a real sense, Elizabeth was not far off the mark. Her concern for him was genuine, if intrusive. She warned that "His candle goeth not out by night" and she feared he would ruin his eyes. She deeply appreciated his "high sense of honor" and "great abilities well cultivated" through his travels. "In him I see the wise politician, the grand statesman, and the patriot in embryo."[41]

Elizabeth and her husband would feel John Quincy's absence more than that of any pupil who had ever lived with them. If she were to speak plainly, she wrote to her sister, she wished "Mr. JQA had never left Europe . . . that he had never come into our family. Then we would not have known him. . . . Then we should not have been so grieved" at his departure. He used to read to her on some evenings, which always gave her pleasure. His comments were good, he was respectful of the author and "in company Mr. JQA was always agreeable, pleasing, modest, and polite." It was only in private conversation that the imperfections of youth "were perceivable," for he did have some rather peculiar opinions and was a little too decisive and tenacious about them. In fact, his brother Thomas had said to him one day, "I think brother you seem to differ most always from every one else in company."[42]

One evening, on the subject of courtship and self love, John Quincy had argued that "Self was the ultimate motive of all actions, *good, bad,* or *indifferent*" and maintained his position, contradicting his uncle to the point that Mr. Shaw questioned why he should so firmly take issue with his elders.[43]

In retrospect, John Quincy thought the charge was partly true. He feared he was too tenacious, making people suppose he was "obstinate, and dogmatical, and *pedantic*." But in self-defense, he wrote in his diary, he had only wished "to own my thoughts," not to impose them on others. While he did not believe it impolite to think differently from a person older than himself, he recognized the discourtesy in openly combating his uncle's opinion. Grown sour on the subject, "Reverence for age," John Quincy supposed, "is one of the most important and necessary qualities a young man can have: and a deference to their sentiments, ought, apparently to be shown to ones elders, even though, they were absurd and ridiculous." Obviously dissatisfied with this notion, he had added "N.B. To think more upon this subject."[44]

While meticulous in his diary entries, in preparing for his entrance exams, John Quincy went for months without writing his sister. He began again as soon as he was done, waxing cynical about a process in which it was not necessary to know anything but what was found in a certain set of books—which some of the best scholars, after having taken their degrees, forgot and could not have qualified for a place back in the freshmen class. He had not, since the first of January, left the Shaw house four hours a week, Sundays excepted, but now he would write more often.

On March 14, John Quincy had ridden half a mile up the river where a path for the boat was cut through the ice and arrived at Cambridge a little after sunset. The next day, between nine and ten, he was examined in Latin, Greek, logic, geography, and mathematics before President Willard, four tutors, three professors, and a librarian.[45]

"After they had done with me, they laid their wise heads together to consult whether I was worthy of entering this University, the president came marching as the heroes on the French stage do, and with sufficient pomposity said: 'Adams, you are admitted.'" And though he had already resolved to show all the respect and deference to every member of the government of the college that they could possibly claim, it would be different with Nabby, to

whom he could give his real sentiments, "such as arise spontane-
ously . . . and that I cannot restrain."[46]

His candid opinion of President Willard was less than flattering. Though a man of great learning who promoted the honor and
interest of the university, Willard had "little knowledge of mankind." Exceedingly stiff and pedantic, he was even ridiculous at
times, especially in refusing to call any undergraduate by any but
his surname. John Quincy concluded his report to Nabby rather
benignly: "he is often laughed at for affecting so much importance,
yet he is esteemed and respected for his learning."[47]

One week later John Quincy returned to see Harvard's president, "as he had commanded me. Said he, speaking with an emphasis upon every syllable, 'Adams, you may live with Sir Ware,
a Bachelor of Arts.'" John Quincy was quite delighted, as Ware,
who had graduated from Harvard and was now a schoolteacher
in town, was "very much esteemed and respected in college and
had an excellent chamber" which he was very fortunate to share
with him, as it was "more agreeable and less expensive than living
in college."[48]

On learning of his son's "Admission into the Seat of the Muses,
our dear alma mater," John Adams was elated and hoped, he wrote
from London: "you will find a pleasure and improvements equal to
your expectations. You are now among magistrates and ministers,
legislators and heroes, ambassadors and generals, I mean among
persons who will live to act in all these characters. . . . You are
breathing now in the atmosphere of science and literature, the float-
ing particles of which will mix with your whole mass of blood and
juices. Every visit you make to the chamber or study of a scholar,
you learn something."[49]

The immediate reality was different. John Quincy had spent
the evening of his acceptance in the college with the sophomore
class at what was called a "high-go." They had gathered in the
room of one of its members, some of whom got drunk, then went
out and broke the windows of three tutors, and after this sublime
maneuver, staggered to their chambers. Unimpressed, John Quincy
noted in his diary that "Such are the great achievements of many

of the sons of Harvard, such the delights of many of the students here."[50]

But soon he was a complete convert to the college, founded in 1636. John Quincy followed in the tracks of three generations of Quincy men, and of his father. His brother Charles had already been admitted; his brother Thomas wasn't far behind. Despite some reservations, he reassured his father that he was "strongly confirmed in your opinion, that this university is upon a much better plan than any I have seen in Europe."[51]

Chapter 11

"STUDY IS MY MISTRESS"

*W*riting a century later, Henry Adams opined, "For the large and increasing class of instructors, or persons interested in the improvement of instruction in this country, few more entertaining and suggestive books could be written than a history of instruction at Harvard College." However, primary sources beyond the college's own records were scarce—with one precious exception being a student's diary covering 15 months in the years 1786–1787. Never mentioning his grandfather by name, Henry goes on to describe John Quincy as having "a fair share of youthful crudities, but was as free from extreme prejudices as could be expected from a young man of his age, while his manner of looking at things occasionally betrayed a mind which had come into closer contact with grown and educated men than with people of his own age. . . ."[1]

After nearly a year at Harvard, John Quincy would question, amid the quantity of trivial events which he had noted in his diary, whether there was sufficient matter worthy of remembrance to compensate for the time he spent in writing it down. At all costs, he wished to avoid "insipid narrative."[2]

But while he fretted over his privacy—he could not keep his diary under lock and key, safe from his brother Charles and other curious eyes—he could not resist recording his intimate thoughts,

thereby creating an extraordinary self-portrait during his formative Harvard years.

John Quincy had set out from Braintree with his cousin Lucy at
10 a.m. on March 22, purchasing some furniture upon arriving in
Boston three hours later. From his corner room on the third floor of
Hollis Hall, he could see as far as Charlestown and Boston and the
spacious fields between. After time spent "fixing things to rights,"
he reported to Nabby on the most prized part of his first day at
Harvard: "We have had one of the most extraordinary northern
lights that I ever saw. It is now ten o'clock, no moon, yet I can read
a common print in the street."[3]

The adjustments to this strangely welcome world were numerous. Unused to rising at 6 a.m., he did not hear the bell ring the
next morning and was tardy for prayers. He learned that every time
a student was tardy for prayers, he was fined a penny. As a result,
Harvard's newest scholar quickly decided "that a student must prefer not attending prayers at all to being a half minute too late." He
later complained that the bell was insufficiently loud to wake him
for a Saturday seminar. But while he may have skipped other prayer
sessions, this was the last class he would miss until a month before
graduation.[4]

His trunks from Haverhill would eventually show up on March
29, "very apropos as I began to be quite scanty for clean linen." And
though comprehension of Harvard's customs, traditions and laws
might prove elusive, John Quincy's indoctrination began immediately. It was customary for two students, chosen alphabetically, to
speak passages from an English author; his turn came on Friday,
his third day of college. Having decided to recite Jacques's famed
soliloquy from Shakespeare's *As You Like It,* he was bemused by
the response at his expense: at "the description of the Justice, in
fair round Belly with good Capon lined," every person present,
tutors and scholars alike, burst into a loud laugh, as though "I myself, truly represented the character."[5]

But no one, he learned, took lightly the sanctity of Harvard's traditions and the zeal with which they were enforced by seniors. His
diary lists several, including locked door at the start of lectures, and
prohibitions against whispering, spitting on the floor, and freshmen

wearing hats in the college yard. These rules and regulations seemed to have limited effect, however. After a meeting to review them, "several of the class went and had a high go. In consequence of which the librarian had a number of squares of glass broke in his windows. Drunkenness is the mother of every vice."[6]

At college for ten days, though he admitted that "a person fond of studying will never want for employment," John Quincy was overwhelmed by the structured environment in which he was so compulsively embedded. To give Nabby an account of one day was similar, he insisted, to that of a month:

> One week we recite to Mr. James, the Latin tutor. The next to Mr. Read, in Euclid. The third to Mr. Jennison, in Greek, and the fourth to Mr. Hale, in Locke. Then begin again:
>
>> Monday morning at six, bell for prayers; from thence reciting; half after seven, breakfast; at nine, go to Mr. Williams upon practical geometry; at eleven, a lecture upon natural philosophy; half after twelve, dinner, and reciting again; five, prayers.
>>
>> Tuesday, instead of practical geometry, at nine, it is a lecture from the Hebrew professor; at two in the afternoon, a lecture from the professor of divinity.
>>
>> Wednesday, at nine, another lecture upon divinity; at eleven, lecture on philosophy; two, afternoon, lecture on astronomy.
>>
>> Thursday, reciting in the morning.
>>
>> Friday, nothing but a lecture on philosophy.
>>
>> Saturday, reciting in the morning to Mr. Read, in Doddridge's *Lectures on Divinity*, a pretty silly book, which I wonder to find among the books studied here.[7]

And "So they went from day to day," he seemed to sigh. "If there was once a week an episode, such as going to Boston, or dining out, this was the greatest show of variety" that he could make.[8]

A month later, he was more at ease, telling his mother "I never was able any where to study, more agreeably, and with so little interruption." As to the students, he found a "confused medley" of good and indifferent. He knew all his own classmates and sought out those with the best reputation, intellectually and ethically.[9]

That his personal appearance, of perpetual concern, had suffered as his studies grew more demanding, was obvious to his family, especially to his cousin Elizabeth Cranch. At tea with him, she reported to her Aunt Abigail: "I could not help laughing at Cousin John, for the learned dirt (not to say rust) he had about and around him. I almost scolded, however we seized his gown and jacket and had a clean one put on. I took my scissors and put his nails into a decent form, and recommended strongly a comb and hair-string to him. He invited me to come once a quarter, and perform the like good services [for] him again. Charles by contrast, though not too strikingly so, is naturally and habitually neat." But, very sweetly, proud of all her beloved and respected "brothers," she concluded, "they are all good—as yet."[10]

Betsey's sister Lucy, though less bothered by her cousin's appearance, worried instead about his obsessive "steadiness," his "very great attention to his studies" that she feared would injure his health. "He is determined," she told her Aunt Abigail, "to be *great* in *every particular.*"[11]

There was no question that had John Quincy arrived three months earlier, he would have entered the senior class and graduated in June. But he had no regrets. He would have missed practice in public speaking in chapel, classroom, at his clubs, on a stunning breadth of subjects which he wisely surmised would be "advantageous." The topics noted in his diary, posed by the tutor in metaphysics to affirm or deny in two or three pages, included: "Whether the immortality of the human soul is probable from natural reason"; "Whether internal tranquility be a proof of prosperity in a republic"; and "Whether inequality among the citizens be necessary to the preservation of the liberty of the whole."[12]

He obviously relished this kind of intellectual jousting. His membership in the A. B. Club, presumably a rival to the more famous Speaking Club, had given him the chance to speak memorably

on the subject of education, his family's supremely enduring avoca-
tion. Indelible parental teachings chimed in the background as he
declared: "The advantages which are derived from education is one
of the most important subjects that can engage the attention of mankind; a subject on which the welfare of states and empires, as well as
of small societies, and of individuals in a great measure depends."[13]

Invited to join the Phi Beta Kappa Society on June 21 along with
his classmate Josiah Burge and his cousin William Cranch, "There
was in the admission," he wrote, "a considerable degree of solemnity." In his first talk to this group the subject was "Whether civil
discord is advantageous to society," and he could not think on
first view of one topic more unfavorable to the person who must
support the affirmative.[14]

Yet paragraphs later, in example after example, he concluded
that "as discord, sometimes proceeds so far as to be very injurious
to society, so when it is kept within proper bounds it is productive
of the happiest consequences."[15]

To illustrate, he pointed out that a ship was frequently used
as the "emblem of an empire," and the metaphor was very appli-
cable: "When the serenity of the ocean is ruffled by a moderate
gale, the vessel pursues its course steadily, and is in perfect security;
but a total calm, is almost always the forerunner of an outrageous
tempest."[16]

So it was, John Quincy reasoned, "where the heads of government were never wholly in peace, never quite secure in their power,
the empire was safe. Where there were two parties or more, continually watching each other's conduct, always endeavoring to pry
into each other's secrets, it was very difficult to intrigue against the
State without being discovered."[17]

This nascent theorizing about the "proper bands" of government was unexpectedly put to the test only a month later. According to Samuel Flagg Bemis, John Quincy's "bookish studies of
history and politics brought to bear for the first time on the political situation of his own day in his own country," by the tumultuous
uprising known as Shays' Rebellion.[18]

On August 29, 1786, in Northampton, Massachusetts, a body of 300 or 400 armed men had "prevented the Court of Common Pleas from sitting and bruised the high sheriff dangerously," John Quincy wrote in his diary one week later; as a result, "the Commonwealth is in a state of considerable fermentation." Similar action was taken against the court in Worcester, where its members adjoined to a tavern but were prevented from meeting the following day.[19]

By early September, unable to raise the local militia to quell the rebels, the governor of Massachusetts issued a proclamation calling upon the people at large to support the state constitution and directed the state's attorney to prosecute the abettors of these riots. At least the militia in Boston had offered their services and declared support for the government. "Where this will end time alone can disclose," but, John Quincy feared, "it will not before some blood is shed."[20]

The rebels, led by Daniel Shays, were a bitterly disillusioned and impoverished group consisting mostly of farmers who were former soldiers. The profound grievances that prompted their revolt included, as John Quincy noted, foreclosures on their farms and homes and the high cost of legal defense plus the intolerable penalty of servitude in debtor's prison. They wanted lower taxes and the issuance of paper money to cover their indebtedness.

At his most pessimistic, John Quincy supposed that idleness, dissipation and extravagance had led to their desperate plight. On further deliberation, he came to think that such disturbances, if properly managed, might be advantageous to a republican government—but if allowed to gain ground, they must inevitably lead to a civil war with all its horrors. "Such commotions," he thought, "are like certain drugs, which of themselves are deadly poison but if properly tempered may be made highly medicinal."[21]

By the end of October, the insurrections were far from silenced; he feared that unless some vigorous measures were taken, the commonwealth must perforce fall. But in another month there was a more promising turn of events. Just before prayers the evening of November 27, 40 horsemen under the command of Oliver Prescott, a Groton physician, rode into Cambridge to protect the court at its next day's sitting from the anticipated onslaught of 1,500 rioters, reported to be within four miles of the town.[22]

The unrest ended with the capture of rebel leaders. But when he heard that all prisoners convicted of treason would receive a full and free pardon, John Quincy wondered: "Is it much to the credit of our government, that a man who has stolen . . . should die for the offence, while others commit treason and murder with impunity?"[23]

The "tumults" sparked by Shays and his "ignorant restless desperadoes," as his mother referred to them, had undermined John Quincy's confidence. According to his grandson Charles Francis Adams, John Quincy was badly shaken that "a new set of men had come forward who could neither write English nor grasp principles of political action [but] breathed the full communistic spirit of the time."[24]

Although the danger had passed, John Quincy questioned the viability of a government that had lacked sufficient vigor and energy to immediately suppress the insurrections; he also noted a degree of timidity and irresolution, "which does no honor to the executive power of a commonwealth."[25]

Reluctantly, he questioned the so-called Articles of Confederation, drafted a week after the Declaration of Independence and ratified only in 1780, that permitted each state of the 13-member confederacy called "The United States of America," to govern itself as free, sovereign and independent.

Much as the idealistic, 19-year-old John Quincy hoped that in two or three months public tranquility would be completely restored, he confided to his mother his concern that the present form of government would not continue long. While the poor complained of government oppression, "men of property" thought the Constitution gave too much liberty to unprincipled citizens. He worried "that a pure democracy appears to much greater advantage in speculation than when reduced to practice . . . and bids fair for popularity."[26]

John Quincy also questioned his own position politically. He had feared that having received so large a share of his education in Europe, his countrymen might find him insufficiently devoted to a republican government. Instead, he had found, "that I am the best republican here, and, with my classmates, if I ever have any disputes on the subject, I am always obliged to defend that side of the question."[27]

His unvarnished intellectual honesty in this matter could have uncomfortable consequences. In one such case, an academic debate resulted in stinging criticism by a classmate, relayed to John Quincy secondhand.

He had spoken on the question of "Whether inequality among the citizens, be necessary to the preservation of the liberty of the whole." In the course of the talk he addressed the critical question of "What protection can any laws afford a citizen in a state where every individual thinks he has a right of altering and annulling them at his pleasure, and where nothing is wanting but the capricious whim of a vile rabble, to overturn all laws and government?"[28]

At this point in the debate, John Quincy turned to his opponent, William Cranch, and acknowledged that popular opinion would likely be against him, but that the logical extension of uncritical allegiance to equality was "manifest absurdity." As nature had, in every other particular, created a very great inequality among men, he did not see on what grounds they all should share an equal degree of power. Accordingly, he had reached the conclusion that "too great a degree of equality among the citizens is prejudicial to the liberty of the whole, the present alarming situation of our own country will I think afford us a sufficient proof."[29]

The overheard assessment of John Quincy's performance— "Adams's forensic at the last exhibition was the meanest . . . ever delivered in the chapel"—hurt John Quincy. Painfully aware that it was "a most unhappy circumstance, for a man to be very ambitious, without those qualities which are necessary to insure him success in his attempts. . . . Such is my situation," he wrote on September 29:

> If it be a sin to covet Honour
> I am the most offending Soul alive.[30]

He mused further on his inability to convince his circle of friends that his deserts were equal to his pretensions. Often he wished that he had "just ambition enough to serve as a stimulus to my emulation, and just vanity enough to be gratified with small distinctions."[31]

Often perhaps, but not very often. Getting by was not a tolerable concept for this son of famous patriot parents. His values on this matter were absolutely clear: better to strive and fail, because the man who would settle for fifth or sixth place and be content, while he has an equal chance of obtaining the first, "must be despicable."[32]

Intermittently, John Quincy mentioned various diversions: picking blueberries, hunting, fishing, dancing. By far, music was his favorite pastime. His cousin William had bought him a flute on a rainy day during his first school vacation, and he had taken lessons on his new prized possession. He had never had an opportunity, he explained to Nabby, of paying steady attention to any musical instrument, and now that he was settled in one place, he was glad for the relaxation from study to amuse himself with a little music,

> When the soul is press'd with cares
> Awakes it with enlivening airs.[33]

By March 1787, he was able to copy flute music by hand, played for family and friends and performed with the Musical Society at Harvard. He complained that the flutes and violins were usually so difficult to keep in tune "that we can seldom play more than three or four items at a meeting." They had lasted for only an hour on March 28 because "it would not be easy to collect a set of worse instruments than we have, among eight or ten violins and as many flutes . . . not more than two or three that will accord together, without scraping and blowing. . . ." Still, despite the failure to meet his perfectionist standards, and Nabby's worry that it might be harmful to his health, he had found that the flute was his "greatest amusement and the chief relaxation after study, and indeed it affords me so much pleasure that I cannot think of giving it up."[34]

His concern about musicianship was ongoing. Some years later at a reception in Holland, he would tell a French diplomat, as the band played the "Marseillaise," that he was extremely fond of music and by dint of great pains had learned to play the flute very badly, but he could never learn to perform on the violin, because he lacked the ability to tune it. He consoled himself with the idea that he was American and therefore not capable of great musical powers; American genius was more inclined toward painting.

"Oh, do not say so!" the diplomat had countered. "You will be chargeable with high treason against the character of your country for such a sentiment, especially if you were to deliver it to an Italian or French connoisseur and virtuoso." But John Quincy held his ground. The sound of the "Marseillaise" was forcible proof, he said, of the fact he had stated. The Americans fought more than seven years for their liberty, and if ever a people had inspiration for combining harmony with the spirit of patriotism, they had it during that time. Yet never during the whole period had a single song been written that "electrified every soul and was resounded by every voice" like France's patriotic songs. He then genially conceded, in defense of his countrymen, that he knew many who had a musical ear.[35]

In addition to his amusements, he wrote his sister a steady stream of commentary on his superiors: "my real sentiments, unterrified by authority, and unabridged by prejudice." Thus, a young preacher who looked already one foot in the grave, "appeared plainly to suffer while he spoke in a whining manner," and governors with important airs and haughty looks seemed to have a maxim among them to treat the students pretty much like brute beasts. Of an unpopular tutor in college, reputed to be very ill natured and severe in his punishments, the rumor that he was leaving college was "too good news to be true," whereas Mr. Read, who retained a little of the collegiate stiffness, "endeavors to be affable, and is very sociable." In general, he concluded, "these people when distant from their seat of empire, divested of that power which gives them such an advantageous idea of their own superiority, are much more agreeable. . . ."[36]

As for his social life, he assessed one evening of dancing from seven until two in the morning by saying, "Of the ladies, some had beauty without wit, and some wit without beauty; one was blest with both, and others could boast of neither. But little was said . . . when the feet are so much engaged, the head in general is vacant."[37]

The wise and sympathetic caution of Nabby's response might have surprised her brother. It gave her great pleasure that his conduct was not marked with any youthful indiscretions, but she advised that "it might be politic in you not to prejudice the heads of the university against you by being satirical upon their foibles." She nonetheless commiserated about the difficulties of paying attention to people who have not earned respect commensurate with their authority: "the mind revolts at the idea." She ruefully assessed her own shortcomings, admitting, "I could never bring my countenance or my actions to oppose the sentiments which I possessed. I have almost envy'd some persons, that innocent and necessary *art* which could conceal under the veil of politeness, the opinions they possessed."[38]

The weather had turned cold, leaves were falling from the trees, and it was not his preferred choice to spend his time reading, writing, walking and playing. "This is dull life, and convinced me, how grossly the whole herd of novel and romance writers err in trumping up a country life. Let them say what they will: the most proper situation for man is that which calls forth the exertion for faculties and gives play to his passions. A negative kind of happiness, like that of the brutes, may be enjoyed in the country, but the absence of pain or anxiety is not sufficient for a man of sensibility."[39]

Even as he ruminated, he worried, as he told his mother about his correspondence with his sister, "I address almost all my egotism to her; and indeed seldom make mention to her of any thing or anybody besides myself." After a worrisome three month silence, he responded to Nabby's letter of the past September only to repeat what he had so frequently said: "that the noiseless tenor of a college life, and the unvaried uniformity of circumstances, cannot furnish a subject, either for interesting relation, or brilliancy of sentiment."[40]

And then, in wry humor, forgetting his fear of being self-reverential, he noted:

On the 17th of October the fall Vacation began, and I went to Brain-tree. On the 1st of November the Vacation being ended I returned to Cambridge. Remarkable events! are they not. "But" say you, "how did you spend your time at Braintree during that fortnight"? Why Madam, I read three or four volumes of history, and Burlamaqui upon law; I wrote a few letters, but as they had not a voyage of 3,000 miles to undertake, I was not as much trouble in equipping them; I went a fowl-ing once or twice, and had my labour for my pains. I prick'd off a few tunes and blew them on the flute. And further the deponent saith not.[41]

Then, weary of his playful patter, he grew pensive as he continued with his letter to Nabby.

I now return to my history. For six weeks after my returning here I went once to Mr. Gerry's (he has bought a house and farm in this town, and came to live here about five months' since). Excepting this visit and two or three at Mr. Dana's, I went nowhere.—Upon recollec-tion, I must also except one dancing party, that we had with a number of the young ladies in the town: I would describe it to you, and might possibly raise a smile, by characterizing the ladies; but I must avoid it, for fear of having another lecture for severity.—In December two vio-lent snow storms which happened in one week; stopp'd up the roads in the country so effectually, that no wood came in town for three weeks. Many families in town, and two thirds of the students, were entirely destitute. I was without any, four of the coldest days we have had this season.

On Wednesday the 13th of December, the students were dis-missed, for eight weeks. The vacation commenced three weeks sooner than common, on account of the impossibility of procuring wood. I determined to remain here through the vacation, for several reasons. I thought that four of us going at once to Mr. Cranch's would make it troublesome, and inconvenient to them: and although I have always been treated there with as much attention and kindness as I could pos-sibly wish, yet it was not like home; the absence of my parents and sis-ter deprived Braintree of its chief attractions, and the place by reviving so frequently the idea of their absence caused too many melancholy sensations, to be an agreeable residence.[42]

He did not want to leave Cambridge and undertake the social obligations that would follow, but remaining in college entirely alone
was not appealing. Fortunately, James Bridge, a classmate of excellent repute as a scholar and a gentlemen, was in similar circumstances, and the two young men agreed to chum together during
the vacation and board at Professor Wigglesworth's. "This gentleman is equally free from the supercilious frown of the president
and the distant reserve of a tutor. He treats us with an unaffected
complaisance, which is not the most remarkable characteristic of
all the governors of the university; he commands respect, but not
by insisting on it as a highwayman, who demands your purse."[43]

In the professor's house were two young ladies—his niece and
daughter—and he could give Nabby a few traits of their characters:

> Miss Catharine Jones, just turn'd of eighteen, has a share of wit, and
> a share of good nature, which is however sometimes soured by a small
> tincture of caprice. She is not wholly exempt from vanity; but as her
> understanding, rather than her person is the object of this vanity, she
> endeavours to appear sarcastic, because she supposes, a satirical tal-
> ent must imply an uncommon share of wit. To sum up my opinion of
> her: I could esteem her as a friend, I could love her as a sister, but I
> should never think of her as a companion of my life.
>
> Miss Peggy Wigglesworth is two years older than her cousin. Her
> complexion is of the browner order; but this defect, if a defect it be, is
> compensated by a rosy variety of colour; her face is not beautiful, but
> is remarkable for expressing all the candor, benevolence, and sincerity
> of her heart; her shape, would be genteel in France or England, though
> her size, would seem to give her the title of a pretty woman as Fielding
> expresses it. . . .
>
> Notwithstanding all this, she is almost universally the object of,
> friendship and esteem, rather than of love. I am sensible of this fact
> myself, and when I search my own mind to find the causes of it, I am
> reduced to condemn either the passion of love, or the sentiments by
> which it is produced.[44]

There was a third young woman who had captured his attention. In the course of the vacation he had frequently been at Mr.

Dana's, where he had encountered Miss Almy Ellery. She was unfortunately somewhat deaf, but uncommonly sensible, and "(what I am griev'd to say is still more uncommon in this country) her mind is much improved by reading; so that she can entertain a company with a large variety of conversation, without having recourse to the stale, and trivial topics of common-place, or to the ungenerous, and disgraceful topic of scandal." She wasn't handsome, and he supposed her to be 27 years of age; yet if asked to choose a seat among 20 of the most beautiful young ladies in the state, it should certainly be by her side. "I have been endeavoring, my sister, ever since I returned from Europe, to find a female character like this, unite to great beauty of person." His search so far had been unsuccessful, and he was beginning to have the same prejudice against beauty, "as you have expressed in one of your letters against handsome men."[45]

Though he might protest, he was fascinated by young women within and outside of his circle, and despite his former infatuation with Nancy Hazen, he had been able to promise his mother that "with a little resolution and some good luck, your young Hercules has till now (that is the past summer) escaped the darts of the blind deity—and will be for 15 months very secure—there is now no lady with whom I am acquainted around here that I consider as dangerous. Study is my mistress." It was against the law, he told his sister, for him "to look at a young lady till the 20th of July," the date on which he would graduate from Harvard.[46]

In response to his sister's advice, on several occasions John Quincy affected some concern of her tendering him "another lecture for severity." Actually, their regard for one another's well-being was mutually affectionate and sensitive. On John Quincy's part, he had worried for months about his sister and her future with Royall Tyler. In May he had been relieved to receive a letter from his mother, of February 16, brimming with praise of Colonel William Smith's courtship of his sister and the announcement that he must have anticipated: "Know then my dear son that this gentleman is like[ly] to become your brother."[47]

His sterling credentials followed. His character was not only fair and unblemished but highly regarded wherever he was known; at the early age of 21 he had commanded a regiment through the war with prudence and bravery. A friend had said, "it would take more proofs and arguments to convince him that he would be guilty of a dishonorable action than any other man he ever knew in his life." As to Nabby's memory of former affections, they proved not to be founded upon a durable superstructure and had properly vanished "like the baseless fabric of a vision."[48]

In response, John Quincy told his mother he had never "felt such strange sensations, as to reading the first page of my sister's letter, where in the most delicate manner possible, she informed me of the connection." He was thrilled by the news, given Tyler's poor reputation. "The contrast was striking. Surely if there is a providence that directs the affairs of mankind, it prompted your voyage to Europe."[49]

That summer, newly married and settled about half a mile from her parents on Grosvenor Square, Nabby supposed, "Mamma will inform him of every particular that he may wish to be informd of." Meanwhile, he must continue to favor her with his daily journal with as much freedom as ever "for your sister is not altered, only in name. She feels, if possible, an additional attachment to her family. . . ."[50]

John Quincy's college education continued: debates took place; tutors lectured on magnetism and electricity; the Phi Beta Kappa group met, as did the A. B. When he was honored by his class for a mathematics-related project, he wrote his father that their Euclid suppers at Auteuil and their Greek breakfasts at The Hague had been surprisingly productive. He also continued to fill his diary with detailed sketches of his classmates, none so admiring, affectionate and respectful as that of James Bridge. This friend clearly epitomized the qualities John Quincy most admired:

As a scholar and as a gentleman, he is inferior to no one in the class. . . . His natural abilities are very good, and they have been greatly improved by study. His passions are strong, but in general he keeps them well under command. His genius is metaphysical rather than rhetorical; in reasoning with him, we are rather convinced by the force of his argument than seduced by the brilliancy of his imagination. He is possessed of much benevolence, and ambition occupies a large share of his mind; he does not endeavour to conceal this, but freely owns his expectations, which are so sanguine, that I somewhat fear he will not entirely realize them all. His advantages however will be peculiar, and it is I think very probable that he will one day be eminent in the political line. Law will be his study and I have long hoped that we should be together in one office, but many difficulties attend the scheme, and I fear much that it will not take place. My friendship for this gentleman, and three or four more of my classmates, saddens very much the anticipation of commencement, when we must part, perhaps forever.[51]

By April he complained of waning interest, of sameness—highly entertaining lectures of the previous year afforded little amusement or instruction this time around—and of poor weather, lack of exercise and fatigue. Yet, in the very last weeks, he grew increasingly nostalgic. He was continually reminded of the ending of this particular journey, such as when he took books from the library for the last time on June 8.

He hoped that in two or three years more, he would have "taken down, without any violence, all the elegant castles which my imagination had built in the air, over my head, and which for want of a foundation, were liable to be overset and crush the builder, if any accident had happened." In short, he was now so firmly persuaded of the superior advantages of a public education, that his only regret, he told his mother, was that, "I did not enter the university a year and a half sooner."[52]

In preparation for commencement looming in July, President Willard on the morning of May 17 had assigned 18 seniors special roles in the ceremony. These included several orations in Latin, one in Hebrew, and two in English, one of which was allotted to John Quincy on the importance and necessity of public faith to the well-being of a community.

Commencement Day, Wednesday, July 18, was fair, cool and pleasant. At about 11 o'clock the procession began from the door of Harvard. The succeeding classes went first; the graduating class of 41 (several did not attend) preceded the president, professors and fellows of the university, who were followed by the governor and council of the commonwealth. The president opened the ceremony for prayer and the performances began.

His cousin Lucy had all along thought John Quincy resembled his mother, but she had never seen the likeness so striking as when he delivered his oration. "It was his mother's mouth that smiled when he addressed the ladies, his mother's eyes that glistened when he bade his classmates adieu—he spoke with great fire and energy, with a spirit that did honour to the son of a patriot and states-man." His Aunt Elizabeth was sure no one could be a judge of her nephew's eloquence unless they kept their eye fixed upon his face and "saw each passion, & each feeling called up" as he spoke.[53]

The *Massachusetts Centinel* weighed in on the ceremonies two days later.

> The two principal performances were the orations by Mr. Adams and Mr. Freeman. The first of these certainly declaimed upon a well cho-sen subject . . . in a manly, sensible and nervous style of eloquence. The public expectations from this gentleman, being the son of an ambassador, the favourite of the officers of the college, and having enjoyed the highest advantages of European instruction, were greatly inflated. The performance justified the preconceived partiality. He is warmly attached to the republican style of his father, and descanted upon the subject of public justice with great energy.[54]

The orator himself was delighted. "I found our chambers as full of company as they could hold and was complimented and flattered on every side. One such day every year would ruin me."[55]

John Quincy and his parents had discussed his future over many months. Back in August 1786, he had asked his father for recom-mendations of an office in which to study the law. His first choice would of course be his father's, but if John was still detained in Europe, he needed to find an alternative. John Quincy wanted to avoid Boston for several reasons—it was "unfavorable to study, and . . . it would be almost doubly expensive."[56]

His mother suggested either the office of John Lowell of Boston or Theophilus Parsons of Newburyport, both "gentleman eminent in the profession." Mr. Lowell, however, was said to have a natural indolence that prevented pupils from learning as much as they might from a more active character. Mr. Parsons's character was equally high as a lawyer; he had an insatiable thirst for knowledge and was known to enjoy young people of similar taste and inclinations. Both parents encouraged John Quincy to choose Newburyport over Boston.[57]

John Quincy did not look forward to long years ahead, having to study in order to qualify for business: "And then Oh! and then; how many more years, to plod along, mechanically, before getting into the world?" He was appalled at the idea of spending one third of a long life preparing to act a part during another third; and the last to be passed in rest and quiet waiting for the final stroke, "which places us just where we were 70 years before. Vanity! Vanity! all is vanity and vexation of spirit."[58]

He arrived in Newburyport just before sunset on August 13, in decidedly low spirits. He was to live in this place without friends for three years; and whether happily or not, he fretted, "time only must discover; but the presages within my breast are not such as I should wish realized."[59]

He had gone to see Mr. Parsons that afternoon and rented a place at Mrs. Leather's, widow of shipwright Joseph Leather, on State Street, a block below Mr. Parson's office, where he would board for the next several years. She was, in her new boarder's eyes, "a good old woman, who even a hundred years ago would have stood in no danger of being hang'd for witchcraft." She was, however, as he later reported to his mother, "civil and obliging, and what is very much in her favor, uncommonly silent so that if I am deprived of the charms, I am also free from the impertinence of conversation."[60]

Before his final departure from Boston, Aunt Mary Cranch had found her nephew more affected at leaving his family than she could have imagined for someone. "Having been toss'd about the world," that is, traveled so much. She seemed surprised by his anxiety about going to a place "where he knew no one & where he cared for nobody, & nobody cared for him," and when he "found it necessary to draw the back of his hand across his eyes when he said it—& from sympathy" she had done the same. By way of comfort, she had reminded him not to forget that he would be within 14 miles of his Aunt Shaw, who loved him like a parent, and to whom he must go if he was unwell at any time. He had promised to write and to visit them in the winter. They had fixed him off so well that she thought he could not want too much done for him till then.[61]

John Quincy's sorrow at yet another leave-taking did not, however, diminish his curiosity or penchant for analysis. Waking from a strange dream, he wrote in his diary on August 30, "I cannot conceive where my imagination ransack'd the ideas, which prevailed at that time (and which remained secret) in my mind. This part of the action of the human soul is yet to be accounted for: and perhaps has not been scrutinized," he supposed, "with so much accuracy as it might have been."[62]

Chapter 12

"A STUDENT IN THE OFFICE OF THEOPHILUS PARSONS"

*I*nterest in John Quincy's days as a law student skipped a gen-eration. To his son Charles Francis, they merited only a single paragraph. For though they gave "a curious and not unattractive picture of the social relations prevailing in a small New England town at that period," they did not "seem to retain interest enough to warrant the occupation of space" in the 12-volume, painstak-ingly abridged version of the diary Charles Francis called *Memoirs*. By contrast, to John Quincy's grandson, the second Charles Fran-cis, they were worthy of a volume of their own. Attempting to ra-tionalize his father's omission, perhaps, the grandson supposed he had overlooked them because they contained "little of, so-called, historical value."[1]

More likely, Charles Francis senior feared their disclosure might blur the heroic image he meant to foster in his father's name. For, in fact, they were disturbing, intensely revealing of the strug-gles of a shatteringly vulnerable young man during one of the most emotionally charged periods of his entire life.

With the passage of 30 or so years, the younger Charles Francis viewed the diary from a far different perspective. Asked to speak at the 175th anniversary of the First Congregational Church of Newburyport in October 1901, in commemoration of his grandfather's student years in the seaport town, he had gathered some extracts from his grandfather's two small octavo volumes, bound in calf, bought in Paris and entitled "Ephemeris," which he would publish under the title *Life in a New England Town, 1787, 1788.*

Unlike his father, he had been "greatly interested" in his grandfather's record of his time as "a [law] student in the office of Theophilus Parsons." John Quincy's diary gave "a curious and graphic picture of social, everyday existence in a small Massachusetts seaport during the closing years of the eighteenth century. Its maturity of tone is perhaps its most noticeable feature." Possibly, it was the heartbreaking candor of John Quincy's revelations regarding his depressed mental state that moved the protective grandson to solicit sympathy for his esteemed grandfather's plight by way of exploring his unusual background. "It is well to bear constantly in mind," he advised, "that not only was the writer an exceptional character, but his experience had been so very unusual as to be . . . almost, if indeed not altogether, unique." He had passed the period between 11 and 18 in a "curiously diversified and roving life in the Europe of Louis XVI, Catherine II, and George III"—separated from family, associated with men of distinction much older than himself such as Benjamin Franklin and Thomas Jefferson—"and then suddenly transferred at his own volition to America."[2]

In addition, to highlight the breathtaking physical and implicitly cultural differences involved in John Quincy's transition from the great cities of Europe to the towns of America's northeast, the younger Charles Francis noted that in the time covered by the diary, "Boston, not yet a city, numbered some eighteen thousand inhabitants, and Cambridge a little over two thousand. The town of Quincy had not yet been incorporated, but was still the North Precinct of Braintree, its population a little short of three thousand." As for Newburyport, between 1787 and 1790, it was a community of some 5,000 "of the old New England type," and "while distinctly provincial . . . it had an individuality."[3]

But also, Charles Francis continued, "The period was critical." The country had emerged from the revolutionary troubles only a few years before and was still in the formative stage. The land was poor, and the taxes burdensome. "Hence the spirit of unrest was great; crude theories of money, government, and the rights of man were in the air, and it yet remained to be seen whether the people of Anglo-Saxon descent in America would prove equal to the occasion and develop into a nationality, or whether, victims of a morbid jealousy of all centralized authority, they were to sink into a state of chronic anarchy."[4]

John Quincy found the first few days in Newburyport long and tedious and had in fact gone to bed early that Sunday "merely from ennui." The weather did not help. Alternately very warm and very cold, these New England transitions were almost intolerable to foreigners, as he wittingly included himself. He had begun his studies in Theophilus Parsons's office with the first volume of Robertson's *History of Charles the V,* an account, Parsons recommended, of the feudal institutions that influenced current laws of contemporary Europe. In the next days he read for the second time the Reverend Hugh Blair's *Lectures on Rhetoric and Belles Lettres,* took up Emmerich de Vattel's *Law of Nature and of Nations,* and pronounced Rousseau's *Confessions* "the most extraordinary book I ever read in my life." His fingers grew so sore from copying extracts from Blackstone's that he thought he might throw out his pen.[5]

With his fellow students, Horatio Townsend and Thomas Thomson—only three students were permitted in an office simultaneously—he attended the Court of Common Pleas, where he heard cases about stolen sheep; about real estate (valid vs. invalid deeds) and a mason's suit for payment for building and plastering a brick house; and about four men arraigned for different thefts, all of whom pleaded guilty and were sentenced to whipping and hard labor.

Evenings he walked and dined with friends, and one night toward the end of September, a group of them got to singing after supper, "and the bottle went around with an unusual rapidity, until a round dozen had disappeared." Deciding it was time to leave, he slipped away, and took a walk with Townsend, arriving at his lodgings about 1 a.m., where the two friends sat for an hour and smoked a pipe or two together.[6]

The next morning, though he thought he had not been intoxicated, he was dismayed to find himself suffering from a severe headache. He could neither attend meetings, nor read, nor write. He "pass'd the day with much tediousness" as he did the following two days, the consequences of his Saturday evening "frolick." Given his tragic family history of alcoholism—his mother's brother William Smith was already ravaged with the disease—he knew that "inseparably in all cases of intemperance is the punishment allied to the fault!"[7]

With relief, days later, he had recovered his "usual tone," able to attend to the very uninspiring task of copying declaration forms, admittedly an unrewarding piece of drudgery that was, he consoled himself, a necessary piece of work the sooner finished, the better. He resented it nevertheless. He had hoped before he came to study with Parsons that he would have time to read for entertainment but, after passing eight hours a day in the office and four more in writing minutes and forms at home, he had energy for only the most menial tasks. And indeed, if for three years he continued to work at this rate, as he had since the day he had entered this office, "the de—l [devil?] will be to pay," he wrote in his diary, "if I have not some stock of law. Health is all I shall ask."[8]

But very far from the entertainment he sought, Parsons's recommendations included Coke's *The First Part of the Institutes of the Laws of England, Or, A Commentary upon Littleton,* the standard elementary treatise for law students since 1628, superseded only by the more (comparatively) modern Blackstone's *Commentaries on the Laws of England,* published between 1765 and 1769. The contrast between Coke and Blackstone was "like descending from a rugged, dangerous and almost inaccessible mountain, into a beautiful plain, where the unbounded prospect on every side presents the appearance of fertility."[9]

In ensuing days, he complained of being distracted, of the year fading away, of proceeding rapidly on a decline. By October 20 he had left Newburyport, heading for Boston with stops in Haverhill and Hingham. Not the way to acquire the science of the law, he admitted, but he excused himself on grounds that "dissipation is so fashionable here that it is necessary to enter into it a little in order not to appear too singular." Also, as Mr. Parsons would probably be away for the next three weeks, he did not know a more "eligible" time for a vacation.[10]

During the next ten or so days of his self-appointed holiday, he dined and chatted with friends and relatives, sang, smoked, played cards, passed an enjoyable afternoon in his father's library reading some of his journals from 1769 to 1776. At one party he felt lucky to draw a Miss Smith of Sandwich for a partner and dance with her for most of the evening. At another party, in honor of his beloved cousin and former tutor John Thaxter's forthcoming marriage, he drank from "big bellied bottles," and though very moderately, he felt it necessary to walk at length with his good friend Leonard White.[11]

Once back in Newburyport, his thoughts were searching, sad, and deeply pessimistic. One night in late fall he was in such a poisonous mood that his demons—whether real or imagined, political or social, is unclear—propelled him to the doorstep of his neighbor and friend Dr. John Barnard Swett. While he had described the events of the previous day as "quite uninteresting," they must have been quite alarming, triggering "an opportunity to observe the effects of the Passions. How despotically they rule! how they bend, and master, the greatest and the wisest geniuses! 'Tis a pity! 'tis great pity! that prudence should desert people when they have the most need of it. Tis pity, that such a mean, little, dirty passion as envy, should be the vice of the most capacious souls."[12]

Whether he was scolding himself or a colleague, or bemoaning a disturbing incident is not known. But clearly miserable, he pondered "Human Nature": "how inexplicable art thou! Oh, may I learn before I advance upon the political stage, (if I ever do) not to put my trust in thee!" Addressing himself—or perhaps an unwelcome reader of his diary—he continued: "the lines that precede . . . may be mysterious to you sir, but if so, remember that it is none of your business. And so I wish you good night."[13]

John Quincy trusted Dr. Swett, with whom his Harvard class-mate and future surgeon Moses Little lived and studied. Swett, a 36-year-old graduate of Harvard who had trained at the University of Glasgow with the distinguished Scottish physician and professor William Cullen, was in John Quincy's estimation "a man of learning, and ingenuity." He had traveled in different parts of Europe, and had "a mean idea of human nature," by which he meant that Swett was keenly conversant with the physical defects and infirmities of mankind, viewing humanity, as all doctors did, "in a state of humiliation." But Swett told him that his complaints "were not worth speaking of," and John Quincy left, having no choice he thought but to "let them take their chance." Not for long, as it turned out.[14]

By December 6 he faced a new and more frightening challenge. He was seriously depressed in a way unknown to him ever before. The evening had started off cheerfully, spent with Harvard class-mates Thompson, Little and Putnam at the latter's lodgings. They had talked on diverse subjects in a gathering, which like many "renew the recollection of those happy scenes, which we have all gone through in college; and in this manner, I now pass some of my most agreeable hours."[15]

But back at his own lodgings at Mrs. Leather's, and after reading an hour or two, he felt "a depression of spirits to which I have hitherto been entirely a stranger." He had frequently felt dull, low spirited, in a manner out of tune; "but the feelings which I now experienced were different from what I ever knew before, and such as I hope I shall never again experience." They kept him awake a great part of the night, and when he finally fell asleep, they disturbed his rest "by the most extravagant dreams."[16]

Another week passed and his anguish deepened. "The question," he wrote on December 18, "what am I to do in this world recurs to me very frequently; and never without causing great anxiety and a depression of spirits: my prospects appear darker to me, every day, and I am obliged sometimes to drive the subject from my mind, and to assume some more agreeable train of thoughts." He did not covet fortune, and honors, he began to think, were not worth seeking. And at Christmas, almost a non sequitur, he wrote, "I suspect I shall soon drop this journal."[17]

It was undoubtedly his mother to whom he best described the challenges that so bedeviled him these days. First the good news, as he always tried to temper his concerns when writing to either of his parents. Reviewing the past months, he explained, he could not possibly have an instructor more agreeable than Mr. Parsons. His chief excellency was that no student could like asking questions more than he liked answering them. He was never at a loss, and always gave a full and ample account of the proposed subject as well as all related matters.

As for the study of law itself, it was more interesting than he had been led to expect. He had read three or four authors with pleasure as well as improvement, and the imaginary terrors of tediousness and disgust had disappeared. But in their stead, other fears had arisen that created greater anxiety in his mind, which was only increasing.

There were two problems, as he saw it, of enormous weight. One was the degree to which lawyers, no matter how innocent and upstanding, evoked the hatred of their fellow citizens. The very despicable writings of Benjamin Austin Jr., who (under the pen name Honestus) had published *Observations on the Pernicious Practice of the Law* a year ago, were calculated to spread "a thousand lies, in addition to those published in the papers all over the country, to prejudice the people against the order."[18]

The other reason for his great ambivalence about his legal studies was the ogre of competition. The number of lawyers was growing, but with little business to be divided among them, he thought they were in danger of starving one another. When he considered these particular disadvantages, as well as the time-honored need for great skill, enormous effort and good luck to achieve sufficient professional standing to earn a living, he confessed he was sometimes discouraged and wishing he had chosen a different occupation.

He started the New Year, Tuesday, January 1, 1788, at his office, and read until one in the morning. He was troubled about his daily obligation to his diary. It was especially difficult to keep up with it in the winter—hands stiff with cold made it so hard for him to write. And yet the diary gave him satisfaction. When he looked back on the volumes, he was at least able to say "that day I did something."[19]

The diary, Samuel Flagg Bemis has suggested, was "a secret tuning-fork for his pent-up emotions." Certainly to some extent, as John Quincy was without a close confidant at that time. More urgently, his diary was the work of an obsessive writer and self-critic—regrettably, to his mind, not skilled at invention and at a loss at this time for a suitable narrative to understand his current situation.[20]

Oddly, though, he made few if any references to his exotic past; it must have seemed another lifetime when he thought of his dinners with Franklin, Jefferson, Lafayette and the grandees of the diplomatic world, of the great theatre, opera, treasured art and palaces of Europe, of fraught adventures on high seas and in foreign lands. And now, as though abandoned in this tiny seaport town of Newburyport, he felt himself staring at an opaque wall, with little promise of transparency or future light.

He grew inconsolable in the passing days. "Nothing," he wrote. "It would be a fine theme to expatiate upon." The ruminations that follow are bleak: "In the moral world, what is honor, what is honest, what is religion?—nothing. In the political world, what is liberty, what is patriotism, what is power and grandeur?—nothing. The universe is an atom, and its creator is all in all. Of him, except that he exists, we know nothing, and consequently our knowledge is nothing." And then, most cruelly, he added, "Perhaps the greatest truth of all is, that for this half hour, I have been doing nothing."[21]

In an effort to combat his frightening hollowness, he accepted a friend's invitation to a party of gentlemen and ladies, although he loathed the singing in these mixed companies, the "few very insipid songs, sung in a very insipid manner." A "stupid" game of pawns had followed, in which kissing was the only condition for redeeming pledges, which he found deeply disappointing. As he complained at a later date: "The art of making love muffled up in furs, in the open air, with the thermometer at Zero, is a Yankee invention, which requires a Yankee poet to describe."[22]

His overall opinion of the young ladies of Boston and Newburyport was not flattering. Though vastly appreciative of their appearance, his assessment of their conversation and personalities was often disparaging, especially when compared to the young women he had encountered abroad.

Fundamentally, he found little pleasure in partying and even less in his daily life. On January 12, with Mr. Parsons gone to Boston, he reached an alarming state of depression. "I hope to god," he prayed, that he would not go on in this way, "squandering week after week, till at the end of three years I would go out of the office, as ignorant as I entered it."[23]

He would arrive at his office at nine each morning, perhaps chat with fellow law clerks, and then take up his Lord Coke and "blunder along a few pages with him. At two I return to dinner. At three again attend at the office, where I remain till dark." The routine changed when Mr. Parsons did not permit a lighted fireplace in his absence. In these instances, as soon as daylight began to fail, he and his fellow law clerks put up their books and spent the rest of the day "as best suits our convenience and the feelings of the moment."[24]

He had begun to seriously doubt the quality of his intelligence, and worried that as he aged, the dullness of his mind would likewise increase. To add to his general frustration, he had failed yet again "to ascend Parnassus" by writing creditable poetry. Some years before, he had confided to his mother that he was "addicted to the rage of rhyming." While ambitious, his efforts could be puzzling. In response to the copy he sent to Nabby, "An Epistle to Delia," his sister had wondered "is Delia a real or feigned character." Fifty-two lines long, marking the end of his frustrating attraction to Nancy Hazen, his poem declared "Let poets boast in smooth and labor'd strains / of unfelt passions and pretended pains / To my rude numbers, Delia now attend, / Nor view me, as a lover, but a friend."[25]

He had begun "A Vision," a composite, satirical sketch based on nine young women of Newburyport, cloaked in fanciful names, in January 1787 and would finish it in June 1790. Among the characters, there was a disdainful Narcissa, a chatty Vanessa, a Lucinda, whose "form my fond attention caught . . . who wanted nothing but a feeling heart." There was also "Belinda's voice like grating hinges groans, / And in harsh thunder roars a lover's moans. . . ."[26]

Fifty years later, by then the master of self-deprecation, on re-reading a copy of "The Vision," he thought that he had never since written anything equal to it—and that his apogee as statesman, orator, philosopher and proser was of the same quality: He had left nothing to live after him "but aims beyond my means, and principles too pure for the age in which I have lived."[27]

In this "dull and low spirited" state, there were inklings of respite and broader concerns. The newspapers were full of the public discussion of the new continental form of government, the Constitution. Fifty-five delegates had met the previous June 21, at the State House in Philadelphia, the precise site 11 years earlier of the signing of the Declaration of Independence. John Quincy feared it would be adopted. In discussion with Mr. Parsons, he noted that his mentor "favors very much the federal constitution lately proposed by the Convention of the States," which was hardly surprising, as it was calculated, in John Quincy's opinion, "to increase the influence, power and wealth of those who have any already."[28]

Coming to terms with the Constitution was a problem for John Quincy. As he saw it, its adoption would be a grand point gained in favor of the aristocratic party: Though there would be no titles of nobility, great distinctions would be made and soon become hereditary. For his own part, he was willing to take his chance under any government, "but it was hard to give up a system which I have always been taught to cherish, and to confess that a free government is inconsistent with human nature."[29]

Parsons left for Boston on January 10 for the purpose of assenting to and ratifying the federal Constitution. About 300 attended the convention; it was adopted and ratified by a majority of 19 members on February 6. When church bells rang and the mob cheered so insistently, John Quincy seemed surprised by the volume of enthusiasm. It was as though "with the adoption of the Constitution everyman had acquired a sure expectancy of an independent fortune."[30]

He acknowledged himself "converted though not convinced," and was surprised to learn in early March that his father had written strongly and at length in favor of the Constitution. The son's response was respectful: "I did not expect it, and am glad to find I was mistaken, since it appears probably the plan will be adopted."[31]

From a 40-year perspective, on rereading those early letters, he thought their best use was to teach him a lesson of humility and forbearance. "I was so sincere, so earnest, so vehement in my opinions, and time has so crumbled them to dust that I can now see them only as monumental errors. Yet the spirit was such as even now I have no reason to disclaim—a spirit of patriotism, of order, and of benevolence."[32]

His legal studies remained pure drudgery. With depleted energy, willpower, and ambition, he felt his friends far surpassed him. James Putnam, for example, read law faster and would make greater improvements in his three years. In his imagination, John Quincy had written volumes and read books without number. In reality, he had written scarcely anything aside from his diary. Though he had begun Gibbon months ago, he was not halfway through the second volume. In Lord Coke's *Laws of England,* he trudged along at the rate of about 80 pages a week and did not understand a quarter of it.[33]

One night in May, walking with his friend Benjamin Pickman up to Sawyer's Tavern, their "future prospects in life were the subject of our conversation." Though Pickman's father's large fortune was bound to be divided among his several children, there was a sum enough for starting forward. Besides, he was courting a young lady of sufficient fortune that the two might marry before long.[34]

The fact that even Pickman was anxious about his future welfare gave John Quincy much greater reason to look to his own future "with terror." He had two long years of study ahead in order to qualify him for anything. He had no fortune to expect. His father had made this absolutely clear, warning his son: "You must prepare yourself to get your bread," and that "I think it very probably that in a very little time, I shall find it very difficult to provide for myself."[35]

The subject of family fortunes was a longstanding preoccupation. The way fortunes changed was similar to revolutions within empires. It often seemed as if fortune was resolved to put the republican system into practice in Boston. The wealthiest and most politically important citizens could not "trace a genteel ancestry or even such as lived comfortably and creditably for three generations." By contrast, it was common to see descendants from honorable and opulent families now in the greatest obscurity and poverty. And there was a great chance, "that I myself shall at some future period service as an additional example of this truth."[36]

But for all his despair, he was keenly looking forward to his parents' return to their home in Braintree. According to his family friend, the historian Mercy Warren, John Adams would be "employing the short respite from the field of politics & intrigues of statesmen: to the momentary delights of rural peace and the cultivation of his own grounds."[37]

John Adams's resignation as minister plenipotentiary to Britain had been accepted on October 5, 1787, and he had embarked with Abigail at Weymouth, England, on April 27 on John Callahan's *Lucretia*. John Quincy, faithfully monitoring their voyage, left his office just before two on the afternoon of June 18 and went "with trembling hope" to the post office. He was soon made happy by a letter from his brother Tom, which confirmed their arrival on the previous day.[38]

He set out on horseback early the next morning and arrived in Boston at 10 a.m. He found his mother at the governor's house; his father had already gone to Braintree, and enjoyed, as he had anticipated, "all the satisfaction that can arise from the meeting so near and dear a friend after a long absence."[39]

John Quincy would spend the next week unpacking "to make a home of the house" which his family had bought while overseas. In between chores—unpacking furniture and books, some moist and somewhat moldy—he and his brother Charles spent the warm summer days shooting birds, reading (very little and of a light kind), playing their flutes, bathing in the creek. The cherry trees were full and so inviting to the birds that there was very good sport with little trouble. In Cambridge for his brother Tom's graduation from Harvard, John Quincy's pleasure was such, his "spirits so much exalted," he slept very little that night. By mid-July, he prepared to return to Newburyport with regret.[40]

Writing on his birthday, July 11, he had seemed sadly resigned to his problems. As he wrote in his diary,

> This day completes my twenty first year. It emancipates me from the yoke of paternal authority which I never felt, and places me upon my own feet, which have not strength enough to support me. I continue therefore still in a state of dependence. One third of the period of my professional studies has also now elapsed; and two years more will settle me, should life and health continue, in a situation where all my expectations are to center. I feel sometimes a strong desire to know what my circumstances will be in seven years from this: but I must acknowledge, I believe my happiness would rather be injured than improved by the information.[41]

Surprisingly, in the midst of his ongoing surges of depression, John Quincy made a meaningful admission of his interest in a young woman named Mary Frazier. On the evening of May 16, he had met his friend Putnam walking with "the young girls," two daughters of Moses Frazier, and joined them to pass the rest of the evening, as he had many times before, at their home. He had mentioned the Misses Frazier most casually four months earlier without a hint of their first names, Elizabeth and Mary.[42]

Now he wrestled with his ambivalence: "These young misses have assumed an importance rather above their years. I receive not much satisfaction in their company, and as they are handsome, I had rather look at them for five minutes than be with them five hours." With more than a tinge of envy, he wrote that "Putnam is not too difficult to please. He can conform to their manners, and enter into all their debates: he is consequently a favorite." Soon it would be apparent that Mary's preference, if she ever favored Putnam, had changed and John Quincy would be writing in the coming months of their serious commitment to one another.[43]

On Wednesday, September 3, he informed Mrs. Leather of his intention to temporarily move back to Cambridge—his friend James Bridge would join him—where he was to deliver "An Oration,

Spoken, at the request of the Phi Beta Kappa Society" that Friday, September 5, 1788. He was pleased by the size of his audience: about 40, including Governor Hancock, two men from Dartmouth College, officers of the French squadron now in Boston harbor and the French consul de L'etombe who, afterward, offered his special compliments.

A week later he returned to Newburyport and "did not sleep a wink" that next Sunday night, his nerves "in a very disagreeable state of irritation." After lying around for three hours he got up and went over to Dr. Swett to request an opiate—possibly derived from the bark of a magnolia or white willow tree commonly used to treat depression—that gradually helped him compose his nerves and gave him a few hours of sleep. The following nights were no better; his diary is a dirge of desperation: "Sleepless. Could do no business / Strolling about all day. Idle / Can neither read or write . . . Unwell out of spirits." By Saturday, weary and "indebted to soporific draughts" for the little rest he enjoyed, he mounted his horse and headed out to Haverhill—Braintree was a far greater distance—where he was determined to spend a few days with the Shaws to see if he could revive his health, and "to experience," as his Aunt Elizabeth explained to his mother, "a little of my maternal care."[44]

Lest her sister should hear of it from someone else, and be too anxious, Elizabeth wrote the next day to tell Abigail that her son "had not been well since he left Braintree." But for all the severity of her nephew's condition, she was cheered that her patient was "the best man to take his medicine that she ever saw—He hardly makes a wry mouth. . . ." As his reward and to amuse his mind, she sent him riding and visiting family. She was afraid he had studied too hard, for "He is so avaricious in coveting the best gifts that I fear such intense application will injure his health, more than he is aware of."[45]

There was a follow-up letter. If she had not felt too great a tenderness for the parent, Elizabeth Shaw would have told her sister that her son on his recent visit was very sick but she did not want Abigail to "travel the road with an aching heart." John Quincy had left for Newburyport contrary to her advice, and she had been very uneasy about him ever since. She thought it was highly necessary for him to be exceeding careful as to "diet, exercise," and as to study, "that most certainly must be laid aside at present."[46]

John Quincy had come to the same conclusion. On one sleepless night, Shakespeare's *Henry IV* "obtruded" on his mind: "Oh gentle sleep / Nature's soft Nurse, how have I frighted thee / That thou no more wilt weigh mine eyelids down / And steep my senses in forgetfulness." He left on the stagecoach on Thursday, October 2, reached Boston that evening and was indeed home in Braintree the next day.[47]

While in Braintree he rode, tramped fields and marshes, continued to read Gibbon's *Decline and Fall of the Roman Empire,* Justinian's *Institutes,* and Cicero's *Cato Major de Senectute* (A Treatise on Old Age). On October 14 he wrote that his "occupations have been very regular, and similar for a week past," and with the help of medicine and constant exercise he thought he was on the way to recovery. But he was too hopeful. His next sentence trails off. "This evening, my . . ." is the three-word fragment that concludes his diary. The next page is blank.[48]

From here on, he kept to the premise of his "line-a-day" notebook with staccato postings: "Madam and Tom went to Boston. Violent Thunder," or "Mr. A. went to Boston. Charles to Cambridge," or "Rode my horse" or "Rode as usual" or "Variable weather. Gibbon's history." Or he named guests or Sunday's preachers. He stayed on in Braintree until December 8, and on the tenth: "Got to Newbury-Port. Ordination [of his friend John Andrews]. Dancing." This burst of activity quickly faded. On the eleventh, obviously still troubled, he sought help: "Dined with Mr. Tufts. Not very bright. Dr. Swett's."[49]

Chapter 13

"EXPOSED TO THE PERILS OF SENTIMENT"

On April 6, 1789, the Senate elected George Washington as president and John Adams as vice president, 69 unanimous votes for the one, 34 votes for the other. That June, "from a proper modesty," John Quincy explained to his father, he had allowed several months to elapse before bringing up any insignificant details about himself, hoping, perhaps, "a moment's relaxation from the affairs of a nation, to attend to those of a private and domestic nature may not be disagreeable."[1]

At this stage, rather than the academic, he was concerned about the actual practice of the law, for he believed that the skill to apply general knowledge to particular cases was no less important than the knowledge itself. Furthermore, he was bedeviled by another problem: his state of irresolution and suspense about where and how he was to settle to practice law and to live. The judiciary bill, "An Act to Establish the Judicial Courts of the United States," had been signed into law the past September 14. He had consulted Parsons, who had hinted that if Parsons were moved up in the judiciary system, either as district judge or attorney general, he would recommend his place to his pupil John Quincy. Then again, John

Quincy supposed that those appointments had been made and he would not therefore appear in the humiliating light of a solicitor which he wished to avoid.[2]

But setting this issue aside for the moment, he asked his father's permission to pay him a visit in the fall, about the beginning of October. The next week brought him a thoughtful, affectionate response. His father was thankful for the letter. As for his advice, it was "to give yourself very little thought about the place of your future residence . . . a few months will produce changes that will easily settle that question for you." As for John Quincy's proposed visit, his father would be very happy to see him whenever the journey might be most convenient to him and to Mr. Parsons, but he wished him to come when the House was sitting, that he might hear the debates and know the members.[3]

John Quincy arrived in New York the morning of September 16, 1789. He had walked and with some difficulty found Richmond Hill, the tall, tiered, columned house his parents inhabited, with 11-foot ceilings, flower gardens and a majestic view of the Hudson and the farms of New Jersey. His mother was pleased to "live in a most friendly intercourse" with President Washington and his wife, she would later write, adding, "Let not the busy fiend envy propagate reports so basely false as that there is any coldness subsisting between the families."[4]

By coincidence, his parents were entertaining the Washingtons the night of his arrival. Weary from a mostly sleepless voyage and feeling unfit for company, he chose to eat alone. But he did stay the month, and was not lacking in opinions or certain political wisdom in response to his visit at the House of Representatives in the old city hall on the corner of Wall and Nassau Streets. Hearing the debates on a judiciary bill—James Madison was one of the voices—he "did not perceive any extraordinary powers of oratory displayed by any of those gentlemen" and thought the "little new eloquences" were actually exhausted old ones "while a spirit of contention still remained." As for the subject of the salaries of judges, it wasn't the subject of the debate—an old one—but its resolution, the art of compromise, that interested him. It showed "the difficulty of men living in different climates and used to very different modes of living."[5]

Before leaving New York City to head back north in early October, John Quincy had visited "at the president's" a number of times. At the end of October he had further contact with him during Washington's stopover in Newburyport. His proud mother's supposition of his important role in the formalities of Washington's reception had met with protest and humor in their spirited exchange of letters.

On October 30, Newburyport welcomed George Washington with a parade, fireworks, and John Quincy's reverential tribute to "the friend, the benefactor, the father of his country," for which Washington was "much gratified with the attention shown him." "This I have it from his own mouth," his mother had reported, hoping also that her son "was one of the choir who so aptly serenaded him with 'the hero comes.'"[6]

"Trifling" with his mother, at first John Quincy assured her that he was "not one of the choir who *welcomed* the president to New England's shore" upon his arrival. He was, however, one of the procession which was formed to receive him, in humble imitation of the capital. And when he left, "I was one of the *respectable citizens* (as our newspapers term them) who *escorted* him on horseback to the lines of New Hampshire."[7]

Then in a more accommodating spirit he allowed that

> I had the honor of paying my respects to the president, upon his arrival in this town, and he did me the honor to recollect that he had seen me a short time before, at New York. I had the honor of spending part of the evening in his presence . . . I had the honor of breakfasting in the same room with him the next morning . . . I had the honor of writing the billet which the major general of the county sent him to inform him of the military arrangements he had made for his reception. And I had the honor of draughting an address, which with many alterations and additions (commonly called amendments) was presented to him by the town of Newburyport. So you see "I bear my *blushing* honors thick upon me."[8]

Then he turned from trifling to a subject very serious. More than six months had passed and the matter of his future residence was becoming more worrisome. His mother (and his father) well knew the objections he had about Braintree under the present situation: he and his cousin William would have to divide the small pittance which either of them singly might obtain. Nor was Newburyport a more alluring prospect, though he would enjoy the advantage of being more extensively known there than in any other town of the commonwealth. Boston, on the other hand, was strongly recommended to him by several of his friends. But he agreed to postpone full discussion of the subject until Parsons's fate was known, after which he meant to state his case fully to his father, and reach a decision based on his final opinion.

Obviously, Abigail had shared John Quincy's letter and concerns with his father who hoped, he wrote in February, that "your anxiety about your prospects of future life will not be indulged too far." If, after his term with Mr. Parsons expired, the "judgment, inclination and advice of your friends lead you to Boston," he would have his father's full consent and approbation. And more, if he could arrange to get a small family into his father's house, reserving the best room and chamber for his own office and lodging room, John would not be displeased with the arrangement. "An office you must have, enquire into this matter, and let me know upon what terms you can board, and have an office. Upon this plan, you might make an excursion sometimes to Braintree, and pursue your studies there, especially in the heat of summer when the air of Boston is unwholesome."[9]

More advice followed on February 19, but first a reading list. There was a set of Scottish writers deserving his attention in a very high degree, "speculations in morals politicks and law that are more luminous than any other" he had read: Lord Kames, Sir James Stewart, and Adam Smith's *An Inquiry into the Nature and Causes of the Wealth of Nations*. As for his project of going to Boston—John Adams thought of it every day—he might divide his time between Braintree and Boston to great advantage, or reside constantly at Boston if his business should require it. Physical arrangements were the easy part about which the father could offer his support to the best of his financial resources. But he was less as-sured though tender in his concern for his son's morale: "You must expect an interval of leisure, and ennui. And whether those who ought to be my friends will be yours or not, I can't say—Whether they are mine or not is at least problematical in some instances—yet I think you will find friends in Boston."[10]

In March John Quincy acknowledged his father's February letters. He hoped, he wrote on March 19, that he would always feel "suit-ably grateful for the tender solicitude" his father expressed regard-ing his future prospects. Reviewing his options, he recognized that he could live less expensively in Braintree, would have a wider cir-cle of friends in Newburyport, but concluded that Boston remained his choice. He had consulted with Dr. Tufts, Judge Dana, and Dr. Thomas Welsh, and all agreed that he could do no better than to fix on Boston. And as his father had approved, he had little doubt in his mind that he would move there.[11]

He had painstakingly thought out the details regarding his liv-ing and working quarters. He hoped to set up his law office in the front room of his father's house in Boston and to rent a bedroom from Dr. Welsh who, he presumed, would not demand more than three dollars a week. He hoped also, with his father's permission, to bring his law library to Boston from Braintree. Such a collection of books around him would allow opportunities "which few of the young gentlemen of the profession have possessed."[12]

John Quincy's father was pleased with his son's prudent delib-eration; he found his judicious decision to board with Dr. Welsh very agreeable and that of taking the best room in his house for his office equally so. As for his law library, his son could take it to his new Boston office and keep it there until he called for it. And again, he thought John Quincy might find it agreeable to go to Braintree and spend a week or a month there, presumably as a change of rou-tine, and especially in summer. Further, as soon as John Quincy's term ended and when he had completed his clerkship, he would ask Dr. Tufts, who frequently handled the family's finances, to pay Mr. Parsons a fee of 100 pounds.[13]

In an April letter to his father, John Quincy reported on the early and bitter struggle to govern the nation according to the United States Constitution signed into law on September 1, 1787. He had happened upon a subject, he thought, "that might at least not be unentertaining," and its vision of a provocative new party system may ring true for fellow citizens far centuries away.[14]

Somewhat apologetic about his pressing ardor (too much, he admitted) for public events since early youth, he had accidentally witnessed conversations on subjects from which he collected some information he described as "trifling" when he truthfully meant urgent, if not alarming. As it appeared to him, "the hostile character of our general and particular governments each against the other is increasing with accelerated rapidity." The spirit and premise at the time of the adoption of the Constitution, that of a balanced government, had already almost totally disappeared "and the seeds of two contending factions appear to be plentifully sown." People were dividing into two parties, the names of Federalist and Anti-Federalist (or self-government) were no longer expressive of the sentiments which they were so lately supposed to contain, and he expected soon to hear a couple of new names.[15]

In October, with his "spirit of speculation" unabated, he observed to his father, people (himself foremost perhaps) with a fondness for the subject of politics—"the prospect was glorious"—were turning their attention to politics in Europe, to France, which seemed now as much as ever it could be since the storming of the Bastille, *"un repaire d'horreurs."* That nation might finally be free but not, he was persuaded, until they had undergone another revolution. A nobility and a clergy, church and state, leveled to the ground in one year's time, blown to the winds by the single breath of a triumphant democracy were inauspicious for the erection of an equitable government of laws. Moving far too swiftly and violently toward revolution, it seemed to him that "the National Assembly, in tearing the lace from the garb of government, will tear the coat itself into a thousand rags."[16]

Independence and self-sufficiency were more meaningful than ever at this particular time. He wished for more financial security. He was in love and considering marriage to Mary Frazier, the 16-year-old daughter of Moses Frazier, and had confided his intentions or at least hinted of his "attachment" on his return to Newburyport to his "unalterable friend," his cousin William.[17]

On April 7 in Newburyport, John Quincy sat down to write a letter to his cousin. First he placed a crosshatch at the top of the page and wrote in the margin sideways: "observe that in the future, all my letters marked thus # are either to be burnt or kept in such a manner as will expose them to the sight of no body but yourself."[18]

To begin he supposed that he would harp on that inexhaustible subject of all his letters to his cousin: "I mean my single self. . . ." He wished William would imitate his egotism, for the employments, the studies, the adventures, the passions, and even the amusements of a friend were always interesting. Or at least he found this so, and it was in the hope of gratifying a similar taste rather than from an irresistible fondness of talking about himself that he filled so great a proportion of his letters with his own affairs.[19]

And now he got to the subject nearest his heart. William Cranch, he suspected, in their time together in Boston and Braintree might possibly have been witness to the struggle he had between his *sentiments* and his *opinions*. He could not, owing to their friendship, which he trusted would keep forever, attempt to conceal his feelings, which he wished not to be known to the world in general. Those feelings had, since his return, been acquiring additional strength, and he was more than ever convinced of the absolute necessity that he leave town very soon. "Flight, and speedy flight too is the only resource that is now left me."[20]

He had attended three assemblies since his return, and they had afforded him as much pleasure as he could have expected. These assemblies were dangerous places, not only dangerous to females but to males as well during those moments, quoting Pope, "when music softens and when dancing fires."[21]

Awkward, helpless and frightened, he did not mean to say that "assemblies were immediately dangerous to our honor and reputation, but rather to the mind, possibly fatal to the peace of a person whose welfare consists in preserving a perfect indifference." His friend Samuel Putnam was in the same boat, only he was struggling with a passion deeply rooted and confirmed by habits of almost three years standing. The two ladies though very intimate friends were widely different in character, and daily increasing in attraction. While the one was acquiring graces and virtues in addition to incomparable beauty (presumably Mary Frazier), the other was increasing her power and influence through her system of coquetry. "Is it not a hardship that the best of the two characters should be by much the most dangerous," he asked his cousin.[22]

If he thought Cranch might have guessed at his feelings for Mary Frazier, the depth of his commitment is revealed in his letter of August 25 to James Bridge. Indeed, his Harvard classmate did not believe it possible for him to have formed another so short a sentence, which Bridge quoted back to him on September 28, that could have afforded him a greater surprise as the following: "*You* may know (though it is known to very few) that all my hopes of future happiness in this life center in the possession of that girl."[23]

He might even have thought of it as a joke, Bridge continued, but for the solemnity of John Quincy's style "which would not admit a suspicion that you were trifling with my curiosity." Now, he had no alternative but to consider his friend's fate "as fixed with respect to the important article of matrimony" while, at the same time, he was reminded with some embarrassment of earlier talks, of "having done injustice of your Goddess by supposing her heart to be cold and unfeeling."[24]

Acutely aware of the consequences of having expressed such a negative opinion to his close friend, Bridge was eager, he said, to justify himself in his own mind. Reflecting on the course of his acquaintance with Miss F, it had been too general to give him any opportunities of knowing the qualities of her heart "which might have contained the seeds of the most engaging sympathy."[25]

But stumbling aside, it was clear that Bridge thought the young and beautiful Miss F spoiled and overly flattered in Newburyport, with guardians who might not have been vigilant enough to counteract its influence. He had seen her twice, he continued, and implied that nothing had happened to change his opinion since John Quincy had become her avowed admirer. He would bargain, therefore: "You may grant that my judgment was agreeable to appearances and I will agree that it was superficial."[26]

At his most conciliatory now, with seemingly guarded optimism, Bridge was sure that the above-mentioned seeds of sympathy must shoot forth vigorously, "encouraged by your genial 'warmth' if they have a place in the soil of her heart."[27]

Besides letters to Cranch and to Bridge, John Quincy must have confided to his sister his attachment to which "reason and prudence would oppose their influence," judging from her response on April 18. Caught by surprise, her brother must excuse her, she said, "if I do not give any belief to your confession." She could not advise him to permit himself to become speedily engaged in an attachment which would influence his entire future, his happiness, prosperity and success.[28]

Instead, if it was not too late, she was in favor of his first settling in business and taking time to form a more extensive acquaintance with the world. She was aware that his knowledge of mankind was more enlarged and extensive than perhaps any young man of his age. Still, he might yet be deficient in practical knowledge, and as one who was much interested in his prosperity and welfare, she would wish to see him "a few years further advanced in life" before he engaged in a connection that, if formed at present, "must impede your progress and advancement." She hoped he did not think her too explicit, or would not permit her sentiments if they did not accord with his opinions to interfere with the future confidence of his letters.[29]

His letters to Bridge, Cranch and Nabby vouch for John Quincy's devotion to Mary Frazier, and yet sometime that spring something had gone critically wrong. Though his diary is silent on the subject, he confided to Nabby on May 1 the challenges to his problematic love affair. His abrupt change in plans reconfirmed her opinion of his "prudence, discretion,—and caution, upon *all* subjects of importance, when the heart is so deeply interested."[30]

She also must have interpreted her brother's remarks as suggesting that money, or lack of it, and consequently his inability to make an immediate commitment to marry Mary Frazier, was the root of the problem. (This was shortly to be confirmed.) She was sorry indeed, she said, that a first impression of partiality and attachment inspired by so amiable and deserving an object—"there was nothing so like perfection, in human shape since the world began," according to their brother Charles—"should meet *eventually* with any effacement from mercenary views."[31]

Which would explain why, of the five assemblies he attended the first week of June in Newburyport, John Quincy danced four with a Miss Newhall who helped him to pass his time tolerably. But there was a weight on his spirits that he could not remove. This he revealed to his cousin William when he also quoted a passage from *Hamlet*: "I have of late, but wherefore I know not, lost all my mirth."[32]

Cranch was tender and wise beyond his 21 years in his concern for his cousin. "Whence comes the listlessness—this depression of spirits? What can relax the elasticity of your mind?" He sought to comfort him by example, his own when he found himself in a like situation.[33]

Cranch felt so yesterday, he wrote on June 10, without being able to trace the least cause. The connection between the soul and body was so inexplicable that he believed it impossible to account for the peculiar temper of mind which a man will frequently find himself in. But whatever may be the cause, he promised he "would not make it a subject of derision," not from the motive of pure friendship alone but because he thought it "a disorder or disease to which a man may as necessarily be subjected as to the stone or the gout." As for the best remedy: He believed in "determined opposition" (he had first written then crossed out "resolution"). His own depressions seldom lasted more than a few hours, and he could generally reason them away. But if neither "reason nor opposition will prevail," he would just "run away from them—convert some passing trivial circumstance into a source of pleasure soon able to dissipate the gloom." On ending his letter, it was his wish that "cheerfulness & peace be with you."[34]

But a month later, a saddened John Quincy was still pondering his fate as he faced a critical period in his life. In a rare omission, he made no mention of his birthday on July 11; his line-a-day diary for this month is blemished with words like "Indifferent," "Disappointed," "Not extraordinary."[35]

On July 15, 1790, age 23, John Quincy was "Sworn into court. Dined at Robinsons tavern, returned to Newburyport." With his formal admission to the practice of law in the courts of Essex County—wishing all the while that he had been "bred a farmer, a merchant, or 'an anything' by which he could earn his bread"—he had ended his three-year peripatetic clerkship to Theophilus Parsons of Newburyport.[36]

In Boston on the morning of August 9—having taken possession of his office, the front room in his father's old house at 23 Court Street, which the tenant had given over to him for an abatement of 15 pounds—John Quincy wanted to devote the first few moments of the day to write to his father. It was an awkward letter expressing gratitude for past and future support. In truth, he felt himself to be in an awkward position. Clearly, at his age, a man ought to rely for his subsistence upon his own exertions, and yet, after all the trouble and all the expense that his father had so liberally bestowed on his education, he remained dependent on him to make every necessary allowance for the peculiar circumstances in his education, which had slowed his advancement, and for the unfavorable situation of the profession which he had embraced.[37]

The principal message to his mother was the same regarding his gratitude and dependence on further material support, but more bluntly revealed his state of mind. Settled in his office, he told his mother, with little expectations at present from business, he was sometimes tempted to regret that he came to a place where the profession was so crowded and expenses so considerable.[38]

Both parents rallied. His mother wrote from Richmond Hill with a kind of cheerful urgency: that she was pleased to find him so well accommodated; that he had a good office, a good library, and an agreeable family to reside in; and if he would be patient and persevering, he would get business in time. And "when you feel disposed to find fault with your stars, bethink yourself how preferable your situation to that of many others." Although a state of dependence must ever be irksome to a generous mind, when that dependence was not due to idleness or dissipation, she wrote, "there is no kind parent but what would freely contribute to the support and assistance of a child in proportion to their ability."[39]

His father also clearly meant to be supportive of his troubled son. With the best of intentions, though endearingly academic, it was his "solemn advice" to John Quincy that "you make yourself master of the Roman learning. Begin with Livy—take your book, your dictionary, your grammar, your sheet of paper and pen and ink, begin at the beginning and read the work through—put down in writing every word with its meaning, as you find it in Ainsworth. You will find it the most delightful employment you ever engaged in." The writings of Cicero were to be added. By all means he was to make himself "master of the Latin tongue." And Polybius and Plutarch and Sallust as sources of wisdom and Roman history were not to be forgotten. "Read them all in Latin." Nor would he by any means consent that he forget his Greek; "keep it alive at least, and improve it by degrees."[40]

In a more pragmatic gesture, thankfully, John Adams offered a supply of wood that might be collected from his various properties, as well as other articles to be reviewed, and most meaningful of all, whole management of his estate if he would take it—though he would not urge it upon him for fear that it might interrupt his studies too much. "Above all things," his father wished for him to "keep up your spirits and take care of your health."[41]

Abigail encouraged John Quincy again in a September letter. She did not doubt, she assured her son, that "you will do very well—only have patience, and I will prophesy for you, that you will be able by the close of one year to pay your own board, and if you do that tis as much as you ought to expect, and if you not, why don't worry your face into wrinkles about it. We will help you all we can, and when you are better off than those who assist you, you shall help them again if they want it, so make yourself easy and keep free from entanglements of all kinds."[42]

There was another reason for Abigail's September letter. Thomas had told her that John Quincy was in love, and she now stammered away as tactfully as she could manage to advise her son on this obviously bewildering news. It was agreeable enough "so far as it will serve to make you attentive to your person, for you are a little inclined to be negligent . . . besides, it may keep your head from rambling after other objects, but if it makes you anxious &

uneasy, and when you are reading, slides in between your subject and you, then have cause to be alarmed, so take heed—."⁴³

In contrast to his explicit letters to Bridge, Cranch, and Nabby about his love of Mary Frazier, his line-a-day diary only records his frequent visits to the Frazier household with comments that initially vary from "quite smart" to "somewhat dull" to "Frazier's very good." On July 8, 1790, he "saw the ladies in the forenoon; evening at Mr. Frazier's"; on October 29, "M.F. came to town, some perplexity"; on November 1, "Evening at my office, critical period"; on November 15, underlined somewhat ominously, "Letter from my mother."⁴⁴

In Abigail's letter of November 7, she advised her son with greater conviction, for the news had spread. Her sister Elizabeth Shaw had confirmed in September the unwelcome news that John Quincy had been "vastly attentive to the ladies of late, & that *one happy fair* was distinguished—aye my sister, what will you say, should *your Hercules* be conquered?" Abigail had been ill in the fall or she would have chided John Quincy sooner. Elaborating on her earlier objections with more than a little passion, she was sorry such a report should persist because whether there was or was not cause for such a rumor, "the report may do an injury to the future prospects of the lady as your own are not such as could warrant you in entering into any engagements. . . . Believe me, my dear son, a too early marriage will involve you in troubles that may render you & yours unhappy the remainder of your life."⁴⁵

Moreover, even if he said that he had no idea of connecting himself at present—and Abigail would believe him—"why gain," his mother asked, "the affections of a woman, or why give her cause to think you attached to her?" Did he not know that "the most cruel of situations to a young lady is to feel herself attached to a gentleman when he can testify it in no other way than by his actions."⁴⁶

Sadly, Abigail was cautioning John Quincy by example: Nabby's example. That she was very anxious for her daughter and her family was "most certain." Nabby had had a third son four years earlier, following her marriage to Colonel William Stephens Smith, and "heaven grant that she may add no more to the stock until her prospects brighten." President Washington, the year before, had appointed Colonel Smith as marshal for the district of New York, a position which poorly fed a family. If only Smith had followed his father-in-law's advice while in England three years ago, he would have entered himself at the Temple and attended the courts at Westminster, reading law at home. Then, on his return, he would have been sworn into court to practice law in New York State, gone into an office, and had no need to look for government employment.[47]

Burdened with concern for his sister's welfare, John Quincy thought he could at least safely assure his mother: "my dear Madam, that I am as resolutely determined never to connect a woman to desperate fortunes, as I am never to be indebted to a woman for wealth" and "you shall never be requested," he promised, "for your consent to a connection of mine, until I am able to support that connection with honor and independence."[48]

He also tried to reassure his sister, in a long-owed letter, of his ardent and sincere brotherly affection, "which no length of time, no absence, no course of circumstances, shall ever impair." He had not wanted to try her patience with peevish complaints, given his inability to bring her accounts of his own happiness or success. Under these circumstances he hoped she would understand his apparent neglect for so long, And in a subtle way, allowing for their shared disappointments, he offered promise to his "dear Sister, [that] better days will come: we shall all in our time, have comforts and enjoyments to boast of, and as time and chance happen to all men, the time must come when some favorable chances will occur to us."[49]

The Court of Common Pleas was sitting in Boston on October 5 and 11 when John Quincy made his first attempt at addressing the jury. Afterward, he wrote his mother that he wished he had acquitted himself to his own satisfaction. He had very little time for preparation and did not know the existence of the cause three hours before he spoke to it. The novelty of the situation added to his diffidence about his talent at "extemporary speechifying." He gave no further details other than the fact that he had lost the case to Harrison Gray Otis. He was too agitated to be "possessed of proper presence of mind," and he left it to her to "judge of the figure I made."[50]

His mother had obviously shared this letter with his father, a matter of deepest concern to both. One evening a few weeks later, Charles, on his return from the Law Society in New York City, found his father in his room with a letter in his hand from John Quincy to his brother. He asked Charles to see what John Quincy had written concerning his "downfall." On opening his letter, Charles soon learned what his father alluded to but, to his own and his father's relief, "could find no marks of any downfall." Instead, he was gravely solicitous in his response. "That you should have been somewhat confused upon your first exertion," he kindly reassured his brother, "was by no means a matter of astonishment to any of us. The person who is unintimidated upon such occasions has not the common feelings of human nature. There is a pride, a respect, required by the auditors, which makes a little confusion rather pleasing than disagreeable. I think that an harangue of fifteen minutes is by no means despicable for a first essay." Also, he could not conclude "without wishing you could persuade yourself to take the world a little more fair and easy" for he was confident "you raise hills in your imagination more difficult to ascend than you will in reality find them. May you have great fortitude and a more peaceful mind is the wish of your brother."[51]

But it wasn't merely his disappointing debut in court that bothered him—Dr. Welsh had remarked on his diffidence and his tremor, his father told him later—and had alarmed his parents. It was his frightening state of despair. He was one letter in debt to his mother but, he had written on October 17, he had no good news to tell about himself, and very little about anyone else. Instead, he had the advantage of being 300 miles distant from every member of the family, alone in the world, without a soul to share his few joys, or to participate in his anxieties and suspense, which were neither few nor small.[52]

"Time was the answer"—his father's solution. "The world cannot be forced. Time must be taken to become known in any situation." As for his sensibility at his first essay at extemporary oratory, "your agitation, your confusion, if they are as lively as you describe them," were not at all surprising. Had he been calm and cool, unaf-fected and unmoved, it would have been astonishing.[53]

At a comparable age, his father also had despaired over his expectations for "Happiness, and a solid undisturbed contentment amidst all the disorders, and the continual rotations of worldly affairs." The son, heir to the father's ambitions and frustrations, was full of gratitude for the "innumerable favors" he had received from the "best of parents," but, by his own bitter admission, grati-tude was the only return he could make for all their trouble and expense, their labors and cares on his behalf. And certainly, this gratitude did not qualify him to think of marriage to Mary Frazier, for whom he cared more deeply than perhaps even he realized.[54]

In late autumn, after learning his mother had been ill, he wrote that he was pleased she was feeling better. He also was apologetic about having upset her on his account. In regard to one of "the other circumstances"—that is, the rumor "common fame" had carried to her ears regarding his attachment to a young lady—he wished to assure her that the "Lady will be henceforth at the distance of 40 miles" from him, and that he would have "no further opportunities to indulge a weakness, which you may perhaps censure, but which if you knew the subject, I am sure you would excuse."[55]

But he could talk about this and several other things with more freedom than he could write and, if it met with his parents' ap-proval, he would be happy to pay them a visit of three or four weeks this winter in Philadelphia, the new federal capital as of that fall. The expense would not be much more than if he stayed in Boston, and the change of air, the exercise, the novelty of the place and the variety of scenes might have a favorable effect on his health and spirits.

He left Boston on January 22 by stagecoach and reached Bush Hill, his parent's residence, seven days later. While in Philadelphia, apart from an intensely social schedule, he visited Congress in ses-sion, celebrated George Washington's birthday—"Splendid Assem-bly at Night," according to his diary. He also indulged in what he called his "poetical effusions" as well as rebuses, acrostics and elegies. But he no longer wished for their publication. He told his

brother Thomas, "I must bid a long and lasting farewell to the juvenile muses. It is to the severer toils of the Historic Matron that I
must henceforth direct all the attention I can allow to that lovely
company," to justice, to "the eyeless dame who holds the balance
and the sword." He had been motivated for some time now to write
in defense of his father against the outrageous accusation of "political heresies" by Thomas Jefferson.[56]

While in Philadelphia he had taken some pains to make a complete collection of books and papers relative to the national government. But back in Boston in March, on finding some documents
were missing, he asked that Thomas, who was heading to Quincy
the next month, might find spare room in his trunks to bring him
a set of the laws and journals of both houses of the last session:
*Acts Passed at the Third Session of the Congress of the United
States of America, Begun and Held at the city of Philadelphia, December 6, 1790* and the *Journal of the House of Representatives
of the United States, Philadelphia 1791*. Also, he was in need of
missing numbers from the first volume—he was caught up on the
second volume—of the *United States Gazette,* which the 40-year-
old John Fenno published to defend the new government under the
Constitution.[57]

But even as he spoke of gathering together his research, he was
far from certain that he could afford to pursue his "inclination."
Fortunately an April 18 letter from his mother fortified his spirits
and his interests considerably. She had spoken to his father on the
subject of an annual allowance and had agreed that he could draw
on Dr. Tufts for 25 pounds each quarter, his first quarter to begin
on the first of July. In June there would come further support: his
appointment as an attorney for his father, empowering him "to
ask, demand, sue for, and recover and receive" all rents and arrears
of rent due now or in the future. With relief and gratitude, he twice
memorialized his father's support. "Power, from my father," he
wrote across the top of the document, and again, in the top corner:
"Powers from my father to let his house."[58]

While John Quincy vowed to abandon juvenile muses for the embrace of the "Historic Matron," he never could entirely forsake

Mary Frazier. Throughout his lifetime, he thought back on the melancholy story of those "troubles of the heart" that were "deep and distressing."[59]

He paid Mary Frazier eloquent tribute when he wrote a friend before leaving for Europe in 1794:

> far be it from me however, to intimate anything unfavorable about the lady, who was then the beloved of my heart. . . .
>
> With respect to her, my *opinions* have never shared in the revolution of my *sentiments*. Her wrong to me (which indeed never originated with herself) I freely forgave at the moment when I resigned her affections . . . I hear her name mentioned without an emotion; I see her without a throb of the heart; I speak to her without a faltering of the voice . . . but I remember that I have *loved* her with an affection surpassing that of women.[60]

Decades later, on a Sunday in the White House on November 18, 1838, John Quincy, then 71, recalled "the most affecting incident of a recent visit to Mt. Auburn Cemetery in Boston," when he had been moved to tears of tenderness and melancholy by the sight of a gravestone bearing the solitary inscription of Maria Osborne Sargent, born in 1804, deceased at the age of 30 in 1835. This was the daughter of Daniel Sargent and Mary Frazier, "once to me the most beautiful and most beloved of her sex. In the 15th year of her age, she gave me, then 22, the assurance of her affection and the pledge of her faith. A year afterwards she withdrew them, from distrust instilled into her mind by an anxious cousin. Twelve years afterward she married Daniel Sargent, and in 1804, at the age of 30, died of consumption consequent upon the birth of this only child," who died, too, the same age as her mother.[61]

At this point, John Quincy imagined what would have been their fate had their union been accomplished. In all probability, he guessed, he should have lost her in the prime of life and lost perhaps a child, cut off like this, in the blossom. "Dearly! how dearly did the sacrifice of her cost me, voluntary as it was, for the separation occasioned by my declining to contract an unqualified engagement forbidden by my father and by the advice of her cousin to insist on a positive engagement or a separation. Four years of exquisite wretchedness followed this separation nor was the wound healed, till the Atlantic ocean flowed between us."[62]

There are no likenesses of Mary Frazier, not even a silhouette. We only know, because Charles Adams told his sister Nabby, that "there is nothing so like perfection, in human shape appeared since the world began." What is certain is that she was the daughter of Moses and Elizabeth Frazier of Newburyport, and that John Quincy was despondent over their parting. That he disposed of relevant correspondence must account for the skimpy, passing reference to his father's powerful influence. His mother's antipathy may have been rooted in her feelings, expressed decades later, of having married "much too young for the proper fulfillment of duties which soon devolved upon me."[63]

Possibly, his Aunt Elizabeth Shaw alone, in whose home he had sought peace of mind, understood the depth of her nephew's love and sacrifice, and knew how critically his health suffered. Some years later, on the eve of his eventual departure abroad, Aunt Elizabeth had teased him about his claim that "cold apathy" had taken possession of his breast, and "If real," she commented dryly, "it must be extremely advantageous to your peace and tranquility." Not a likely state for a young man of his nature, the one she recalled on his visit to Haverhill, "when I beheld you nobly struggling with those tender passions, which few at your age would have thought of contending with—& seen you sacrificing your own inclinations, to situations, & filial duty."[64]

As to his latter day fears that he might not have another love, his aunt would not hear of them. Instead, she chose to reassure her beloved nephew that he would find "all your sacrifices—your anxieties—your daily labors—midnight toil amply rewarded in the love of this happy fair one," in a "new candidate for the nuptial state."[65]

Chapter 14

"ON THE BRIDGE BETWEEN WISDOM AND FOLLY"

ooking back on his move to Boston, John Quincy recalled, "though I cannot say I was friendless . . . I was without support of any kind. I may say I was a stranger in that city, although almost a native of that spot." And he had struggled. For the first year he could hardly name any law practice he had at all. In fact, "Very busy with nothing to do," he "wasted time at court," took walks and dined with friends and family, and seemed cheered only on the November day he "wrote all day and evening. Tolerably satisfied."[1]

On April 1, 1791, he decided once more that he would keep a journal of his "transactions." He often found himself wishing to "fix the fleeting reflection which originates in some transient occurrence"; he had decided to attempt again "an undertaking which indolence had so often rendered abortive."[2]

Under the pseudonym Publicola, Roman friend of the people, John Quincy would publish 11 impassioned essays in Boston's *Columbian Centinel* from June 8 to July 27, 1791, in response to which his "steadfast friend and earnest well-wisher," James Bridge, supposed that "Dear Publicola" must have struggled with his conscience before he "clasped his sickle to reap in the field of politics."[3]

In truth, Publicola's motivation was far more complex, fired not only by ideological and philosophical differences with Thomas Paine, but more acutely by a heartbreaking sense that his father had been betrayed by Thomas Jefferson, the family friend whom he had once loved to be with because he was "a man of great judgment."[4]

Thoughts of Jefferson evoked his youth in Paris where he had learned to speak French like a native and lived gratefully and uniquely with his parents and sister in their all too fleeting reunion. For him, France was a keepsake of fond memories. At present, with the future of the French government at stake, he feared to think of the fate of its people.

The unraveling of France's old regime had begun more or less officially in May 1789 when the States General, comprising Three Estates (the First, the clergy; Second, the nobility; Third, the so-called commoners) had dissolved into a National Assembly. On July 14 a mob stormed the Bastille; the night of August 4 saw *la Grande Peur,* the peasant uprising that signaled the end of feudalism; three weeks later, on August 26, the National Assembly published the Declaration of the Rights of Man and of the Citizen. The influence of the United States was unmistakable.

France in tumultuous revolt launched a fury of responses. Word had traveled swiftly across the English Channel (and on to Boston and Philadelphia) to be exalted with supreme enthusiasm by the eminent, 68-year-old British philosopher, preacher, Protestant dissenter, pamphleteer and advocate for American independence, Richard Price, minister of Newington Green Unitarian Church. In his "Discourse on the Love of Our Country," Price was thankful, he said, after sharing in the benefits of one revolution, that of 1688 (England's Glorious Revolution); he now thought he saw the love for liberty catching and spreading, and the dominion of kings changed for the dominion of laws, and the dominion of priests giving way to the dominion of reason and conscience.[5]

Price's discourse, read in London just two months later, in January 1790, "set in motion the avalanche of [the Irish born, Protestant statesman Edmund] Burke's eloquence against the Revolution." As "an observer of the wonderful spectacle exhibited in a neighboring and rival country, that is England gazing with astonishment at a French struggle for liberty and not knowing whether to blame or to applaud," Burke found the spirit impossible not to admire. But the old Parisian ferocity that had broken out was shocking and insupportable.[6]

Burke wanted more from the "dissenting divine," as he called Price, something deeper than "the agitation of a troubled and frothy surface." He looked on that sermon as a "sort of a porridge of various public opinions and reflections"—but the revolution in France was the grand ingredient in the cauldron—as the "public declaration of a man much connected with literary caballers, and intriguing philosophers, with political theologians and theological politicians, both at home and abroad." He was set up as a sort of oracle because, Burke concluded, he naturally "chants his prophetic song in exact unison with their designs."[7]

Burke's stormy rebuttal of Price, *Reflections on the Revolution in France,* published in November 1790, was printed in Philadelphia the following March. Abigail was the first to mention it; her response was judicious though shaded. She had read Burke's letter and though she thought "he paints high, yet strip it of all its ornament and coloring, it will remain an awful picture of liberty abused, authority despised, property plundered, government annihilated, religion banished, murder, rapine and desolation scourging the land."[8]

As for Richard Price, her "worthy and venerable divine" so admired when she had lived in London, she was sorry he should expose himself at this late period of his life to so severe a censure. Though she loved and venerated his character, she did "think his zeal a mistaken one."[9]

John Quincy had obviously read Burke, too. He did not have the leisure to pursue his inclinations, he thought, that is to venture on some speculations in the newspapers because, quoting Burke on Ecclesiastes, "He that hath little business shall become wise."

Personalizing this advice, it was "at least incumbent upon him who is in that predicament, to endeavor to obtain wisdom."[10]

And he had kept his word. He had remained essentially on the sidelines on the issue of the French Revolution, at least for one month, until *The Rights of Man*, Part I, the work of Thomas Paine, surfaced in Philadelphia in May. In a kind of rebuttal of a rebuttal, Paine defended Price against Burke's attack.

Paine was one of the most polarizing figures in all of early America. Author of *The Common Man,* variously regarded as "pamphleteer laureate" of America, propagandist, opportunist, meddler and gadfly, Paine had been introduced to the colonies as an "ingenious worthy young man" by Benjamin Franklin. In John Adams's contrary opinion, Paine was a "Star of Disaster." In the preface to his current work, the British publication of *The Rights of Man,* Paine felt compelled to answer Burke because of the latter's thundering attack and "outrageous abuse on the French Revolution" and the principles of liberty: "Notwithstanding Mr. Burke's horrid paintings, when the French Revolution is compared with revolutions of other countries, the astonishment will cease when we reflect that *principles,* and not *persons,* were the meditated objects of destruction."[11]

As for the English constitution so powerfully defended by Burke and "the bulwark of reactionary government," Paine wrote, there "never did, there never will, and there never can, exist a Parliament, or any description of men, or any generation of men, controlling posterity to the end of time, or commanding for ever how the world shall be governed or who shall govern it." Further, all such clauses, acts or declarations by which the makers of them attempted to do what they had neither the right nor the power to do, nor the power to execute, were in themselves "null and void." Moreover, "the vanity and presumption of government beyond the grave was," he continued, "the most ridiculous and insolent of all tyrannies."[12]

To John Quincy, Paine's wishful annihilation of the tenets of the English Parliament of 1688, and of the English constitution that his father believed to be the only workable form of government, was disturbing in itself. But the endorsement of Paine's work by the trusted, beloved friend of his youth was intolerable. Now John Quincy read to his utter dismay that Thomas Jefferson was "extremely pleased to find it [*Rights of Man*] will be reprinted, and that something is at length to be publicly said against the *political heresies* which have sprung up among us. I have no doubt our citizens will *rally* a second time round the standard *Common Sense*."[13]

John Quincy all too clearly understood, as did his parents, Jefferson's reference to "heresies." These were the serialized installments of John Adams's *Discourses on Davila,* his seeming defense of the monarchical rule of Great Britain, which Paine construed to be a shameless endorsement of the tyranny and arrogance inextricably linked with a monarchy. Immediately on publication of the first installment of the *Discourses,* John Adams knew he was in trouble and was made to feel foolish, pompous, almost treasonous in his advocacy of Great Britain's government. Popular support of France, enhanced by both Jefferson's and Paine's encouraging rhetoric, pointedly marked Adams's published articles as an obvious target for misinterpretation. John defended himself to his friend Dr. Benjamin Rush, on April 18, 1790: "I am a mortal and irreconcilable enemy to monarchy. I am no friend to hereditary limited monarchy in America." As he had written in January 1776 when he had recommended a legislature in three independent branches, he was, he assured Rush, still attached to the same theory.[14]

John Adams felt quite alone, though he had "acted in public with immense multitudes," he had "few friends," and those few were "certainly not interested ones."[15]

He was mistaken. The writer who called himself "Publicola," who attacked Jefferson's inscription in Paine's *Rights of Man* with caustic precision, was not only his friend but also his son. With shrewd deliberation, Publicola pleaded his case. The late revolution in France, an event "so astonishing and unexpected in its nature, and so important in its consequences," had arrested the peculiar attention of the whole civilized world, including philosophers and politicians who speculated on what foundation this newly acquired liberty would be rooted. Two among these were Edmund Burke and

Thomas Paine, whose separate publications, "founded upon very different principles," were received with "the greatest avidity."[16]

At no point in his implacable denunciation did Publicola mention Jefferson by name. But there was no mistake about the identity of the "very respectable gentleman" to whom Publicola addressed himself: "I confess, Sir, I am somewhat at a loss to determine what this very respectable gentleman means by *political heresies.* Does he consider this pamphlet of Mr. Paine's as the canonical book of political scripture? As containing the true doctrine of popular infallibility, from which it would be heretical to depart in one single point? . . . [does it] compel all countrymen to cry out, 'There is but one Goddess of Liberty and Common Sense is her prophet?'"[17]

Initially Jefferson was convinced that the author of the *Davila* discourses and Publicola were one and the same—none other than John Adams, as he wrote to James Madison on June 28, 1791. But in mid-July, Madison supposed, "If young Adams be capable of giving the dress in which Publicola presents himself, it is very probable he may have been made the editor of his father's doctrines. . . . There is more of method also in the arguments, and much less of clumsiness and heaviness in the style, than characterize his father's writings."[18]

Madison's conclusions were confirmed in John Quincy's last essay, July 27, in the *Columbian Centinel:*

> The papers under the signature of Publicola have called forth a torrent of abuse, not upon their real author nor upon the sentiments they express, but upon a supposed author, and supposed sentiments. With respect to the author, not one of the conjectures that have appeared in the public prints has been well grounded. The Vice-President neither wrote nor corrected them.
>
> With respect to the sentiments, to those who have read the pieces with attention, it is needless to say that they are simply an examination of certain principles and arguments contained in a late pamphlet of Mr. Paine's, which are supposed to be directly opposite to principles acknowledged by the constitutions of our country. And the author challenges all the writers who have appeared in support of Mr. Paine's infallibility to produce a single passage to these publications

which has the most distant tendency to recommend either a monarchy or an aristocracy to the citizens of those States.[19]

Publicola's essays were reprinted in New York and Philadelphia and eventually London, Edinburgh and Dublin. They added "fuel to the funeral pile of Liberty" in Jefferson's opinion. On the other hand, the Adamses thought Jefferson's support of Paine favored "a mere popular tyranny," bordering too closely on social disintegration. Crossroads, though signs were not clear, had been reached; "general types" known as conservatives and democrats from hereon would marshal the people of the United States in opposition to each other, "when not affected by disturbing influences from without." But this was hindsight on John Quincy's part. For the moment, raw personal wounds required immediate attention.[20]

Jefferson took up his pen a dozen times, and laid it down as many again, "suspended between opposing considerations." He was determined finally, on July 17, 1791, to write from a conviction that "truth, between candid minds," could never do harm. And also that the "friendship and confidence" that had so long existed between them required his explanation.[21]

To begin with, he told John Adams, it was James Madison who had lent him Paine's pamphlet. When he had finished reading it, he was to send it to a Mr. Jonathan B. Smith, whose brother meant to reprint it. Because he wanted "to take off a little of the dryness of the note," he thought it proper, as a stranger, to add a few comments, and he had done just that. He was glad the pamphlet was to be reprinted, that something was to be publicly said against the political heresies which had sprung up among them. But subsequently, he had been "thunderstruck" on seeing his note reprinted at the beginning of the pamphlet and hoped it would not attract notice. Unfortunately, it had been reprinted not only in New York and Philadelphia, but also London, Glasgow, Edinburgh, Dublin and Dordrecht.[22]

In conclusion, Jefferson wrote, "That you and I differ in our ideas of the best form of government is well known to us both; but we have differed as friends should do, respecting the purity of each other's motives, and confining our differences of opinion to private conversations."[23]

Jefferson, who had pledged privacy "in the presence of the almighty," did not keep his word. On May 8, 1791, he had written to George Washington and mentioned Adams's "apostasy to hereditary monarchy and ability." On May 9, 1791, he had confided to James Madison that he had Adams in mind when he mentioned "political heresies." As late as July 3, to his son-in-law, Thomas Mann Randolph Jr., he had elaborated on the problem of his so-called note of endorsement and how he "knew immediately that it would give displeasure to some gentlemen, fast by the chair of government, who were in sentiment with Burke, and as much opposed to the sentiments of Paine."[24]

John Adams answered Jefferson at great length on July 29, 1791. Regarding his prefatory note to the Philadelphia edition of Paine's pamphlet, the person who had committed the breach of his confidence by making it public, "whatever were his intentions," had sown the seeds of more evils than he could ever atone for. Thanks to the pamphlet and Jefferson's renown, his own writings were deliberately misinterpreted. Thanks to Jefferson, he was held up to the ridicule of the world for his "meanness," for wishing to subjugate the people to a few nobles, for favoring the introduction of hereditary monarchy and aristocracy in America and, ultimately, suffering "as fiery an ordeal as I did, when I was suspected of a blasphemous doubt of Tom Paine's infallibility."[25]

There was no question in John's mind that Jefferson's writings had cost him readers and believers. An agonizing sense of failed justice permeated a ringing passage of his letter to Jefferson: "Of the few who have taken the pains to read them, some have misunderstood them and others have willfully misrepresented them, and these misunderstandings and misrepresentations have been made the pretense for overwhelming me with floods and whirlwinds of tempestuous abuse, unexampled in the history of this country."[26]

It had been Jefferson's hope to prove himself as innocent "in effect" as he was in intention, and that their friendship would never be "suffered to be committed," whatever use others might think proper to make of their names. At the end of his July 17 letter, he had wished John to present "Mrs. Adams with all the affections I feel for her," a gesture unwelcomed by Abigail. Her silent condemnation would be suspended only momentarily by her note of condolence in response to the tragic death of his daughter Mary, known as Polly, 13 years later, long after she had stopped believing that there could be "any event in this life which could call forth feelings of mutual sympathy" between herself and Jefferson.[27]

John Quincy, though he maintained a remarkable objectivity in regard to his political policies, never again trusted Jefferson personally. After reading about 50 pages of the first volume of Jefferson's memoirs, he concluded that Jefferson "tells nothing but what redounds to his own credit. He is like the French lady who told her sister she did not know how it happened, 'mais il n'y a que moi au monde qui a *toujours* raison.' Jefferson, by his own narrative, is always in the right." Probably, John Quincy assumed, it was Jefferson's college professor William Small who "initiated him in the mysteries of free-thinking and irreligion, which *did* fix the destinies of his life. Loose morals necessarily followed. If not an absolute atheist, he had no belief in a future existence."[28]

That fall of 1791, troubled for some time about his weak eyesight, almost blind he claimed at one point, John Quincy was frequently unwell. His worrisome notation of October 20—"Constant at Court. Evening at my office. Dr. Swett"—suggests that his visit to the physician for medical attention was the result of being under pressure. A week later, rather shyly, he acknowledged to his brother Thomas "my confidence in myself growing much stronger," and that he had acquitted himself at the Suffolk County Court of Common Pleas "more to my satisfaction than I had ever done before."[29]

Three months later, he would write Thomas again, asking if his brother might have observed in the *Columbian Centinel* of January 14 that a "committee of 21 inhabitants of this town was chosen in town-meeting to report to the town what measures it might take to reform the present state of the police"; and "you may have noticed that my name was among those of several of the most respectable characters in this town upon that committee."[30]

The issue, ultimately voted down, was a request of certain citizens for a city charter. His nomination by Dr. Charles Jarvis ("the first public notice ever shown me") had been a surprise, but the physician's speech more so: "that this country was under great obligations to my father, and he thought it very proper that some notice should be taken of his son; that he observed I generally attended the town-meetings, and appeared to interest myself in the affairs of the town; that I was a 'sensible young man' (excuse the vanity of the relation) and he wished to hear my sentiments on this subject."[31]

And yet, proud as he was of being asked to serve on the committee, he had declined the assignment. Though the occasion, he recognized, offered a very good opportunity, possibly even the opening to a political career, he had chosen to postpone to some future period his appearance as a speaker in town-meeting—the principal reason being "a want of confidence in myself, which operated most forcibly upon me." He hoped, however, "the time will come, when I shall not be so much oppressed by my diffidence."[32]

In April 1792, while John Quincy had been soberly reading Cicero's orations, Spinoza for law and Shakespeare transiently, and amusing himself with his flute, he reminded himself that "more than 11 months have elapsed since I put pen to this paper," that is, to his diary. But then, in self-defense of his truancy, he questioned whether "events perfectly trivial, or barely rising beyond the level of insipidity . . . painful occurrences and mortifying reflections"—in other words, his dull and dreary life—were worthy of record, of "stability and duration."[33]

No matter how much he hoped to rationalize his position, he remained inconsolable. On Tuesday, April 17, he wrote that "The Court of Common Pleas sits this day. I entered about half a dozen actions. More than I have ever done hither-to, but still very small. My business has an aspect a little more favorable than it has had but still remains for me abundant occasion for anxiety."[34]

Some days he tried to divide his time, reserving the latter part of the day for what he called "mental amusement for the investigation of those parts of science, which have no other relation to the law than the universal chain." Other times, he was determined to make himself a complete master at least of all the Latin classics. He was, for example, much pleased with reading Lord Kames's *Elements of Criticism.*[35]

Then again, at his office in the forenoon, when he solemnly vouched that he made inquiries into the laws relative to executors and administrators, he broke off, as though to plead to an unknown genie for help to fulfill his lofty goals and earnest needs, or possibly just to save him from miserable boredom. "Support me," he wrote, "ye powers of patience, through these sandy deserts of legal study, from whence I am to pick up a scanty subsistence by forcing an unnatural cultivation."[36]

Yet by May 16, he was still dissatisfied with the manner in which he employed his time, calculated as it was to keep him "forever fixed in that state of useless and disgraceful insignificancy" which had been his for some years past. Close to age 25, a time when many of his contemporaries had made a reputation, he still found himself "as obscure as unknown to the world, as the most indolent or the most stupid of human beings. In the walks of life I have done nothing."[37]

For a time, his intense self-examinations were suspended despite his promised commitment. Still, he sustained, and would continue to do so faithfully, his line-a-day pages, a kind of alternate, brief and frankly worded memoir, a daily calendar of his aches and pains, sorrows, private failings and public ventures. He suffered a toothache, sleepless nights, low spirits, poor vision, rheumatism and "melancholy reflections." He played chess, whist, the flute, learned shorthand, and despaired that smallpox had begun to ravage friends and that he too was affected by pocks on his face.[38]

About the evening supper parties, assemblies and dances, he listed the usual complaints of "conversation sentimental & insipid" or dull, or being too large, or when he danced with the Misses Pierce, Shattuck and Breck—"be it forgotten"—or that he found the telling of fortunes a silly amusement, or that he was ill dressed on another occasion, in complete dishabille in large and splendid company yet "I cannot help it."[39]

After, as he termed it, a "somewhat busy" day, both afternoons and evenings, he frequently walked in the mall, a promenade that wound its way through the breadth of Beacon Hill, shaded with double rows of lime, elm and poplar trees. The craggy western and southern slopes gave way to meadow and pastureland; the north slope ended at water's edge and a thriving seaport of wharves, rope walks and sailor's lodgings sometimes disapprovingly known as "Mount Whoredom."[40]

John Quincy took walks alone and, more usually, with friends. But there are increasing hints now of hesitant but potentially embarrassing encounters with women who frequented a certain area of the mall. "I am," he wrote on April 26, 1793, "on the bridge between wisdom and folly." Walking in the mall the evening of September 3 he was "fortunately unsuccessful"; of other evenings, "not so wise as sometimes"; "no harm"; "a foolish but fortunate walk." By New Year's Eve he was "determined upon a course of more discretion": his friends drank champagne with him at his own house.[41]

Fortunately for his parents, their son guarded his most feverish private concerns between the covers of his diary. Outwardly, though somewhat obsessed about his finances (and understandably so), to their knowledge he was a hard-working, conscientious, brilliant and future star of state, country and the world. John Quincy hoped that his father would not consider it as trifling with his time to spend hours on translations of French political writings and on the defense of theater in Boston. Louis de Rousselet, a Catholic priest, editor of *The Courier Politique de l'Universe*, which published news of the French Revolution, had asked him to work on some of the English translations. Resolving the legal problems of the theater would be a far greater challenge.

On December 7, Boston's *American Apollo* carried the final advertisement for "a comic lecture," a performance of David Garrick's *The Lying Valet,* and "a musical lecture," *The Padlock,* by David Bickerstaffe. The next day, actor Joseph Harper advertised in the *Columbian Centinel* that while he lamented the necessity he was under, "thus early to leave this hospitable capital," he was "grateful to the people of Boston for their many favors." Actually, Harper had departed under arrest and the theater was shut down. A dismayed John Quincy reported to his father that after three months of virulent argument to legalize theater in Boston, "The Governor has at length prevailed in routing the players."[42]

Cast-iron opposition to theater in Boston dated back to 1750 when the General Court had passed "An Act to Prevent Stage-Plays, and Other Theatrical Entertainments," which imposed five-pound fines on anyone running, acting in or attending a theatrical production. And opposition persisted in 1767 because "a majority of the members of the Legislature believed that such exhibitions had a tendency to corrupt the morals of the people and were inconsistent with the sober deportment which Christians ought to maintain."[43]

Twenty-five years later, in January 1792, Boston was no more hospitable. When the Massachusetts Legislature declared, in rejecting the most recent challenge, "that it was not expedient to repeal the law," it was clear that if Boston was to have a theater, it must be in defiance of the authorities. As a result, the New Exhibition Room, a theater in all but name, built in a converted stable in the plank-floored, marshy passage called Board Alley (today's Hawley Street), opened to the public on August 10, 1792.[44]

Still, the pro-theater group persisted in pressing its case to no avail. Rival and wrathful factions had argued until Wednesday, December 5, when Governor John Hancock ordered Attorney General James Sullivan to prosecute immediately the violators of the law. By evening, Sheriff Jeremiah Allen had arrested Joseph Harper mid-performance and demanded, under threat of punishment, the instant dispersal of the rest of the company.

Chaos ensued. An infuriated audience, resenting the interruption of the performance, tore down the state's coat of arms and trampled a portrait of Governor Hancock. Two nights later, Boston's town clerk and seasoned justice of the peace, William Cooper, read the Massachusetts Riot Act of 1786 to restrain an opposition contingent from destroying the theater. In the end, the company decided that obedience to the law was safest, and Harper was released when Justices Benjamin Greenleaf and Samuel Barrett of the Court of Common Pleas declared the warrant illegal. With everyone connected to the theater mostly dispersed, John Quincy had hoped the argument had ended but found himself quite mistaken.

Not content to let it be, the governor sought the public's approval, and toward this end Attorney General Sullivan published an article as "A Friend to Peace," to justify the executive authority. Writing in the *Independent Chronicle,* on December 13, Sullivan stubbornly maintained that even if the law was unconstitutional, there was ample provision for a remedy for "the violent measures which have been resorted to," and that the open defiance to a law established by the legislature, and recognized several times as proper and expedient, could not be justifiable.[45]

Having lost patience with Hancock's and Sullivan's "whimsical passion against the theater," John Quincy notified his father that he would probably see in the next two *Centinels* a couple of pieces signed "Menander." "Perhaps an interest in the success of the writer may induce you to peruse the discussion."[46]

As Menander, after the Athenian general and poet, John Quincy meant to do battle, as he would all his life, intensely and with supreme courage, for the causes he was committed to, in this case, for the very existence of the theater, an institution he was happily acquainted with from his earliest travels abroad. And though the New Exhibition Room's *Hamlet* had exceeded his expectation, his line-a-day diary reveals his displeasure with several other productions—on October 8: "*Miser,* & a pantomime very ill performed, the best bad, the worst inexpressible."[47]

His passion, however, was unstinting for the company's right to exist. And so he argued:

> The friends of the theater in Boston have publicly contravened an act of the legislature, which they do not consider as the law of the land; they have not eluded the regular and constitutional discussion of the point; they have not betrayed a consciousness of doing wrong, by shrouding themselves in secrecy; they have not fled from the vengeance of the government which they have provoked. . . .
>
> The observation relative to the dangerous tendency of an open disregard to established laws is just, but in its application to the

present subject, it begs the question in dispute, for no obedience is due to an unconstitutional act of the legislature.[48]

John Quincy's notes on December 24: "Very angry answer to Menander." But he had done admirably in the opinion of his family. His father thanked him for his history of "Tragedy, Comedy and Farce." The translation of the French account of the revolution was well done. In fact, he scarcely knew "of a greater service that could be now rendered to the people of this country than a faithful and impartial account of French affairs would be." As for his Aunt Elizabeth Shaw, she had a favor to ask of her sister Abigail: "Whenever you may chance to see the sensible Menander, please to tell him that since he is so great an advocate for the theater, there are many friends in Haverhill who would wish to see him act his part there . . . any character which he may think appropriate to assume will please . . . but in none can he please your sister more than in that of an *affectionate nephew*."[49]

There were still more compliments for Menander. His mother thought his articles were written "in a masterly style." On further thought, his father rejoiced that John Quincy had taken the unpopular side of the questions concerning the incorporation of the town as well as of dramatic entertainments. It would serve, in his judgment, to hold back his prospective political career for some time and "give you leisure for study and practice, in your profession."[50]

But John Quincy differed somewhat on how best he might use his leisure, given his instinctive preference for current events over law; best, he wrote his father in February, to give him an account of the commercial catastrophe now taking place in Boston. The bubble of banking was breaking; the pernicious practice of mutual endorsements on each other's notes had been carried, it appeared, to an extravagant length. Also, the alarming passions and rivalries of some of the most prominent citizens made him apprehensive for the fate of their country. But this was not a subject on which he could dwell with pleasure. He desired to remain unconnected with political topics, because his sentiments in general were as unpopular as his conduct regarding the town police or the theatrical question.

Not that he had a predilection for unpopularity as such, he explained, but he held it preferable to the popularity of the day, which was his country's obsession with the French. Suspicious of their efforts to despoil their neutral stance, he had persisted in refusing to appear at what he called the "anarchical dinner," the civic feast that a committee of Boston citizens had organized for Thursday, January 24, to celebrate "the SUCCESSES of their French brethren in their glorious enterprise for the establishment of EQUAL LIBERTY." Most emphatically, "We have Jacobins enough," he told his father.[51]

Once again, his father could not but approve of his son's "refusal to appear at the delirious dinner." But while both feared the menace posed by the French—the new French republic's minister to the United States, Edmond Charles Genet, was already on the high seas—their ways of coping differed considerably. John Adams thought "we cannot be too cautious in forming our opinions of French affairs, and we ought to be still more slow in discoursing on them." Angrier by far, John Quincy pictured the beastly local supporters of the French republic with "teeth and claws," the propriety of their acceptance a matter of deepest anxiety.[52]

Minister Genet arrived in Philadelphia on May 16, 1793, in good time to read John Quincy's three essays published in the *Chronicle* between April 24 and May 11 under a pseudonym, this time of the young Roman warrior Marcellus, in ardent defense of American neutrality. John Quincy's son, Charles Francis, would note that these essays "gave a new turn to the course of his life." He would assume the name of Columbus to publish five more essays from November 30 to December 14 to denounce foreign influence on American affairs, and as Barneveldt he defended Columbus against the rage of Americanus, Attorney General James Sullivan, who was a champion of Genet's.[53]

This time there was no secret about authorship of the papers. Or, in the words of Samuel Flagg Bemis, "It was the impact on the United States of the French Revolution . . . that gave to John Quincy Adams the first profitable topic for his scholarly pen." And, at last, the recognition for which he had been destined since his birth.[54]

Chapter 15

"I, TOO, AM A SCRIBBLER"

*F*oremost, the Adamses were humanists, not monarchists, and the specter of France's "fire, impetuosity and vehemence" haunted the thoughts of John Quincy's entire family.[1]

From London, New York, Philadelphia, Boston and Braintree—Thomas was living in Philadelphia, studying law with Jared Ingersoll; Charles had opened his law office on Hanover Square, just off Wall Street, in 1792—they reported to one another the critical current news from Paris, both improbable and bizarre in its ramifications.

Nabby had given warning the past September. Having accompanied her husband on a business trip to London, she had forwarded the English newspapers by which, she wrote to her mother on September 13, 1792, "you will see the distressing situations in which the French are at present . . . too dreadful to relate." One hoped that the English newspapers exaggerated in their accounts, but feared they did not. An acquaintance, returned from Paris, had heard and seen scenes so shocking as to appear "to have refined upon the cruelties of the savage." Yet, for all the turmoil, there were those in London who would say the French were doing fine. All of which, she told her mother with somewhat dry humor, led her to wonder, "what Mr. Jefferson would say to all these things," knowing full well of his support of Thomas Paine.[2]

The next spring, as Thomas wrote to his father on April 7, 1793, the situation in Paris was such that "nothing can be thought too mad or extravagant for the National Convention to commit" and "the conjecture is not unfair that the royal family is e're this extinct."[3]

Actually, Thomas was correctly informed about the king— Louis XVI having been executed by guillotine on January 21—but premature about the queen, who would meet the same fate on October 16. Nevertheless, this same April, official dispatches at last confirmed France's surprising declaration of war on England and Holland the previous February 1, along with the appointment of the 30-year-old, English-speaking Parisian Edmond Charles Genet as minister from the new republic.

It was the propriety of establishing policy and acknowledging and receiving the new minister from the new republic—"that is, if indeed it could be called a republic, where no laws existed, or if they did, where there was no supreme power to enforce obedience to them"—that had mostly angered Thomas. It was a heated topic of conversation: some said they could not but receive Citizen Genet, out of gratitude to France for its early recognition of America's independence, while others wondered whether this might risk drawing all the nations of Europe into a war with America.[4]

On April 18, President Washington posed grave and pointed questions before his entire cabinet on "Respecting a Proclamation of Neutrality, and The Reception of a French Minister." In addition, was the United States obliged to consider prior treaties with France, such as the 16-year-old Treaty of Alliance between the United States and France, fortifying the two against the British back in March 1778?[5]

The response was unanimous. At a meeting of the heads of departments and the attorney general with President Washington on April 19:

> it was determined by all, on the first question, that a proclamation shall be issued forbidding our citizens to take part in any hostilities on the seas, with or against any of the belligerent powers; and warning them against carrying to any such powers any of those articles deemed

contraband, according to the modern usage of nations; and enjoining them from all acts and proceedings inconsistent with the duties of a friendly nation.

On the second question, "Shall a minister from the Republic of France be received?" it was unanimously agreed that a minister from the Republic of France be received.[6]

Three days later, according to Washington's formal and official Neutrality Proclamation issued on April 22: "duty and interest of the United States require, that they should with sincerity and good faith adopt and pursue a conduct friendly and impartial toward the belligerent powers."[7]

Citizen Genet, as it turned out, was received with open arms—so Charles Adams had heard—on his arrival by carriage in Philadelphia on May 16. Which was alright with Charles, as long as it did not convey the idea of acquiescence to the transactions in France. No person could be more of an advocate for civil liberty and civil equality than himself, "but name not the French as models; name not that barbarous, that cruel people, as examples worthy to be followed by Americans." Fiercely passionate on the subject, Charles was very much pleased, he told his father, with a writer who signed himself Marcellus.[8]

If Charles did not know the identity of Marcellus at the time of that letter to his father, he would learn shortly that it was his brother John Quincy writing in the name of the young Roman warrior. Actually, Charles had read in the Philadelphia paper the third installment of the series published originally in the *Columbian Centinel*—the first of which had appeared on April 24, two days after Washington's Proclamation, the next two on May 4 and 11—in which John Quincy explored "the interesting question" of what line of conduct should be pursued by the United States as a nation and by its citizens as individuals when all the European powers with whom they had considerable commercial intercourse were involved in war. He had concluded that "a rigid adherence to the system of neutrality between the European nations now at war is equally the dictate of justice and of policy to the individual citizens of the United States, while the nation remains neutral."[9]

John Quincy had no illusions about Genet's mission, which was to co-opt the United States as an ally in France's illegal ventures on the high seas. "There have indeed been certain suggestions in the public papers, and in private circles, of an intention among some of our fellow citizens to arm privateers, and commit depredations upon the commerce of one of the parties under the authority of another. It is to be hoped that this violation of the laws of nature and nations, this buccaneering plan of piratical plunder, may not in any instance be carried beyond the airy regions of speculation, and may never acquire the consistency of practical execution." Convinced that "the natural state of all nations, with respect to one another, is a state of peace," he thought that to digress further on the natural injustice and wickedness of privateering would be as idle as an attempt "to add perfume to the violet."[10]

Repeatedly, insistently, John Quincy had preached the cause of neutrality at the same time that he acknowledged feelings of gratitude on the part of Francophiles toward a nation "which assisted us in the days of our own calamity. We may be disposed to throw a veil over their own errors and crimes, and wish them that success which their frantic enthusiasm has rendered so improbable," and "we may be willing to forget as descendants of Englishmen the miseries they inflicted upon us in our just struggle against them." But, he concluded: "as the citizens of a nation at a vast distance from the continent of Europe, of a nation whose happiness consists in a real independence, disconnected from all European interests and European politics, it is our duty to remain the peaceable and silent, though sorrowful spectators of the sanguinary scene."[11]

Indeed, his father had agreed with Charles and thought that Marcellus deserved as high an encomium as that of Publicola, whose essays, he had been informed, Mr. Pitt, speaker of the House of Commons, and several other characters in high office had pronounced "one of the ablest things of the kind they ever read. . . . Your brother has great talents, and equal industry . . . is destined to be celebrated and consequently envied and abused."[12]

Even as John Quincy's reputation was growing, his qualms as a writer seemed to nurture and further his evocative craftsmanship. At the invitation of his townsmen, he had completed "An Oration in commemoration of July 4th." While writing it, he told his brother Tom, he had thought himself quite brilliant. Now, with ten days to go, it appeared "a mass of dull commonplace . . . with scarce a single gleam of originality shooting through the solid darkness of the composition."[13]

But he had remained on message at Boston's Old South Meeting House and made an incisive distinction between the American Revolution and that of the French, then in progress: "It was not the convulsive struggle of slavery to throw off the burden of accumulated oppression, but the deliberate, tho' energetic effort of freemen, to repel the insidious approaches of tyranny."[14]

Despite his misgivings, *The Massachusetts Mercury* reported the next day: "The elegance and spirit of the composition, and the forceful elocution of the speaker, excited such a burst of admiration as would have flattered Cato." It had brought him, his brother Charles said, "universal applause," as well as his personal admiration for "the prudence which you have observed in steering so cautiously between the Scylla and Charybdis of public opinion."[15]

On November 25 and for weeks later, John Quincy was writing for the public at large "in a manner that will be of no avail to me."[16]

The very foundation of the country, the Constitution, had been assaulted, and feeling it his moral and religious duty, he would publish his next three essays in five parts, from November 30 through December 14, under the pseudonym Columbus, to speak about the French minister whom he called "the most implacable and dangerous enemy to the peace and happiness of my country."[17]

As a pragmatic lawyer, he opened his "case" with the heartfelt conviction, fundamental to his being, that it was the "unquestionable right of every individual citizen to express without control his sentiments upon public measures and the conduct of public men" and, accordingly, "I, too, am a scribbler," he wrote. "I too as a citizen of the United States have the right to express my opinion upon the pretensions of Citizen Genet."[18]

In his view, it was tolerable so long as the agent of a friendly nation confined himself within the circle of his own rights, however offensive the demands he was instructed to make may be. On the other hand, matters took an ominous turn:

> if the ambassador descends from that station: if he threatens to negotiate with the *people,* without any authority or commission from his own sovereign for that purpose, if he is constantly pouring forth in the public prints, a stream of abuse, under the shape of letters, of addresses, of remonstrances, and protests, against the very government to which he was accredited, he thereby renounces all the privileges which surrounded his public character, and makes himself obnoxious to every feather in the wing of wit, and every shaft in the quiver of satire. . . .[19]

Genet had crossed the line irrevocably when he chose to appeal to the people over the decision of the regular and constituted authority, thereby insulting the character of their "common friend and benefactor," President George Washington. It was an insolent outrage "when a beardless foreigner, whose name was scarcely enrolled upon the catalogue liberty; a petulant stripling . . . presumed to place himself in opposition to the father of their country."[20]

An evaluation of the Constitution followed. Like its Athenian role model, the American Constitution was purely democratic. Furthermore, the American Constitution did not permit any of the states "upon any terms whatever to enter into a treaty, alliance, or confederation; nor without the consent of Congress so much as to enter into any agreement or compact with a foreign power."[21]

"But there let it rest," John Quincy concluded. Yet, he had to drive home his ultimate point, in emphatic confirmation of the president's eight-month-old declaration:

> The interference of foreigners upon any pretense whatever, in the dissensions of fellow citizens, must be as inevitably fatal to the liberties of the state, as the admission of strangers to arbitrate upon the domestic differences of man and wife is destructive to the happiness of a private family. . . . [22]

If inquiries were made about the cause, within the past quarter of a century, fatal to the liberties of Sweden, of Geneva, of Holland and of Poland, the answer, he continued, was "one and the same. It was the association of internal faction and external power." And while all these terrible examples of national humiliation and misery were staring us in the face, "we behold a foreign agent among ourselves, violating the spirit and intention of our Constitution, and pursuing every measure which can tend to involve us in the same ruin, and add us to the melancholy catalogue of subjugated freemen."[23]

John Quincy's cautionary sentiments had been couched more officially and decisively when Washington delivered his December 5 "Message to Both Houses of Congress; Respecting the French." In essence, the president asserted, the nation would no longer tolerate "the vexations and spoliation understood to have been committed on our vessels and commerce" or the reprehensible actions of one man whose name he left unspoken but was clearly that of Edmond Genet. It was with "extreme concern," the president informed members of Congress:

> that the proceedings of the person, whom they have unfortunately appointed their minister plenipotentiary here, have breathed nothing of the friendly spirit of the nation which sent him; their tendency, on the contrary, has been to involve us in war abroad, and discord and anarchy at home. So far as his acts, or those of his agents, have threatened our immediate commitment in the war, or flagrant insult in the authority of the laws, their effect has been counteracted by the ordinary cognizance of the laws, and by an exertion of the powers confided to me.[24]

Four days after the printing of his final, December 14 essay, Columbus was attacked in the *Independent Chronicle* on December 18. Americanus (the Attorney General James Sullivan), a champion of Genet on all counts, challenged his interpretation of the Constitution and questioned whether his arguments were "founded on the law of reason." A week later, on December 26, and for some weeks to come, Columbus's cause was taken up quite mysteriously by a writer who called himself Barneveld (probably a variation on the name of the hero of Dutch independence) and who staunchly upheld the president's Constitutional right "to receive and dismiss foreign ministers and consuls." Somewhat playfully John Quincy informed his father, "Columbus and Barneveld, we are told, are one and the same."[25]

Certainly, at this stage, it was not difficult for any family member to identify the author of the pieces signed Columbus. "They are very highly esteemed and have been reprinted in all our papers but one," Charles had written his father, who admitted he had the exact same thought as the friend who said "there is but one man capable of writing Columbus."[26]

In a wryly put compliment, having read two essays by Columbus, John Adams had observed that it was mortification to reflect that "a few ironies, a merry satirical story, or a little humor will make more impression than all these grave reasonings, polished eloquence and refined oratory." The similarity of his son's fearful reckoning with the French and with Genet in particular to that of Washington did not, of course, escape John Adams. In his summation of Washington's speech, for the benefit of Abigail, the father was proud that "The President had considered the conduct of Genet, very nearly in the same light with Columbus and has given him a bolt of thunder." Indeed, President Washington's formal request for Genet's dismissal would be granted by the French government the following October.[27]

At this point, early in the new year of 1794, both applause and criticism propelled John Quincy through another cycle of intense introspection. A sonnet, published in the *Chronicle* and signed U.S.A., had described Columbus as "Patriot of the world, the friend of man."[28]

On the other hand, he had to cope with "the saturnine genius of Americanus," whom he knew perfectly well to be James Sullivan who, after assuring the "juvenile author" that he would not be rescued from contempt even by the "high station of his sire," had gone on to describe the "petulance and affected wit of Columbus and Barneveld most of which . . . was a sort of literary plagiarism from

Junius . . . the aspirations of family pride." Though John Quincy claimed that he was not much affected by Sullivan's harsh words, he did admit that he resented the response of so-called friends who would be clamorous enough to praise him "if they were not disposed to check his aspirations as a writer."[29]

As for his writing—he circled the question of why he wrote a number of times. He wrote neither for political gain or fame, he confessed to his brother Tom. But it would be "false and absurd to deny" that a literary reputation was an object of his ambition.[30]

In a reflective mood, it was as though this February 13, 1794, was a day of reckoning. "Advanced almost to the age of thirty," he was warily judgmental: He had "no political existence and his ideas of liberty and government are so widely distant from the fashion of the day that they are much more likely to be injurious than beneficial to my advancement." When it came to rating himself at the bar, he was just as pitiless. After nearly four years of practice, he remained obscure and unknown. "Surely then as far as success is the criteria of talents," he told Thomas, "I have no reason to be vain."[31]

In spite of his dismal account, he trusted that his brother did not think him discontented with his present situation. He did allow that his profession at present gave him bread, and that his business, however slowly, seemed gradually to improve. He had cases in three different courts, had won a case on behalf of the Massachusetts Commonwealth and two for private clients, and planned to argue two or three important cases before the Supreme Court in the next week. "So that you may conclude, I am not entirely idle but still, however, upon probation and still consider all my professional employment as accidental and precarious."[32]

In early March, without being overburdened (as he put it) with business, John Quincy could report to his father that he had on hand enough work to employ almost all his time, but "to keep upon my mind, a continual anxiety, which unfits me for any thing else." He took note of the arrival of the new minister from France, Jean Antoine Joseph Fauchet, and the recall of Genet. His father thought Fauchet a very different character—reserved, cautious, discreet, young, not more than 33 in comparison to Genet, "gay as if nothing had happened to him." He was hopeful that the new plenipotentiary would pursue a different course, and that their country would still be permitted to remain at peace.[33]

John Quincy was also consoled—judging from a recent town meeting—by the lessening influence of the French, as shown by the postponement of a civic festival fostered by the Jacobin–Anti-Federal faction. But optimism flickered to pessimism; if the British persisted in seizing their ships, he saw no alternative but war. Indeed, he thought "it is of itself a state of war, to have every thing that passes under the denomination of supplies liable to capture," he told his father. And a few days later, he pronounced the news of the capture of 30 American vessels on the Island of Nevis alone "beyond all toleration."[34]

Perpetual and nagging, John Quincy's innermost concern about his life's work inevitably surfaced in his letters. No matter how casually introduced or phrased, it did not escape his father. He told John Quincy that he hoped his business would increase, but he strenuously recommended a far more aggressive approach. "You must hustle in the crowd to make speeches in town meeting, and push yourself forward. Meet with the caucuses and join political clubs, not the Jacobins however." Some people, he continued, "have a faculty of making friends and dependents: some marry fortunes; some marry into connections. Others find ways of making money in twenty honest plans. Much more depends on little things than is commonly imagined—an erect figure, a stead[y] countenance, a neat dress, a genteel air; an oratorical period, a resolute determined spirit, often do more than deep erudition or indefatigable application. . . ."[35]

But all, he did concede, "have not the same gifts." Taking stock of the future of his three sons, he did not mince words or the truth. They must be content to crawl into fame and be satisfied with mediocrity of fortune, like their father. Either nature had not bestowed on them her most exquisite favors, or they had some awkwardness in address, or some peculiarity of feelings, which condemned them to perpetual drudgery, without much fame, fortune or attention from the world. So be it. "We are under so much less obligation to others."[36]

His father was not to worry. John Quincy had hope, he wrote a week later, of more business. As for his father's recommendations of town meetings and speeches and caucuses and political clubs: "But I am afraid of all these things," he explained. They might make him a better politician and give him an earlier chance of appearing as a public man, but they would throw him completely in the power of the people, and his future "would be a life of dependence."[37]

There was no question of his intention to serve—only the matter of timing: "I would rather continue some time longer in obscurity and make some provision for fortune, before I sally out in quest of fame or public honors." Moreover, "Mediocrity of fortune" would certainly be sufficient to satisfy his desires, and he would be content if, like his father, he could "crawl into fame" and serve so essentially the cause of humanity and of liberty, as he had done.[38]

His father, in turn, was polite but sternly unyielding. He understood his son's caution in political matters. But in regard to the "mediocrity of fortune that you profess or affect," he reminded John Quincy that he had come into life with advantages which would disgrace him if his success were mediocre. If he did not rise to the head not only of his profession but of his country, "it will be owing to your own laziness, slovenliness and obstinacy."[39]

The question of their son's bearing was somewhat of a preoccupation of both his parents. As John Adams wrote to Abigail, Mr. John must take care, he must learn "silence and reserve, prudence, caution—above all to curb his vanity and collect himself." These were admittedly virtues that he himself had wanted, and he had often thought their son had "more prudence at 27, than his father at 58."[40]

He was hardly one to talk, Abigail scolded. Her husband would curb their son's vanity when, in her opinion, he did more with his praise to excite it, coming as it did from the father he held in such great respect and veneration. For her part, she had complete confidence in John Quincy and, while she would not say "that all my

geese are swan," she hoped that she had no occasion to blush for
the conduct of any of her children.[41]

On May 30, his father sent momentous news of a profound change
that would meet with great wonder and, given John Quincy Adams's nature, not a little anxiety. John Quincy noted in his diary
simply, "the President of the United States had determined to nominate me to go to The Hague as resident minister from the United
States."[42]

The day after writing John Quincy, John Adams thought it
only proper that he inform Abigail, then at home in Quincy, of the
president's plan to send their son to Holland. He was writing to her
in confidence, at the desire of the president, and she must keep it
secret until it was announced to the public in the Senate's Journal.
And John Quincy, meanwhile, must hold himself in readiness to
come to Philadelphia to converse with the president, the secretaries
of state and the treasury, and receive his commissions and instructions without loss of time.

His father advised John Quincy to go to Providence in the stage
coach, to New York by water and to Philadelphia via the stage. This
plan had one caveat: Just to be on the safe side, he would not advise
him to set out until he was officially informed of his appointment,
allowing "Perhaps the Senate may negative him," and then his journey would be unnecessary. He himself intended to go on Saturday
by the stage to New York, and be home, he hoped, by June 12.[43]

Understandably, both parents were elated by the appointment.
His father, somewhat reliving his own past, did not overstate his
promise "to drop hints, broken hints from time to time," nor conceal his ambition for his son. It was a serious trust; it ought to make
a deep impression on his mind; he ought to be very cautious in his
dispatches, and he ought to employ all the elegance and art of his
pen. Still then another thought: "a few years spent in the present
grade will recommend him to advancement to highest stages and
larger spheres."[44]

Abigail's response took a different form, a rare exchange
with Martha Washington. Uncompromising in her pride, unsparing in her praise of her son, she wrote to the president's wife to

acknowledge the honor of the unsolicited appointment the president had conferred on him. To her mind, John Quincy had already served his nation, for "at a very early period of life I devoted him to the public" when, in the most dangerous and hazardous time of war, she had consented to his accompanying his father in his embassies abroad.[45]

As a result, she had the satisfaction "to say to you, Madam, perhaps with the fond partiality of a parent, that I do not know in any one instance of his conduct either at home or abroad," that he had given her any occasion of regret. She hoped from his "prudence, honor, integrity, and fidelity" that he would "never discredit the character so honorably conferred upon him." Above all, "painful as the circumstance of a separation from him will be to me, Madam, I derive a satisfaction from the hope of his becoming eminently useful to his country."[46]

John Quincy had hand-delivered his mother's note. Martha Washington's response was more than kind; it was sensitive and appreciative, both encouraging and vastly supportive of John Quincy's future. "That parental feelings should be put to the test at a separation (perhaps for years) from a dutiful and meritorious son," was not to be wondered at. On the other hand, her son's prudence, good sense and the high estimation in which he was held left her nothing to worry about as to his character and his abilities. Given the prospect ahead, he would prove himself among the foremost in their country's councils. This, Martha Washington knew, was "the opinion of my husband from whom I have imbibed the idea."[47]

On May 30, the day the Senate unanimously advised and consented to the appointment of John Quincy Adams to The Hague, John Adams wrote to his son: "If this event should affect your sensibility as much as it does mine, it will make a deep impression upon your mind, both of the importance of the mission and of your obligation to gratitude, fidelity and exertion in the discharge of the duties of it."[48]

John Quincy had indeed been deeply affected for several reasons. On the helpful side, the meeting with his father in Quincy on June 10 had convinced him that family influence was not a factor in his appointment. His father had also promised him introductions to various officials that would make his stay in Philadelphia more rewarding. But then he wondered after their conversation if his father was "more gratified than myself at my appointment."[49]

In fact, it proved to be a torment rather than a pleasure. Uneasy from the start and almost ill within 24 hours of the news of his appointment, he was burdened "with very unusual reflections." He felt himself the next day "disqualified both for business and amusement by the late event;" and on another evening, "much affected by the sentiments of my friends on the present occasion, but unwell." He had supposed on June 7 that he felt better but found himself "much mistaken"; on June 14, he did not go to Dorchester to dine with his club but "Commenced a new process, the last resort of hope.—Its affect rough." The next day with "Dr. Lathrop and Mr. Clarke perusing my system," he was "reduced almost to the extremity of despair."[50]

On the morning of June 18, after a "very bad night," he was bled and felt a little better. He walked in the mall, attended his club, saw friends, went out to Quincy to talk once more with his father. The day before he left for Philadelphia, June 29, he continued to make preparations for his departure, but he found the idea of leaving all his friends "very painful."[51]

Chapter 16

"THE TIMES CHANGE AND WE CHANGE WITH THEM"

*O*n Monday, June 30, John Quincy left Boston for Philadelphia to report to President George Washington for instructions, traveling first to Providence, then down the river to Newport. He then sailed toward New York on the *Romeo* and, owing to a dead calm, had to row from Hell Gate into New York City, where he stayed for three days with his sister Nabby and her husband, Colonel Smith, in their home at 18 Cortland Street. Dinner guests that day included Charles Maurice de Talleyrand-Périgord and Bon Albert Briois de Beaumetz; also Louis Saint Ange Morel, Chevalier de La Colombe. John Quincy wasn't surprised finding these famed Frenchmen at the Smiths' table. His father had commented on the great number of men of talent in the United States—not only from France but from Switzerland, England, Scotland and Ireland—and feared they would do more harm than good "if 'we are not upon our guard.'"[1]

Still, they were an impressive group with memorable pasts: Talleyrand, bishop of Autun and ambassador to England; Beaumetz, a prominent member of the National Assembly of France; Colombe, aide-de-camp to the Marquis de Lafayette during the American Revolution, who had escaped from Austria where Lafayette remained imprisoned. Both had been promoters and victims of the French Revolution. John Quincy found Talleyrand reserved and distant, Beaumetz more sociable and communicative. He and Colombe had spoken for half an hour before they realized they had been fellow passengers on the *Sensible* nearly 16 years ago. Now banished from France and from England, it seemed that America, "this country of universal liberty, this asylum from the most opposite descriptions of oppression," was the only one in which they could find rest.[2]

Obviously quite taken by his formidable companions, it was natural to look with reverence, or at least with curiosity, so John Quincy told himself, on men who have been so highly and so recently conspicuous upon the most splendid theater of human affairs. But parties had successfully destroyed one another, and in the general wreck it was not easy to distinguish between those whose fall has been the effect of their own incapacity, and those who have been only unfortunate. As he wrote his mother, "*tempora mutantur et nos mutamur in illis,*" "The times change and we change with them." Presently, Talleyrand and Beaumetz were exploring business opportunities on behalf of themselves and friends abroad, particularly investments in land. That probably accounted for their presence at the Smiths, the colonel momentarily being a vastly successful landowner in 1794.[3]

But truly, he thought the times unique, that "Perhaps there never has been a period in the history of mankind, when fortune has sported so wantonly with reputation, as of late in France." The tide of popularity ebbed and flowed with nearly the same frequency as that of the ocean, though not with the same regularity. The list of the fallen was long, including Necker, Lafayette, Pétion, Condorcet, Brissot, Danton and "innumerable others [who] have in their turns, been at one moment the idols and at the next the victims of the popular clamor. In the distribution of fame, as in everything else," he wrote in his diary, "they have been always in extremes."[4]

John Quincy also spent time with his brother Charles, dined early and alone on July 8, and made no further comment on his brother-in-law, sister, or their establishment, though he knew very well of his family's increasing concern for the well-being of their daughter and family.

Nabby had married in London eight years before, on June 12, 1786, to the relief and approval of her parents. Both parents delighted in the "circumstances and connections respectable" pertaining to their daughter's marriage. From all appearances Colonel Smith was a brave soldier, accomplished and charming. Only a letter to his close friend hinted at a different man entirely: ambitious, impecunious, entrepreneur and adventurer. He was staying in Pall Mall near the St. James's Palace "thinking it best to strike at the highest peg at once." On the rebound himself from a romance gone awry and vastly pleased with his reception by the Adams family, he seemed to imply that he would try harder or behave better this time around. "You need not fear I'll make another slip with her," he reassured his friend, the Prussian general, Baron Friedrich von Steuben. Though admittedly part of a "very extreme and gay theater," he fully intended "to move with great caution lest I should stumble."[5]

In the next years, the colonel had teetered between prosperity and embarrassment. In 1791 he bought 150,000 acres in central New York State; in 1792 he suffered financial pressures from an uncertain market. The following year, the colonel's display of affluence, such as traveling in a coach and four, led John Adams to comment on his son-in-law's preference for "monarchical trumpery" and Abigail to write John Quincy, "I am very anxious for your sister and family."[6]

John Adams grew impatient with his peripatetic, real-estate-speculating son-in-law, with his questionable political connections and foreign allegiances, and lack of financial stability. But for all his criticism, he was fascinated by the charismatic colonel. He wished that his sons had a little more of his activity. He thought, in fact, that he "must soon treat them as the pigeons treat their squabs—push them off the limb and make them put out their wings or fall. Young pigeons will never fly till this is done," he told his wife. Fourteen months later, John Quincy was on his way.[7]

John Quincy continued on to Philadelphia, a nine-day trip in all. On July 10 he reported at the president's house on the south side of High Street between Fifth and Sixth, originally built by Richard Penn, grandson of the founder of Pennsylvania, and rebuilt by financier Robert Morris, whose questionable real estate investments would land him in jail. Washington said very little to John Quincy about his appointment, but he did invite him to the next day's reception for Piomingo (also known as Mountain Leader), one of the heads of the Chickasaw nation, and a number of his tribesmen.

On July 11, his twenty-eighth birthday, he received his commission from Secretary of State Edmund Randolph. He did not miss a nuance of the reception, awkward, amusing and altogether riveting, held in the splendid upstairs parlor.

The president, an imposing, six-foot figure, and John Quincy, the young, bemused new minister to The Hague, completed the circle of seven warriors, five chiefs, four boys and an interpreter. He found nothing remarkable in their appearance, he claimed. Some of them were dressed in coarse jackets and trousers, and some in the uniform of the United States. Some of them had shirts, and some had none. Four or five wore rings in their noses, one or two sported silver breast plates. He did not remember any other ornaments and, to his relief, no one was "painted or scarified."[8]

As soon as they were seated, the ceremony of smoking began. A large East Indian pipe was placed in the middle of the hall. The tube, which appeared to be of leather, was 12 or 15 feet in length. The president began, and after two or three whiffs, passed the tube to Piomingo; he to the next chief, and so on all around. "Whether this ceremony be really of Indian origin, as is generally supposed," John Quincy confessed to some doubt.[9]

"At least these Indians appeared," he continued, "to be quite unused to it as if they were submitting to a process in compliance with *our* custom. Some of them smiled with such an expression of countenance as denoted a sense of novelty and of frivolity too; as if the ceremony struck them, not only as new, but also as ridiculous." When it was finished, the president addressed them in a speech which he read, stopping at the close of every sentence for the interpreter to translate it."[10]

They then made several inquiries respecting the Cherokees who had recently been there. Their questions were a mixture of curiosity and of animosity. These two nations were at war, and the Chickasaws spoke of the others as a perfidious people "who had the *fides punica* [Punic faith]." Treachery, it seemed to John Quincy, "is not confined to civilized nations."[11]

While wine, punch and cake were served, the president told the Chickasaws that they had "always been distinguished as sincere and faithful friends, and that the United States always valued such friends most highly." In return, John Quincy wrote, "They said nothing of their own sincerity, and made no answer to the president's compliment. These formalities employed about an hour; after which they rose, shook hands with us all, and departed."[12]

John Quincy stayed on in Philadelphia longer than he wished, awaiting the return of Secretary of the Treasury Alexander Hamilton, who had taken his son to the country for a change of air from the city, rampant with smallpox. Meanwhile, he read six volumes of his father's dispatches to the Continental Congress while he was their commissioner and minister in Europe, which proved, he wrote his father, "such a fund of information and of entertainment . . . as I have seldom met with in the course of my life."[13]

He also wrote to his mother that he would be gratified to have his brother Thomas go with him and hoped this plan would be agreeable to his father. He would pay his expenses of traveling, his board and lodging, if his father would continue with the same allowance he gave him at present. He thought Tom would be glad to go, that he certainly never would have an opportunity when he could spare a year of his time with so little inconvenience. Both parents had responded positively; his mother thought the opportunity "would be mutually beneficial [and] . . . not so solitary to you." To his additional pleasure, John Quincy learned that he was officially permitted a private secretary with an allowance of $1,350.[14]

Waiting for Hamilton, who was expected hourly, as patiently as he could, which was hardly at all—he wrote his father on July 27: "lolling away my time, and sweating away my person"— allowed for a treacherous period in which to analyze in excruciating detail how his mission abroad would affect his future. At its core, there was the matter of the lack of prestige, having been told by Secretary of State Edmund Randolph that the mission was "almost exclusively reduced to a pecuniary negotiation."[15]

Most acutely, John Quincy was conflicted about his appointment and its relation to the legal profession he was abandoning. The timing seemed all wrong, for it was just when prospects were brightening, when he was at least on footing of equal advantage with others in the profession. Elevated to a public station much beyond his own wish and expectations, and invested with a character more conspicuous than those of his fellow citizens of equal years and standing in the world, he worried that his absence would carry him back on his return to the obscurity in which he began.

But if he was worried about being less of a lawyer on his return, he was even more deeply troubled by the thought of being less an American after living in Europe. Unquestionably reflecting his own experience at a younger age, he worried that "habits, manners and affections insensibly undergo an alteration until an American abroad gradually becomes a stranger to his own country, and, on his return, finds himself an alien in the midst of his own fellow citizens."[16]

His father, in response, was sympathetic, wise and encouraging; he thought that Secretary Randolph underestimated the responsibilities of the new minister. John thought the post at The Hague was an important diplomatic station, which might "afford many opportunities of acquiring political information and of penetrating the designs of many cabinets of Europe." His father would prove correct in that assessment. John also believed John Quincy would, in three or four years, be promoted to the rank of a minister plenipotentiary; possibly in less time, if the president became aware of his talents and principles suitable for so high a trust.[17]

As far as John Quincy's observations on his law practice, they were "very sensible," his father said. Should he return in three or seven years, or more or less, he wished him to return to the bar and counseled patience. "Submit to the mortifications you justly foresee: Open your office and be always found in it, except when you are attending the Courts of Justice."[18]

Meanwhile, focusing on his new assignment, his father advised, "Endeavour to obtain correspondences with able men in the southern and middle states as well as in the northern ones, and these will inform you and advise you." And if his life should be spared, he hoped to be one of them to give him his "best opinions and advice as circumstances occur." "With constant affection, your friend and father," he wished his son "a pleasant voyage and much honor, satisfaction and success in your mission."[19]

The diplomatic instructions signed by Edmund Randolph on July 29 included John Quincy's letters of credence to the Stadtholder and States General and also a cipher. His duties were hardly as innocuous as John Quincy had anticipated, given Randolph's tactful warning that:

> the administration of the Dutch government was not only liable to the fluctuations which the administration of every government undergoes, from the passions and views of individuals at the helm of affairs, but the peculiar situation of Holland in relation to the present European war lays it open to the chance of sudden revolutions, and very sudden and new courses of policy. If therefore the germ of any important change should be foreseen, it will be honorable to yourself, and may be advantageous to the United States to apprize us of it, as early as possible. . . .
>
> Among other things, which may be contemplated, as worthy of observation, if any symptoms of increasing liberty, of dissatisfaction with any of the combined owners, or of an inclination to make peace with the French republic should be found, you will hasten to us the intelligence of them. . . .
>
> But I must entreat you and urge you, to make it your first and unremitting duty, to forward by all the means in your power the loan, opened for 800,000 dollars and destined to the ransom of our fellow citizens in Algiers, and the effectuating of a peace.
>
> It is the wish and instruction of the president, that a memorandum be daily taken of every circumstance, which may be deemed proper for his information, and a letter commenced and continued, so as to be ready for conclusion and sealing, upon a moment's warning of a conveyance. . . .[20]

On July 29, John Quincy told his mother that, accustomed as he was to writing freely, he found it difficult to realize that henceforth his correspondence "must be armed at all points," or confidential, and that it would take him some time to ease himself "into diplomatic buckram completely," especially in his frustration over the critical $800,000 Dutch loan whose laggard repayment would still be in negotiation when he moved on to London.[21]

John Quincy returned to New York City on August 9 and left on the packet *Sally* on the morning of August 16, arriving in Providence on August 18 and in Quincy the next day. Hamilton had given him the powers necessary to negotiate the loan, and from Randolph, dispatches to be delivered abroad, adding, in a private note dated August 13, that he was to carry to Europe "a precise account of the insurrection" that had occurred in western Pennsylvania. What John Quincy had described to his mother as "a very serious opposition"—in which a thousand men violently protested the excise tax on domestic distilled spirits—would become known as the Whiskey Rebellion after it was quelled by President Washington's militia on November 9, with several lives lost in the turmoil.[22]

On September 17, John Quincy boarded the *Alfred* for London with his brother Thomas Boylston and their servant, Tilly Whitcomb. Family and friends accompanied him on board the ship, then returned to shore to wave him off, except for Daniel Sargent—Mary Frazier's husband—and Nathan Frazier—her brother—who sailed as far as the lighthouse. Frazier, alluding to the new French Revolutionary Calendar, told John Quincy: "The name of your ship is auspicious. You depart on the day of Virtue, I hope you will return upon the day of Rewards."[23]

At that moment, on bidding final farewells, John Quincy thought that, "The pain of separation from my friends and country was felt as poignantly by me . . . as it ever has been at any period of my life. It was like the severing the last string from the heart." He looked back at their boat, and when it was out of sight, he did not, but he could have, he wrote, "turned my eye and wept."[24]

On October 14, they sailed past the lighthouse of Dungeness between noon and one and were soon abreast Dover's white cliffs. After 28 days aboard the *Alfred,* considering the flimsy, crazy condition of the old ship and the mistakes of their captain, their safe landing had been extraordinary.

They had liked the Royal Exchange Inn opposite their landing place in Deal, but John Quincy was too pressed to enjoy its comforts. He had been entrusted with highly confidential documents regarding critical negotiations with Great Britain on the subject of depredations of American commerce; President Washington had asked John Quincy to make a stopover in London en route to The Hague to assure that certain papers reached the president's special emissary, the eminent American John Jay, then the minister plenipotentiary and envoy extraordinary of the United States. The papers concerned what would become known as Jay's Treaty. Earnest, dutiful, admittedly filled with anxiety, John Quincy and his brother Tom decided to leave Deal in early morning.

Part II

Chapter 17

"THE MAGNITUDE OF THE TRUST AND MY OWN INCOMPETENCY"

*E*leven years had passed since John Quincy had traveled almost the identical route from nearby Dover to London in the fall of 1783, age 16. Now he found the countryside most remarkably improved, and it was very possible to say the same about John Quincy himself when education and experience were taken into account: at age 27, he was a Harvard College graduate, a lawyer, a writer of esteem and controversy, and the recently appointed minister to the Netherlands.

At his side was his genial and thoughtful younger brother, 22-year-old Thomas, a recent graduate of Harvard, a lawyer "rather from necessity than inclination" with literary interests. Both men tended to be overweight, as did their third brother Charles, who was, said their father, "fat as a squab or duck." While both parents were pleased for Tom to have the experience of living abroad, they both cautioned about "that mighty novelty Europe." "Let me tell you a secret Tom," his father added, "It will either make or mar you. If you prove superior to its blandishment, seductions and false charms, it will make a man of you." In particular, Abigail did not want him to come home with a European wife: "You must take care & not get fascinated." She warned him especially against the English ladies: "Every thing is enchantment upon that ground, beware however of their snares."[1]

Toward the end of their 78-mile journey all pleasure gave way, just before London Bridge. At around 7 p.m., in the shade of night, in the bustle of a London street, their carriage rattling over the pavements, along with 20 others confusing their sense of hearing, they suffered a "dexterous felony." A preview of Dickensian London, recounted in stirring detail, both in his diary and to his father, it was as though John Quincy regarded the incident as a test of his character, self-esteem and, indeed, whether he was worthy of the presidential trust placed in him with his appointment.[2]

The trunks, one bulging with the dispatches, had been lashed to a seat ahead so that he could keep his eyes on them. Suddenly, he heard an unsettling noise, instantly looked ahead and saw that both trunks were gone. Somewhat stunned, Thomas found the missing trunk of dispatches directly under the carriage. The second was a few yards behind, and half a minute more it would have been crushed to pieces by the horse's hoofs of the next carriage. Securing them inside the chaise for the rest of their trip, their driver assured them that the trunks could not have fallen unless the straps had been cut away.

The brothers booked a room for a night at the Virginia and Baltick Coffee House on Threadneedle Street, but after such an accident, John Quincy hired a hackney coach to take him to the Royal Hotel in Pall Mall, where he found John Jay recuperating from a bout of rheumatism. John Quincy appreciated and respected John Jay, an esteemed family friend, his father's close colleague and a valued mentor. While others found him at times a stubborn, prickly, cold, formal, and somewhat taciturn public figure, John Quincy thought him wholly congenial.

Jay had served as president of the second Continental Congress and minister to Spain. With Benjamin Franklin and John Adams, he had negotiated the 1783 Treaty of Paris, an achievement "like a lull of the boiling waters of the deep after a furious storm," which "dispersed all possible doubt of the independence of his country."[3]

He had also served as secretary of foreign affairs, and with James Madison and Alexander Hamilton wrote the *Federalist Papers,* the series of essays published in New York journals between October 1787 and April 1788. He had been serving as chief justice of the Supreme Court since 1789, when President Washington sent him on his urgent mission abroad to reinforce the position of 40-year-old Thomas Pinckney, the current minister of the United States to the Court of St. James's, to quell Great Britain's ominous threats of war that might endanger the future of their vulnerable, six-year-old nation. Pinckney, "a worthy and excellent man," a South Carolina lawyer and planter educated at Westminster and Oxford, was considered "highly persona grata" by the English.[4]

What would be known as Jay's Treaty was intended to resolve the bitter and enduring conflicts regarding trade and commerce, and interpretations of the burning issue of the freedom of the seas. With the ever-predatory Great Britain looming darkly, Pinckney, Jay and John Quincy studied the plan of the new treaty in progress, article by article.

John Quincy had no inflated idea of his position or contribution at this meeting. Particularly with respect to Jay, he thought of himself, he told his mother, as "something like the candlesnuffer," a reference to the celebrated David Garrick in the role of Peter Pindar, the king's detested satirist. But he was being treated as an equal, and he was flattered "to think and speak" on behalf of his country.[5]

It was precisely Great Britain's flouting of the principles established in the treaty negotiated 11 years earlier that precipitated the present critical negotiations. The revised plan had too many compromises regarding boundaries, compensation for illegal seizures and provisions for reciprocal freedom of trade between the United States and the British dominions in Europe. John Quincy thought the agreement was far from satisfactory, but in the opinion of the two plenipotentiaries, it was preferable to war: "The national honor will be maintained." Coping with complexities of such magnitude, John Quincy did not feel himself competent to form a proper judgment without further study. Yet, when Jay had asked his opinion of the new treaty, John Quincy told him that although he felt inadequate to offer a decision, he must readily agree with his two superiors to their assessment *"that it was better than war."*[6]

He was, however, far from content with the terms and believed that many Americans would be dissatisfied with the gradations and limitations of the negotiations. Signed by both the United States and Great Britain, by John Jay and Lord William Wyndham Grenville, in London on November 19, 1794, the treaty would be debated in a special session of the Senate held on June 8, 1795. Two weeks later, on June 24, it was ratified with one exception by a bare two-thirds majority. George Washington added his signature on August 14, 1795. Two months later, on October 28, 1795, it was ratified in London, though not without searing criticism from the newspaper editor Benjamin Franklin Bache. Writing in the *Aurora,* John Quincy's former schoolmate Benny, nicknamed "Lightning-Rod Junior" after his illustrious grandfather, would later claim that any advocate of Jay's Treaty must be as foolish as the "napping old negro woman" and that Jay had been sent to the Court of St. James's "to throw himself on the magnanimity of the British Kings."[7]

It was with some regret—despite frustration over his first venture in diplomacy—that John Quincy and Tom "made out to escape from that fascinating city" on October 28. John Quincy would have especially liked more time to show Tom, the first-time visitor, more of the "curiosities" of London. But they hadn't a moment, he assured his mother, what with daily invitations to dinner, letters to deliver and to write, and the time he was compelled to devote to conferences. Still, in spite of great pressure, they had "filched" two evenings for theater. Interestingly, it was the audience that elicited criticism, to say nothing of discomfort, from the dissonant American. "In this country," John Quincy wrote his mother, "Loyalty is yet very fashionable," and when the tune "God Save the King" was played by the band, "the whole audience rose, & stood all the time it was performing, clapping their hands, and crying bravo, as if it had been the scene of a favorite play," though he suspected "the heart, did not in every instance, join in the applause."[8]

There were also two accounts of John Quincy's evening with the artist John Singleton Copley (who had left America prior to the

American Revolution to live in London) and his family, where he found the eldest daughter "handsome, if not beautiful, and . . . very pleasing in her manners." But he had left the Copleys early to prepare for his departure the next morning, and both wistful and relieved, he observed "something so fascinating in the women I meet with in this country, that it is well for me I am obliged immediately to leave it." This remark was confined to his diary. Unquestionably sensitive to his mother's aversion to early romances or marriages, he wrote of having the pleasure of seeing Copley's two daughters, the eldest particularly was pretty and engaging and that he supposed his brother "will write you more about her than I shall," for he was so captivated, "that I did not know but I should have had to leave him behind."[9]

It had been one thing to read at home in Massachusetts of the volatile Dutch situation, another entirely to learn in London that the successes of the French armies in every quarter had exceeded all predictions. This meant that the Dutch government was indeed in transition, if not infamous jeopardy, beset with "tarnished ideals, forsworn pledges, devious stratagems and counter-betrayals." The Hague had become and would possibly exceed that "perfect testing-ground" his father had predicted, for obtaining political information and learning the intentions of European governments, particularly those of the suspect, post-revolutionary French Republic.[10]

There was turmoil within and without the Netherlands. The federation of seven provinces ruled by the Stadtholder William V, Prince of Orange, head of the pro-English Estates party since their separate Treaty of Paris of 1784 with Britain, was dangerously challenged by the Patriots, the French Revolution-inspired liberals dedicated to routing the monarchy at most any price, their citizenship included. Further, ever since the marriage of William II to a daughter of Charles I of England, the House of Orange had sought the support of Great Britain while the liberals turned to the rival power of France. Now, both nations were already under siege by the French, and John Quincy was keenly aware of the distinct possibility that the Stadtholder and the States General (the provinces' delegates) might have sought exile before his arrival at The Hague. In reality, with the French already in full possession of all of Flanders and Brabant, with Nijmegen and Maastricht under attack, Amsterdam was next.[11]

As for the future of the war, every advantage seemed to be on the side of France over the English and, therefore, of the Patriots over the Stadtholder's government. Their numbers seemed inexhaustible; the loss of ten thousand men seemed to have no effect other than that of calling out myriads more. For the British, their lack of seamen was without remedy and would increase greatly despite the most brilliant victories. As strongly as they were bent on the success of the war, and inveterate as they always were against the French, they did not have the enthusiasm that had driven the French to level all the boundaries of private property. "In short, Sir, the situation of this country external and internal, appears to be perilous, and its prospects looming in the extreme," John Quincy reported to his father.[12]

Understandably, John Quincy had wondered about his own prospects, given his unique position as novice commissioner to a country in upheaval. Just hours before his departure for The Hague on October 28, in need of advice (and also cash), John Quincy had paid a call on the sympathetic, resourceful John Jay who, not surprisingly, counseled caution at every step.

John Quincy was to take no part whatever in internal dissensions nor do business with any new power until he received further instructions. If the French took complete possession of Holland, and the government actually dissolved, it was best to stay in London, Jay counseled, foreshadowing the challenges of the uncertain years ahead.

With his arrival at The Hague on October 31, John Quincy's work officially began: to fulfill Alexander Hamilton's instructions and to report "interesting intelligence" to the secretary of state. New at his job and somewhat intimidated, he confided to his father that in official correspondence with the secretary of state, he felt a restraint "owing perhaps to the natural awkwardness of novelty." Also, the constant dread of committing some impropriety to paper prevented him from saying many things which naturally flow from a confidential communication. On the other hand, if his father thought any facts or observations contained in his letters were worthy of being known, of public interest, he had no doubt he would impart them to the president.[13]

Very specifically, he wished that his letters would preserve a chain of general intelligence concerning the most important political affairs of Europe. And though the Dutch revolution might be dismissed as a "footnote to the foreign policy of revolutionary France," it would prove to be an invaluable preface to John Quincy's long and unique diplomatic career. Holland before his astonished eyes actually did turn into a listening post "in the resounding amphitheater of European power politics."[14]

To John Quincy's immense surprise, everything was much the same as it had been 11 years ago—perfectly quiet at The Hague. No confusion, no agitation, no crowds in the streets. He could almost say "no symptom from any part of the people of feeling an interest in the fate of their country."[15]

The government met with no internal resistance—for John Quincy, this was perhaps the most tantalizing aspect of the phenomenally disturbing situation. When news came that the opposition at Amsterdam had been completely crushed, that the petitioners had tamely delivered up their arms at command, John Quincy feared that the Dutch had lost "that energy of character which once so honorably distinguished them." Had there been a common share of spirit displayed by the petitioners at Amsterdam, he had been told, the consequences would have been extremely different.[16]

To him it was a dreadful puzzle. The so-called Patriots scarcely concealed their wish to be conquered, and the partisans of the present government cursed their allies but did not so much as lift a finger in their own defense. They seemed to think that an orange cockade in their hats was equivalent to the most heroic self-devotion, and besides, they could scarcely be induced to lend a *stuyver* of their money.

He had sought and found Monsieur Dumas, his family friend and tutor, and United States agent at The Hague, who no longer lived together with his wife. The old gentleman's health was good. But oppression had taken its toll, and he could not, to John Quincy's dismay, "write, think, nor talk about anything" except representative democracy and Joel Barlow, the 41-year-old radical associate of the loathsome Thomas Paine and ardent proponent of the revolution in France. As for the Dumas's daughter Nancy, very probably his first love, she was married with three children and, according to John Quincy's awkward explanation, "to avoid the appearance of singularity or affectation[,] I shall see her, I doubt not, with composure; perhaps with indifferences, but not," he assured his mother, "with pleasure."[17]

While he appeared to dismiss Nancy Dumas so openly and negatively, he seemed unable to resist a teasing reference to his present status. Speaking for Tom as well, he assured their mother: "We do not find here as yet any of the nymphs of the country whose attractions are like to steal our hearts." Nor did he perceive that "either of the Graces yet assumed the shape of a Dutch milliner, wearing a hoof, a long petticoat, white stockings included."[18]

They had seen, however, some very beautiful women in the streets but understood them to be refugees from France. The number was very great and he thought their poverty must evoke compassion considering their former opulence. He had heard it said and really believed it to be a fact that in general women bore this extreme reversal of fortune with more magnanimity, and submitted to it with more dignity, than the men.[19]

For the moment, however, John Quincy's most urgent problem was establishing a time to present his credentials to the king, a process more or less begun on November 5. After several attempts, he was notified that his papers would not be acknowledged because their high mightinesses received communications in three languages only: Dutch, French, and Latin. As his papers were in English, they were found unacceptable. At first John Quincy had refused to rework them, claiming that he could not use another language than his own without authority from his superiors. But with some face-saving machinations back and forth, he had turned the requisite papers into French.[20]

The Stadtholder, Prince William V, returned to The Hague around November 12. Two days later, John Quincy found him "civil enough." Two months later he and his family were gone. A revolution had taken place. From a visitor, John Quincy had learned "some particulars of the Stadtholder's departure" and rushed them into his diary.[21]

The Stadtholder had left The Hague on January 16 at about ten o'clock and embarked in fishing boats at Scheveningen for England. He took formal leave of the States General and demanded their acceptance of the resignation of his two sons. The next day, the Princess of Orange, his wife, along with the wife of the eldest son and her child, a boy, went to Scheveningen, heading for England. Prince William V had been gracious,

> talked to many of the people as he went along, said he always had their happiness at heart. The Princess was furious. The hereditary Princess resigned to anything but going to England. Prince Frederick, the younger of their two sons, was very averse to going at all. Said he had done nothing but his duty. Had served his country, and had committed no faults unless of inexperience, which could not be criminal. He could not bear to fly like a malefactor; and finally submitted only upon the express and positive command of his father.[22]

Concluding that these anecdotes, whether true or false, were characteristic of the several reputations, John Quincy continued:

> The Stadtholder himself is well disposed, with a good heart, and a feeble mind. He is the man of his councils, and not of his own energy. The Princess,[23] detested almost universally. Haughty, domineering incapable of submitting to misfortune with dignity, when she found her power at an end, and no resource for personal safety but inglorious flight in an open, paltry fishing boat, in the extreme severity of a season almost unexampled, she could no longer contain her passions, but broke out in transports of rage, until she was totally exhausted and sank into a state of sullen apathy. The hereditary princess was beloved. Her youth, beauty, innocence, and affability of disposition, all recommended her to compassion; and the interest in her favor is increased by attributing to her so popular a sentiment as an antipathy against England.[24]

The French had moved their base of operations from The Hague to Amsterdam, where John Quincy arrived on Saturday, January 18, at "a moment of crisis." A Batavian, a physician by the name of Cornelius Krayenhoff, had pronounced himself commander of the city; by evening, the three-colored cockades were worn openly, the streets noisy with lusty stanzas of "La Carmagnole"—"Madame Veto" (the queen) promised to "To cut everyone's throat in Paris. But she failed to do this. Thanks to our cannons—and the *Marseillaise* heard everywhere."[25]

On January 22, the states of Holland gave orders to all their officers and commanders to make no further resistance against the French armies, and all had capitulated. No disorders, no massacres, no pillage; not even any personal insult to the conspicuous characters of the previously dominant party. In short, at this moment, "it is scarcely possible for us who are spectators to conceive that what we have witnessed is in reality the complicated transaction of a foreign conquest and an internal revolution," John Quincy reported to the secretary of state.[26]

John Quincy's meeting with the French representatives had gone well. He had proven himself an agile, witty and certainly conscientious diplomat. The French, who were "Principally complimentary in their fashionable cant," in their language had told him, according to his diary:

> they received the visit of the *citoyen ministère* of a free people, the friend of the people *français,* with much pleasure. That they considered it *tout à fait* as a *visite fraternelle.* I told them that hearing of their arrival, I felt myself obliged to present my respects to the *citoyens representants* of the people *français,* for whom my fellow citizens have the greatest attachment, and to whom they were grateful for the obligations under which they felt themselves to the French nation. . . .[27]

The substance of the business was his demand for safety and protection to all American persons and property in Holland. They reassured him that all property as well as persons and opinions would invariably be respected, and that if there should be any occasion for exceptions, they would make the strongest representations to their constituents on behalf of Americans.

Among other things, they had spoken of President Washington whom, like all Europeans, they called General Washington. They had asked about his age, and on being told that he was 63, they said he might still long enjoy his glory; that he was a great man, and they had great veneration for his character.

They also asked John Quincy if he had ever been in France. He answered that he had, that he received part of his education and had resided there for several years; that he "had therefore from infancy every possible reason to have admiration and affection for the French nation."[28]

Pleasantries had stumbled, however, when they spoke of the English and the Treaty of Commerce lately concluded between Great Britain and the United States by Mr. Jay. One of the French representatives said England was their most obstinate enemy; another, that she was their only remaining enemy; a third, that she had always been their enemy; a fourth, that she was the enemy of all the maritime powers. Yet collectively, they were respectful of America's unwillingness to side with either their country or England. Without a navy sufficient to protect her commerce against Britain, she was right in maintaining peace.

The winter had been unusually severe, but by mid-February things had eased up. Tilly, their servant, had gotten to be very serviceable. His uncommon honesty was vastly appreciated, and John Quincy could report that he and Tom were in good health and spirits.

He also supposed that the state of the Batavian people was undoubtedly a subject of considerable attention in the United States, that "the arrival of the French army in Holland, as the friends and allies of the Batavian People, and the revolution" would occasion many groundless rumors and reports. Actually, the streets of the cities were as quiet as those of Boston, that even the partisans of the former government were not injured, molested or insulted— only disarmed.[29]

But something else was amiss, of deeper concern by far: "we seem to be entirely secluded from the rest of the world," John

Quincy told Abigail in mid-February. Letters went astray (he had written at least 40), and nothing could be trusted to the post offices. The practice of reading letters was so openly admitted that nobody thought of sealing a paper sent through that channel.[30]

Understandably, as the crisis deepened, John Quincy had concluded that behind the façade of "profound tranquility" the people were, in fact, subjected to the usual consequences of conquest: the municipal governments were all crushed and the ancient constitution was to be destroyed. He wrote, "it vanishes before the light of a single luminous principle. It was founded on the rights of princes, of nobles, of corporations, of the church, in short upon a motley jumble of every possible right, except the only rights upon which any legitimate government can rest, the rights of man."[31]

There were still other complications. More than once, he had been urged to become a member of one or another faction of either the Patriots or the Orange party, but he had excused himself on grounds of being a stranger, and of the impropriety which he should commit in taking any part personally in the politics of the country. As he wrote home to Dr. Thomas Welsh, his country's system of neutrality "which struggled so hard with foreign influence, foreign insolence and injustice, before it could obtain a solid and immovable footing, has proved as glorious to the honor as it has been advantageous to the interests of the United States." The issue of neutrality was, in truth, a core and heartfelt belief of John Quincy's, which would resonate most famously in the epic Monroe Doctrine.[32]

That May, reviewing the last six bizarre months, he allowed that if he hadn't been warned that the post of an American minister at The Hague was in its nature "tolerably insignificant," it would have been made clear to him by his introduction there. In fact, mindful if not resentful of the far-from-cordial Dutch he had met these past months, the only total exception he could mention was the Stadtholder himself. He did not have business with him, saw him only three or four times, but had every reason to be satisfied with his reception. From all the rest, it was ill-will, "always covered with forms of decency, often aiming at the disguise of politeness, but never concealed successfully."[33]

Nor did he entirely make exceptions of Wilhelm and Jan Willink, two of the Amsterdam bankers with whom his father had negotiated loans for America in 1782. He remained guarded, skeptical of their friendship, especially after their meeting this first day of May when he refused to accede to Wilhelm Willink's demand of a "sacrifice" of 10 percent as a premium for the renewal of a financial plan. He had accepted, somewhat reluctantly, the Willinks' invitation to visit them at their country houses in Haarlem, which he allowed were handsome but not magnificent. But he remained intrinsically unimpressed with these people who "generally spend the Saturday and Sunday throughout the year at country seats; the remainder of the week in the city, drudging for the accumulation of enormous wealth."[34]

He was hardly more forgiving when he toured the grounds. He considered the hothouses the most useful part. As for the gardens, they had nothing remarkably agreeable: "Everything was cut up and fashioned by the rule and square." Which was probably John Quincy's ultimate opinion of the Dutch: measured, methodical, but hardly inspiring.[35]

Toward the end of May, John Quincy had grown restless, dispirited, felt sadly remote from family and friends. It had been three months since he had heard from his father; two from his brother Charles. But in general, information from America was indirect, the means of conveyance few, also "difficult and uncertain," which, in a way, described the ten-page letter he sent his father: a compelling brief of sorts, poignant and diffuse testimony, both personal and political.[36]

First, while he did reassure his father that he knew his appointment was undoubtedly respectable and much beyond his pretensions, still, he had paid a price. Not in terms of possessions or money, but "a fair and rational prospect, infinitely more pleasing than those now before me," he wrote on May 22. And though his sacrifice was merely of an expectancy, it had been "a very valuable one in every point of view: it was independence, usefulness and personal consideration, but above all increasing attachment to friends, which every probability led me to expect would be durable."[37]

He had also been deprived of the benefit of his father's advice and instructions, and the companionship of his mother and the rest of his family—in this instance he was resigned to their loss, felt severely but inevitable given his absence beyond the Atlantic. Nor was he more positive when he turned to the subject of his service as minister. "To speak the sentiments of my heart without equivocation, an American minister at The Hague is one of the most useless beings in creation."[38]

After four months of suspense about the fate of Holland, John Quincy could report that the Treaty of The Hague, signed on May 17, acknowledged the independence and sovereignty of the Batavian people without a Stadtholder. It was signed by two members of the French Committee of Public Safety and four deputies from the States General, and John Quincy hoped, when it was published in the American newspapers, that it would show in the clearest light the price of friendship and assistance from the French.

> Let it be remembered that from the commencement of the war they have declared themselves the enemies of the Stadtholder and his government, but the *friends* and *allies* of the Dutch people. These friends and allies . . . finally exact as conditions for acknowledging the liberty and independence of their friends and allies, a very considerable dismemberment of territory, a perpetual pledge of political subservience, and one hundred million of florins in cash.[39]

These facts were the more deserving of consideration because he had several reasons to suppose that the policy of the French government at that time was to make use of the United States as a passive weapon in her hands against her most formidable enemy, Great Britain.

John Quincy was as fearful of the British, whose government seemed to consider military operations as the least essential part of war. The pride, pomp and circumstance of their hostility consisted "not in the neighing steed . . . but in forgery and famine." But then again, every man had his predilection for some particular species of glory. That of conquering by famine and forgery might have its charms too, and however destructive such a contest might be, the victory, John Quincy concluded, "would at least have the advantage of being bloodless."[40]

Meanwhile, since the conclusion of the treaty between the French and the Batavian Republic, John Quincy noted that "nothing very material has taken place." The project of making a new constitution was in the works, a plan of so little consequence that it had not even been published in any of the French newspapers of the country. But John Quincy had translated the document from Dutch to English and sent copies to the secretary of state and to his father, both as an object of curiosity and because he was glad, he said, to have the chance to show him that he had not entirely neglected the language which he had learned as a youth but almost had entirely forgotten until he had arrived in Holland the previous October.[41]

For all the vast political changes that had taken place since his arrival in Holland, the drama that really intrigued John Quincy lay elsewhere. Paris, for instance, was in a state of violent agitation, and the song that was being sung, the real badge of popularity, "Le Réveil du peuple"—which had neither the poetry nor the musical merit of "La Marseillaise"—was a bitter expression of hatred for the Jacobins, the terror and the carnage of it all. It had therefore become a great favorite among the people of Paris. Within the last few weeks people frequently refused to hear "La Marseillaise" and called constantly for the other.

As for the rest of Europe, John Quincy followed: the armies of Spain; the negotiations of Germany with France under the mediation of the King of Prussia; the Russian fleet that, according to the recent treaty with Great Britain was to be sent to the North Sea; the British government fueled by nothing but national hatred against France in the continuation of the war. These were the events that sparked his imagination and his vision of a stunning new society and convinced him, he told his father, that "The prophecy of Rousseau, that the ancient monarchies of Europe cannot last much longer, becomes more and more infallible."[42]

Not surprisingly, John Quincy's "encyclopedia of politics" was glowingly acknowledged by his father. "I have no language to express to you," John Adams wrote, "the pleasure I have received from the satisfaction you have given to the President and Secretary of State, as well as from the clear, comprehensive and masterly accounts in your letters to me of the public affairs of nations in Europe, whose situation and politics most concerns us. Go on my dear son, and by a diligent exertion of your genius and abilities, continue to deserve well of your father, but especially of your country."[43]

John Adams had, in fact, proudly forwarded four of his son's letters to President Washington whose appreciation was golden. "They contain a great deal of interesting matter," and one especially, he wrote that August, "discloses most important information and political insight. . . . Mr. J. Adams, your son, must not think of retiring from the walk he is now in. His prospects, if he pursues it, are fair; and I shall be much mistaken if, in as short a period as can well be expected, he is not found at the head of the diplomatic corps; let the government be administered by whomever the people may choose."[44]

Five days later "A Letter of Credence To our Great and Good Friend His Britannic Majesty" was issued on behalf of John Quincy: notification of the transfer of the "Minister Resident of the United States of America at The Hague to London." As the ratification of the Treaty of Amity, Commerce and Navigation had been concluded and signed on the previous November 19 by the plenipotentiaries of his majesty and of the United States, the said John Quincy Adams was instructed "to take the necessary measure for the exchange of the ratifications." The notice was written in Philadelphia on August 25, signed by George Washington and Timothy Pickering (newly appointed secretary of state owing to Edmund Randolph's scandalous forced resignation over his rumored collaboration with the French).[45]

Whether it was the excellence of John Quincy's correspondence that had influenced Washington to post him to London or coincidence or proximity was never mentioned. But as Thomas Pinckney, the accredited envoy of America at the Court of Great Britain, was in Spain negotiating another treaty, the government had decided to

call on John Quincy to cross the Channel to complete the operation and to confer further with her majesty's minister on matters
"essential to the establishment of the good understanding between
the two countries."[46]

John Quincy only learned of his appointment two months
later. On October 14 he wrote in his diary, "Received this morning to repair without delay to London where I shall find directions
and documents for my government." And added, "This business is
unpleasant and unpromising but I have no election."[47]

On October 19 John Quincy presented Thomas as chargé
d'affaires of the United States during his absence to the president of
the States General. He took the boat for Delft the morning of October 21, reached Rotterdam the same day but would be detained
at Helvoetsluys most unhappily for nearly the next three weeks.

To his father he wrote of his "principal concern," that "the
magnitude of the trust, and my own incompetency" might end up
harming his country. He wished he had brought more books along
and could not concentrate on some poetry.[48]

"Did you ever know what it is to be cooped up a fortnight or
three weeks, in a paltry little European seaport, waiting for wind
and weather; and cut off from all human communication, almost
as entirely as if you had changed your world?" he asked his mother
in his letter. He had lost touch with news of the world.[49]

Then he voiced a different concern to his mother in possibly
the most moving and personally revealing letter of his entire life:
the subject of past and future "connections." As for his father's letter expressing his wish that his elder son should at an early period
return home to assume in like manner the cares and enjoy the felici-
ties of a family state—he would, he told his mother, take the liberty
of addressing to her his answer. In so doing he at last acknowledged
the devastation of the loss of Mary Frazier, "radically torn from
the bosom by voluntary violence." And, in effect, the hope for his
mother's consent for him to love again, as he wondered: "Can a
widowed heart, a heart which at the admonition of parental solicitude and tenderness has offered up at the shrine of worldly prudence the painful sacrifice of an ardent affection, and pronounced

by mutual consent the acquiescence [in] an irrevocable separation from the object of all its hopes and all its wishes; can such a heart readily submit to the control of other bonds?"[50]

If after such wounds had been healed, after all impressions once so dearly cherished had been effaced, except those "that last till life shall be no more . . . then let my conversion to the matrimonial faith not be despaired of as impossible." He had made his sacrifice to duty and now he made a vow, most prescient in regard to his imminent meeting with Louisa Catherine Johnson, that if his heart could choose again, "its election must be spontaneous, without receiving any direction from the will." And added: "as to a marriage of *convenience,* it will be time enough to think of that at five and forty," should he live to that age.[51]

Meanwhile, he hoped his mother would not think him romantic. At the same time she now had a clear idea of his sentiments and principles on this subject. "The inference as far as it is my personal concern, need not be drawn here, but might be left to your own judgment." Perhaps a polite but firm way of telling his mother that the next time there would be no interference.[52]

John Quincy finally boarded the schooner *Aurora* on November 9 and arrived, two sleepless nights later, via Margate and Canterbury, in London, at Osborne's Hotel. After breakfast, he went immediately to No. 1 Great Cumberland Place to see William Allen Deas, Pickering's chargé d'affaires, but only caught up with him at the home of the American consul, Joshua Johnson and his wife Catherine, in the company of the esteemed American painter John Trumbull. That same evening, obviously unaware of its momentous significance, he was introduced to his future wife, Louisa Catherine, and casually noted that he "Dined with Mr. Trumbull, at Johnson's . . . after dinner Mr. Johnson's daughters entertained us with good music."[53]

The next morning John Quincy met with Mr. Deas and learned that the primary reason for his trip to London had been nullified. Because he had arrived in London beyond the specified deadline of October 20, Deas, according to official instructions, had signed the ratification of the treaty negotiated by John Jay. Left to await further word of his future "destined duties," he was forlorn at the thought of having "nothing to do on my mission here."[54]

But just days later, with London as his listening post, he was back to writing his timely, voluminous and keenly opinionated letters to the secretary of state, to colleagues, and to his family. Almost simultaneously, he would also be confiding in his diary the dread pressures of his nearly calamitous courtship of 20-year-old Louisa Catherine, second of the Johnsons' seven daughters.

*Louisa Catherine Johnson
at the time of her marriage
to John Quincy Adams.
Oil by British miniaturist
James Thomas Barber, 1797.
(Cincinnati Art Museum).*

*Louisa Catherine Adams in her
mid-40s. Her son Charles said,
"Her face wears a sorrowful
appearance too common to her."
By Gilbert Stuart, 1821–1826.
(The White House Historical
Association)*

John Quincy Adams at 16, on his return to The Hague from St. Petersburg, where he had served as secretary to Francis Dana, first U.S. Minister to Russia. Pastel by Dutch artist Isaak Schmidt, 1783. (National Portrait Gallery, Smithsonian)

John Quincy Adams, Minister to the Court of St. James's, a year before returning from London to the United States as Secretary of State. By American Charles Robert Leslie, 1816. (Diplomatic Reception Rooms, U.S. Department of State)

Emperor Alexander I, grandson of Empress Catherine, was vastly admired by John Quincy, who faithfully recorded their impromptu chats together when he served as Minister Plenipotentiary to Russia from 1809 until 1814. By Francois Gerard, 1814. (Musée National du Chateau de Malmaison)

William Vans Murray, beloved and esteemed friend of John Quincy, succeeded him as Minister Resident at The Hague. By American Mather Brown, 1787. (National Gallery of Art, Andrew W. Mellon Collection, 1940)

Birthplace (right) of John Adams, born in 1735 in Braintree, Massachusetts, later called Quincy. Birthplace (left) of John Quincy Adams, born in July 1767. Painting by Godfrey Nicholas Frankenstein, 1849. (Adams National Historical Park)

A Westerly View of Harvard College. John Quincy graduated Phi Beta Kappa, taught there as Boylston Professor of Rhetoric and treasured a lifetime association with the institution. By Samuel Griffin, c. 1783–1784. (Harvard University Archives)

The first American Embassy abroad on the Fluwelen Burgwall, at The Hague, where John Quincy Adams served as Minister Resident. (The Adams Papers and Massachusetts Historical Society)

"Entry of Napoleon . . . through the Brandenberg Gate," Berlin, where John Quincy was first U.S. Minister to Prussia. By Charles Meynier, 1810. (The Grand Palais)

John Quincy visited the Hermitage Palace in St. Petersburg innumerable times while serving as U.S. Minister to Russia from 1809 to 1814. Engraving, "View of Palace Embankment," by Karl Petrovoch Beggrov, 1826. (The State Hermitage Museum)

The first, if unofficial, presidential library: the one-room Stone Library at the family house in Quincy, built in 1870 according to John Quincy's will of 1847 to preserve his and his father's papers and books. (Adams National Historical Parks)

In tribute to the infant Louisa Catherine Adams, who died on September 15, 1812, the U.S. Consul General in St. Petersburg unveiled a new gravestone on September 15, 2012 at the Smolenskoye Lutheran Cemetery. Photograph by Elena Smirnova, U.S. Consulate General, St. Petersburg, Russia.

View of the Village of Passy, just a few miles from Paris, where John and Abigail lived together with John Quincy and Nabby for a brief, nine idyllic months in a vast and picturesque chateau. By Nicolas Jean Baptiste. (Musée Carnavalet)

Charles Francis Adams, youngest of John Quincy's sons, ambassador to Great Britain during the administration of Abraham Lincoln, was the third generation to hold this post. By American painter Charles Bird King, 1827. (Adams National Historical Park)

John Adams II, Harvard graduate, lawyer and businessman, died an alcoholic at age 31. By Charles Bird King, 1823. (Mrs. Gilbert T. Vincent, Cooperstown, NY)

George Washington Adams, eldest of John Quincy's sons, Harvard graduate and lawyer, jumped or fell to his death in the Long Island Sound at age 28. By Charles Bird King, 1823. (Mrs. Gilbert T. Vincent, Cooperstown, NY)

Chapter 18

"THE USUAL MIXTURE BETWEEN SWEET AND BITTER"

Joshua Johnson, the United States consul, lived on Cooper's Row on Great Tower Hill—both Roman and medieval in its structures, and the sometime habitat of Chaucer—on the eastern edge of the city of London and the north bank of the River Thames. Of the brothers' introduction and first evenings together at the Johnson household, there are two distinct versions. According to John Quincy's spare testimony in his daily diary, dated November 11, he dined with Mr. Trumbull at Johnson's and a few weeks later pronounced all the daughters "pretty and agreeable," and he admired the way Nancy played the pianoforte, Louisa sang, Caroline was at the harp.[1]

For Louisa, the memory was more vivid, despite penning the details a distant 30 years later in the "Record of My Life," July 25, 1825. As she recalled, the painter Colonel John Trumbull (formerly aide de camp to General Washington, whom the French servant called Colonel Terrible) had introduced them, and when John Quincy first supped with her family, "he was in high spirits, conversed most agreeably and after he retired all the family spoke well of him. His dress, however, produced some mirth as it was completely Dutch and the coat almost white." In fact, when Trumbull joked with the girls and said Mr. Adams was a fine fellow and would make a good husband, Louisa and her sisters did not take his recommendation seriously for "his dress did not impress us agreeably as it made his person appear to very great disadvantage."[2]

Also, for some strange reason, Louisa said, her sister Nancy had nicknamed John Quincy "Cain" and his brother Tom "Abel." Louisa also mentioned in her memoir, "merely to show how little idea or desire there was in the family to plot or plan a marriage between the families," that they were "too entirely happy to make marriage a *want* and we only looked forward to it as . . . evidence that we were not devoid of those attributes which generally are the operating causes of affection." What she does not mention is her family's pressure on John Quincy to marry Louisa within four months of their introduction.[3]

John Quincy went to the Johnsons', in the shadow of the looming Tower of London, to collect letters from home that brought "the usual mixture between sweet and bitter." In a sense, that mixture described the state of affairs abroad that John Quincy would report in seven-, eight- and eleven-page, tightly scripted, densely newsworthy, encyclopedic letters to the new secretary of state, Timothy Pickering, and to colleagues, friends and family—such news as the alarming fact that England's state was not much less critical than that of France, that grain and flour were scarce, that riots had taken place in different parts of the kingdom and, on the first day of the current session of Parliament, the king had been personally insulted, the glass of his coach shattered by a stone.[4]

As for France, the establishment of a new legislature was predictably neither stable nor harmonious, nor assembled under the fairest auspices. A civil war in the heart of Paris had been stifled in blood, and a paper currency depreciated to the lowest extreme of sufferance. In regard to France's political influence on the United States, which was John Quincy's nagging concern, "a tendency as pernicious . . . as if it had been invented in the councils of the

Prince of Darkness," it had in fact taken its toll directly in regard to President Washington and in rumors of his resignation triggered by that of the recently disgraced former secretary of state, Edmund Randolph.[5]

John Quincy was especially sensitive about President Washington, who had not resigned but appeared to be under a most violent attack. In England, the same people who had derived so much pleasure from the 1794 western Pennsylvania insurrection (the Whiskey Rebellion) took an equal satisfaction in this current controversy, anticipating with delight the fall of a man who had formerly been the boast of republicans.

Fiercely defensive, John Quincy asked angry questions: Wasn't it more than a little remarkable that the attack on the president was still carried on when the national prosperity continued to grow to a degree entirely unique in the annals of the world? And, wasn't there reason to wonder that the American government, and the president in particular, did not receive the acclaim so richly deserved? Especially in the case of the president—for if the country's neutrality was preserved, it would be due to the president alone. Nothing, in John Quincy's opinion, but Washington's weight of character and reputation combined with his firmness and political intrepidity could have stood against the torrent that was still "tumbling with a fury that resounded even across the Atlantic."[6]

Furthermore, as to the future: "If his system of administration now prevails, ten years more will place the United States among the most powerful and opulent nations on earth."[7]

From the start, it was quite obvious that John Quincy did not enjoy sparring with the British. Worrying about his conduct as a diplomat, he tended to suffer acutely over the question of whether he said too little or too much, and how to defend without offending. Scolding himself accordingly, on November 22 he wrote: "To myself at the close of this day—I can only say Oh! Stupid Vanity! When will thou learn to be silent."[8]

Three days later, he found himself in diplomatic combat with the worldly, 34-year-old George Hammond, veteran of service in

Paris, Vienna, Copenhagen and Madrid. As the first British envoy to the United States, he had recently returned to London and was now posted as undersecretary of state in the office of the foreign secretary (and future prime minister) Lord William Grenville. John Quincy found Hammond not only patronizing but, worse, intrusive on so many of America's most critical issues and about important officials. Meeting with Lord Grenville proved an even greater test of his confidence, the combination of the two British men altogether daunting.

As for his three-hour session with Lord Grenville on November 27 with Hammond in attendance, it wasn't surprising that John Quincy was distrustful of the British statesmen's seemingly wily explanations and arguments in response to the critical issues he had raised: the need for clarification of some controversial points on the Jay Treaty, on violations of territorial rights, on the mistreatment of an American consul, on the impressment of American seamen, and more.

But what really alarmed John Quincy was the way the British, speaking "unofficially and as an old friend and acquaintance," said they were not satisfied with William Allen Deas, chargé d'affaires of the United States—his letters being "too violent and fractious, and expressed in irritating terms"—and sought to flatter John Quincy with the thought that he might supplant his American colleague and serve more agreeably. As he notes in his diary on November 27 about "Some conversation afterwards with Mr. Hammond":

He told me he wished Mr. Pinckney would go home, and that I might be placed here in his stead. Enquired whether I should not like it as well as being at The Hague . . .

He asked if I had any news from America. I answered, none. He said he heard the democrats were quite cock-a-whoop—talked very high of impeaching the President, etc.

"There always will be in all countries," said I, "people that will talk very high. You find that in this country, as well as elsewhere."

"Ay," said he, "the best way is to let them talk."

"Your Government seems to think otherwise," I might have said, but I preferred saying nothing, not choosing to imitate his conduct.

He suggested that the place of ordinary minister here would be very agreeable to me, because it would be succeeding to the station my father had held.

"That may do very well for you," said I. "You may be an aristocrat with propriety; but in my country, you know, there is nothing hereditary in public offices."[9]

John Quincy had found all of this "foolish talk." He was not to be misled by this Shakespearean character: "I do see to the bottom of this Justice Shallow." And, if he did stay on, Hammond, he vowed, "will learn to be not quite so fond, nor yet quite so impertinent." And he wondered further: "What sort of a soul does this man suppose I have?"[10]

But then, Hammond, he had decided, was "a man of intrigue." His reference to so many politically sensitive issues had more or less confirmed his suspicions. On December 1 he wrote in his diary, "His question, whether Mr. Pinckney had signed the Treaty in Spain, implies at least that he knew there was a treaty to sign. His question on the subject of my having been to theater was probably suggested by some previous information he had received. Mr. Pinckney's letter to Mr. Deas, received yesterday, came by post. My letter to my mother mentioned my having been at Drury Lane. I sent it last Sunday to the New York Coffee House. Had not Hammond seen them both?"[11]

And further, when Hammond inquired how he liked his lodgings in the Adelphi, and whether he did not find them too noisy and ought he not move elsewhere, John Quincy had wondered "does he wish to have facilities for keeping spies over me, greater than my present lodgings give him, or does he fear I *shall* change, and, by advising me to it, think it will deter me from changing?"[12]

In the ensuing weeks, though the tone might have been considered somewhat more conciliatory, further conversations (and incidents) "of unqualified acid" had followed. The matter of his title and manner of his presentation at court was inflammatory.[13]

John Quincy understood he was to appear at Lord Grenville's office around 11 in the morning of December 2 about the presentation. But Grenville was out, and after waiting an hour John Quincy had returned home where, between two and three that afternoon, he had received a card from Hammond informing him that Lord Grenville was much concerned that their appointment *"had entirely escaped his recollection."* As he had not yet "had an opportunity" of taking the king's pleasure with respect to his presentation, that ceremony would be deferred "until this day a week." Far from accepting Hammond's explanation, John Quincy had concluded that "This escape of Lord Grenville's recollection is a little off, under all the circumstances. The excuse thus chosen deserves some attention. But patience! patience!"[14]

It was the card from Lord Grenville, received on December 8, informing him that his audience with the king would take place the next day, that struck John Quincy as "singular," that, in fact, caused him "real alarm."[15]

This was precisely what he would report to the secretary of state about "the anxiety and perseverance" of the British, and their insistence on recognizing him in a role to which he had neither right nor pretensions, that of "fixing" him as the negotiator for the remainder of the treaty. Hammond, in fact, had said as much: Mr. Pinckney was viewed as unfriendly to the British government, and there was "a decided preference for treating with me, rather than with him."[16]

In fact, the whole thing had the taint of a formal conspiracy. John Quincy wrote back immediately to Lord Grenville to set the record straight: he could not be the minister plenipotentiary. His credential letter, which he had the honor to bear from the president of the United States to his majesty, styled him as minister resident of the United States of America, at The Hague. If this circumstance were to preclude him from an audience, he requested that they notify him, as he could not by any acquiescence or assent on his part claim that he was "vested with the character of a Minister Plenipotentiary."[17]

The more he brooded on the subject, the more determined he was to make it absolutely clear to Hammond that there should be no misunderstanding between them. Again, as he had with Grenville, "If this be not sufficient let us stop here—no harm done." And to emphasize his position: "The thing with us is *Constitutional*."[18]

John Quincy did not exaggerate when he said that he could hardly wait for Pinckney's return, as though it were a rescue operation. He was extraordinarily relieved to welcome Pinckney back to London the following January 13—Pinckney, he thought, with his experience and character, as well as his talents, was much better adapted to treat with men to whom "action is an ambush and thought a stratagem." Meanwhile, he did not know how long he could stand this state of "*peine forte et dure*." Considering his ridiculous situation, "surrounded with man-traps and spring-guns," what he did know instinctively was that "Extreme caution becomes more and more necessary," and that he could not take a step "without risk of error."[19]

As he explained to his father, all his life he had been accustomed to plain dealing and candor, and he was not "sufficiently versed in the art of political swindling to be prepared for negotiating with a European Minister of State."[20]

As it turned out, the British had acceded to his position. John Quincy had made his point and proudly so, pleased at the thought that the fair warning he had given was sufficient to prevent any future improper conclusions. Lord Grenville introduced John Quincy into the private closet of the king on January 9, nearly ten years after his father's presentation on June 1, 1785. Three profound bows—one at the door, one halfway, the third directly before the stout George III—and John Quincy found himself presenting his credential letter.

> He afterwards asked to which of the states I belonged, and on my answering, Massachusetts, he turned to Lord Grenville and said, "All the Adamses belong to Massachusetts?" To which Lord Grenville answered, they did.
>
> He enquired whether my father was not Governor of Massachusetts. I answered, "No, Sir; he is Vice President of the United States."
>
> "Ay," said he, "and he cannot hold both offices at the same time?" "No, sir."
>
> He asked where my father is now. "At Philadelphia, Sir, I presume, the Congress being now in session."
>
> "When do they meet?" "The first week in December, Sir."

"And where did you come from last?" "From Holland, Sir."

"You have been employed there?" "Yes, Sir, about a year."

"Have you been employed before, and anywhere else?" "No, Sir."[21]

Some weeks later, however, on January 13, in complete contrast to former occasions when he had sensed he was to be "cajoled into compliance," the king did not speak to him. Which was all right with John Quincy; it "flattered my pride as much as the former fawning malice humbled it."[22]

The next morning's papers said that he took leave of the king the day before and that he was about to return home, a hint, John Quincy supposed, that he was meant to go away. Aware of being caught in a bind—Pinckney having just arrived—he realized that he could do no further good. On the other hand, he could not leave without receiving further orders from home. By February 10 he would tell his father: "I have hitherto been tolerably patient. But can hardly answer how much longer I shall be so."[23]

At this juncture, John Quincy's son and editor, Charles Francis, shut down volume 1 of the Memoirs, his judiciously edited version of his father's diaries. While noting that John Quincy "did not receive permission to return to The Hague until the 26th of April, and he remained in London until the 28th of May [1796]," Charles Francis fills the gaping hole of more than four months with a single paragraph in which he posts an engagement announcement: "This delay was partly occasioned by [an] attraction in the family of Mr. Joshua Johnson, then consul of the United States in London. . . . The result was a betrothal between himself and Louisa Catherine, the second daughter of Mr. Johnson."[24]

But contrary to the impression Charles Francis might have fostered that his father had abandoned his pen during this interval, it is more likely that the son found aspects of his parents' love story so clouded, so puzzling or even troubling, that he could not honor his avowed promise "to suppress nothing of [my father's] own habits of self-examination, even when they might be thought most to tell against himself." The provocative confessions of the troubled suitor had obviously gone too far. The depths of self-examination had, after all, their boundaries.[25]

The wretchedly ambivalent fiancé and his strangely anguished relationship with Louisa Catherine Johnson and her family within weeks of their meeting hint at differences so mutually provocative and painful as to raise alarming questions about the couple's future together. All of this most certainly explains the reason Charles Francis crafted on his father's behalf—by the strict process of elimination, if not censorship, from his diary—the muted memoirs of a statesman safeguarded from the vagaries of his personal life and temperament. It is as though the lover and husband of these next months and years did not exist.

With Pinckney's return from Spain after successfully negotiating the Treaty of San Lorenzo (or Pinckney's Treaty) on behalf of United States, John Quincy felt completely displaced. Still, there was "some consolation in meeting with an old friend" such as Nathan Frazier and several other visitors from Boston, to walk in Hyde Park and to dine together at the London Coffee House. His health, he thought, was the better for their excursion to Cambridge University. He was also "very highly gratified" after spending three or four hours in the Shakespeare Gallery at 52 Pall Mall, in which he admired the paintings of George Romney and Joshua Reynolds among others. At Covent Garden he found *The Comedy of Errors* better on the stage than in the book—though acted much as it was printed, loud scenes bordering on indecency were indeed left out.[26]

Also, on a positive note, he was entirely amenable to posing for his portrait by family friend James Singleton Copley, which Mrs. Copley promised to send along to his mother. Begun on February 11, Copley "had made a good picture of it" on its completion on April 4. Besides, John Quincy had rather relished their conversation "political, metaphysical and critical"; though the artist's opinions were not accurate, he did find them "well-meaning."[27]

Beginning in mid-December, he most often visited the Johnson family on Cooper's Hill—so frequently that by April 22 their home was, he ruefully admitted, "more I think, than my own lodgings." Suppers were followed not only by music but by card games or backgammon or whist, and soon John Quincy was taking frequent walks, carriage rides with "Mrs. Johnson and the young ladies." At Mrs. Johnson's ball on December 22, John Quincy danced until 3 a.m. and complained two days later that he was "quite stiff in my limbs" from the ball of Tuesday and felt "quite unwell" the next, Christmas day. About Mrs. Johnson's second ball on January 27—honoring Louisa's twenty-first birthday the next month—there were no complaints. John Quincy found the "evening very agreeable," had danced with a Miss Church and with Louisa until past three in the morning; went home with the Misses Bancroft; was "Abed at about 5."[28]

But very early on he was feeling constraints about his lifestyle. And though his spirits might occasionally lift on hearing what he judged to be "excellent music," he was fighting depression. One evening he was cross with himself for staying up too late; on another he wrote: "Not in the best temper," to which he added mysteriously one word "Revolution."[29]

Another night his feelings went beyond discontent. With Mrs. Johnson and her four oldest daughters at Covent Garden, on hearing Handel's "Allegro & Il Penseroso," he was "Not much pleased with the music. Displeased with several trifling incidents. Above all dissatisfied with myself." But then, he was also "puzzled" by others' behavior. He did not know why Nancy was "very much affected" and thought Louisa pretended a headache for the privilege of being cross; he wondered that Mr. Johnson was in very good spirits during the earlier part of the snowy March 28, less so in the evening. "Reflections perplexing." If he sensed his feeling of alienation was due to his failure to meet the Johnsons' expectations, he did not say. He was especially troubled the evening of February 25, insisting, "Some end must be put to the present state of things. It has got to the end of my patience." A few days later, after walking in the park with "the Miss Johnsons," as John Quincy put it, he "Rallied till angry."[30]

And yet, he seemed most strikingly and provocatively to hint to his mother, without mentioning Louisa's name, at a meaningful relationship. That February 20 he had written to her that he had been idle for so long, he had almost entirely "doff'd the world aside and bade it pass." The first month or six weeks after his arrival had been a period of considerable anxiety and occupation, but since then a time of almost total "fantasy." Neither state was conductive to health. "Perhaps I may tell you the reason of this at a future day; or perhaps you may guess at it without being told."[31]

But he did not quite leave his mother in mid-air about his new romance. A week later he wrote again to tell her that the cloaks she had requested for herself and for his cousin Louisa were on their way. They had been chosen by Mrs. Johnson and by her second daughter, a very amiable young lady bearing the name of Louisa Catherine, one of his reasons for asking her to select the cloak for her namesake in Braintree. Both cloaks were meant to be presents, in the case of his mother, "a mark of grateful affection."[32]

As it turned out, Louisa and her family very clearly had marriage in mind. Contrary to Louisa's middle-aged recollection that John Quincy made his choice "decidedly public" by taking her hand at a ball the prior month, his diary tells a different story. To begin with, the timing was most inauspicious. He had been complaining almost daily and bitterly of "indolence & dissipation," and according to John Quincy's abysmally joyless but of-the-moment account of Tuesday, March 2, he had done a little writing before noon, spent the evening—there was some music and dancing—at the Johnsons where he played cards with much luck, when Louisa made the gesture: "Ring from Louisa's finger. Tricks played. Placed in a very difficult dilemma. Know not how I shall escape from it." All of which gave "cause for uneasiness."[33]

Nor did his tension ease on the following days. He had tea with the "young ladies," but some "conversation did not close well . . . sullen on our return." The situation remained embarrassing; Louisa was ill; Louisa recovered. There were differences with Louisa that were repaired, however, but another evening was "Dull from various causes."[34]

On April 10, he noted something resembling reproach from Mrs. Johnson, and he thought an explanation would be necessary. Three days later he received a card, "partly apologetically and partly spirited," asking to see him. Having given a full explanation of his views and intentions to Mrs. Johnson "upon the subject—the word marriage unmistakable though merely implied—she said she was satisfied." Only plainly he was not. Suffering such "Depression of spirits such that I can do nothing," he had required from Louisa an explanation of the past evenings' "singularities."[35]

On April 18 John Quincy dined and spent the evening at the Johnsons. "Conversation with Louisa. Was explicit with her, and obtained her acquiescence. The same with him [her father]. Upon one point however, the only one to which I *must adhere,* neither of them was satisfied. The right and the reason of the thing"—most probably the logic of Johnson's financial situation—"are however indisputably with me, and I shall accordingly persist."[36]

The next day was very warm but no less gloomy. Mrs. Johnson was in low spirits and unwell, as was the family. But days later, on April 26, though the evening was as usual—that is, John Quincy repining at a situation which seemed as if it never would end—the Johnsons seemed partly recovered. Or perhaps this tinge of optimism on his part was colored by the fact that, miraculously, "certain singular phenomenon [were] still discernible," by which he meant that on his return home that evening he found a letter from the secretary of state dated March 9 that he thought sufficient to authorize his return to The Hague, "upon which I accordingly resolved immediately."[37]

The next morning he was out early to check on transportation to Holland. But even Mr. Pinckney was unable to help, and he would wait a full month, until May 28, to board the small schooner with "very indifferent accommodations" for which he would pay a price, he complained, "of real extortion." Meanwhile, he felt his "Patience must be drained to the very dregs."[38]

And obviously nothing was more distasteful than the way he spent his days:

Rise between 9 and 10. Spend about an hour in dressing. It is one of the necessities of the time and the place. Breakfast. Read the *Morning Chronicle* for opposition news & *The Times* for the ministerial. This brings me to nearly twelve. Read or write about an hour. Then walk two more to pay a foolish visit, or two from thence till 5 my dinner time, read again or write. Generally dine at home or at Mr. Johnson's.

Am sure at least to pass the evening & sup there, return home between 12 & 1 at night . . . Smoke my segar, and just before 2 in the morning retire to bed. What a life![39]

As for time with the Johnsons: There were more lessons of dress. The usual asperities arose on May 10, and John Quincy wrote, "I must get away." Members of the family were often "dull and out of humor," though John Quincy did suggest that perhaps his own temper came out too offensively the evening of May 11. Another time, he "affected as much as I could good humor," but "succeeded no better than usual."[40]

He had also said that he thought himself "deemed unaccountable and meet with unaccountables." These thoughts perhaps refer to the Johnson family's inexplicable moods that might be better understood in time—in fact, in the coming year, with the revelation of Joshua Johnson's calamitous financial state. This accounts for the Johnson family's urgent hope to settle Louisa in a suitable marriage before their somewhat abrupt departure for the United States, prompted by their need to flee from bill collectors and by their desperate attempt to salvage a supposed family fortune stateside.[41]

Finally, on the evening of May 27, "one of delight and of regret," he took his leave of all the Johnson family "with sensations unusually painful," ending in a private conversation with Mr. Johnson about which there were no further details.[42]

John Quincy left London on Saturday at noon. Riding 25 miles from Osborne's Adelphi Hotel to Gravesend, he arrived at four to find the Dutch vessel, after waiting for him for three or four hours, had just departed. Luckily, the custom-house officers had rallied, and he found boatmen to row him the six or so miles downriver below Gravesend to meet up with Captain Garmers. After a "boisterous but not unpleasant" voyage of three days, more seasick than he had been for the past ten years, he had landed in Rotterdam, taken a boat for Delft, and arrived at The Hague the last day of May. Happy to find his brother in good health and despite past sleepless nights, he kept Tom up chatting about various things until one in the morning.[43]

The confusion of "sweet and bitter" had only begun. Already in his post was his mother's letter acknowledging the safe arrival of the cloaks he had ordered and that she was "much pleased" with them. But more than the satisfactory cloaks was on his mother's mind. Judging from the close of his letter of March 20, she suspected that "Some fair one has shown you its sophistry, and taught you to admire!" And in still another letter from his mother less than a week later: "I will speak out if you will not, it is one of the Miss Johnson's who has become your flame." But for all her disappointment—she knew perfectly that Louisa was the daughter of an Englishwoman—she allowed her son "years sufficient to judge for yourself. And whom you claim yours shall be mine also," but in the same breath cautioned that he "only weigh well. Consider maturely of the most important action of your life."[44]

That Louisa was indeed "half blood" would turn out to be the least challenging part of her own and her family's history. Though Abigail frankly admitted her unease about her son's "foreign connection," she could not know how alien this prospective daughter-in-law was to her vision of the wife she had in mind for her son, namely, one "whose habits tastes & sentiments are calculated for the meridian of your country."[45]

She couldn't know unless she and John had been able to read Louisa's later versions of her early years in which she described herself as a young woman of delicate, uncertain sensibilities brought up "to live in luxury without display, too much beloved by my family for my own good," and educated "in those accomplishments which properly used are an ornament to female loveliness" which prepared her for a marriage like that of her parents.[46]

Tormented with contradictions, Louisa herself wondered why it was so easy to be spontaneous, almost an unwilled act one day, yet laborious another, to recall "a childhood in which flowers so concealed the thorns that I knew not, that they lurked beneath their fragment and bewitching loveliness."[47]

Probably John Quincy's grandson Henry Adams put Louisa's plight most affectionately and succinctly, just as he respected his grandparents' concerns. As a small boy in Quincy, Henry had liked her refined figure; her gentle voice and manner; her vague effect of not belonging there but rather to Washington or to Europe, like her furniture and writing desk with little glass doors above the little eighteenth-century volumes in old bindings labeled *Tom Jones* or *Hannah More* or *Peregrine Pickle.*

But try as she might, Henry believed, she could never be Bostonian, and it was her cross in life. No question that she was charming, "but among her many charms that of being a New England woman was not one." Her future in-laws, Abigail and John, were both troubled by the fear that Louisa "might not be made of stuff stern enough, or brought up in conditions severe enough to suit a New England climate, or to make an efficient wife" for their paragon son. Their great-grandson Henry concluded, "Abigail was right on that point," and "the defect was serious."[48]

Chapter 19

"THE AGE OF INNOCENCE AND THOUGHTLESSNESS"

*N*ot surprisingly, Louisa's deeply romanticized, puzzling, conflicting, melodramatic and ultimately tragic accounts of her
early and late life—including harsh, mean-spirited indictments of
the Adams family and her husband, furiously presented in her two
memoirs—vary in mood and interpretation. Louisa endured numerous failed pregnancies and heartbreaking losses during the first
25 years of marriage. Undoubtedly suffering from depression, she
kept a diary when she was most troubled and in need of solace: from
October 12, 1812 through 1815; from January to March 1819; and
from December 6, 1819 to January 8, 1824. Living in Washington
in the winter of 1821 while her husband served as secretary of state
for President James Monroe, she felt "totally unable to meet the
exigencies of the bustling season." By July 23, 1825, at 50, she had
begun *Record of a Life, or My Story,* as "a slight sketch" on a day
of "unparalleled heat that made it scarcely possible to pursue any
occupation whatever. . . ."[1]

In the course of recording a second memoir, *The Adventures of
a Nobody,* 15 years later, in July 1840, at 65—the title an instant
reflection of her own punishing self-esteem—she would tell her son
Charles that he shared her tendency to choose the emotional rather

than intellectual response to a situation: "My temper is so harassed and I am I fear so imbued with strange and singular opinions, and surrounded by persons with whom it is decidedly impossible for me to agree, I feel that I am a torment to myself, and a still greater torment to your Father, who bears with me with the patience of Socrates."[2]

Subsequently, in a third and more succinct summation of her life, she advised her daughter-in-law Abby that she "must take my journal for better or worse as a man takes his wife; or as he must take everything in this life. . . . But you will find in it enough of love to make up for all other deficiencies." Tragically for her and especially for John Quincy, there would also be acid enough to permanently deface his image while she, on the other hand, lost in helpless melancholia, would gain sympathy and stature.[3]

At various junctures, in journals and letters, Louisa did write of John Quincy's "fine qualities, his easy temper, his quiet home habits, and his indefatigable powers of application," and as a ministering angel always at her side who read books of travels and novels. But in a shockingly different mood at the time of their son Charles Francis's engagement to Abigail Brooks in 1827, she addressed this devastating appraisal to her son as a warning: "It is a painful thing to state but it is nevertheless the fact that as it regards women the Adams family are one and all peculiarly harsh and severe in their characters. There seems to exist no sympathy, no tenderness for the weakness of the sex or for the incapacity of occasional exertion which is a part of their nature arising from the peculiarities of their constitutions."[4]

Sorrowfully aware in those latter years of her emotional instability, she was "forever ashamed" of herself for suffering her heart to crave for some social comforts, some soothing influence to fill up the lagging hours. At her age, she observed, those hours hung with a tedious weight upon her time, and left her with a "too vivid and too painful contemplation of the past."[5]

Still, Louisa's deeply felt (and even fantasized) versions of her life have prevailed, the life "fraught with bliss" poignantly remembered in the two memoirs which stylistically may owe something to the popular novelists of her era. Louisa did speak of her passion for reading everything she could get hold of in her youth: "novels and romances but only characters of lofty excellence" who "excited her ambition or produced emulation. . . ." Tobias Smollett, who included "The memoirs of a lady of quality" within *The Adventures of Peregrine Pickle*, wrote: "By the circumstances of the story which I am going to relate, you will be convinced of my candor, while you are informed of my indiscretion. . . ." There was more than a faint echo of the British author in tone and phrasing when Louisa wrote: "Do not, children, read this as a romance for every word is true." As for Louisa's *Adventures of a Nobody,* it seems not coincidental that Fanny Burney, author of the eighteenth-century best seller *Evelina* (the story of a 16-year-old woman of marriage age), addressed the first entry in her own journal on March 27, 1768 to "Miss Nobody."[6]

At the start of her *Record of a Life,* Louisa firmly stated that she did not have "pretensions to be a writer and no desire to appear anything more than a mere commonplace personage with a good memory. . . ." Immediately—and contradicting what she, several pages later, wrote about the truth of her "every word"—she gave warning that some suspension of belief was inevitable on her part and essential to her readers: "All the scenes of my infancy came with such faint recollections, they float upon my fancy like visions which never could have had any reality, yet like visions of delight in which all was joy and peace and love." She was "writing for amusement" she said, "as we all love to dwell on that age of innocence and thoughtlessness when all is fresh with hope. . . . It is easy," she admitted, "to skip what we do not wish to read and view it only as a blank."[7]

And skip she did. She not only filled but crowded the blanks in both memoirs in such a way as to render a disturbing portrait of an emotionally challenged young woman with a frail grasp of the truth of her early life. She simultaneously exalted and defended her father's life, as she did her mother's: "O home! sweet home! . . ." Her "beloved parents" placed a picture of domestic felicity constantly before her eyes, "truly enviable and in no one instance during my life have I ever met such an example."[8]

Louisa traced her father's life and character in loving detail. Her father was the handsomest man she ever beheld. His temper was admirable, his tastes simple, his word sacred, his heart pure and affectionate as that of the most unsophisticated child of nature—and the greatest fault he had was believing everyone was good, as correct and as worthy as himself.

Also, she wrote, his establishment was not sumptuous or extravagant, but such as the first merchants in London at that day usually had. He kept a neat carriage and one pair of horses, and everything was conducted in the family with regularity. His entertainments when he made any, which was not often, were handsome; but his usual way of receiving company was unceremoniously social and almost limited to his own countrymen who, whether in England for business or pleasure, "found a home and a friend in him at all times."[9]

On the surface, at least on the one she provided, descended as she was from a "wealthy and impeccable" Maryland family, Louisa was an entirely eligible young woman. She was American enough by ancestry and with her father's unquestioned patriotism to be considered a flawless candidate for marriage into the Adams family—more than enough, in fact, to bolster Abigail Adams's pride in the connection.[10]

Two members of Joshua Johnson's family had served in Parliament before his grandfather Thomas Johnson migrated from Great Yarmouth, Norfolk, England, in 1689 to the deep tobacco country of Calvert County, Maryland, on the Patuxent River near St. Leonard's Creek. Joshua Johnson, born in 1742, was the eighth of eleven children. The star of the family, however, was his brother Thomas Johnson III, ten years his elder, who had served as a delegate to the second Continental Congress in 1775—his colleagues in the cause of the colonists included Benjamin Franklin, John Jay and John Adams. He also served as the first governor of Maryland and then a justice of the United States Supreme Court. In June 15, 1775, he was honored to nominate his friend and neighbor, Colonel George Washington, precisely his own age, to be general of all the Continental forces.

But Joshua Johnson's life was far different. Louisa's father did not have the advantage of a classical education because, Louisa explained, not without a tinge of bitterness, that her grandfather "retaining many of the English prejudices in favor of the eldest son" (Thomas III was actually the second son) had "lavished all the expense to make him an object of consequence in the country."[11]

Instead, Joshua Johnson was destined to join one of the enterprising English or Scottish merchant houses in the precarious business of trading tobacco, wheat, grain, flour, iron—in truth, of trading whatever would turn a profit in a fiercely competitive market at the mercy of political upheaval locally and abroad in Europe and the West Indies. Maryland ranked sixth among the 13 colonies in shipbuilding and was then less competitive than other port states.

Early in life, Joshua Johnson was placed in the counting house of "a very respectable merchant." In Annapolis, he was involved in real estate—he had invested in a warehouse then under construction—and in the wholesale and retail sales of British goods. He formed a partnership with Charles Wallace and John Davidson, and "in consequence removed to London as second partner in the firm" in April 1771, age 29, fortified with a working capital of 3,000 pounds and an allowance of 30 pounds for rent.[12]

From the time of his arrival in London and his letters home, Louisa's sublime portrait of her father takes on more provocative coloring. The peerless father turned speculator and entrepreneur was proud, ambitious, tenacious and prosperous, or so he must have appeared to buyers and creditors, to visiting Americans and native Englishmen. In reality, he was pitifully insecure, unprepared and even awed by his new responsibilities.

From the start, Joshua Johnson was pressed for money and never seemed to have enough credit to finance any purchase comfortably. He seemed never to count on the vagaries of the competition or deliveries dependent on the caprice of the winds by which a dozen or more captains navigated their ships through the narrow, unpredictable English Channel waters. Most immediately, he complained about his health, his bad leg, a severe cough and fear of consumption, and about needing a new wardrobe.

He had arrived in Bristol on May 29. Several weeks later, on July 22, 1771, he wrote a "small sketch of my observations" that conveys to his partner, John Davidson, the intense anxiety that unfortunately characterizes almost his entire 27 years abroad: "I am frighted at the expense attending one's living here; O Joney, you have no idea of it. They may talk of 18d. [pence] per day but it is impossible and to support the character I must, why, the washing of clothes alone will come to 18 pounds or 20 pounds per annum; then where is the first purchase, house rent, meat, drink, etc." However, he promised, "I will never flinch while I can serve you two, if I get nothing but my support."[13]

He was also homesick, obviously nostalgic for more companionable times, as he told Davidson. The duty on hams had been removed: "So that, if any of my friends would be so polite as to present me with one now and then, you may assure them there is no danger from the Customs House officers. I likewise have discovered a method to get safe a few bottles of such good old spirit as we used to have."[14]

Johnson also wondered about what had become of his building in Annapolis, its completion critical, it appeared, for storage of the goods he would be shipping home. At the same time, he seemed resigned to the fact that he would be obliged to mortgage it to be able to finish it.

Several months later, there was a change in tone, a demanding implication of loss of confidence on the part of his Maryland partners which Johnson could not "omit" noticing, nor fail to answer in self-defense. Both naive and apologetic, his response was the sum of all his enormous frustration: "Admit it: can you blame me? Did I not always tell you I was doubtful of it through my ignorance in the business and was I not loath to undertake it for those reasons?"[15]

But the situation only deteriorated. The mercantile business had settled into a full-blown depression, and as he traveled in April 1772 to Gloucester, Tewkesbury, Bromsgrove, Birmingham, Coventry and Woodstock, he had never met, he said, with anything that fell so short of his expectations. Instead of finding large warehouses well stocked, it was quite the reverse, and "such devilish strokes make me afraid of the commission business," he would tell his partners. In the ensuing months, times grew worse: "the situation makes me tremble for the future," he wrote on June 4, 1772.[16]

That October, the mercantile business in full depression, Johnson informed his partners that he had been arrested and obliged to enter bail. By January 1773, his situation was "very ticklish," yet he could support it with a good face under expectations that his partners would exert themselves "and forward me the needful." But in February: "We shall go to pot"—they owed more than 4,000 pounds.[17]

Fortunately, Johnson could be amazingly resilient in crisis, and curiously, both an exuberant extrovert and a measured loner. In November, as far as the firm's news went, "we are in top credit" he told his colleagues; in regard to his personal life, he was remarkably reticent. He did not mention that he was about to become a father, that a very young Englishwoman, Catherine Young (probably 16 years of age) was about to give birth to their child in the next month. In fact, as far as female company, he had told his friend Denton Jacques soon after his arrival in London only of his interest in "Quanturns" whom he had found "exceedingly pretty and genteel," and whose great advantage was that he could "use them with impunity."[18]

Somewhat later he dismissed all rumors of his impending marriage as "the last of my thoughts, & if I continue in the same mind I believe I never shall." And when his partner John Davidson accused him of slyness and hinted, with displeasure, his knowledge of his relationship with the Creole ladies, Johnson was quick to explain: "A man must possess true courage indeed to engage the matrimonial way, in those hard times," and he was "content to let the more enterprising enjoy the charmer with all her charms," he wrote on September 4, 1773.[19]

But apparently he would have a change of heart on this score. It has been assumed that the couple did marry, though whether before or after the birth of their first child Nancy on December 2, 1773 is unknown; four of their nine children—Nancy, Louisa Catherine, Carolina Virginia Marylanda and Mary Ann—were baptized as legitimate; only their son Thomas Baker seems off record.

In stark contrast to Joshua Johnson's very public family history, Louisa's mother Catherine's ancestry has remained a mystery.

Louisa does pay her respect and affection: "Beautiful, her person very small, exquisitely delicate and very finely proportioned, she was lively, highly cultivated, her wit brilliant though sometimes almost too keen." But it was her variable given maiden name—Nuth or Young—that remains a challenge to generations of her descendants, most particularly to her grandson Henry Adams, the legendary historian. "My own chief curiosity," Henry Adams had informed a friend, "is to know something about my great grand-mother Catherine Nuth, wife of Joshua Johnson and mother of Mrs. J. Q. Adams. If any of your Maryland genealogists would solve me that difficulty," he wrote, "I can quite fill out my family tree, although the other Johnsons are still troublesome enough."[20]

Two years later, his quest still unrequited, Henry hired a professional genealogist in London, with equally frustrating results—not a trace of her to be found under either Nuth or Young or Johnson in London Parish records or elsewhere, whether "in marriage or out." And still, seven years later, the question of "Who was Catherine Nuth," remained "one of the deepest mysteries of metaphysical theology." Put another way, "What was Catherine (Nuth) Johnson?" he asked his brother Charles.[21]

According to Louisa's brief account:

My grandmother was Mary Young. She was the daughter of a brewer, a partner in the house of Sir Felix Calvert and was engaged to marry his son—but owing to some misunderstanding rejected him and married Mr. Nuth. They had twenty-two living children born but only reared two, Mother Catherine Nuth and a son who at fourteen years of age was sent out to the East India Company as a cadet and was always supposed to have perished in one of the expeditions sent up into the back country. I remember my grandfather who died at the age of ninety-six—I think when I was about 12 or 13 years old. He lived at Camberwell and left at his death the use of 500 pounds sterling to my mother which my father permitted her to use as her own.[22]

Louisa's version of her family history was one of Louisa's many inventions. In the first place, no one by the name of Nuth (or Knuth) was employed at the India House between 1750 and 1775; nor was anyone sent on an expedition. Nor was there a Calvert partner named Young. Which provoked another question: If Mary Young married a Mr. Nuth, why wasn't she named Mary Nuth? Instead, it was a "Dame Catherine Young, née à Londres" whose name is on the birth certificate of Harriet Johnson, Louisa's younger sister, born on January 3, 1782, which suggests the possibility that Catherine, Louisa's mother, was illegitimate. Then there is the almost farcical intrusion on the entire misbegotten story—that the man Louisa called Nuth (her mother's benefactor) may have been one George Lookup, a wealthy London surgeon who had done business with Joshua Johnson in March 1772.[23]

Louisa's ingenuous account of her mother's family is clarity itself compared to that of her own early days. Her multifaceted self-portrait, ranging from pitiable waif and beleaguered sister to proud daughter and marriageable Jane Austen-ish character, owes everything to her quixotic temperament and willful imagination. It has both provoked and defied history's consensus without tempering, over the centuries, any of its fascination and influence.

For example, to a small boy, Henry Adams's grandmother, Louisa Catherine Adams was "Louis Seize, like the furniture," exotic as the Sèvres china. He identified with the complexities of her turbulent strain of mind and was nearly in awe of their emotional and psychological kinship. Before he knew anything of her interior life, he wrote that he "never dreamed that from her might come some of those doubts and self-questionings, those hesitations, those rebellions against law and discipline, which marked more than one of her descendants." But he might even then have had a vague suspicion that "he was to inherit from her the seeds of the primal sin, the fall from grace, the curse of Abel, that he was not of pure New England stock, but half exotic."[24]

Louisa begins her own history in Nantes when she was three. Given Britain's passage of the Intolerable Acts in reaction to the Boston Tea Party, and "with every apprehension of dread, sorrow & fear that we behold the steps taken here to crush our fellow subjects," Joshua Johnson feared the increasingly hostile environment would decimate his sales to the point where he felt he must leave the country. And though wary of the very heavy expense of moving his family, and in hope of one day taking them across the "heaving pond" that was the Atlantic, by March 1778 he had settled in the vibrant French seaport town of Nantes, on the Loire River, where he would both prosper as one of the leading American merchants in France and complain to his partners that his children "will be beggars whilst yours will be rich and happy." They would live there until the peace treaty was signed in 1783.[25]

They lived, Louisa recalled, in "an immense building . . . called the Temple de Gout" on L'Iles Feydeau, a bridge across from inner town. A six-story, grand baroque, Nantes-style mansion of sandstone, granite and marble with intricate carvings and lacework iron balconies, just the name was enough, Louisa wrote, to turn the head of a beautiful and much admired woman such as her mother. And probably, she supposed in retrospect, it inspired tastes and ideas calculated to lavish on her children a more expensive and higher order of education than her father's station in life as a commission merchant prudently authorized.[26]

She said she could "perfectly remember the school to which I was sent, the strong impressions made upon my imagination by the Roman Catholic church, the heartfelt humility with which I stood before the image of the tortured Jesus and the horror I felt at the thought of being with heretics. . . ."[27]

Unfortunately, in the very act of kneeling before the "heretics" she had fainted; two severe illnesses left her very weak. While her sisters who enjoyed fine health were very lively, they "had little of that sensitiveness . . . which has proved so great an obstacle to my happiness."[28]

Louisa was a thoughtful, grave child and a creature of ardent affections and strong impulse, according to her mother. Her earliest recollections were in French, and the little knowledge she had of that language was soon "obliterated by the requirement of the new one." As for education: "My mind was of a different stamp, everything in the shape of work I abhorred. Dancing and singing I was very fond of but the mere mechanical drudgery of music was utterly beyond me . . . as proof of which I was one year learning to play one song from the opera *Rosina*." The only way she could forgive this excessive stupidity was that she could read music with the greatest facility, and her voice was so flexible, she could execute almost anything at first reading and before she could learn the accompaniment on the piano.[29]

In April 1783, the family left Nantes for London. With the United States War of Independence at an end, the Johnsons once again settled back in London with the addition of two, her sisters Eliza Jennet Dorcas and Adelaide, Louisa noted. Back at studies in England, in consequence of their extraordinary deep and utter ignorance of English, she and her sister Nancy became objects of ridicule to the whole school of 40 young ladies from the ages of 7 to 20. "To this cause," she wrote: "I am convinced I owe the haughtiest and pride of character which it has been impossible for me to subdue; to the suffering I then underwent living in a state of constant torment, and being perpetually punished or mortified for those very things which had always before been subjects of admiration. . . . I became seriously melancholy and almost gloomy—which caused me to be called Miss Proud by my schoolfellows. . . ."[30]

On August 7, 1790, Joshua Johnson was informed by Thomas Jefferson that the president of the United States, "desirous of availing his country of the talents of its best citizens in their respective lines, has thought proper to nominate you consul for the United States at the port of London."[31]

As for the house on Cooper's Row, her father's establishment was so perfectly regulated that everything in it moved like clockwork—with eleven servants, three of whom had been with him from the time of his marriage, all of them devoted to him. A very indulgent master, although strict; as everything was methodical, everything was easy. In this Louisa's mother had played a memorable role, superintending everything though her health was so delicate.

Time flew on, Louisa wrote, and one winter both Nancy and Louisa, with so little difference in age, were introduced "into what is called society." Timid, shy, reserved and cold, though "when pleased delighted to ecstasy," her disposition, however, was not half so amiable as those of her sisters—but it was her father's idea that she was more steady, and this induced him to treat her as if she was the eldest, which aroused some jealousy. And though she did not have the advantage of possessing the personal attractions which adorned her two sisters closest to her age, she was so entirely happy that she "never looked or dreamt of anything beyond the hour, and thoroughly detested everything like society beyond my own home, unless an occasional visit to the theatre."[32]

And then Mr. Jay came to England, and while he was there John Quincy and his brother arrived in London on their way to Holland. Louisa and her sisters were far from dreaming of a future connection with the Adams family and seemed uninterested in marriage, especially as her father had always told them that the fortunes he would be able to give them as dowry would not be large enough to prove a motive for an offer. In other words, they would be loved for themselves, but, on the other hand, as they were constantly told that they would have 5,000 pounds sterling apiece, they were confident in meeting society's expectations. And so thoroughly was her father convinced of possessing that sum, that even when all his calamities came so suddenly upon him, he still believed that his children would be provided for. And so would Louisa, to her everlasting despair.

After their introduction, John Quincy came frequently. He was a great favorite of Louisa's mother but she did not think her father admired him so much—"he always had a prejudice toward the Yankees and insisted that they never made good husbands." Initially, Louisa continues, she had never observed anything in Mr. Adams's conduct that indicated the smallest preference for her. And once engaged, even her first lessons in the "belle passion" were pretty thickly stewed with thorns. Love seemed to chill all the natural hilarity of her disposition, and those hours which had been spent in cheerful mirth were passed in gloom and anxiety.[33]

If lovers' quarrels are a renewal of love, they also leave a sting behind, in this case, for her, a sense of unnecessary severity of character, which often led her to fear something: "I know not what and put a damp upon my natural spirits which I never overcame. I loved with all the affection of a warm and untried heart. . . ."[34]

The time arrived for John Quincy's departure for Holland and to take leave of Louisa. He recommended that during his absence she attend to the improvement of her mind and a course of study. Instead, she dwelt on all these circumstances, she said, to explain why she would rather have married than be left behind. And that was because, she wrote, she had a "horror of banter to which a young woman is exposed who is known to be engaged."[35]

Louisa and her family might have been the classic prototype of the novel Jane Austen had begun to write that year of 1796. Fanatically burdened with the pride and prejudice implicit in the ruling British social protocol of the day, the young Johnson women's genteel education had embraced the harp, pianoforte, song, poetry, dance. But unlike the independent Elizabeth Bennet, Austen's heroine of similar background, Louisa would have been intimidated by the novelist's presumptuous Lady de Bourgh and cowed by her snobberies.

Resigned to the conventions of so-called respectable society, Louisa, the daughter of a British mother of obscure lineage and a Maryland-born father in trade, could have no pretensions to being an aristocrat, but at least her promised dowry gave her some hope of an eligible marriage. Without funds, according to the unwritten rules, securing a husband of any position was out of the question. And, apparently, no young woman, as it would turn out, would take this convention to heart and mind with graver consequences than Louisa C. Johnson, as she signed her letters to John Quincy during their 13-month separation between London and The Hague.

Chapter 20

"ALBEIT UNUSED TO THE MELTING MOOD"

The morning that John Quincy was to leave London, he had set himself to performing his "indispensables." Among them was an hour devoted to his last sitting for the artist Thomas H. Hull for the miniature he would exchange for one of Louisa in return. He had arranged for her father to deliver it to her, and he hoped she would "Accept it as a token of an affection," he wrote, "which will cease only with the last pulse of the heart of him whose image it is. And may it often meet your eye with one half the delight which at this instant he derives from a look at the precious corresponding pledge of your regard, which now lays on the table before him."[1]

On the whole, the miniature of Louisa, oil on ivory, copied by William Birch from Copley's romantic portrait, was more pleasing to the sitter than the original. He thought it less flattering, "in want of a little assistance from The Graces," in this instance, "a capital qualification." As for his gazing at the young lady in the miniature and using all his eloquence, trying to elicit a smile from her countenance had become one of his favorite occupations and challenges. In this portrait of a mere girl with towering and tumbling hair, grave in wistful thought—in spite of all his efforts, she "continues inexorable," and seemed to tell him "that she knows her power and is sure to please me let her look how she will." As a result, he had given up the hope of a perpetual smile from the image and comforted himself with the hope of an occasional one from the original.[2]

From The Hague, he wrote tenderly and lovingly that "Six days have elapsed since I last enjoyed the happiness of seeing you." It had been his hope that meanwhile, in sharing his need for comfort at their separation, she too "exercised and discovered the species of fortitude" of which they had often conversed. Back at The Hague, in the midst of a great deal of business, he realized that it would be some time before he was able "to bend myself properly to it."[3] Instead, discipline wanting:

> My imagination cannot help flying from the flat realities around me to the scenes which have been recently familiar to me, which however highly prized while they were enjoyed, are still more valued now that they are past.
>
> I see you sitting on the sofa with the table before you working at a Vandyke, and Caroline at the other end and with her silken net-work pinned before her, while Nancy calls the very soul of harmony from the forte piano.[4]

It was as though he had forgotten the misanthropic record he had left behind of a nearly hostile captive of his last months in London and its irresistible dissipation. Though he scornfully mourned "too much time spent in relaxation, perhaps lost," he allowed himself one tentative apology: the state of his health. Then again, he would concede that "weakness of the heart is only a plea for me— much more might have been done by me." But on the whole in regard to the past year, he wrote in his diary on his twenty-ninth birthday on July 11, none of its predecessors had been so innocent, "yet none of them have been more exposed to temptation." In other words, John Quincy was in love and, at the same time, riddled with guilt and disapproval of his obsessive capitulation to the possibilities of marriage.[5]

Since his return to The Hague, he found himself determined to make the remainder of his stay as short as possible, as he saw no prospect for an increase in his earnings. But he meant to write home to his friends in America to explore other prospects "that would enable him to indulge the wishes of my heart," he told Louisa. He would, he continued, "cheerfully resign a career of public life which forbids that private happiness, the first object of my hopes and which you only can confer." He also asked to be remembered with respect and gratitude to Louisa's mother, and "with kind attachment to all your lovely sisters." As the bearer of his messages, he hoped she would tell Nancy that the new sonatas "yet vibrate upon the ears of Mr. Quiz," as he was called, and Caroline, that he would with rapture hear once more her deep toned execrations on the Dutch language. "To yourself, Louisa, say in his behalf everything that can give you the most pleasing and unmingled gratification, and be assured that however warm and eloquent the language may be, it will fall far, far short of the feelings which fill the breast of your ever faithful and affectionate friend John Q. Adams."[6]

In a most congenial mood, he also wrote that same June evening, to his prospective father-in-law, Joshua Johnson, requesting him and Mrs. Johnson and all their family to accept his gratitude for the "numberless marks of kindness" he had received during his stay in England. Also, he hoped to hear from him as frequently as convenient.[7]

Weeks later, he reaffirmed his commitment to Louisa and his future plans in his letter to his mother. Rather discreetly, but nevertheless with passion: "From considerations of necessary prudence," he had left "a highly valued friend behind."[8]

"Albeit unused to the melting mood," he found the separation "not a little painful. It is meant however that it shall only be temporary." Looking ahead, he proposed to pass one year more in the Netherlands, to complete the three years that he had committed to his present mission. In the meantime, he would try to make arrangements that might afford him greater support. He knew, of course, that he would have it in his power to return to the bar, but he would give preference to other choices. Three years of total abandonment of both the practice and study of the law, and a pretty constant pursuit so different from it, would deprive him, he knew, of whatever fitness he had for that profession, which certainly offered no alluring prospect in the first place.[9]

Being back at The Hague was more of a struggle to adjust than he had anticipated. It would take much of his time to recover the general information of the state of affairs which had been interrupted by his long absence, he apologized to his father. But he was, he assured him, paying formal visits to the president and secretary of the National Assembly, meeting with officials from Denmark, Sweden and Portugal, attending the weekly tea of the French minister and his card party. He had also met up with several old friends, including Mr. Dumas and his daughter. All of this was a little wearing to the confused young man, trying to sort out what he owed his family, his country, his brand new fiancée Louisa. Comparing the solitude at The Hague to the bustle of London, he concluded somewhat wistfully that his present life, on the whole, was infinitely better suited to his taste, or so he rationalized.[10]

He did note in his diary on June 30:

> On my return from England, I determined to resume a life of application to business and study, which, during the principal part of my residence there [was] altogether impossible. . . . Rise and dress at six. Read works of *instruction* from thence till nine. Breakfast. Read the papers and translate from the Dutch till eleven or twelve. Then dress for the day. Write letters or attend to other business that occurs till between two and three. Walk till half-past three. Dine and sit till five. Read works of *amusement* till between eight and nine. Walk again about an hour. Then take a very slight supper and my segar, and retire to bed at eleven.[11]

He was also devoting an hour a day to the study of Italian with his friend Baron de Bielefeld whom he thought a "not very brilliant natural genius," but learned. And yet, he was still dissatisfied: "Too much of this time is devoted to reading and too little to society. But I was not formed to shine in company, nor to be delighted with it; and I have now a considerable lapse of time to repair. . . . I hope and intend at a future time to take some of my present reading hours for the purpose of writing. I wish no other change."[12]

Having also resumed his duties as trusted sentinel of his listening post at The Hague, John Quincy faithfully fulfilled his obligations with copious letters in cramped hand, crowded with intelligence on the state of Europe, on commercial relations with numerous maritime nations, on France's persistent attempt to involve America in its war with Britain, on Bonaparte's march toward Rome through the Tuscan territory. The issues were numerous and he was ardent about them. With elections looming and news of President George Washington's retirement, he feared (obviously protective of his father) that his successor would be exposed "to the most tempestuous political season that the world perhaps ever witnessed." And then, the passage of Jay's Treaty was critical. Under no circumstances did he wish the United States to be drawn into war with Great Britain. Just the thought posed terrifying questions: "I am unwilling to look the prospect in the face," he told his father.[13]

And yet, in an aside to his father, though he distrusted the French (and absolutely loathed the British), he could understand why they had made such powerful inroads on the American public. To begin with, French manners were captivating while the English were "always cold and distant, generally insolent and overbearing, and not infrequently contemptuous and malignant." Though his fears were allayed with news that the House of Representatives had at last signed the Treaty with Britain, on April 30, 1796, he still did not consider their country out of danger of "being yet involved in the war that still rages in Europe." Justly so in light of his father's future and bitter challenge from the French, who would annul the Treaty of Amity and Commerce written into the Franco-American Alliance of 1778, refuse to recognize America's minister to France, and, given the looming and sensational events of the notorious XYZ affair, help to cripple his presidency almost from the start.[14]

And in this connection, John Quincy mentioned to his father that their old friend Dumas, to his abject dismay, appeared to be retained in the service of the French Republic, a position he found difficult to justify either as a pensioner of the United States or as an old personal friend of his father's or himself. With some tenderness, he added, "He imagines I am not aware of it, and I must so far do his heart the justice to believe that he is not altogether aware of it himself."[15]

To his mother, John Quincy raised the subject of the treaty with Britain. He was happy to find that "after all there was a majority in that House of Representatives (a feeble one, indeed) who could make a distinction between the *right* to *ratify* or reject and the *power* to *violate* a solemn national engagement, a majority who did not think it proper to construe the latter which they certainly possessed in the former, which the Constitution had explicitly placed in other hands."[16]

"But enough of politics for the present at least," he wrote on July 25. "Let us come to something about ourselves." His mother had guessed right as to the object of the attachment which had been intimated in his formal letters—an attachment which had now become irrevocably fixed, and on which much of his future destiny would depend.[17]

Then there was the fact that his father *"wishes in his heart"* that his attachment had been made in America. He wished so too, if he could have had control over his affections. He could only hope that neither his friends nor his family, nor he himself would ever have any other reason to regret his choice.[18]

But it was his father's prospects for election as president of the United States that stirred his greatest anxiety. "Whatever of humor, of fame or of any benefit, which that station can bestow upon its next possessor will be counterbalanced," he feared, by so many oppressive cares, by so many formidable dangers, by so much malevolence and envy, and by such boundless abuse and scurrility, that he was torn—his filial affection really and sincerely dreaded what his love of his country could not but strongly desire. As for his own prospects for promotion under his father's presidency—"it must be altogether out of the question" and there were to be no exceptions. With his brother heading home, if he still found himself without means to support a family, he thought he too would return home to pursue his own concerns and serve his country in a private station.[19]

And then came his blunt response to his mother's recent (but not first) inquiry as to whether "Maria? Has she no claim?"—clearly referring to his once beloved Mary Frazier: "She had none, but to my fervent and cordial good wishes for her welfare." Seeming to have forgotten the pain of his youthful love affair, he assured his mother that they had parted forever: "it was a mutual dissolution of affection: the attractive principle was itself destroyed, the flame was not covered with ashes, it was extinguished with cold water."[20]

Chapter 21

"OH MY LOUISA!"

"Happy indeed would it have been for Mr. Adams if he had broke his engagement, and not harassed himself with a wife altogether so unsuited to his own peculiar character, and still more peculiar prospects," Louisa would write 43 years later in her memoir, *Adventures of a Nobody*. By then Louisa, submerged in bitter memories and flailing for her sanity, said that her health at the time of her engagement was already injured by anxieties "by no means trifling." Among these she specified her father's ship idling by and her wedding trousseau in storage. But in a stunning omission, she failed to mention her father's catastrophic bankruptcy.[1]

She also remembered her discovery of views that totally differed from John Quincy's in many essential points. There was a severity bordering on injustice in some of the opinions that she heard him express, and minor concerns of life which grew so intense at one point that a rupture of their engagement had nearly taken place. She claimed proudly that she had shown enough spirit to defend herself in that instance, and more than enough to embarrass herself into apology after each outburst.

What had been theoretically her minor concerns were the essence of John Quincy's very being. Louisa had an instinctive distaste for his "boasted philosophy," his pervasive morality, intense patriotism, and even his bookishness which, to Louisa's mind, endangered his health. The subject of "spirit"—that is, temperament or disposition—was a minefield. Given how painful John Quincy found "so essential a wideness of sentiment between them"—Louisa, a girlish romantic of 22, and John Quincy, a scholar and a dedicated patriot who had turned 30—it was logical to wonder that the couple's engagement should have survived their stormy correspondence.[2]

Before their marriage, John Quincy intuitively might have sensed the swaying moods of her emotional makeup. Apart from her later erratic journal-and-memoir writings, her first letters to John Quincy, written at age 21 during their separation of one year and a month, comprise a candid record of their own and pitilessly illuminate the couple's chasm of differences as well as the would-be bride's quixotic temperament. Beyond the question of her British birth, her French language, her "taint of Maryland blood," her cloistered education, her rebellion against the Adams's political allegiances and philosophy, bitterness, guilt, anger and insecurity stain near and far corners of her letters and, tragically, presage her lifetime of emotional stress.[3]

At the same time, these letters were truly love letters—even John Quincy seemed surprised at his own eloquence. His affection is unmistakable, his warmth beguiling as he addresses Louisa as "The Companion of my Life," "My lovely friend," "dear friend," "gentle friend," "amiable friend," "best friend." On her part, she responds to her "most tender and most faithful friend," "loved friend," "dearest friend." There was passion in abundance, all of which disproves one historian's claim that "as in many a successful marriage it cannot be said that the nuptials [of Louisa and John Quincy] sprang from any deep romantic love on either side." In fact, it appears to be the reverse. There was passion in abundance and though John Quincy claimed a happy marriage, in Louisa's version it was at times both heartbreaking and maddening.[4]

A *year before* she and John Quincy were to be married, Louisa spent the summer "in a very retired way," in Clapham, then a suburb about four or five miles south of Westminster, while her parents and her two older sisters remained on Cooper's Hill. It was a very small house, as Louisa described it, rented expressly for her to devote herself to such studies as she—or perhaps her father—hoped "would lessen the immense distances which existed in point of mind and talent between herself" and her future husband. Tended by Celia, her governess, and one other servant, she also seemed to be learning something about cooking lighter fare.[5]

She was miserably unsure of herself, most immediately about her first attempt to write a letter to John Quincy in response to his query about her opinion of the miniature portrait of himself he had given her. Though she rose to the challenge, she did explain:

"So totally incapacitated do I feel myself for writing were it not through fear of giving you pain I certainly should indulge any avowed aversion to it and decline the task, but judging of your feelings by my own, think it incumbent on me to avail myself of every opportunity of testifying my affectionate esteem for you. 'Oh Philosophy where art thou now.'"[6]

As for his picture: she approved the likeness, though the complexion was much too dark and the figure altogether too large. Friends who saw it recently said they should never have known him. She remembered in middle age "the anxiety with which I awaited a letter from Mr. Adams and the terror which assailed me at the idea of answering it." She claimed further that her governess undertook to correct her letters and to give them such a turn as she thought would be most elegant.[7]

John Quincy read her first letter ten or fifteen times, so he told her, was entirely sympathetic and agreed that the trouble of writing letters was more than sufficient to counterbalance the pleasure of receiving one. Yet, an ardent and gallant advocate, he predicted that the day would come when instead of being compelled to write, she would take delight in it. Meanwhile, the only fault he could find with her letter was its shortness. "Instead of wishing you had not answered me, I wish you had answered me three times as much, but even for what you did write, I thank you over and over again." It had what was at all times important to him, "the assurance of your constant affection."[8]

Of her second letter—it was more charming than the first and he was sure if she would have the resolution to practice a little, she would form a really elegant style. "No friend to hereditary honors, but a great partisan for hereditary practices," if she did not write with eloquence, "It would be entirely owing to yourself if you should not." As for her remarks about his picture—he could hope it would convey the feelings of the original, expressed his affection for her "beyond the reach of any expression that can be given to the pencil, the pen or the tongue." He never could be happy far from her, it was a consolation to have her share that sentiment.[9]

Louisa did dare to broach (more graciously) the probability that John Quincy's father would be the next president, and should that be the case, she offered John Quincy with sincere pleasure her congratulations. "You *know* my friend I am not ambitious of any thing but your affection and in that my wishes are unbounded." Her Mamma and sisters united in best wishes for his health and happiness—"For my own I leave you to imagine."[10]

Judging from John Quincy's response, Louisa had touched a nerve. "You tell me you are not ambitious, but will offer me your congratulations of my father, should he be placed at the head of the American government," he had written on July 9. "Indeed, my friend, that is a high station, but I have no ambition to see him placed in it. For like all other high stations it is planted with thorns and surrounded with dangers." Besides, the more conspicuous his father became in the world, the more incumbent it would be on John Quincy to prove himself not unworthy to be his son. And already, he had "a heavy burden on that account to bear" and did not wish to see it increased. For himself, he was not ambitious of rank, "but it is impossible to be indifferent on the point of reputation."[11]

Perhaps the burden he perceived was the legacy or the destiny that he hoped to fulfill in partnership with Louisa—his parents being his inspiration—as he defined in a single paragraph the ideals and goals of his life that would endure until his death, but the dream and reality of those ideals she tragically could never appreciate or fully embrace. Gravely envisioning "the American nation one of the first upon Earth . . . as far as may ever be in my power," he wrote Louisa, "I will strive to promote it." He spoke to her with entire confidence, because whatever his conduct or his fate might be, "your interests are now united to mine, to be separated only by death."[12]

By July, there was a gap of "five tedious weeks," as Louisa wrote, between letters, their delivery being utterly dependent on the whims of sea transport. In response, John Quincy apologized: the next time he would try to write by Hamburg. But, he wrote, she was never to believe for a moment that absence could erase her memory from his heart. "No, my best friend; to you it is devoted; from you all its hopes of domestic happiness in this life are received."[13]

There was a second letter from Louisa dated July 25, far more cheerful in tone, written to congratulate him on his appointment as minister plenipotentiary to Portugal. George Washington had proposed the nomination on May 28, 1796, and the Senate passed it on May 30. Which meant, Louisa joyfully assumed, that he would soon return to London.[14]

The official letter, dated June 11, had informed John Quincy of his appointment but that for several reasons the transfer of his services to Portugal must be postponed. He was to remain on as minister at The Hague until notified otherwise, possibly by early autumn. Somewhat startled by this news, he noted the next morning that he had not been able to pay attention to his Italian studies, and supposed that he might perhaps find it necessary to suspend them entirely at least for the present. "The circumstances mentioned yesterday," he realized, "give an entirely new turn to my affairs, and presents new objects which must command my immediate application."[15]

It was as though he suddenly awakened to the gravity of his commitment to Louisa. With plans to remain until spring, and an attempt at bolstering Louisa's faltering spirits, he wrote on August 13 of his hope of terminating sooner than he would otherwise have expected "the vile embarrassments which made our separation absolutely necessary."[16]

For her own happiness in facing these diplomatic obligations and delays, he asked her to acquire the faculty not merely of acquiescence to unavoidable inconveniences, but even of a cheerful conformity to things that must be endured, and above all to establish an invariable rule never to express an opinion of general or national nature. He hoped she would forgive him this "intimation," but he had often found that nothing was more natural and nothing more offensive than tactless comments about foreign nations or on numerous classes of people. Further, he knew her heart was so good that he could not conceive of anything said by her would "ever give dissatisfaction to anyone."[17]

Having dutifully reviewed financial matters and those of diplomatic protocol, John Quincy now turned to matters of Louisa's education. Knowing that she was spending part of the summer at Clapham, he was positive that she had used the time to advantage, and it would give him pleasure to hear in detail of everything she found interesting to herself, for example, her progress on the harp. But she was not in all of this to think he was setting himself up for a mentor, for he was at the same time asking for her advice and opinions with equal freedom in return. Perhaps he sensed that he was treading on sensitive ground and hoped to leave Louisa in a happier place for, curiously, though he had repeatedly warned her of his lengthened stay at The Hague, he now allowed for the possibility that his leave might come earlier than expected.[18]

Louisa was totally charming, candid and humble in response. She took pleasure in the thought of his return. But, she had to confess, it aroused fears that had never before presented themselves. When she reflected on the part in life she would have to act, given the little she had seen of the world, her conscious deficiency was manifest, and she already thought she saw him blush for her awkwardness. But then she knew the generosity of his disposition and could count on him to forgive and encourage her "by your kindness to mend."[19]

She faltered but rebounded somewhat on his next question: how she spent her time in Clapham. She wished her friend had touched on any other subject, for she must candidly confess she had profited little by her retirement but then, she said, it is "yourself who are the cause by (shall I say it) intruding too often in my thoughts."[20]

The letters both parents had written to him in a week's span in August emphatically reconfirmed their doubts about Louisa, every

nuance of which they had already made known to him in prior
months. Suspicion that the senior Adamses' opinions may have
been colored by their knowledge of Louisa's parents' elaborate lifestyle had already been hinted at in Abigail's thanks for the cloaks
she had received the previous May. At that time, she had written
to her son, "The young lady who undertook the commission shows
that she inherits the taste of elegance which her Mamma is conspicuous for."[21]

His father wrote on August 7, 1796, congratulating John
Quincy on his appointment to Portugal and for what he knew of his
proposed marriage by this time. How a "young lady of fine parts
and accomplishments, educated to drawing, dancing and music,"
was to fare under the restrictive circumstances of being the wife of
a minister in a foreign country was the next question. However domestic and retired from the world she may have been in her father's
house, when she came to shine in a court among the families of
ambassadors and ministers of state, "if she has not some prudence
and philosophy, uncommon to her sex, she would be in danger" of
involving him "in expenses far beyond your appointment."[22]

From his mother, he received a letter (written just three days
after his father's) that clearly suggests that the two in Quincy had
not only discussed but wholly agreed on their concerns about their
son's choice of bride. But, at least the first paragraph brought news
that John Quincy was longing to hear. His appointment as minister
was the last nomination President Washington made before Congress ended and had taken place after his father had gone home
"without it ever being hinted to him." Proud in response, hoping
his mother would not attribute it to anything like filial ingratitude,
that idea gave him singular pleasure. He could support very well
the thought of being indebted for his advancement to his father's
merits, but he could not bear that of attributing it to his father's
"agency."[23]

What especially pleased his mother was the unanimous vote he
had received, added proof, she said, of their country's confidence
in him and of the approval of the president who had honored and
promoted him. But then, she was also worried. She readily admitted "This new appointment my dear son has filled my mind with a

thousand anxieties on your account." The engagement he had made in London would no doubt lead him there on the way to Portugal, and she wondered too, echoing her husband shamelessly, about the young lady's adjustment: "Without any knowledge of experience of the world, to be introduced into the manners, luxuries, dissipations and amusements of a foreign court? Placed in an elevated station with examples before her eyes of a style of living altogether incompatible with her future views and prospects in America?"[24]

As if that picture wasn't bleak enough, and even allowing that the wife he would eventually bring home stateside was born of an American father, how might she assimilate to their manners, customs and habits without too much pain? Abigail remained unconvinced. "Who can answer for her, after having been introduced into the dissipations of a foreign court?"[25]

John Quincy had tactfully considered his mother's observations "full of tenderness as well as of the prudence" as were usually to be found in her counsels. He also reassured her that he had thought it his duty to be very explicit with the lady on the subject of his future prospects in America.[26]

Very soon and increasingly, John Quincy would find he misjudged Louisa. All may have been explained, even understood, but all was not approved. His moralizing made her irritable; she felt diminished by his assumptions, depressed by his gloomy thoughts. Obviously he was the beneficiary of far too many parental lectures on the subject of prudence and, as a dire result, the debonair, even flirtatious suitor had turned moralizing, arch, would-be mentor, who insistently raised nagging issues that seemed unfriendly, if not hurtful, in Louisa's opinion.

Louisa, as it turned out, was not the only one eager to meet with John Quincy in London. Though casually broached initially, the desire to meet was almost in fact quite desperate where her father was concerned. In response to his several inquiries, John Quincy told Joshua Johnson that letters from America made it more uncertain than ever how long he would be detained.

As of November 9, he had reason to believe that he would not be leaving until quite late in the spring or the beginning of summer. And as Johnson mentioned the need of going to America early in the spring, John Quincy was resigned to the necessity of postponing until his own return to America "those arrangements which I had hoped might be settled at an earlier period, and upon which the happiness of my future life will essentially depend." He had received no letters from Louisa, and he hoped, he told her on November 15, that he might attribute her silence to her usual aversion to writing, rather than to any remains of the temper which he had been sorry to observe in her last letter. He also addressed the painful prospect of his detention at The Hague.[27]

And so their minuet had begun. Up to this point, though Louisa had not disputed the integrity of his advice, she frankly was in no position to absorb, let alone practice, what he advised. With her, every reference to postponement gave her more uneasiness than she was capable of expressing. She told John Quincy on November 29, that "stronger judgment enables you so happily to philosophize," and so her weakness must appear to him in an unfavorable light. But in self-defense, when she reflected how few lessons she had received from the school of disappointment, he might be more inclined to pardon than to blame.[28]

From this open admission, he was not to imagine she was supinely yielding to the tyranny of unavailing complaint. On the contrary, she would prove that she had not neglected her dear friend's repeated lessons, and was still worthy of his much valued affection. Her sentiments on his retreat into books ran deeper. If he valued her happiness, he would relinquish a habit that must ultimately prove so injurious to his health. As to the mental improvements he so justly recommended, she would if possible acquire them, though she was too distracted at the moment to pay the requisite attention to profitable study.[29]

As for his future plans—it is here for the first time that she hints at her knowledge of her father's financial plight, which dictated that she would receive no dowry—she implores John Quincy, "whatever might be their mutual uneasiness, never to resign any situation on my account, as it is not my lot to add to your future welfare."[30]

Louisa's letters were delivered to John Quincy the morning of December 20. He had risen after eight, just at daylight, late for him—he had to forgo his feast on Tacitus before his breakfast, but he knew perfectly well that "late evenings make late mornings." First off, he apologized to Louisa for what seemed to be an inevitable continuance of their separation. It had been his hope, he explained, that they might in the interim establish in this exchange of letters a "free, open and unlimited confidence in each other" which he had always sought in their relationship and still thought necessary.[31]

That mutual confidence in one another was never more necessary than now, apparently, but with dire consequence, judging from Louisa's volatile response. According to four bulky paragraphs, jarringly polite with lawyerly logic and incendiary wording, John Quincy totally negated Louisa's proposal that her father embark for America by way of Holland that they might meet once more for a few days.

While it was unpleasant to explain, to go over the same reasons again as he had many times before to her dismay and that of her parents, he knew it was in her best interests that he do so. Though it pained him to knowingly displease her by dashing her wishes and plans, he was convinced that it was in her interest and satisfaction to be "clear and explicit." Obviously firm, he sought in deep frustration to convince Louisa that there was no way to reconfigure their circumstances for the simple reason that "My present situation is not improved in point of fortune." Furthermore, while he remained at The Hague in his present unsettled condition, without orders, without authority, without power to move—exposed to dismissal from public service by a probable "revolution" in the administration of the American government—"it was an act of absurdity" toward himself and of cruelty toward her to connect the fortunes of any amiable woman indissolubly with his." In short, he put their marriage on hold.[32]

The last of December, the weather remarkably mild, John Quincy took a walk, wrote a letter to Louisa and spent the evening at home "to close the year with sober meditation. Not perfectly well," he added. But he seemed quite content in his review of the past months in The Hague, which, contrary to the indulgence of London, had been "a time of as steady and constant application" as ever oc-curred in the course of his life.[33]

One month later, on January 31, the picture of contentment gave way to despair, and he wrote in his diary, "A profound anxi-ety has taken possession of my mind." No doubt his wrenching correspondence with Louisa in the intervening month accounted in part for his turbulent spirits. But looking ahead, a note in his diary of March 4 was also telling. It was the day the new administration of the United States was to begin, and still uncertain about the elec-tions and his father's fate, he wrote, "Everything has contributed to accumulate anxiety upon this event in my mind. Futurity laughs at our foresight. I can only pray for the happiness and prosperity of my country."[34]

Clearly, John Quincy had been savaged by concern over the machinations of his father's candidacy as well as the uncertainty of his own role and his own future. As the son of the president, promotion, as he told his mother, "must be altogether out of the question."[35]

Meanwhile, as of January 7, John Quincy had not heard from Louisa since early November. Her father's letter had told him that she was unwell, and he wrote that he hoped she had recovered her usual good spirits and had reconciled her mind to the longer sepa-ration which they "were doomed to suffer."[36]

Somewhat to this point, he recommended a book—"I must read a little, though with your admonition always in mind," he apologized—recently published by the Swiss-born Parisian writer, Madame de Staël. It was a treasure, he thought, on the influence of passions on the happiness of individuals and nations, "all passions being merely sources of unhappiness that the love of glory, ambi-tion, vanity, love . . . confer on us mortals." And that if we must live, "nothing but philosophy, study and the practice of beneficence could make life tolerable or give us a semblance of happiness." Ma-dame de Staël, being very much addicted to passions, was of course very unhappy "but thought herself for that reason the better quali-fied to warn others."[37]

As he had believed the book very ingenious, he thought Louisa would find it well worth her time. It would show her what a figure one of her sex can be when she undertakes to philosophize, although he allowed affectionately that "you should continue susceptible of one passion at least," rather than adopting altogether the philosophy of Madame de Staël.[38]

Perhaps Louisa's silence provoked further concern about her proposed meeting at The Hague and accounts for the apologetic tone of John Quincy's next letters. He was sorry, knowing she waited with such great expectations, that his letters only confirmed disappointment. But for all his amiable rationalizing, besides objections beyond their control, he did remind her of another flaw in her plan: She must be aware, in the eyes of the world, that her coming to The Hague would have an appearance "consistent neither with your dignity, nor my delicacy."[39]

And then there was the question of how much John Quincy knew at this time about Joshua Johnson's devastating financial plight. More than he wished, most likely, judging from their earlier correspondence in which Johnson mentioned sales of tobacco that had put him "very much at a loss."[40]

Quite direct about his intentions, Johnson had pressed John Quincy for specific plans about when he should see him in London and how long he would stay. Polite in response, hopeful that Johnson would find in America a more favorable settlement than he expected, John Quincy said it was impossible to gauge the time of his return.

Two weeks later, when Johnson had supposed that "it was more than probable" that he would see his prospective son-in-law at The Hague, John Quincy's response was entirely negative. The same message went off to Louisa: "The purpose for which I presume you intended the journey is impracticable."[41]

Several letters of Louisa's had crossed with John Quincy's. At first, buoyed by his assurance of affection, she was ardent in reciprocation. But this was mid-January and just days later, on January 17, she was shattered on reading his "very decisive letter" of the past December 20, so intensely "astonished and mortified" by him that she could scarcely believe he knew to whom he was writing.[42]

She was also very sorry to discover that they had not perfectly understood each other, that he had misinterpreted her intentions. As far as the trip to Holland was concerned, he had indulged himself in unnecessary apprehension concerning her expectations. In fact, she implied, it was occasioned in the first place by his letter to her father in which he wrote that he would be "compelled to relinquish the hopes so fondly raised" that had moved her kind and honored parents to try to alleviate their distress.[43]

As a result, her father had generously told her that his affairs might oblige him to quit Holland and offered to embark from England that they might have the satisfaction of meeting once more, which she "fondly and foolishly imagined would have been mutual." But as things stood now, she would go to America and he to his embassy where, she prayed, "to the great disposer of events to grant that peace to *your bosom*. . . ."[44]

But she was far from finished. Though she apologized, she had long since, she assured John Quincy, "ceased to think writing trouble." She clearly had not overstated her claim when it came to communicating: five pages worth of the fullness of her anger, in particular in the case of his frequent repetition of the words "suspicion and distrust" in several of his former letters. She could not conceive what he meant by them or to what he alluded. When she had looked to her beloved friend for every indulgence, from whom she least expected unkindness, he only added to her distress by the peremptory harshness displayed throughout his letters.[45]

"Believe me," she added, she should be wary to have him or anyone in the world say that she wished to force herself upon any man or into any family. As to further grievances—he appeared to regret plans for her to go with him to Lisbon, and if such was the case, he had certainly taken an improper method of showing this regret. But if this was not so, she begged his pardon for having even thought it.[46]

Regarding his recommendation of Madame de Staël's book— she intended to read it though she could with pleasure inform him that he had been a more able instructor in philosophy than the author could be. She had acquired a great deal of knowledge lately and thought after perusing her book, that she would become adequate to every trial.

And more, if he had found it painful to write to her in such a harsh style, could he judge what it must be to her, "whose mind must be doubly wounded at the idea of having give rise to it." Then too, this boasted philosophy that she had heard so much of, "Ah my beloved friend," it was "indeed a *dreadful* thing." She had too much reason to dislike it, as she saw too plainly that it dictated his every motion and guided his pen in contradiction, she hoped, to his feelings. She also remembered the time when he could see no fault in his Louisa, but alas how he had changed, charging her now with impropriety of conduct and even hint of want of *delicacy*.[47]

But she was determined to heal their precarious relationship. She asked John Quincy to destroy and if possible to erase from his memory the unfortunate letter which had been productive of their mutual anxiety, and to rest assured that she would never again offend him with anything of the sort. However long their separation might be, she would find that she was as capable of bearing it as himself, and she hoped in time to convince him that she possessed both fortitude and dignity sufficient at least to conceal any unbecoming emotions, if not entirely to conquer them.

But the damage was done and her apologies did not hold. He had decided, and told her so, but for the profound affection and indissoluble attachment he felt for its writer, that he must reply to a letter he thought most kindly used by leaving it without any reply at all. Sensing that he had no alternative, he had begun his answer that noon and finished only after dinner. Obviously, both hurt and offended by her assertion of spirit, "Let us," he pleaded, "understand one another, Louisa."[48]

He had always expected and intended that the communication of sentiments between them should be free, candid, open and undisguised: "and if on either side they should occasionally give pain I have trusted that the certainty of mutual affection would at least secure the most favorable instruction, that nothing sarcastic, nothing bitter, nothing invidious would ever pass between us, that expostulation itself would speak the language of love, and that *spirit* would never be needed or called in aid for the settlement of *our* differences."[49]

At the same time, he continued that he could assure her that he never thought her disposition deficient in *spirit* and was fully convinced she had as much of it as could be consistent with an amiable temper, but there was such a thing as going too far. "I do most cordially wish my amiable friend that you may never have occasion to know whether I should possess a proper degree of spirit or not in opposition to you."[50]

He also took exception to her claim on several occasions of thinking herself *honored* by her connection with him. "My *dignity*, my *station* or *my family* have no sort of concern with any subject of debate between you and me." When he spoke of her dignity in a former letter, he meant, and could mean only, the dignity of her sex and of her personal character.[51]

As to her complaints, John Quincy found both sides "remote from the sober medium of reason." Her proposal to come to The Hague was adopted by her without a full consideration of its natural and inevitable consequences, but, he assured her, without the faintest shadow of indelicacy in her heart. He apologized "from the deepest of my heart for every word which may have continued one particle of superfluous asperity." He had always believed in "you, my Louisa," and still believed she possessed "a virtuous heart, an intelligent mind, an accomplished person and a gentle disposition, all of which qualities contributed to inspire the strong affection" that he has for her. But he never seriously believed or pretended that he believed her exempt from the common and universal imperfections of humanity, from occasional errors of the mind and varieties of temper.[52]

The letter had been a challenging one to write, so much so that in his diary the next day John Quincy found himself "somewhat relieved from the pressures of correspondence which I have for some time labored."[53]

Fortunately, Louisa's "kind and affectionate letter" of January 27 which offered congratulations on the certainty of his father's election seemed also to suggest a ray of hope that their tribulations might be at an end. "Oh my Louisa! Let us forever discard a subject of correspondence, which tends mutually to excite sensations of a nature so different from these. Let our only exchange of sentiments," he begged, "be that of tenderness and love."[54]

And the following month, his February 20 letter too was an apology of sorts, and a confession and confrontation as well. If the restoration of sober reason counted for anything, then he had to admit that the time of the latter part of his residence in London, though indeed a time of delight, had also been a time of too much indulgence. Yet, he assured her: "I am the man I was when you *first* knew me," but now much more estimable, and much more respectable than he had been for two or three month before he left her.[55]

Louisa, too, wished to make amends. She had burned her previous letter, wished she hadn't sent others: "I regretted my folly, and felt sincerely ashamed of my ridiculous conduct—Dictated by anger, without time for reflection." But she also wanted to deserve his esteem, for "by doing this I am convinced I shall secure your affection." Asking his pardon, she promised never again to try his temper nor assert her spirit, and trusted that he would "never again have occasion to write any thing but what the tenderest love dictates, and what your Louisa may peruse, without feeling the painful sensations which this moment agitates her bosom."[56]

On a cold, windy March 11, John Quincy took a walk to the seashore, about three miles from The Hague. The English coast was opposite, and though far beyond the reach of sight, his eyes settled on the borders of the horizon while his imagination carried him the rest of the way to Louisa in London.

Thinking about Louisa, he obviously sensed their many differences, worrisomely so, and wished to clarify these concerns. For one, her attitude toward what she called his "bookishness" (which implied a preference for solitude versus socializing) was seriously bothersome. He had to try to have her understand that "the ardent love of literature tended to confirm, to increase, to exalt every virtuous and laudable affection." He told her what books meant to him, and how he could always return to them with pleasure, how they left "no languor, no satiety, no littleness of indolence upon the mind." Further, they were often the only refuge of one to whom the common course of society was now more than ever insipid. But he had noted in two or three different letters that she was not satisfied with this propensity of his and inclined to use her influence over him to divert him from his books. He should not have thought it necessary to review the discussion between them on this subject, except for Louisa's remark that his attachment to them was "hurtful *to my temper.*" He did not agree.[57]

It was still more painful to see her consider the time which he dedicated to improvement as a time lost to her. He considered the union for life between two persons of sense and honesty as something more than a mere living together, and that one of its greatest objects and of its charms was a mutual exhortation and encouragement of each other to every honorable pursuit and every laudable employment. The subject he thought important with regard to her happiness as it was to his own in their future connection, and he wished her to adopt at once the conviction that he considered arguments to the contrary as little better than frivolous.

Finally, while in London John Quincy had repeatedly talked to Louisa about serving his country, that it was not merely "an ambition but a duty," that "every interest and every feeling inconsistent with it must forever disappear." He could not refuse to perform, especially at a moment when there was danger and inconvenience attending it. At the same time he was aware of its inherent sacrifice, since it touched not only on his own happiness but hers as well. It was, after all, what required his continued presence in Europe.[58]

Though Louisa could not help but agree "respecting your attachments to your country," that his impassioned commitment was most certainly a virtue, "virtue," she thought, "may be carried to too great a height."[59]

Chapter 22

"FOR THE FRIEND
OF YOUR LIFE"

*O*n the morning of April 9, 1797, John Quincy received a letter from the secretary of state containing his recall from the mission at The Hague and his commission as minister plenipotentiary of the United States to Portugal. Four days later, he broke the news to Louisa of his plans for departure. He was now trying to get to London where he might have the pleasure of meeting her and end a separation so painful to them both.

In turn, Louisa, having informed her father of John Quincy's new post, and Joshua Johnson, nearly ready to return to the country of his birth with the hope of settling his family, were both anxious to see John Quincy before his departure. Prudence, Johnson concluded, would direct him to arrange his worldly matters to be divided among his family in a will, a gloomy subject, he thought, and he was taking the liberty to nominate John Quincy as one of his executors, to protect the fortunes and morals of all his children. As Louisa's father, he added, he was anxious to see her happy and united to the man *"I am sure will make her so"* and whom he esteemed. He would therefore do anything in his power to promote his intentions. And, if his schooner *Mary* wasn't too small to take

John Quincy to Lisbon, he would send it immediately to Rotterdam to wait for his departure.[1]

The schooner would suit him but, John Quincy replied, for a lady used to very delicate living and unused to the sea, he feared it would be a trial. He found himself unwilling to give up any possibility to allow his wish to come true. And to Louisa, if the expedient met with her father's approval and her consent, they might yet complete their union. Having already observed, with regret, the breadth of their differences, but willing and even eager to marry, he had left the final decision to Louisa. There was one catch—with courage and compelling honesty, he begged that she understand the man she was marrying in all his foibles and prospects: "You know the man you have chosen for the friend of your life. You have known him the better for that absence, which has at once shown you a trial of his affection and of his temper. He has disguised to you none of his failings and weaknesses. . . . Choose, Louisa, choose for yourself, and be assured that his heart will ratify your choice."[2]

He would probably remain at The Hague long enough to receive her answer. If the opportunity for a passage turned up, he would immediately come to her. If not, "let us submit with resignation to the will of Providence and acquiesce in the separation. . . ."[3]

For Louisa, there never was or could be a question. Their difficulties had ended so, "Why my beloved friend do you tell me to choose." What more did he need to convince him that his return would make her happy? She only feared he would find her a troublesome companion. In regard to his temper she could only say that the "more I know you, the more I admire, esteem, love you and the greater is my inclination to do everything in my power to promote your happiness and welfare." "Be but as easily pleased my friend," John Quincy replied, "after marriage, as you are before, and together we shall live as well as can be expected."[4]

When at last his final plans were set, he would quit this country with some regret, he wrote his mother on June 26. The mission was not a station of splendor, yet on the whole agreeable to him, both by the good disposition of the Dutch government and the "indulgence and approbation" of his own government, in particular that of President Washington. The president had urged his father "not [to] withhold merited promotion" from his son, "the most valuable public character we have abroad." Indeed, that such a man of character as Washington had repeatedly praised him had left him nothing to wish for, but he was also alarmed. For how much, he asked, was required of him to support and justify such a judgment? Further, she might rest assured he would never hold a public office under his father's nomination.[5]

William Vans Murray, his successor at The Hague and a beloved and esteemed friend, had accompanied John Quincy and his brother Tom to Rotterdam, wishing them genial weather when they boarded the *Alexander and Alexander* under the Prussian flag. Due to unfavorable winds, they would only inch about 15 kilometers (a bit more than 9 miles) toward the North Sea before they were more or less marooned at Maasaluys, where John Quincy thought of his second day as "imprisonment," the third as "detention." The eighth day, a Friday, was worst of all for reading some "very unpleasant intelligence personally concerning myself." Murray had forwarded news with the comment that it was not Lisbon but Berlin "for him who is imprisoned by the viewless winds."[6]

Murray's second letter of the day confirmed the nomination and the "high probability of a change in your destination," which he supposed was a real inconvenience for his friend. But surely, though he could predict that Benny Bache, the *Aurora* newsman and his kennel, would "bark a little," Murray thought the new president, John Adams, did right in this business and would be supported by the American world. A mere change of place with the same grade where Washington had already placed him should leave no room for "sensibility."[7]

Support, as Murray predicted, had been forthcoming. The king of Prussia, although a great villain, he said, was powerful, especially in northern Europe, and their treaty having expired was in need of renewal. Of critical consideration was keeping a steady eye "on the intriguing, insidious and convulsed government and people," better learned in Berlin than at The Hague, or any other court, wrote Uriah Tracy, then the United States senator from Connecticut. "John Q. Adams, placed at Berlin, can do us much service, as he is unquestionably the most intelligent, and at the same time most industrious man, we have ever employed in a diplomatic capacity."[8]

But Murray had underestimated the private and personal inconvenience of the new appointment, John Quincy having "totally disconnected" all his arrangements. He had already bought his passage and shipped his personal effects to Lisbon, including his cherished library, and had made a financial commitment of $2,500 (possibly for housing). Moreover, in spite of his formal and deliberate declaration to both his parents, he had broken his resolution and accepted a new appointment. He had hoped, he wrote Abigail, that "*my mother* knew me better," that given his personal sense of delicacy, he had not wished to receive a promotion from his father.[9]

His letter had given his mother great pain. She had not known that the change in his embassy was personally so inconvenient but had thought he would find it more agreeable than he anticipated. His father took a different tack. Far from apologetic, he was adamant on the subject.[10]

A masterful lawyer in crafting his case, John Adams was respectful of his "client's" integrity, understanding of his pride and protective of his future. He was also famously forthright in his convictions. He did not think John Quincy's opinion, putting it mildly, was "well considered." He marshalled the facts: "1. In the present case you have no greater emolument, no higher rank than you would have had if you had gone to Lisbon under the nomination of President Washington. 2. You will not occasion one farthing more expense to your country. 3. You are not more dependent upon me now than you would have been because I should have had the power to recall you." Furthermore, "Your reasons will not bear examination. Your own disqualifications, if they had existed, would have been the same at Lisbon as at Berlin. . . . Your qualifications and title to the mission either to Portugal or Prussia are equal to those of any one of your fellow citizens, be he who he may." Having argued, in a sense, at the top of his lungs, he concluded, "Your disapprobation of a nomination by the President of his own son is founded on a principle which will not bear the test. It is a false principle. It is an unjust principle, the sons of presidents have the same claim to liberty, equality, and the benefit of the laws with all other citizens . . . it is well understood that Mr. Washington appointed you not only without my solicitation, but without my desire as the creature of favor; because you stand exactly as you did, and there is no favor in it."[11]

Or, as Abigail explained further to her sister Mary Cranch: In the president's judgment, the north of Europe was more interesting than the south, the neutral powers of Denmark, Sweden, and Prussia being more naturally allied to American interests. Therefore, John Quincy, with his "talent, sagacity and industry" might be more profitably engaged in Berlin, where the treaty renewal was pending, than in Portugal, collecting and transmitting intelligence of the "views and designs" of those courts and nations.[12]

John Quincy arrived in London at Osborne's Hotel in the Adelphi complex at six the afternoon of July 12. Presumably so weary that he could not go out and retired early, he wrote cheerfully of the next day when he "Went down this morning to Mrs. Johnson's. . . . Found my friends there and particularly my best friend, well."[13] Filling his days with meetings with colleagues and friends, evenings with the Johnsons, he apparently had avoided setting a wedding date, judging from Joshua Johnson's letter dated July 19, in which he wrote:

> In consequence of what a discussion Mrs. Johnson tells me has passed between you and her on Sunday, I am induced to believe that a matter of delicacy on your part retards your union with my child. The uncertainty how long you may remain here, together with the shortness of my stay, makes me ardently wish to see it completed. Do not then lose sight of peace and happiness, by the supposition that the request made by her mother (to make my house your home) can possibly be attended with the slightest inconveniency. On the contrary, believe me that your acceptance (*en famille*) of the small comforts we have to bestow, will diffuse general joy and delight through our little circle.[14]

He had been thus particular, Johnson continued, because he wanted John Quincy to feel "perfectly free from restraint." In other words, he wasn't pressing him, so he said, but the implication was clear.[15]

At nine o'clock, Wednesday morning, July 26, 1797, John Quincy and his brother Thomas, faithful companion and secretary, called on Louisa at her home on Cooper's Hill. Together with her family, they continued on to the modest Church of the Parish of All Hallows, founded in 675 AD, a brief walk downhill in the hulking shadow of the ever-looming Tower of London. Married at about eleven o'clock by John Hewlett, and with the addition of their friends James Brooks and Joseph Hall, they had gone immediately to see Tilney House, "one of the splendid country seats for which this country is distinguished." They had returned at four, dined together that evening. In view of the Johnsons' financial plight and imminent departure, the bridegroom understandably found "The day was a very long one."[16]

Two days later, on July 28, he wrote to his "dear and honored parents" that he had the happiness of presenting "another daughter, worthy as I fully believe of adding one to the number of those who already endear that relation to you. The day before yesterday united" them for life, and his recommendation of her to their kindness and affection he knew would be unnecessary. At the end of his letter, Louisa had added a note: "The day before yesterday by uniting me to your beloved son has given me a claim to solicit your parental affection, a claim I already feel will inspire me with veneration to pursue the path of rectitude, and render me as deserving of your esteem and tenderness, as those who stand in the same relation. . . . to meet the approbation of my husband and family is the greatest wish of my heart. Stimulated by these motives (your affection the reward) will prove a sufficient incitement never to sully the title of subscribing myself your Dutiful Daughter, Louisa C. Adams."[17]

John Quincy now divided his days between Cooper's Hill and the Adelphi. Louisa was too ill to accompany him on August 6 and again on August 17. But the Johnsons continued to entertain, and at one point John Quincy was so fatigued that he found himself hardly capable of thinking. Now one or another member of the family fell ill—"the cause an unhappy one" as they began to pack up and make preparations for their departure for America. On the last day of the month, the situation had become so painful that John Quincy was determined to stay at the Adelphi and take Louisa with him. Louisa finally moved in two days later, then to a furnished house costing four guineas a week. They were joined for dinner by the Johnsons. After supper on September 8, John Quincy witnessed the "distressing scene" when the whole family, scheduled for departure at 4:30 the next morning for Gravesend and America, took leave of Louisa.[18]

Both of Louisa's parents wrote to the couple. Joshua Johnson from Margate Roads on September 12, expecting a rough passage, wrote: "I need not attempt describing to you my sufferings on this occasion of leaving England, you have seen and witnessed them." He did not expect to hear from him often but whenever an opportunity offered, he hoped he would drop him a line. He asked that he would deliver an enclosed a letter to "my dear child and your wife, with the attendance of the most sincere affections of a fondest loving father."[19]

Catherine Johnson wrote from the Orkney Islands on September 18: "My Dear Son: Driven by adverse winds and what was still worse, adverse fortune," they had been "obliged to take refuge" on one of the Orkneys. The town was "a miserable poor place," but to her "at this moment magnificently grand. So do we measure happiness, from the transition of pain to pleasure." Knowing his "time can be better spent" than in reading her letter, she concludes "with this great truth, that no event of my life has given me more heartfelt satisfaction, than that which enables me to subscribe myself your affectionate mother."[20]

Unfortunately, Joshua Johnson's fear that he would be censored for his unseemly business practices was confirmed in a letter to John Quincy from Fred Delius, a Bremen merchant, on September 29. The information that Mr. Johnson and his family had sailed for America was certainly not very agreeable, as Mr. Johnson had gone off largely indebted to him. And now "it was impossible to describe to you," he told John Quincy, "the horror I feel at such a low, mean and unpardonable conduct." He had mistaken Johnson's character, always took him for being "open, upright and candid." Now Delius had found Joshua Johnson's records inaccurate and revealing "a certain pattern touching tender points of commercial ethics."[21]

Thomas Adams told his mother that Louisa was "indeed a most lovely woman" and, in his opinion, "worthy in every respect of the man for whom she has with so much apparent cheerfulness renounced father and mother, kindred and country to unite her destinies with his." Quoting Thomas's earlier letter, Abigail in turn reported to her sister that John Quincy had married and given him "an accomplished sister. . . . He is very happy and I doubt not will remain so, for the young lady has much sweetness of temper and seems to love *as she ought.*" Thomas had also spoken highly of her family and of their kindness and attention to him, that they were about to embark for America and settle in the city of Washington where Mr. Johnson had property. All this was welcome news to Abigail who thought they would be "an agreeable acquisition to the city at which I rejoice." And further, thinking Mrs. Johnson a "very amiable woman," she meant to welcome the Johnsons most cordially.[22]

Nabby wrote that she was a little piqued as John Quincy had not told her personally of his wedding plans. But then he must excuse her for not writing; for two years there had been many trials and struggles with which to contend. Nabby, mother of three, did not exaggerate her plight. These last 18 months she had felt marooned, "that existence was a burden" on a farm in Eastchester (modern day New Rochelle), 20 miles from New York City. Awaiting the return of her financially overextended and now insolvent husband, "a sore calamity," the pathos of her situation was of incessant concern to her parents who feared she would be "waiting & expecting, expecting & waiting," the rest of the winter, and did not rule out the possibility of her abandonment. Colonel Smith's surprising return the week of February 17 was a relief for everyone. Though Abigail was wary of the colonel's "visions, of ideal schemes, etc." and did not suppose he could satisfy his creditors, she feared that Nabby would "lose herself" if left alone any longer.[23]

Newspaper reports of the marriage of John Quincy and Louisa showed deep political bias. The *Independent Chronicle,* September 14, 1797, wrote: "Young John Adams' negotiations have terminated in marriage treaty with an English lady, the daughter of one Mr. Johnson, on Tower Hill. It is a happy circumstance that he had made no other treaty." Intolerant of insult, the *Columbian Centinel* regarded the rival Anti-Federalist (and therefore anti-Adams) newspaper as "an imposition on the public, who ought to be informed, without derogating from the merits of the ladies of England, that Mrs. Adams is an American lady; that her father is a citizen of Maryland, and brother to his excellency Thomas Johnson, Esq., late governor of that state. All who know Mrs. A. speak of her as a lady of distinguished worth, and if every negotiation Mr. A. makes in Europe terminates as happily for his country as this will for him, we shall have additional cause to praise the wisdom of that illustrious character who selected him from his fellow-citizens as one of the representatives of the United States in the eastern hemisphere."[24]

On September 22 John Quincy received his commission and instructions for Berlin but did not leave Gravesend until October 18.

Chapter 23

"WISE AND IN THE BEST INTERESTS OF THE COUNTRY"

Abigail received a harrowing account of John Quincy's journey:

We reached Berlin on the 7 [of November 1797], and three days after began my severest affliction. My wife and brother one after the other were seized with violent and dangerous illnesses. At a tavern—in a strange country—unacquainted with any human being in it, and ignorant of the language in a great measure, you can judge what we all suffered. Mrs. Adams was so ill for ten days that I could scarcely leave her bedside for a moment, and Thomas seized with an alarming inflammatory sore throat & high fever.[1]

He had first seen Berlin when he was 14, traveling with Francis Dana on his way to St. Petersburg, and he had thought the capital of the King of Prussia's dominion, with its immense green square, baroque-frosted palaces and fabled Tiergarten, more impressive than London or Paris.

This time, he seemed bemused by the dapper lieutenant at the Brandenburg Gate who was mystified by their citizenship until one of his comrades explained what the United States of America was. As his country's first minister to Prussia, John Quincy was obliged "to grope my way as I could" through the maze of diplomatic protocol of a polyglot kingdom whose present monarch, King Frederick William II, was said to be dying. If caught in limbo without credentials for the successor king, John Quincy might not be officially recognized for eight months or more.[2]

He met at five in the afternoon of November 9 with the 80-year-old Count Finck zu Finckenstein, who had served half a century as one of three ministers of state in the department of foreign affairs. The count, whose head was "full of forms and precedence's and titles, and all the trash of diplomatic ceremony," was polite but firm. The king was pleased by this mark of attention from the United States, but regretted that his extreme illness prevented him from receiving John Quincy's credentials.[3]

The second minister, the blunt but not unpleasant Count d'Alvensleben, tried consoling John Quincy with a similar tale—he had arrived in England at the time King George had gone mad, which left him from November till May without being able to deliver his credentials.

On November 16, John Quincy noted: "The King of Prussia, Frederick William II died this morning at nine o'clock, and was succeeded by his son, third of the same name." That same day, private disaster overwhelmed diplomatic challenges. Sadly, he wrote in his diary: "Mrs. Adams appeared to be recovering well all this day, and we had some hopes of escaping the misfortune which we have dreaded, and which threatened. . . . [But] this evening her complaint returned with a violence which no longer leaves a doubt, and reduces us to . . . misery."[4]

The next day, Monsieur le Commandeur de Maisonneuve, the minister representing Malta, recommended Dr. Robert Brown, a physician to the royal family. Brown, an Englishman with three daughters, would prove to be a trusted personal friend of John Quincy and Louisa. In later years, Louisa remembered Dr. Brown as a "very handsome courtly gentlemanly man, highly aristocratic . . .

showy in his manners, proud of his daughters and fond of distinction." She thought him "attentive and amiable to his patients and generally esteemed and beloved."[5]

Dr. Brown's consultation did little to ease Louisa's suffering. Two days later she was extremely ill again, and on November 30 John Quincy marked the month "as one of the most unfortunate that have occurred to me in the course of my life" and, tragically, by far not the last. Louisa had miscarried her first pregnancy.[6]

John Quincy's unceasing diplomatic efforts resulted in a note from Count Finckenstein on December 4: King Frederick William III would treat him as designated minister at a private audience the next day. From the antechamber, the count escorted John Quincy into the new king's apartment, made his bow and withdrew. John Quincy told the king of his arrival with credentials to his father with the full power to renew the Treaty of Commerce, and of his assurance that the government of the United States, upon being informed of his majesty's accession, would immediately send new credentials addressed to him. The king, in response, was very happy to maintain friendly relations with the United States, and their shared commercial interests might lead to renewal of the treaty. After further civilities, a query as to how long his father had been president, and another on whether George Washington had retained any involvement in government affairs, John Quincy withdrew.

On the whole, he was impressed with the 28-year-old king and the simplicity of his dress, a plain uniform and boots. Tall and thin, grave almost to the point of severity, his face often lit up with a very pleasing smile. His subsequent royal introductions included the 70-ish Princess Henry of Hesse-Casell, who asked him about General Washington and whether there were any living descendants of Mr. Franklin. The princess obviously made a more vivid impression on John Quincy's brother Tom who, after his presentation at her court, pronounced her "a very antique piece of furniture as are most of the female courtiers whom I saw there . . . the palsied head & hand, the tottering knee & the trembling voice bespeak age & infirmity, which all the glare of rouge or the luster of jewels cannot conceal." A number of royals not only asked about Washington,

Franklin, and John Quincy's father, but also read American newspapers and were current about the epidemic of yellow fever raging in Philadelphia.[7]

It was Prince Henry whose vision of America's future proved most interesting to John Quincy. A resident at Rheinsberg, in Berlin only because of the king's death, Prince Henry predicted that America was a rising part of the world while Europe was a declining one, and that in the course of two or three centuries the seat of art and sciences and empire would be with the United States. Civilization's progress had been westward, beginning in Asia, Prince Henry said, and it was natural that America should have her turn. His one reservation, John Quincy remembered, was, "whether we should have a center of union sufficiently strong to keep us together and to stand the trials of the inconveniences incident to republican, and especially to federative governments." Prince Henry, too, had asked after General Washington, speaking of him with great respect. He also mentioned Franklin, whose bust he said he kept, and asked after John Quincy's father.[8]

By mid-January 1798, John Quincy was tired of his demanding social life: The Grand Maréchal's ball on January 16 was "not very bright," the same as former balls, with the same company. Nor to his mind was "the charm of conviviality" to be found among the company he was keeping. Given the Prussians' "stiffness, coldness, formality, politeness, labored affability, studied attention and everything exact," he treasured his rare evenings at home with Louisa.[9]

She was now well enough to be presented at court. Of this novel experience, Catherine Johnson received rewarding letters from both daughter and son-in-law, Louisa's beguiling for its candor and modesty:

> You know, Mamma, *my partiality for great companies* therefore readily conceive what I felt at the thought of going into a society so entirely strange to me. . . . However, I got ready and went & considering all things, got through this disagreeable business pretty well. But from that day to this . . . we have not been permitted to spend an evening at home, which is so extremely unpleasant to me, that I am obliged

to pretend sickness to avoid it. The King and Queen are both young, and I think the Queen one of the most beautiful women I ever saw. She is now pregnant with her fourth child, and is but just 21 years old. She goes into company, and dances from 6 in the evening until 6 in the morning, notwithstanding her situation. The courts are twice a week one of which is a ball & the other a card party. The etiquette and usage of the court require all ministers & their ladies to attend, so that I am obliged to make one in this *elegant mob*. On every Monday evening I am obliged to pay my respects to the Princess Henry, a great-aunt of the king, where I am necessitated to sit 2 or 3 hours at whist. Once a fortnight we are obligated to visit Prince Ferdinand, who is great-uncle to the King. The Princess is an old lady who has been very handsome. She is remarkably kind to me, and has interested . . . herself very much about my health. Her sister, some years younger than herself, is the most elegant woman I ever beheld. She has been pleased to take such a fancy to me, as to make me sit down with her, at her work table, and talks whole evenings with me. . . .

Yet after all this, my dear Mamma, I do not think I am calculated for a court. To a child educated like yours, for domestic society, such a round of constant dissipation makes me wish I was once more among my beloved friends.[10]

John Quincy's letter of February 7, 1798 to Mrs. Johnson, while concise, brims with pride in his wife's success:

Since the recovery of Mrs. Adams, she has been presented at court, and to the several princesses belonging to it. Her personal appearance, as well as her manners & deportment, which are such unequivocal indications of her character and disposition, have been everywhere pleasing.[11]

John Quincy's diary during this time offers sharp contrast between outward triumph and intimate grief. Louisa was again pregnant and ill that February, and John Quincy wrote about "hopes raised to be dashed to the ground." And on March 21: "My prophetic heart! I have no doubt of the cause—The cup of bitterness must be filled to the brim and drank to the dregs."[12]

Louisa's fond brother-in-law Thomas fully understood and grieved over his sister-in-law's difficulties. "Mrs. Adams," he wrote on July 17, "extremely ill last night—sent for Dr. Brown. He thinks she must miscarry—poor little woman; how she suffers! Matrimony these are the fruits! Bitter Bitter. . . ."[13]

In public, the model of an accomplished diplomat, John Quincy was privately wounded—so distracted by Louisa's illness that he couldn't think, he said at one point, and found that keeping his diary, that is, "minuting down the transaction of every day," was excessively painful at times when there was nothing but distress to record. He walked not only for exercise but to relieve his mind. He was an omnivorous reader and collector of books, not only for their literary value but for the promise of escape between their covers. Possibly, he persisted in his study of German for similar reasons.[14]

These stratagems were of limited use, and when he could bear no more he abandoned German and became "extremely careless about every other study," asking, "of what good is it all?" At one period, he was so deeply affected by Louisa's violent bouts of illness that left him wholly sleepless, he resorted to relief with the opiates prescribed by Dr. Brown.[15]

Yet for all his problems, John Quincy would tell his mother that he was "as happy as a virtuous, modest, discreet and amiable woman" could make him. After seven months, he found their "mutual affection increasing" and described marriage to one friend as "the state of the greatest happiness that this world can bestow." On his "First anniversary of my marriage day," he wrote on July 26, 1798: "The external occurrences of the year have not been fortunate. But from the loveliness of temper and excellence of character of my wife I account the happiest day of my life."[16]

Miraculously, despite private heartbreak, John Quincy managed with steely discipline to tend his ministerial duties in Berlin. His father's words, written on June 2, 1797, were seemingly enshrined on his conscience: "You have wisely taken all Europe for your theatre. . . . Send us all the information you can collect. I wish you to continue the practice of writing freely to me, and cautiously to the office of state."[17]

Officially, according to instructions from Secretary of State Timothy Pickering dated July 15, 1797, John Quincy's commission was to renew the Treaty of Amity and Commerce between the United States and the late Frederick William II, King of Prussia, concluded in the year 1785, for another ten years. In fact, several articles were in need of change. The treaty needed to be renegotiated, not merely renewed, along with a second treaty between the United States and Sweden dating back to 1784 (which had originated with Benjamin Franklin).[18]

But beyond reworking the two treaties, Pickering told John Quincy, the president had another object in mind in placing in Berlin "a minister of your abilities and knowledge in diplomatic affairs." He was seeking correct intelligence and information on "the future system of Europe and how we can preserve friendship with them all, and be most useful to them all."[19]

On December 16, five weeks after his arrival, John Quincy issued his first "intelligence report." On the new king, he wrote:

> though quite a young man, [he] was not without some experience, and was said to have a very military turn. This indeed can hardly be otherwise here, in a country the only basis of whose power is military and which is little more than a nation of soldiery. His habits of life are domestic, distinguished by great simplicity, and a laborious activity. There is in his manner . . . nothing that betokens weakness, indolence or dissipation, the most dangerous of all qualities to a sovereign, and especially at the present time.[20]

And in appraisal of complex European relationships, John Quincy wrote: "There was an apparent coolness between this Prussian court and those of Vienna and of London; the House of Austria seemed indeed the perpetual rival of that of Brandenburg; the English alliance seemed to have been barely temporary and to be altogether dissolved. With Russia, there seemed to be a better understanding than there was before the late Empress." With France, there was "a distant and suspicious amity without cordiality, but without the least probability of renewed hostility," which he could hardly say about his own country's relationship with France.[21]

Given the shocking "misunderstandings and disputes that had been festering to a rupture for some time," he feared that war with France "must be one of the most unfortunate events" that could befall his country. Looking ahead, John Quincy warned that France would soon be under a military government by turns anarchical and despotic, a country ruined and incapable of supporting a large part of its population. With an immense army inured to every danger—its generals, of first-rate talents, unrestrained by any principle human or divine—"It is a grapple for life and death between all the ancient establishments."[22]

Two years later, John Quincy would not mention Napoleon by name in connection with the Battle of Marengo, "the most decisive engagement perhaps fought within a century." But he did concede that "the Corsican ruffian is beyond all doubt a hero in the common acceptation of the word," and supposed in other respects "as good a man as the rest of his class." John Quincy predicted, when Napoleon had elevated himself to First Consul "with a power greater than that of any limited monarch in Europe," that his fate would always depend on the outcome of warfare. "Impossible to consider him as a principled man, his ambition, like that of other conquerors, scruples little what means it uses. . . ."[23]

John Quincy reported to Pickering on January 15 the French proposal that a neutral flag would no longer protect enemy's property, and that every vessel laden wholly or in part with British goods would be lawful to seize. "This measure requires no comment, its character in reference to the laws of nations cannot be mistaken. Its effect must place us at least in a state of passive war with France—but of war unproclaimed."[24]

Nevertheless John Adams, determined to strive for peace, sent a diplomatic mission abroad intended to heal crippled relations between America and France. John Quincy's soulmate in his grave concern over developments in France was his friend William Vans Murray, his successor at The Hague. Probably there was no one besides his brother Thomas and his cousin William Cranch of whom he spoke more warmly, trusted and regarded with greater admiration than Murray.[25]

Murray took pleasure and consolation from confiding in John Quincy over "this monstrous undigested scene of general decadence in European affairs—the times which seem to call for some Mahomet." A militia of two, they had bonded together in a desperate fight against the "infernal French disease." Though aware that it was a very hazardous thing to write as freely as they did— Murray sincerely hoped that his letters might "sleep in quiet in the books"—both men were openly riveted by what would be known as the XYZ Affair. Murray referred to it as "The Envoy Extraordinary's extraordinary situation at present in Paris" in April 1798.[26]

The American peace commission was composed of three members. John Marshall, the lawyer from Virginia, reputed to be a "very fair and honorable man, and truly American," along with Elbridge Gerry, a "friendly-hearted and worthy man" who was substituted for Francis Dana, who had turned down the appointment for health reasons. The third member, Charles Cotesworth Pinckney of South Carolina—a graduate of Oxford University, a general in the Continental Army, a lawyer, who had helped secure South Carolina's ratification of the Federal constitution—was already in Europe. After he had been refused recognition as America's minister to France, the president had asked him to stay on as part of his peace delegation.[27]

The Americans conferred with three agents of the minister of foreign relations, the wily Charles Maurice de Talleyrand-Périgord, on October 18, 1797. These men "doing the filthy business of French democracy" were Jean-Conrad Hottinguer, Lucien Hauteval (rumored to be Talleyrand's natural son) and Pierre Bellamy. These agents were the X, Y and Z of the Americans' dispatches. The one that reached President Adams on March 4, 1798 related France's outrageous price for peace: a $10 million loan plus a fee—actually a bribe—of $250,000. On March 19 John Adams informed Congress of the mission's failure to reach terms "compatible with the safety, honor, or the essential interests of the nation."[28]

Puzzling news followed. According to General Pinckney, the three American peace commission members had unanimously agreed not to accede to such an insulting, unethical offer. In response, the French would negotiate with only one of the three "whose presumed disposition promises the most confidence" in their government.[29]

Murray's letter of April 13 confirmed Pinckney's tale. "Yes, sir, thus it is going. GERRY IS TO STAY." Gerry "who sees not very far into a millstone," was persuaded, Murray supposed, "that he will save his country." Incredulous, Murray saw nothing, he told John Quincy, "but improper things in Gerry's determination to separate and assume to himself in this way."[30]

John Quincy was in complete agreement about this "strange and unaccountable abandonment" of his colleagues by Gerry. It was a miserable justification for Gerry to claim that he had stayed because Talleyrand had threatened him "'that if he did not stay, a rupture would be the immediate consequence.'" Apparently, the French were now sure of having a man to deal with "who dreaded rupture more than dishonor, disgrace, and vile indignity."[31]

A "goblin story" Abigail Adams would call it. John Quincy had expected from the beginning that the mission's aim at conciliation would fail, but he did not foresee an outcome worse than failure through fracturing the envoys' solidarity. It was apparent to him that the French preferred "this mongrel condition between peace and war" in which they "plunder us as enemies and we continue defenseless as friends. . . ." One thing was as clear as the midday sun: There could be no honorable and safe settlement with the French.[32]

Yet, angered as he was by the French, war was never a solution in his mind. "Let us put on the shield and the helmet, and even draw the sword, but never cease to hold out the olive branch." For his own part, he believed that in America the government could never declare war unless the strong, unequivocal voice of the people led them into it. He saw no such inclination.[33]

Internal political hostilities were, however, enormously challenging to John Quincy, ever protective of his father. By voting to print 1,200 copies of the envoys' dispatches from Paris, the House of Representatives created diplomatic chaos. John Quincy wrote

Murray on May 25 that, sensitive to the critical state of things and the safety of the envoys, President Adams had not wished to share the dispatches with the public. Now, "the whole scene of corruption will be unfolded, and why," John Quincy wondered, "should the commissioners be exposed to the unbridled fury of the worst of mankind?"[34]

As he had feared, the Paris newspaper *Le Moniteur* deliberately chose to distort John Adams's statement on March 19 that "the powers of the envoys were extensive, as *liberal* and pacific policy required." By reprinting the word liberal in italics, the French insinuated that the envoys had themselves powers to use bribery.[35]

But John Quincy did not need the French newspapers to alert him to his parents' difficulties with the press. Partisan American newspapers taunted his father as "his Serene Highness," referred sarcastically to Abigail as the "excellent wife of the excellent President" and assured readers that the country was "under the way of the Great Mogul or a Delia Lama." Most punishing was the press's treatment of the president's position on France. Nothing but destruction, his mother feared, was the price America would surely pay for those "contemptible hirelings" who would deliberately misrepresent relations with the French.[36]

If journalists like the venomously anti-Adams Benjamin Franklin Bache and papers like the *Chronicle* were not suppressed, "we shall come to civil war." She was convinced that some sort of penalty needed to be paid by these enemies of America and of the president.[37]

Abigail was not alone in her quest. Alexander Hamilton asked why "renegade aliens connected with some of these presses" weren't sent away. And on June 16, Harrison Otis told Congress that there was greater danger to America from French infiltration than from any other source.[38]

In response, the Alien and Sedition Acts—actually four separate acts—were passed in different stages. The fourth act, the Sedition Act, served as a legal weapon against the press. A fine of no more than 2,000 dollars and imprisonment not exceeding two years were to be imposed:

if any person shall write, print, utter, or publish, or shall cause or procure to be written, printed uttered or published, or shall knowingly
and willingly assist or aid in writing, printing, uttering or publishing
any false, scandalous and malicious writing or writings against the
government of the United States . . . with intent to defame . . . or to
bring . . . into contempt or disrepute . . . or abet any hostile designs of
any foreign nation against the United States. . . .[39]

Though easily overlooked, a single sentence in Section 4 stat-
ing that this act "shall continue to be in force until March 3, 1801,
and no longer" raised powerful arguments from deeply partisan
quarters over the validity as well as the constitutionality of the act.
Thomas Jefferson, for example, along with James Madison, were
in complete disagreement. Together, they argued against a central
government usurping the powers of individual states. Jefferson
resolved that "whensoever the general government assumes undefined powers, its acts are unauthoritative, void, and of no force."
Madison protested that in case of a "deliberate, palpable and dangerous" exercise of powers not granted by the Constitution, the
states had the right and the duty to interpose their power.[40]

Jefferson crystallized his opposition to the Alien and Sedition
Acts in a letter to Elbridge Gerry describing his stance, "for freedom of the press, and against all violations of the Constitution to
silence by force and not by reason the complaints or criticisms, just
or unjust, of our citizens against the conduct of their agents." As
president, Jefferson would pardon James Thomas Callender, the
Scottish-born journalist fined and imprisoned under the Sedition
Law for his Anti-Federalist activities. Now, he enflamed the most
provocative issue of John Adams's administration—freedom of the
press.[41]

Thirty-eight years later, to refresh his memory of those controversies, John Quincy read over the portion of Thomas Jefferson's correspondence during that period, which his grandson had published.
In doing so, old wounds seemed to fester painfully, confirming Jefferson's "craft and duplicity." John Quincy wrote in his diary, "His
success through a long life, and especially from his entrance upon

the office of Secretary of State under Washington until he reached the Presidential chair, seems, to my imperfect vision, a slur upon the moral government of the world. His rivalry with Hamilton was unprincipled on both sides. His treatment of my father was double-dealing, treacherous, and false beyond all toleration."[42]

The more John Quincy read of Jefferson's papers dating from 1793 till August 1803, the "deeper and deeper" Jefferson sunk in his opinion. Jefferson's hatred of Hamilton was unbounded; of John Marshall, most intense; of his father, driven by ambition tempered with occasional compunction. Perhaps at the heart of John Quincy's disillusionment was the fact of the former friendship of the two founders. They had been colleagues in the great cause of independence, as joint commissioners abroad after the Peace of 1783. There had been a warm and confidential intimacy between them that, John Quincy allowed, Jefferson never entirely shook off, but that he sacrificed always to his self-interest, and, at the end of his life, to envy and poverty. Here John Quincy was pitiless: "Jefferson had died insolvent, on the very day of his death receiving donations from the charity of some of those whom he had most deeply injured. The circumstance was not creditable to his country."[43]

Given the steep passage of time, the wounds of partisanship remained open and shockingly raw. In time John Quincy would compare the effect of the Sedition Acts "to the falling of a spark into a powder magazine." An ineffectual attempt to extinguish the fire of defamation, it had instead "operated like oil upon the flames."[44]

In the matter of France, however, publication of the correspondence between Elbridge Gerry and Talleyrand was helpful. By August, 1798, the French, Murray told John Quincy, "have lowered their tone." John Quincy also saw progress. After two years of frustrating negotiations, he reported to Abigail on September 14, 1798, he was hopeful for the first time in months. The published letters of the American commissioners had resounded through every part of Europe to America's favor; in this contest "we are right and France is wrong." The cry of the Americans, attributed to General Pinckney, was "Millions for defense but not a sixpence for tribute." Pinckney's message left no doubt "that France dreads a rupture with the United States."[45]

Victor-Marie du Pont, a 32-year-old French diplomat, left no doubt of the radical change in sentiment among Americans in his report to Talleyrand. Du Pont—whose brother Eleuthère Irénée du Pont would found the Delaware munitions company that became the giant chemical concern—had been refused recognition on his appointment as consul general of the French Republic at Philadelphia. Returning to France, Du Pont's 41-paragraph report of July 21 was in essence a warning that grave differences between the two countries might result in consequences "*fatale*," that a rupture would only strengthen the English party and English influence in America, and that the true patriots, both French and American, wished rather for conciliatory measures on the part of France.[46]

Both French and American diplomats chimed in on the intense discussions that followed. The American Richard Codman's report home that Du Pont's memo "had opened the eyes of the Directory" was significant enough to influence John Adams to write, seeking peace with France. Meanwhile, a mysterious American, recently arrived from the United States, was also trying to exert diplomatic influence.[47]

A deeply suspicious Murray informed John Quincy that a Mr. Droghan had landed in Hamburg and was on his way to Paris with letters to Lafayette; to Merlin de Douai, then president of the Directory; and to Talleyrand from Jefferson and others with the hope of averting war between France and the United States as the only means of salvation of their party. Murray had never heard of Mr. Droghan, but if the intelligence was correct, he was a clandestine deputy from the Jeffersonians. If it cost Murray 100 guineas, he was determined to know what this envoy brought with him, and what his plans were. He had set a friend on the case and would have a little more to tell shortly.[48]

Just four days later, on August 6, 1798, Murray could tell John Quincy that this envoy extraordinaire had reached Amsterdam—but not as Droghan, though so spelled in the letter shown to him, but as Doctor Logan of Philadelphia. His passport, issued by Jefferson and Judge McKean, attorney general of Pennsylvania, was "guardedly worded, as a friend of science and humanity—the gib-berish of hypocrisy."[49]

By December 11 the Senate raised questions about the French who were dealing with "individuals without public character or authority" who were "neglecting and passing by the constitutional and authorized agents of the government."[50]

Impassioned debates followed on the usurpation of executive authority. The bill to be known as the Logan Act was signed into law on January 30, 1799. Unlike the fate of the Alien and Sedition Acts, its message regarding the rights and responsibilities of America's citizens would prove timeless:

> any person, being a citizen of the United States . . . [who] shall with-out authority of the United States, directly or indirectly commence or carry on any verbal or written correspondence or intercourse with any foreign government, or any officer or agent thereof . . . with an intent to influence the measures or conduct of the government having disputes or controversies with the United States . . . shall be deemed guilty of a high misdemeanor. . . .[51]

By early May 1799, things of "no small importance" were begin-ning to happen. The capture of the French frigate *l'Insurgente* by America's frigate *Constellation* had boosted morale at home im-measurably. The seizure convinced the French, John Quincy told his mother, that America's naval power was not as contemptible as they had represented to the world and to themselves. Also, re-maining halfway between peace and war was untenable. He saw no reason to reject new negotiations with the French government.[52]

John Adams, "always disposed and ready to embrace every plausible appearance of probability of preserving or restoring tran-quility," had in fact announced to the Senate the past February 18 his nomination of John Quincy's friend William Vans Murray to be minister plenipotentiary of the United States to the French Repub-lic. The appointment was as daring as it was initially unpopular.[53]

Personally, Murray was profoundly grateful for the appoint-ment as the sole envoy, but readily accepting of additional envoys.

He imagined correctly that his commission had caused "a great stir." In truth, as Timothy Pickering wrote, "every man who had steadily and faithfully supported his and his predecessor's administration was thunderstruck, it was done without any consultation with any member of the government, and for a reason truly remarkable—because he knew we should all be opposed to the measure!"[54]

John Quincy, acutely aware now of the rabid criticism of the new commission by both Congress and the press, was wary. The envoys would find an almost total change of men at the head of the French government since former negotiations, as they tried to repair all the mischief done by their predecessors and, as he told his mother, "bring forth golden days fruitful of golden deeds." John Quincy was satisfied that the bold stroke was proper and "wise and in the best interests of the country."[55]

Regrettably, he could not say the same about a ludicrous incident that had taken place in Congress, filling the English newspapers of the past spring. Headlined in bold type "American Manners," one of many articles reported the scandalous behavior of two members of the House of Representatives: Matthew Lyon of Vermont had spat in the face of Connecticut's Roger Griswold, who then defended himself with fire tongs against his foe's cane.[56]

John Quincy was also distressed to learn about John Fries, who had led hundreds of men in Northumberland County, Pennsylvania, in rebellion against a federal property tax. "Such things as these insurrections," he wrote his mother, "injure very much the estimation of our country with the rest of the world."[57]

By March 1799 he was busily writing out the last copy—he made a rule of doing three—of his notes on the treaty on which he had been working steadily for transmission to the Prussian cabinet ministry. On July 11, the day John Quincy turned 32, he met with Count Finckenstein and his colleagues to sign the new Treaty of Amity and Commerce between the United States and Prussia.

Six days later, John Quincy and Louisa, with Epps, Whitcomb and Andrew, left Berlin for Dresden and Toplitz. Murray thought the idea of his friend enjoying better air, away from the smoke, din and dirt of Berlin, with exhilarating scenery was "delicious." Then too, Murray wrote on August 8, "I believe that like myself you occasionally require that sort of toying and caressing of the mind which it seems always . . . to enjoy on these occasions, alone with one's wife, which were indeed, extremely sweet."[58]

Only it wasn't like that. On better days, Louisa visited with friends, most often with Dr. Brown's family, walked and played whist with John Quincy. More often, she was "unwell," or "very unwell."[59]

The past April, John Quincy had written of having had "a bad night more from concern for my wife who is unwell than from any illness of my own." This entry was just one of many bad days and nights, growing worse in warm weather. As John Quincy explained to his father-in-law, "the residence of Berlin during the summer months is not healthy for any one, and appear'd peculiarly unpropitious to her," so they spent three months away from Berlin, the warm baths of Toplitz in Bohemia having been recommended to Louisa as frequently beneficial in cases similar to hers.[60]

They had enjoyed walks, operas, museums, tea parties with friends, even shopped for bed and table linens, but failed in their main mission, to improve Louisa's health. They returned to their Berlin home on October 12. In his bleak summary of the past months, on the last day of December, John Quincy wrote, "This year would in general have been a pleasant one, but for the state of my wife's health which has been almost continually bad, and concerning which I am even now deeply concerned. The subject preys upon my spirits more than I can express."[61]

Part III

$Chapter$ 24

"TO TURN WEARINESS ITSELF INTO PLEASURE"

Though it grew more moderate after a full month of icy, nine-degrees-below cold weather, things did not improve in the new year 1800. Louisa was bled on January 2, bore the operation well but fainted in the evening and was taken ill the morning of January 8 in the process "of a fourth misfortune like three others" which she had gone through since arriving in Berlin. After a punishing night, John Quincy hoped the worst of her misfortune was over, and he could only pray to God that there might never again be the possibility of another like event.[1]

February brought no respite from "melancholy tidings." News of General Washington's death after a short illness the past December 15 was a "heavy calamity." Saddened as he was, France's formal and public tribute that month to America's first president seemed to ease his spirits. Napoleon, who had seized power as First Consul of France on the past November 9, 1799—the coup of the 18 Brumaire, year VIII, in the French revolutionary calendar—had ordered black crepe added to the flags and colors of the French armies throughout the whole republic for ten days, and delivered a funeral oration at the Hôtel des Invalides.[2]

John Quincy was also somewhat consoled that France's minister at Berlin, General Jacques de Bournonville, with his entire legation had paid him a personal visit to express their regret at the death of America's most illustrious citizen. But John Quincy had interpreted France's homage to George Washington from an additionally positive perspective. He was also thinking of America's trio of peace-seekers, when he reported to Secretary of State John Marshall on March 8 that the outcome of their mission "appears to be more flattering from day to day."[3]

The trio of American envoys—Oliver Ellsworth, former chief justice of the Supreme Court; William R. Davie, former governor of North Carolina, after a torturous journey by way of Portugal; and William Vans Murray, after pushing his way across Holland's marshes and wide chilling waters—held their first official meeting with France's minister of exterior relations on Wednesday, March 3. In general Murray faced the situation with some optimism. If there was to be a time more favorable than another to obtain justice in France, he thought it was the present. As Bonaparte wished from self-interest to establish his credentials among the neutral powers of Europe, Murray knew that America's affairs would be the touchstone.

Still, it had taken until August 20 before Murray could predict that they might bring things to a speedy conclusion. He also made it very plain to John Quincy that he was acutely aware of the twofold nature of the commission's challenges. Though settling a peace in Paris would be great in itself, it also would greatly aid John Adams's reelection. "Do not believe that we sleep over this estimate of the influence of a good end to our labor over the approaching election. We have all felt it and worked to get along." And though Murray was proud of his own role, he had to say that the great turns were contributed by Ellsworth, whose resources, his "clearness, firmness and wisdom" had staggered him. He profoundly admired the neatness and accuracy of his mind, and if he had *l'usage du monde* (the French language) and more literature, he would have been a giant among the diplomats of Europe. That man, he had concluded, "has a head of iron—just iron—that works with the precision of a mill, without its quickness and giddy manner." As for Davie, he found him "a firm, soldierly, and well-informed man."[4]

The treaty of amity between France and the United States was signed at Morfontaine on October 3 at the noble chateau of Joseph Bonaparte, president of the French commission. The impromptu *fête champetre* that followed, honoring the American commissioners, was "highly complimentary in all its features, and splendid and courtly, and friendly," in striking contrast to the terrible treatment of the last commission.[5]

Guests included the ministers of state, generals, the entire Bonaparte family and the foreign diplomatic corps, about 150 in all for dinner. The chateau was illuminated, wreathed in foliage and flowers as fireworks burst skyward from the gardens, and songs were sung in honor of reconciliation, of perpetual peace between France and the United States. With glasses held high in honor of Washington's successor, cannons echoed throughout the night.

The letters of William Vans Murray, John Quincy's cherished confidant, which were messages of the happiest tidings John Quincy had heard in years, especially the one of September 27 of successful negotiations with France, did not reach him "in due season," and he apologized. As his post in Berlin was a place of almost total inactivity, he made best use of the summer to travel out of Berlin, ostensibly to acquaint himself with the most important and valuable province of the Prussian dominion, that of Silesia (after 1945, mostly Poland and a corner of Czechoslovakia). Silesia was a very interesting province, little known to foreign travelers, yet rewarding for its beauty and cultural aspects. Also, as the only Prussian region of commercial interest to the United States, he thought it might, for example, supply linen and broadcloths on more advantageous terms than those of England and Ireland.

But perhaps his more urgent motivation, which he did not mention to Murray, stemmed from his hope that this new travel adventure would prove more beneficial to Louisa than the previous summer's journey. Hinting possibly at her fragile mental as well as physical health, "a state of debility as great as she had been in at any period before," he had thought, as he wrote in a letter to her father, "to try what would be the effect of a long and fatiguing journey . . . to amuse the mind, to make the time seem short, and to turn weariness itself into pleasure."[6]

John Quincy told Murray he thought about writing a series of letters to his brother "without aspiring to the pretensions of a printed type," that would give his friends in America some knowledge at least of a country which by no means deserved the neglect it had experienced. And his brother Thomas, now returned to America and living in Philadelphia and working in partnership with his Harvard classmate Joseph Dennie in the recently founded periodical *Port Folio,* might be in a perfect position to publish his "Letters from Silesia."[7]

John Quincy had attentively read the prospectus and the first three numbers of *Port Folio,* which would be regarded in time as "the most influential of early American magazines." The object was noble: "to take off that foul stain of literary barbarism which had so long exposed their country to the reproach of strangers, and to the derision of her enemies." Flattered to be part of this lofty endeavor, he cheerfully accepted the editor's invitation and promised his "cordial cooperation to promote his success according to the measure of my powers, and of the time left me, after attendance to my other duties."[8]

The 42 letters, dated from July 21, 1801 to January 3, 1803, included as promised "fragments, written at different times and places; nay, 'perhaps, in different humors.'" Contributions "of a miscellaneous nature" had touched on a variety of subjects: attempts at making sugar from beets, the system of manufacturing broadcloths at Grunberg and Hirschberg, the great manufacture of porcelain at Meissen, the misery of the peasants, Jewish filthiness, enmity between Catholics and Protestants, a prominent Englishman's embarrassing marital connection, the highly valued collections of prints to which he wished he might have devoted every morning while in Dresden. They also included translations into English of Juvenal and of Friedrich von Gentz, the admired German author of *Origins and Principles of the American Revolution Compared with the French Revolution.*[9]

John Quincy was surprised and not a little embarrassed by the publication of the both promising and pretentious "Letters from

Silesia" three years later, in 1804. Mostly, he regretted the allusion to the domestic histories of certain individuals he and Louisa had met in Dresden. Humbled by the experience, he hoped that if ever he qualified as an author, it would be through more elevated materials. Rather wistfully, in middle age, having fallen short of his goal, he consoled himself that "Scarcely any man in this country who has ever figured in public life has ever ventured into the field of general literature—none successfully."[10]

John Quincy, Louisa and their servants arrived in Frankfurt an der Oder the evening of July 18, 1800, after an 18-hour journey from Berlin. They traveled on to Crossen, Grünberg, Freystadt, Rottau and Bunzlau, then to Schreiberhau and Warmbrunn. By mid-August they had also visited Schmiedeberg, Landeshut, Grüssau, Glatz and Breslau. Writing from Leipzig on September 24, six weeks before they would return to Berlin, John Quincy found himself in a small, compact town of about 30,000 people, the center at certain seasons of the year of all the commerce of Germany. He had found a very pleasant walk planted with several rows of trees which circled the town. "And this is almost all I know of it as yet," he reported.[11]

It was more than he would know of it for some days. He was ill, suffering a cough and chest pains; Louisa had a bad cold and was quite unwell. On September 20, he wrote: Mrs. A "very ill indeed this afternoon," and added, "We have a dismal month before us."[12]

Obviously he knew that Louisa was pregnant, though he never seemed to use that word, referring to her child-bearing state as her "illness." On September 27 he sent for a Dr. Kapp. He consulted him not only about his own health but Louisa's; resigned to their dismal fate, he concluded that her case "no physician can remedy." The next day was rainy and cold and Dr. Kapp returned: "He prescribed for Mrs. A—Tis to no purpose." John Quincy felt somewhat better the next day, took a walk, called at the circulating library but wrote mournfully, "Mrs. A's illness rapidly approaching. She is already very unwell and will continue until the severe and inevitable trial has had its usual end."[13]

Sad and sadder notations had followed, one day after the other, hidden in the privacy of his diary. Back in Berlin, one day in

December he felt compelled to reveal to his father-in-law, Joshua Johnson, the tragic state of Louisa's health. He had been silent for so long because he was reluctant to become the messenger of ill-tidings, John Quincy wrote on December 10, loath to give pain when the truth would not have proven gratifying to his parental affection. "You have been informed of the afflictions which four times since our residence in this county have befallen us, and the shock to her constitution by such severe and repeated illnesses has occasioned long periods of so much weakness that to have related her situation to you would almost always have been to stress your sensibility."[14]

That John Quincy loved Louisa, there was no question. As her father had always found his Louisa a dutiful and affectionate child, it would be almost superfluous to tell him that she had been invariably to him a tender, faithful, inestimable wife. Their domestic happiness would have been perfect but for the sorrow of her sufferings for his own sake, "and how much more so, for hers!" And in his quest, his most anxious and ardent desire to take every possible measure to find relief, he had thought to leave Berlin, which was not healthy for anyone, but peculiarly unsuitable for her, to spend three months of the summer away in the country.[15]

But far from enjoying herself, apart from ill health, she also suffered for another cause. She was deeply affected by the "unmerited embarrassments . . . her dear and honored father" had suffered from the dishonesty and treachery of his former partners. And on this sore subject, John Quincy begged Johnson to understand that though his silence may have seemed unkind, "nothing could ever be more remote from the feeling of my heart." He had always shared Louisa's anxieties and pain on this account. What John Quincy did not share with his father-in-law was the fact that Louisa was once again pregnant, and for the fifth time.[16]

For months now, John Quincy had discussed his father's chances for a second term and was far from optimistic about the result. Contrary to his expectations, Murray's mission, he concluded, had been the origin of that very strange division of the Federalist party, which would probably transfer the office of president at the impending election into the hands of their opponents. Ever since he had learned that Alexander Hamilton was promoting Charles Cotesworth Pinckney for president, he had been fearful of the division and saddened, especially for his father's sake, to think of the outcome.

Still, John Quincy consoled himself, if the same measure that had given an honorable peace to America should deprive the president of his reelection, "it will but prove the more victoriously that he acted in his station not as the man of a party, but as the man of the whole nation."[17]

Hamilton had published *The Public Conduct and Character of John Adams Esq., President of the United States* in which the contentious secretary of the treasury and inspector-general of the army—from 1798 to 1800, during the unrecognized war with France—acknowledged Adams's "patriotism, integrity, and, even talents of a certain kind." But, he continued, he would be deficient in candor if he concealed his conviction that the president did "not possess the talents adapted to the administration of government," and that there were "great and intrinsic defects in his character, which unfit him for the office of chief magistrate. . . ."[18]

What Hamilton's provocation had been, John Quincy did not know for certain. But he thought it stemmed from his pronounced aversion to this last mission to France, and that it was his weight and influence which probably formed the principal nerve of the Federalist party's dissenters. Further, if a foreign quarrel was necessary as a pretext for keeping the army, then it followed that an army was necessary for keeping Hamilton its commander.

John Quincy also feared the consequences of division from another source, the southern states: the uprisings in South Carolina and Virginia where "the planters have not discovered the inconsistency of holding in one hand the rights of man, and in the other a scourge for the back of slaves." This was an early and seemingly oblique recognition by John Quincy of the hypocrisy of the nation's founders who preached freedom but practiced slavery. He was referring to the insurrection led by the enslaved blacksmith known as Gabriel Prosser, named after his master Thomas Prosser, in the summer of 1800. The blacks were said to be 700 strong; then again

6,000; the revolt had not surprised a young man who wondered why the blacks had not risen before.[19]

But more to John Quincy's point: Any insurrection against the government, whose unity was always tenuous, was a threat to its survival. He definitely thought that so long as the slaves did not break out in formal rebellion, the Virginians would not feel the need, for the sake of maintaining the union, to impose order. Obviously, as of December 1800, John Quincy had not heard that in the aftermath of the uprising among the southern blacks, a number of them had been killed by hanging.

The winter months would prove more dismal than even John Quincy had anticipated. Ideally, through stormy days and frosty nights, he continued on his round of diplomatic engagements, and Louisa received visits from her faithful friends, foremost among them Dr. Brown's daughters and Lady Carysfort, the wife of the British foreign minister and, ironically, the granddaughter of George Grenville, perpetrator of the despised Stamp Act of early Revolutionary times.

But more often than not, plans were disrupted. On his return from a ball given by Lord Carysfort, just after nine the night of January 30, 1801, he found Louisa so very ill that he did not leave her bedside the next evening but finished reading Samuel Butler's *Hudibras* to her and then some of Thomas Chatterton's poems. In a sense, their lives were on hold, summarily ordered according to the vagaries of Louisa's health. As he wrote in his diary at December's end: "Rise between 8 and 9. Seldom earlier; for which a partial apology arises from the very frequent bad nights my wife's state of health occasions—Revise my translation of *Oberon,* about half an hour. Breakfast; dress—Read or write till 2. Walk an hour—Dine—Spend the evening abroad, or reading to Mrs. A—more frequently the latter, until 10. Take a light supper. Bed at 11."[20]

Seemingly too disciplined to allow himself the solace of self-pity, John Quincy was, nevertheless, an acutely sensitive man, apt to turn to prayer when deeply moved. So he had done on February 2 when he received so belatedly newspaper clips of December 6, sent by William Vans Murray with the sorrowful announcement of the death of his younger brother, Charles, and wrote: "May the tender mercies of an ever gracious Heaven have attended him in his passage to the world of spirits." Charles had died the previous November 30, aged 30.[21]

But Charles's death could not have come completely as a surprise. His sister Nabby, at the time of Charles's marriage to Sally Smith, her husband's sister, had reported to John Quincy: "After all the hair-breadth scrapes and imminent dangers [Charles] has run, he is at last safe landed and I believe is very happy." Abigail had also mentioned that "people spoke in grief and sorrow of his habits." Charles had grieved—"my sleep has been disturbed and my waking hours embittered"—over his mismanagement of John Quincy's funds. The facts were vague but John Quincy's savings of 4,000 dollars were clearly lost in an ill-conceived effort by Charles to bolster their brother-in-law Colonel Smith's limp fortune. Charles, in partnership with their trusted family friend and recently bankrupt Dr. Thomas Welsh, had exchanged John Quincy's mortgage for a note from Justus Bosch Smith, the colonel's brother, a prosperous landowner. As values had plummeted, there was good reason to believe Justus Smith's note was worthless, and Abigail was dismayed that John Quincy "should be plundered by every one in whom he has placed confidence."[22]

As Abigail's brother before him, her son Charles had died an alcoholic wreck, of complications of liver and lung disease and dropsy. She took comfort that the once-darling of his father's heart was "beloved, in spite of his errors," which John Quincy's sentiments movingly echoed: He had "cordially and deeply lamented my poor brother," he told his mother.[23]

At the same time that news of Charles's death was confirmed in a letter from his brother Thomas, John Quincy read about the unfortunate election results in both the English and German newspapers: the election of Thomas Jefferson as president of the United States. Also, his father was ill of a fever. He wrote to his mother to assure her: "My mind has deeply shared in all the anxieties, and disappointments, and afflictions, both of a public and private nature which have befallen you, crowded into so short a space of time. The loss of my brother Charles, the illness of my father, and the manner in which his country rewarded a life of labors devoted to their service were all events which, I know, must call forth the fortitude and energy of his soul and of yours."[24]

Beyond sympathy, in turn philosophical and pragmatic, bitter and cynical, John Quincy's intuitive understanding of the complexities of his father's loss of a second term was implicit in all ensuing discussions of this tender subject involving "lynx-eyed statesmen" and "lion-hearted warriors."[25]

He presumed his father cared about the results of the election, but always understood that every man who served in public must look upon the injustice of men in the same light as on the ills of nature—"a fever or a clap of thunder." Also, he realized his parent had known from the earliest period of his political life that he was destined to receive at some point, sooner or later, such treatment in return for every sacrifice and toil. And, that John Adams would be prepared to bear this event with calmness and composure, if not with indifference, and would not suffer, or allow his health to be affected, or think less of his country than she deserved.[26]

"Political disappointment is perhaps one of the occasions in human life which requires the greatest portion of philosophy, and although philosophy has very little power to assuage the keenness of their feelings, she had at least the power to silence the voice of complaint," he wrote his mother. He also reminded his father that in his retirement he would have the genuine pleasure of reflecting that he had left his country in safe and honorable peace.[27]

But along with concern for his father's health and spirits, John Quincy worried about his finances and, anticipating this problem, he discussed it with his brother Thomas. Once out of office their father would be out of income as well. Although his father's principles of economy were as rigorous as he could manage, always free from serious and permanent embarrassment, he had been far from growing rich in the service of the nation, and it was not improbable that he might in his retirement have need for money. In light of John Quincy's own severe losses, his instructions to Thomas were extraordinarily generous: "I therefore authorize and direct you to consider all and every part of my property in your hands whether of principal or interest, as subject at all times to his disposal for his own use. If you are certain (as you have means of information which I cannot at this distance possess) that he will have no occasion for this, you will not mention to him that I have given you this instruction, for wishes not to make a show of offering."[28]

Still looking ahead in mid-March, John Quincy promised "while I remain in Europe" to keep his father informed, to write more often than in the past to compensate for the time his public correspondence no longer crossed his presidential desk. "I say while I remain in Europe" because, he explained to his mother, he was in expectation of his immediate recall after the new president took office. It would not be anything personal—it was just that his mission had been the source of one of the most powerful objections made against what might be called his father's foreign policy, and he presumed therefore it would be one of the first programs subject to reform.[29]

In his opinion, the use and advantage of having some public figure in the north of Europe was, indeed, at this moment more immediate than it had been at any time since he had resided there. Russia, Sweden, Denmark and Prussia were all on the brink of war with Great Britain. This left the United States as the only neutral maritime nation, a situation that might in time convince some large-souled politicians that treaties of commerce with Russia would not be a useless waste of public money. As his colleague Joseph Pitcairn wrote on the last of March: The minister of Russia had taken the occasion every time they met to speak of the American trade: "that the Emperor knew we were very commercial, great consumers of his productions, and that the conduct of our seamen and position of our country made ours one of those intercourses which the policy of the court most disposed them to encourage." But then again, John Quincy realized that those who deemed the mission to Russia inexpedient would probably find motives, if not reasons, equally strong for thinking it still so.[30]

By mid-April, John Quincy's mood had eased. He had learned with extreme satisfaction, he wrote his mother, that his father had regained his health and spirits, that he had known all along that in contributing to found a great republic, he was not preparing a school for public gratitude. Now, as his father thought it advisable, he planned to return home immediately. Obviously torn, both felt there was no choice to be made. John Quincy was deeply wounded but resigned. "Justice," John Adams thought, "would require that [John Quincy] should be sent to France or England," if he should stay in Europe. But in the end, taking charge and sparing embarrassment, he was convinced that it was his duty to call his son home.[31]

Three months later, John Quincy offered news that would bring joy as well as relief to his parents, especially to his mother who had feared after the last news of Louisa that the next would bring an account of her death. On April 14, 1801, John Quincy wrote, "The day before yesterday, at half-past three o'clock afternoon, my dear Louisa gave me a son. She has had a very severe time through the winter, and is now so ill that I dare not write to her mother to give her notice of this event. I will humbly hope that in a few days, I may be relieved from my anxiety on her account and enabled to announce to her mother only news of joy. The child is well."[32]

John Quincy had every reason to be cautious. It had been a winter of dismal notations in his diary. He had passed the period of transition between the two centuries "with prayer for a mind to bear whatever the future dispensations of his Providence might be," and he had tried mightily to avoid self-pity. But with Louisa perpetually weak and unwell he schooled himself: "Hope will intrude upon the slightest occasion and catch at every straw. I have every reason for excluding it."[33]

Pain had come with such great and daily increasing violence that he thought they could not continue: "My wife's health," John Quincy wrote, "is now the object of my greatest concern." The day after the baby's birth and for several weeks, Louisa was alternately excessively ill, dangerously ill, dreadfully ill, and, to complicate matters, she had taken such an aversion to Professor Ribke (a local physician), that she would on no account see him again. In such a weakened state, unable to attend the christening on May 4, the ceremony, John Quincy would explain, was as private as possible, limited to the absolutely necessary persons and family. The baptism was performed by Reverend Charles Proby Jr., chaplain to the British Embassy. The godfathers were the Earl of Carysfort, the British Minister at Berlin, and John Quincy Adams himself; the Countess of Carysfort was godmother. Witnesses included Thomas Welsh Jr. and Tilly Whitcomb. The child's name, John Quincy wrote, was George Washington, and "I implore the favor of almighty God that he may live and never prove unworthy of it." Afterward, John Quincy had walked with Lord Carysfort under the linden trees until dinner time.[34]

Judging from Abigail's remarks to Thomas, his mother was less than pleased that John Quincy had called his son George Washington. His mother had said, "This I think was ill-judged. I feel that it was wrong; children do not know how much their parents are gratified by the continuation of their name in their grandchildren." But she was sure that John Quincy did not have any intention of wounding his father's feelings, though he had done so.[35]

Between four and five the next morning, May 5, John Quincy was on the road to Potsdam where he would deliver his letter of recall to the king, who said he had been pleased with this American minister's residence in Berlin and was well satisfied with his conduct. His interview with the queen had proven slightly more satisfactory. She repeated nearly what the king had said but with "less appearance of saying mere formalities." They had talked about Silesia, Switzerland, sea voyages, and in less than half an hour all was over.[36]

Louisa had remained frail—described as feeble at one point. She walked with help and great difficulty across the room for the first time a month after the baby's birth. "We are not allowed to hope for a long time at best" for her recovery, John Quincy had written on May 15. Three days later, suffering from rheumatism, he found himself "without an occupation and without the resolution and perseverance to give myself one," on the verge of a depression. "Mrs. A's health varying from day to day between bad and worse keeps me in a crucifying state of suspense. My own health suffers from it in proportion." Desperately seeking relief, the weather very warm, he tried a cold bath in the river "as a species of exercise, and as a tonic."[37]

In preparation for their departure, trusted Dr. Brown had inoculated their infant son against smallpox by a new method whose "vaccine matter" troubled John Quincy. Treatment for the scourge, which his father described as "worse than the sword," had recently and radically changed since his boyhood. At nine, in Boston with family and friends, his mother valiantly leading the way in July 1776, he had braved Dr. Thomas Bulfinch's application of the Suttonian method, found to be less harsh than prior techniques—smaller punctures, the use of less virulent matter. But 20 years later in 1796, the esteemed British surgeon Dr. Edward Jenner had substituted live cowpox for smallpox and John Quincy was uneasy about the revolutionary content of this recent vaccine matter.[38]

Generally speaking, "young Mr. Adams," John Quincy reported to Thomas on May 30, was in good health, and when milk was plenty, in good spirits. But who he resembled definitely was an open question and varied according to his papa's and mamma's dearest friends. Thomas would have his turn, John Quincy promised, but meanwhile Louisa was "sorely perplexed to ascertain how he came by his blue eyes."[39]

John Quincy with Louisa, their infant George, Epps and Tilly Whitcomb left Berlin for their homebound journey on June 17. They boarded the *America* on July 8 and would reach the shores of the United States on September 3.

Just three days out, on July 11, 1801, John Quincy had written prayerfully: "I enter upon my thirty-fifth year; with a grateful heart to a kind Providence for its great indulgence through the course of my life and with a supplication for the means of making my future days, days of usefulness."[40]

Early on the morning of September 3, they dropped anchor and, with a faint and irregular breeze, proceeded slowly up Delaware Bay. In the afternoon, at Port Penn a customs house officer came on board. Too late in the evening to disembark, they sailed by Newcastle and Wilmington, where the views from the river were most beautiful. They landed in Philadelphia at noon on September 4, 1801. Happily, Thomas was at the wharf to greet them and take them to lodgings he had found for them at Mrs. Roberts's, at 130 Walnut Street.

Thomas thought his brother unchanged, "though others thought him altered." He had, however, developed a "sort of fatherly look—no doubt it would grow upon him with increase of years." With "so much to say to each other," there was no doubt of Thomas's appreciation and understanding of the "grasping genius" of his brother. And further, "If he does discuss his opinions openly, he will by the Federalist be called a Jacobin and by the Jacobins a Federalist."[41]

Chapter 25

"PAINFUL RETROSPECTION"

"The 11th of September is reckoned among the happiest days of my life," a jubilant John Adams had written in response to John Quincy's report that he had arrived stateside. Louisa's health, though infirm, was better than expected, and his grandson was "as hearty as any sailor of his age that ever cross'd the ocean."[1]

He also promised not to be impatient. Though John Quincy had not spoken of his future plans, just knowing that his son was on American soil seemed good news enough. Whenever their reunion might be, however, he hoped John Quincy would consider "my house as your home, for yourself, your lady and son, as well as your . . . servants."[2]

The couple went their separate ways on September 12. John Quincy had willingly understood that Louisa, with her family living so close by in Washington, must go to see them, taking George, her maid Epps and John's servant Tilly Whitcomb with her, while he headed for Quincy and his own family. It was the first time he and Louisa had been separated since their marriage, and he parted from her and their child "with pain and no small concern and anxiety."[3]

In stages, he headed north, meeting with friends, family and colleagues on the way. He breakfasted with Nabby, who with her six-year-old daughter Caroline was visiting her mother-in-law in New Jersey. Moving on to New York, with his sister and her husband Colonel Smith, he dined with Aaron Burr, the soon to be infamous vice president of the United States, and Edward Livingston, the 37-year-old mayor of New York City. He went to see the steam engine recently erected to supply the city with water, which he found to be "an ingenious and complicated machine." On September 17, he sailed from Crane's Wharf to Providence and took the stage to Boston.[4]

"The appearance of our country," he would report to Rufus King, diplomat and fellow bibliophile, had very much improved since he left it in 1794. "I find everywhere the marks of peace within our walls, and prosperity within our palaces, for palaces they may truly be called." Thanks to Boston's Thomas Bullfinch, future successor to Benjamin Henry Latrobe as architect of the capital in Washington, and to the influence of his grand tour abroad, costly domed and columned neoclassical mansions in contrast to prim white wooden dwellings seemed to John Quincy "to have shot up from the earth by enchantment."[5]

He reached Quincy on the evening of September 21 and had "the inexpressible delight of finding once more my parents after an absence of seven years." He spent the next day almost entirely with his parents. He walked with his father on his farm, which had been much altered and improved. He had enjoyed the luxury of seeing uncles and aunts, cousins, classmates and Dr. Tufts. The passage of time, however, had made great changes among them, especially those he had left as bachelors who seemed to be rearing three to seven children each. He did not need a census, he thought, to tell him how greatly the population of his country had grown, nor to remind him that his "mode of life has of course been altogether various."[6]

John Quincy was not alone in his sense of alienation. Both loving and realistic, John and Abigail had tried to prepare their son, diplomat and lawyer, husband and father, for the dramatic political and cultural transition that they, too, had experienced on their return from France and London. His father had much advice to offer, particularly in regard to his reestablishing his law practice, which must be "all very modest and very humble."[7]

His mother's concerns were more intimate, especially now that John Quincy had to begin anew "in a profession he never loved, in a place which promised him no great harvest, where there are so many reapers." She worried about the sudden change in his life, and the effect it would have on him and his family. She was fearful, too, of his exposure to the catastrophic scourge of pestilential fevers. And she was most anxious about her daughter-in-law "in all respects." Critically aware of Louisa's difficult confinement the past spring, Abigail thought her son "burdened by his poor weak and feeble wife and boy" and told as much to Thomas.[8]

Anticipating Louisa's difficult adjustment, Abigail warned her son, "Mrs. Adams is going to a place different from all she has ever yet visited, and among a people where it is impossible for her to be too guarded." And more, "every syllable she utters," would be received with "carping malice; such is the spirit of the party."[9]

Further, she was obviously concerned about Louisa's response to her own family's situation. Given the new administration, she feared Louisa's father might lose his job. Living in pressed circumstances in Washington, "very very much broke in spirits," Joshua Johnson was supporting his family as superintendent of stamps, an appointment owed to John Adams's presidential largesse.[10]

Meanwhile, not only Louisa but John must be vigilant. The stakes were high. Abigail obviously felt her grand vision for her revered son's future was clouded for the present, relegated during the current administration (meaning Jefferson's) to a private station hardly consonant with her ideals of patriotic service.

But before he could settle his finances, dwelling place, or law practice, John Quincy was bound for Washington. On September 25, Whitcomb had arrived with letters from Louisa. She and George had reached Washington safely and in good health. She liked Washington. When the city was finished she thought it would be "one of the most beautiful spots in the world."[11]

Assurance soon gave way to doubt and pity, for herself and for her father. Her brother-in-law Thomas, she said, was "shocked and distressed" when he first saw her. In turn, she had found her father "indeed very much broke." Altogether, her family was much altered but, she assured John Quincy, they would give him a sincere welcome. And though Epps and her sister Caroline were meant to accompany her to Boston, they apparently were not enough re-inforcement. She could not think of undertaking any part of the journey by herself. "I am too great a coward to venture alone upon so long a journey," she told Abigail.[12]

John Quincy, in the interim, had found a house, but one that would not likely meet Louisa's expectations. Nor was it readily available. "But," he wrote, "it goes to the utmost bounds of my power," and she had so long submitted to inconveniences with him, he hoped she would cheerfully continue to put up with more. Meanwhile, he assured her she would receive a most cordial wel-come and find, he hoped, an agreeable residence in Quincy. He also hoped her sister Caroline would come and pass the winter with her. In conclusion, he bade "Farewell, my best beloved. Remember me affectionately to your parents and family, ten thousand kisses to George, and believe me to the last gasp yours, John Q. Adams."[13]

John Quincy was not alone in his appreciation of Louisa. Thomas had written to tell his mother that she would be "pleased with the sprightliness and vivacity" of John's wife, that her spirits were abundant "when she is in only tolerable health."[14]

Sadly, Louisa was not in tolerable health. She suffered a fever, fatigue, cramps in her hands, and "unusual agitation of my spir-its," aggravated by her reunion with her financially and physically compromised family. Further, her troubled father "had so set his heart upon receiving you," Louisa had written John Quincy, that he would not let her go to Quincy until he came to fetch her.[15]

Most obligingly, to please his father-in-law and, more impor-tant, to most affectionately comfort his apprehensive wife, on Oc-tober 15 he planned, with extraordinary cheer, "to take the wings," he wrote Louisa, "alas! Not of the wind, but of that very earthly vehicle the Providence stagecoach." And then, by land or by water to "creep or wade or swim with all that motion can give to this sluggish lump of matter."[16]

On his arrival in Washington on October 21, there had been a round of calls due to issues of protocol on President Jefferson, Mr. Madison and his family, Mr. Gallatin and Mrs. Washington. Together with the Johnsons and the Madisons, they had attended dinner at the president's that, one guest said, was of "chilling frigidity."[17]

But it was soon apparent that Joshua Johnson was not well. He gave John Quincy some papers to look over and a watch as a token of his affection. The son-in-law was very moved, feeling as he did that Johnson was "unfortunate in his trust, and considered as a prey by every man with whom he has dwelt." At the same time, he was strongly apprehensive about the outcome of his lawsuit against his partners.[18]

At last bound for home on November 3, John Quincy and his family arrived in Philadelphia on November 12, Louisa "quite overcome by the fatigue of the journey" and very ill in the evening. She was better the next day and then worse all the following day, and John Quincy sent for their loyal family friend, the remarkable polymath Dr. Benjamin Rush, to see her. "She is under great apprehensions," he wrote, "and still more depress'd in her spirits than really ill."[19]

Dr. Rush, born in Philadelphia in 1745, patriot and linguist, author and educator, was a pioneer in the study of intemperance, and in psychiatry. He would publish *Medical Inquiries and Observations upon the Diseases of the Mind* in 1812, having already lectured about distinguishing marks between madness and delirium. While this was probably the first time that John Quincy suggested that Louisa's problems might be psychosomatic, it was not to be the last. Louisa's "great apprehensions" would be the enduring challenge of their entire lifetime.

After visiting New York, they arrived at Quincy on November 25, Thanksgiving Day, and John Quincy wrote Thomas on November 28, "I had the pleasure of introducing my wife and child to my parents. The weather was cold but perfectly clear and fine." What John Quincy wrote in his diary, however, described a different picture. Louisa, he wrote, was "quite unwell" and grew worse on successive days. In tacit disappointment and even denial, John Quincy summarized the rest of the stay as "irregular and unsettled."[20]

He might have added "troubled" or worse had he accurately described the meeting between Abigail and Louisa. Witness to the ups and downs of Louisa's days—she was ill, severely in pain, could not leave her room—Abigail was dismayed by her daughter-in-law's pitiful state, the "frame . . . so slender" and "constitution so delicate." She feared "Louisa will be of short duration."[21]

In contrast, the written record of Louisa's corrosive first impression was 43 years in the brewing. Judging from her 1840 memoir, *Adventures of a Nobody*, there had been no peace of mind for Louisa from the time of her introduction to her in-laws, though both Mr. and Mrs. Adams, she readily admitted, had received her kindly and were pleased with the baby. But beginning Thanksgiving Day, "the Quincy visitations were almost insupportable," and she longed for her home "with an impatience that made me completely disagreeable." According to her iconic "painful retrospection,"[22]

> Quincy! Had I stepped into Noah's Ark I do not think I could have been more utterly astonished. Dr. Tufts, Deacon French! Mr. Cranch! and Capt. Beale. It was lucky for me that I was so much depressed, and so ill, or I should certainly have given mortal offence. Even the church, its forms, the snuffling through the nose, the singers, the dressing and the dinner hour, were all novelties to me; and the ceremonious parties, the manners and the hours of meeting half past four were equally astounding to me.[23]

Significantly, when she did get around to writing *Adventures* it had not been intended to be a diary, she insisted, "but merely a sketch of the times long past, and of many who have long laid cold in their graves." She also admitted, with astonishing candor, to making her "observations from a perusal of Mr. Adams's Journal" which was on many days the more poignant for its pitiful and incessant concern for Louisa's well-being. In her version, she was prone to amplify—to correct but also to embellish—her husband's notes: she was not merely critically ill but her life was endangered, if she was not near death.[24]

Beyond Quincy was Boston, where they had moved to 39 Hanover Street in November. Though it might be considered the land of learning, never would Louisa consider it the land of wit. There was something, in her opinion, *"lourd et pesant"* in that scientific atmosphere that destroyed all sympathy for *"les folies brilliants"* that gave "a playful varnish to the somber colorings of real life." Quincy and Boston were too demanding. They disallowed fantasy, which was perhaps the essence of Louisa, who admitted that she would "willingly deceive myself with the idea that the world is young and innocent."[25]

With the floodgates wide open, Louisa allowed that could she have enjoyed health, and fitted herself to perform the duties required by her change of life, she might have been happy. "But I hourly betrayed my incapacity, and to a woman like Mrs. Adams, equal to every occasion in life, I appeared like a maudlin, hysterical fine lady. Not fit to be the partner of a man, who was evidently to play a great part on the theatre of life."[26]

At times of desperation, and there were many, John Quincy sent for Dr. Welsh—sometimes even at midnight. Memorably, on one especially stressful day when Louisa "was seized with extreme violence, with cramps and hysterics which continued for three hours," Dr. Welsh's treatment of drops of laudanum were the only thing that gave her ease. That was also the time John Quincy was frantic that his child, who suffered a cold, sore throat and fever, might be threatened with the dreaded measles, and he had indulged himself in a rare moment of self-pity. "I thank God," he had written that January 8, 1802, "I can yet struggle with the ills of life allotted me."[27]

Chapter 26

"NO SMALL DIFFICULTY"

For days John Quincy had been sorting and unpacking papers and books, and a lashing storm having at last subsided, on the frigid Tuesday of January 5, 1802, he moved into his first-floor office on State Street. His upstairs neighbor was the *Columbian Centinel*, published by the ardent Federalist Benjamin Russell.

He faced his future with grave uncertainty, courage blended with guarded optimism. Though he continued to write in lofty terms, even with grandeur, of the larger issues of his life, on closer view, the challenges, hazards and compromises concerning his travels, his profession, his Louisa and her interminably poor health and the care of their infant George Washington loomed vividly. As he wrote a few days later: "The commencement of my old profession again is attended with difficulties somewhat embarrassing and prospects not very encouraging." The landscape bleak, the cold penetrating, he was immensely frustrated about his books. He had brought some along with a bookcase to his office, but here at home, having spent an evening unpacking a chestful, he had no place to put them and mournfully faced the fact that he was "Much stinted for want of a room."[1]

As to where he would settle, John Quincy had just a few months earlier confided to his brother Thomas his alternate plan to consider Boston as a temporary residence. In this newer plan, he thought of moving to New York State to make his home on lands belonging to his brother-in-law, the compulsively entrepreneurial speculator William Smith, and Smith's brother Justus, property that he might take in settlement for a loan that, due to declining land values, they could not repay.

The lands were "the most promising spot on the continent for enterprise and industry," John Quincy told his brother. They also promised, at least at that moment, "independence, thrift and sport." And, though unspoken, they symbolized his last quest for a different destiny. "What say you to joining me in the plan, and going with me. . . . Why," he continued, "should we wither away our best days, and sneak through life, pinch'd . . . for the sake of a few luxurious indulgences in a large town? Reflect on it and let me know."[2]

Thomas, John Quincy's devoted companion and secretary, now 30, was a game recipient of his brother's invitation. He wanted but little time to look at it, for golden prospects could not sooner tempt him than rustic independence, thrift and sport. He was ready to embrace with "zeal, ardor, any practicable enterprise which may justify a renunciation of my present ill-required labors in an ungracious profession."[3]

He was quite ready to leave the law and the journal called *Port Folio*: "No more words—I am your man, for a new country & manual labor. Head-work is bad business, and I never was fond of it." Almost jubilantly, he had signed his letter: "My capital is chiefly in my hands & feet, and they are at your service."[4]

The plan, however, if it had ever been serious one, fell through. As did John Quincy's earlier determination, also confided in Thomas, that he was "more and more determined not to concern myself whatsoever in politics." Besides, there was not a party in their country which an honest man could join without blushing, for a politician "must be the man of a party—I would fain be the man of my whole country."[5]

But he was already involved. His second week in his Boston office, Dr. Welsh had come round to hint at the probability that Judge Thomas Dawes would quit the Massachusetts Supreme Court to move to a municipal judgeship and that John Quincy might be nominated in his place. This hadn't worked out, but by February 20 John Davis, another respected judge, had personally asked him to join the Commission on Bankruptcy and by March 3 he was formally sworn into office. It was a service that began cordially but would terminate with bitter repercussions, especially, to put it mildly, on his mother's part. As for his election only one month later to the Massachusetts State Senate, and confirmed on April 5, he claimed to have "little desire to be a senator, for whether it will interfere with my duties as a commissioner or not, it will interfere with pursuits much more agreeable to me than politics."[6]

He was in fact striving for some peace of mind, judging from the affectionate exchange mid-March with his father. When the weather and the woods kept them at a distance for days if not weeks, John, in robust thanks for John Quincy's recent gift of the work of the provocative French literary critic Jean-François de La Harpe was nearly ecstatic: "I am in love with La Harpe, I know not there was such a man left. If I had read the work at 20 years of age, it would have had, I know not what affect. If it had not made me a poet or philosopher, it certainly would not have permitted me to be a public man." John Quincy was in complete agreement, in principle. But for the present time, he gently explained, there were other considerations, in need as he was of "repairing the dilapidations of seven years upon my stock of legal learning."[7]

Then too, there was "a second pursuit" that had captured his attention (and he might have added passion). He had been invited to join the Society for the Study of Natural Philosophy, whose members were required to systematically record their experiments, essays or lectures in a *Book of Transactions*. In a sense, the society offered him the same consolation that his father had discovered in the companionship of La Harpe, but with far greater consequences. These amateur experiments would prove to be of lifelong interest, influence and accomplishment. In time, he would be celebrated as "one of the greatest political spokesmen for science, especially for pure and basic science, in the nineteenth century."[8]

On January 7 he had gone with his cousin Josiah Quincy, future president of Harvard, to attend his first meeting: Membership was limited to ten; the textbook was to be Jones's edition of the British scientist George Adams Jr.'s essays.[9]

By the end of the month, he rose mornings between 4 and 7, made his fire, brought up his accounts, wrote in his journal and read Adams's lectures until breakfast at 9. Whether these studies were more challenging than he anticipated he did not say. He had graduated from college with honors in mathematics and would write, as a future secretary of state for whom "science and education were passions and amounted to a religion," his "Report on Weights and Measures" which his father John Adams admired as a "mass of historical, philosophical, chemical, metaphysical and political knowledge" intended to improve man's life through scientific learning. Meanwhile, he did vow that during the course of the present year, he would undertake to do little or nothing: "My object will be to *learn*. It is late, in the progress of my life to complete my education, and perhaps after my age, a man can claim but little—Yet must I not despair."[10]

A quarter of a century later, as president of the United States, in his stirring first State of the Union Address on December 6, 1825, he included what one distinguished historian called the "clearest statement ever made by a president of the government's duty toward knowledge." In that address, John Quincy called on America to contribute her share of labor and expense for "the improvement of those arts of knowledge which lie beyond the reach of individual acquisition."[11]

Half a century had passed, he continued, since the declaration of America's independence, and bearing in mind that France, Great Britain and Russia had devoted the genius, the intelligence, the treasures of their respective nations to the common improvement of man in these branches of science, was it not incumbent upon the United States to contribute "our portion of energy and exertion to the common stock?" He urged most specifically the erection of an astronomical observatory in order to study "the phenomena of the heavens." Europe had 130 of these "lighthouses of the skies." And further, weren't we cutting ourselves off from the means of returning light for light while we had neither observatory nor observer on our half of the globe "and the earth revolved in perpetual darkness to our unsearching eyes?"[12]

Later still, his role in the creation of the Smithsonian was a crowning achievement. Its establishment had been misunderstood, suspect (British money was tainted) and bitterly fought (by British would-be heirs). Its donor of half a million dollars, James Smithson—the British mineralogist and illegitimate son of the Duke of Northumberland—was even "supposed to be insane." John Quincy had wondered about the attitude of his political colleagues: "so strange is this donation of half-a-million dollars for the noblest of purposes that no one thinks of attributing it to a benevolent motive." Whereas he, almost biblical in his reverence, "regarded the bequest as a high and honorable sentiment of philanthropy, and a glorious testimonial of confidence in the institutions of the Union."[13]

Despite John Quincy's nearly negative appraisal of his service in the Massachusetts Senate, his son Charles Francis in editing his father's papers would evaluate that year in office as the "most critical of his whole career." More specifically, John Quincy revealed in that time a maverick's pattern of voting that spanned his entire lifetime of public service: He followed no pattern but only the strictures of his conscience and ideals.[14]

In his own words years later, the first act of his legislative life "marked the principle by which my whole public career has been governed." John Quincy was referring to his second day in office, May 27, when he had proposed adding to the council of the Commonwealth two or three members of the opposite party to his own, in a conciliatory procedure to achieve a proportional representation of the minority as it existed in the two houses. "But no," he wrote in his diary, "they would not hear me."[15]

That same session, the Senate was divided on a petition for the removal of two Republican judges, and while the Federalist members voted in the affirmative, John Quincy had voted with the

Republicans in the negative. In defense of his vote he had written: "Because of the decision of the Senate in this case, affecting in the highest degree the *rights,* the *character* and *reputation* of two individuals, citizens of this Commonwealth ought not to have been taken, without giving them an opportunity previously to be heard in their own defense." Echoing his party colleagues' displeasure, the *Independent Chronicle and Boston Patriot* reported the same day that "The Federal leaders said, 'this man is not our friend, but against us.'"[16]

Again in February 1803, he was not to be considered a party loyalist in regard to the proposal of a new bank, apparently the talk of the town for the past three years, to which his opposition was known and his consent was critical. The ardent Federalist James Otis had taken him aside to win his backing, to tell him that he had "no conception of the interest and agitation which that affair had excited; the application embraced a great multitude of the most respectable persons in this town, and almost the whole commercial interest." But the next day, to the dismay of his Federalist colleagues, John Quincy spoke in opposition to the bank on grounds that the subscription to the stock should be open to all the citizens of the Commonwealth, and again cast a negative vote on the final passage of the bill. As one outraged colleague wrote: "A great bank in Boston, of twelve hundred thousand dollars, is now in debate in the Senate, having passed the House. It is supported by the principal moneyed men in this town, about twenty altogether, and opposed by John Q. Adams, whose popularity is lessened by it. They say also he is too unmanageable."[17]

When in 1825 John Quincy took measure of what he called "the noviciate" of his legislative labors in the year 1802, he had concluded with honesty and humility that he was not able "either to effect much good, or to prevent much evil. I attempted some reforms, and aspired to check some abuses. . . . I wanted the authority of experience, and I discovered the danger of opposing and exposing corruption."[18]

Yet despite his dismal self-appraisal, John Quincy was proud of the two orations he delivered that year that formed, he said, "not inconsiderable incidents in the history of my life." The first, "An

Address to the Massachusetts Charitable Fire Society" on May 28, was a testament to his own horror at finding "their wooden city . . . a vast tinderbox, kindling at every transient spark." It was his rousing plea to his fellow citizens to "secure the lives and properties of our fellowmen from destruction by fire." As a worldly historian, he would remind his audience that Augustus Caesar had "found the Roman metropolis of brick and would leave it of marble." Improvements had followed, and John Quincy believed that the speech "had contributed to rebuild the city of Boston."[19]

In his second notable talk, "Oration at Plymouth . . . of the First Landing of Our Ancestors at that Place," he stated proudly that there was no previous example of a nation "shooting up in maturity and expanding into greatness with the rapidity, which has characterized the growth of the American people." And he also made a brief argument "on the *right* of Europeans to form establishments in the American wilderness, and to extinguish upon just and reasonable terms all the natural rights of the aboriginal Indians conflicting with it." Writing about this premise after a lapse of more than 20 years, "I still think unanswerable" was his puzzling comment.[20]

Heading for Quincy the day before his thirty-fifth birthday on July 11, 1802, which John Quincy planned to spend with his parents, the stage was so crowded that he left it at Milton to walk the rest of the way to Quincy. The next morning he swam, strolled the hills with his father, was visited by family friends and continued his summer reading, Plutarch's treatise (this day, on the tranquility of mind), and more of Madame de Sévigné's *Letters* with which he was very pleased.

Back in Boston the following week it was, more or less, business and pleasure as usual until July 20, when he noted "This day the new appointment of General Commissioners of Bankruptcy arrived here" and that "none of the former Commissioners are appointed" with the exception of Judge John Dawes. Eleven days later, the last of the month, he quite reasonably concluded "As a new set of Commissioners of Bankruptcy have been appointed, I shall henceforth have but little of that business to do."[21]

This would seem to be John Quincy's last reference to the presidentially appointed commission, but not so his family's. That his mother most heatedly resented his not being reappointed as a commissioner, and blamed Thomas Jefferson for it, was revealed in a correspondence two years later that began with her response to the news of the death of Jefferson's daughter Mary (called Polly) on April 17, 1804, whom she had known and loved. Eventually the Commission on Bankruptcy would prove, in Abigail's words, to be "a small object."[22]

In November John Quincy was urged to stand as the Federalist candidate for election to the House of Representatives, a race he lost by 40 or 50 votes due, the party claimed, to a rainy election day and poor attendance in remote parts of town such as Charlestown, Medford and Malden. But such excuses were not acceptable to the failed candidate. In his opinion the loss was "one of a thousand proofs how large a portion of Federalism is a mere fair-weather principle, too weak to overcome a shower of rain." Personally, he admitted, he was somehow relieved from a heavy burden and a thankless task of blind party loyalty. In fact, he seemed to look back on the last year with some pride. "I have been able to preserve my principles and my independence," he wrote on December 31.[23]

Just over one month later, on February 2, 1803, John Quincy would learn that his name was listed for the nomination as United States senator from Massachusetts. After days of negotiations, on February 8, he was elected by the committee to a six-year term, to begin in late fall 1803. John Quincy would speak of it after only two months in Washington as "the only important incident of my political career. It has opened to me a scene in some sort, though not altogether new, and will probably affect very materially my future situation in life."[24]

John Quincy maintained that in the year just passed, 1802, not only had he enjoyed better health than he had for many years before but, most curiously, that his wife also had "on the whole been more favored in this respect than at any period since their marriage." It was true that they had 40 guests to their home the past January— had opened all the rooms, upstairs and down, served refreshments at "prettily ornamental" small tables—and that John Quincy had danced the whole evening. But it was also true that Louisa suffered constantly from headaches, and might be taken very ill after a walk or on a random evening. She had been "excessively affected" when told on April 27, 1802 of her father's death, to such an extreme that she had refused to see Dr. Welsh.[25]

Louisa was pregnant that spring of 1803, and again John Quincy's dismal notations of her physical and mental suffering mirror those of previous years, and obviously they took their toll on him as well.

John Quincy had spent the weekend in Quincy—both parents had been ill—and returned early to Boston on Independence Day, July 4, 1803, to learn that he had a second child, born about three that morning. Mother and child were as well as he could hope: "for this new blessing," he offered his "humblest gratitude to the high throne of Heaven." Thomas, in jovial mood, congratulated the couple, writing that his opinion of Louisa grew more favorable in proportion to the increase of the male branch of her family. Also, in recalling his joyless state of celibacy, he hoped the compassionate regard of his fruitful (he had crossed out prolific) relatives should at least be willing to perpetuate his given name.[26]

By contrast, Louisa's mother, obviously moved by the event, wrote with restraint, editing her words to "My Dear Sir" with great care. "Last evening's mail presented me your welcome letter, announcing the pleasing intelligence of [my dear Louisa] of the safety of my beloved child. Permit me to offer my sincere congratulations on this happy event. The memorable day which gave birth to the little stranger is I hope a presage to his independence, the greatest blessing (health excepted) this world has the power to bestow." Weighing six-and-a-half pounds at birth, the infant was baptized John, presumably after his grandfather.[27]

In the next days, Louisa was "as well as her condition admits;" "unwell," then "suddenly, and for some time excessively ill." On July 11, his thirty-sixth birthday, John Quincy noted "with sorrow to think how long I have lived, and how little purpose."[28]

In September he packed glassware and china, leased the house in Court Street, deposited all letters, letterbooks, journals and diaries in a large trunk in his father's office, and concluded, on the eve of departure, that the past two years, like every other period of his life, "had its pleasures and its pains." His finances, perpetually a challenge to him and to Louisa, would always figure in the latter category. The transition from his European post had not been, as he put it, "agreeable," and yet he found it less mortifying than he might have expected. Easily connecting his mind to it—so he claimed—he was able to endure and surmount with the help of friends the collapse of Bird, Savage & Bird; the London banking firm's collapse had wiped away a significant amount of the Adams family capital, greatly affected John Quincy and his parents, and had necessitated the sale of his Hanover Street house in Boston.[29]

On October 4, John Quincy, Louisa, her sister Caroline, young George, three-month-old John and the maid Patty embarked on the packet *Cordelia*—boisterous weather accounted for grievous delays—and arrived at Paulus Hook (across the Hudson River from Manhattan) on October 9. Nine miles away, at Gifford's Tavern, crowded with people who had fled New York's epidemic of yellow fever, "it was no small difficulty" with which John Quincy was able to find a single room to lodge the whole family. They were barely installed, however, when Louisa, suffering from "violent fatigue and agitation" fell suddenly and violently ill, at which point John Quincy sent for a Doctor Johnson who treated her with a powerful opiate that put her to sleep.[30]

With family and friends to lend a hand—John Quincy had deposited George with his sister Nabby, who lived nearby—they were able to leave on October 12. Planning ahead, John Quincy had written Thomas in Philadelphia to ask him to reserve a private carriage and four horses—Louisa could not possibly travel night and day as they must do if they were to take the stage, and besides they had a lot of luggage—and to make the cost as favorable to them as he could. At last, having traveled since the first week of the month, at dusk on the evening of October 20 they arrived in Washington. It was day four of the session of Congress, and by curious coincidence they had encountered Secretary of the Senate James Otis, who was going from the Capitol to the president's home to inform Jefferson of the Senate's ratification of the Treaty of Cession enabling the Louisiana Purchase, which passed in the Senate with 24 yeas and 7 nays.

Regrettably, the "accidental illness" in John Quincy's family, which detained him on his way to Washington to take his seat in the Senate, had prevented him from voting for the ratification of the treaties, "one of the happiest events which had occurred since the adoption of the Constitution." It would also turn out to be one of the thorniest personally, given John Quincy's scrupulous reading and interpretation of the Constitution.[31]

The family headed for the home of Louisa's sister Nancy and her husband, Walter Hellen, with whom they would board, two-and-a-half miles from the Capitol, located on what would be identified in later years as (approximately) 2600 K Street NW in Georgetown.

At 11 the next morning, October 21, John Quincy proudly took his seat in the Senate immediately after delivering his credentials and being sworn to support the Constitution of the United States. Ten days later, in his monthly review, he sounded almost serene with contentment. Now his mode of life was more uniform. Rising at 7, he wrote until 9, took breakfast, dressed, and soon after 10 began his 45-minute walk. Two-and-a-half miles later, he reached the Capitol around 11 and usually found the Senate assembled, sitting until 2 or 3; when adjournment was earlier, he went to hear the debates in the House of Representatives.

Home at 4 for dinner, he passed the evening idly with George in his room or with the ladies. Supper was at 10, the hour for bed was 11. He noted, somewhat prophetically, "the interest with which my mind seizes hold of the public business is greater than suits my comfort or can answer any sort of public utility."[32]

Chapter 27

"ANOTHER FEATHER AGAINST A WHIRLWIND"

To John Quincy's grandson Henry Adams, the annexation of Louisiana—827,967 square miles for $15 million, officially acquired on April 30, 1803—"was an event so portentous as to defy measurement: it gave a new face to politics, and ranked in historical importance next to the Declaration of Independence and the adoption of the Constitution." Doubling the country's size, it was the making of part or all of 15 additional new states. Never had the United States government gotten "so much for so little." In fact, he concluded, at $15 million, "it cost almost nothing." Unfortunately, in personal terms, the same could not be said for his grandfather.[1]

John Quincy's thoughtful yet torturous resolution of the legal dilemma posed by the Louisiana Purchase came at a wrenching price intellectually, politically and emotionally, with not only sleepless nights but the enmity of both political parties, over his entire lifetime.

Writing about October 20, 1803, his first day as a proud voting member of the national legislature, John Quincy had embraced the Louisiana treaties, "with vote and voice and heart," when every other Federalist in the Senate opposed them. But in supporting these treaties, "the most important that ever occupied the deliberations of Congress," he had done so as an independent, on his own, as far as his duty, his unalterable, unalienable dedication to the principles of the Constitution would allow and no further. Governed, and strictly so, by his sense of honor and truth, compromise was not in his vocabulary let alone his character.[2]

On this point, he had differed dramatically from Thomas Jefferson. "While the Constitution," Jefferson admitted, "has made no provision for our holding foreign territory, still less for incorporating foreign nations into our union," he was convinced, he told a colleague, that it was the duty of both houses of Congress to ratify the Louisiana Purchase and to pay for it, "so as to secure a good which would otherwise probably be never again in their power."[3]

John Quincy was as keen on the acquisition, regarding its object as "the highest advantage to us." Only, his legal palette being pure black or white, there was no sidestepping the Constitution. Convinced that the annexation of Louisiana to the Union transcended the constitutional powers of Congress, he believed that an amendment to the Constitution was needed to achieve "full, undisturbed and undisputed possession of the ceded territory."[4]

The subject of Louisiana had preyed on his mind for some years. Writing from Berlin on April 25, 1801, referring to a report "circulating all over Europe" that Spain had ceded the Floridas and Louisiana to France, John Quincy had warned his father: "We must be upon our guard." France might want Louisiana "in order to obtain a powerful influence over the U.S."[5]

France had long had a tangled and slippery history in the multi-century juggling act that was Louisiana. Though Spain's Hernando de Soto had claims as the earlier explorer in 1543, it was Robert Cavelier, Sieur de La Salle who had taken official possession of the Mississippi Valley in the name of France, and named it Louisiana in honor of King Louis XIV in 1682. As a result of the punishing French and Indian War, it reverted back to Spain by the secret Treaty of Fontainebleau on November 3, 1762.[6]

Thirty-three years later, Spain had guaranteed the United States (in what was known as Pinckney's Treaty) in 1795 free navigation rights on the Mississippi River at the port of New Orleans, the "right of deposit" to store wares between shipments for export. By 1800, Louisiana was back in French hands and the situation had progressed. Given the monumental ambition of Napoleon's French government, John Quincy feared "most imminent danger to the political liberties of all Europe, and even of the United States."[7]

But John Quincy had underestimated Jefferson's awareness and chilling analysis of the potential danger of a French presence so powerfully embedded in American territory. "The cession of Louisiana and the Floridas by Spain to France works most sorely on the United States," Jefferson wrote to the U.S. minister to France, Robert R. Livingston, in April 1802.[8]

There was "one single spot the possessor of which was their natural and habitual enemy"—the port of New Orleans, indispensable to the country's commerce. "[B]y placing herself in that door," France had assumed the attitude of defiance. With Spain, "given her pacific disposition and her feeble state," she might have retained it quietly for years, then yielded it to America's possession. Not so in the hands of France—"the impetuosity of her temper, the energy and restlessness of her character" would make it impossible for that country and the United States to continue as friends, meeting in so "irritable" a position.[9]

The day that France took possession of New Orleans would seal America's union with Great Britain and their marriage to the British fleet. And, under these circumstances, France might consider ceding to the United States New Orleans and the Floridas, which to a great degree would relieve the nation from "taking immediate measures."[10]

This was the case Jefferson wished Livingston to make: "to return again and again" to press for the cession of New Orleans. In this negotiation, Jefferson urged Livingston to "cherish" Pierre Samuel Du Pont de Nemours, one of the most intriguing of the formidable real estate sales force involved in the Louisiana Purchase.[11]

Du Pont, four years Jefferson's senior, born on December 14, 1739, was an economist, journalist, educator, loyal friend of Lafayette, former councilor to King Louis XVI. The elder Du Pont had met Jefferson during his service as minister in Paris. In regard to

Louisiana, in their uniquely affectionate correspondence between April 1802 and November 1803, the American entrusted Du Pont with the deepest of state secrets and said he "always considered him as the ablest man in France." In turn, the Frenchman confided disarmingly of his "need to be free . . . need to be useful . . . need to live with men of lofty feelings."[12]

Du Pont was leaving for his native Paris, and Jefferson thought it safe to trust his letters with him. "You will perceive the unlimited confidence I repose in your good faith [and] in your good disposition to serve both countries when you observe that I leave the letter for Chancellor Livingston open for your perusal." If Du Pont could be the means of informing Napoleon Bonaparte of all its consequences, "you will have deserved well of both countries."[13]

Du Pont's responses were testament to his mastery of the "entire importance" of the subject. According to his analysis, "To say: 'Give us this country; if you do not we will take it,' was not at all persuasive." The argument for achieving a friendly surrendering of France's property needed to be addressed from a different angle: "the poverty with which all great powers are constantly threatened, which only powers of the second rank escape, leave you only one means: that means is acquisition, it is the payment of money."[14]

"Offer her enough to make her make up her mind before she takes possession," Du Pont advised. Furthermore, "these treaties must be quickly made, the longer you bargain and the worse the bargain you make, the more complete would the break be."[15]

The story of the dazzling negotiations in which, contrary to official instructions, the two statesmen, James Monroe and Robert Livingston, bought the whole instead of just part of Louisiana, is the more fascinating for the personal accounts not only of the Americans but of the elite of the French government.

Napoleon's plans for Louisiana began to unravel with news printed in the French newspaper *Monitour* on January 7, of the ruin of St. Domingo (Haiti), the death of General Victor Emmanuel Leclerc and the decimation from yellow fever of his army, originally destined to move on to Louisiana. Napoleon had brooded for some months over the catastrophe until, according to his finance minister François de Barbé-Marbois, on Monday morning, April 11, he declared, "Irresolution and deliberation are no longer in season. I renounce Louisiana. It is not only New Orleans that I cede, it is the whole colony, without reserve." He concluded the discussion with orders to this effect and that Marbois "interview this very day with Mr. Livingston."[16]

Later that same day, it was the ubiquitous Foreign Minister Talleyrand who startled Livingston with the question of whether the Americans wished to have the whole of Louisiana and the price they would pay for such an acquisition. It was not a subject Livingston had thought about (having pressed for New Orleans and the Floridas for the past year), but he supposed they might offer 20 million francs. "Too low an offer," Talleyrand replied, "but he would be glad if I would reflect upon it and tell him" the next day, Livingston reported to James Madison. As James Monroe, appointed envoy extraordinaire by Jefferson, was expected to arrive in two days, Livingston said he would delay any further offer.[17]

Monroe, having sailed for France on March 8, reached his Paris hotel at one o'clock on Tuesday, April 12, joined Livingston in meetings that resulted in the April 30, 1803 agreement of the French finance minister Marbois and the two American negotiators on a $15 million purchase, culminating on May 22 with the formal signing of the treaty for the Louisiana Purchase in French (and a week later, the formal signing of the treaty in English).

After the formal signing and a round of handshakes, Livingston told his colleagues Monroe and Marbois: "We may live long but this is the noblest work of our lives."[18]

Though Livingston was deservedly proud of his role in the Louisiana Purchase, there were angry questions in Congress about the fact that Florida was definitely lost for the time being, boundaries remained undefined and an alarming group of northerners— members of the arch-conservative Essex Junto—were even then secretly plotting secession from the Union.

By no means did John Quincy qualify as one of "the inflexible Federalists" Jefferson spoke of. His only issue with the Louisiana Treaty was its incompatibility with the Constitution, which the addition of an amendment might easily resolve, a solution he would pursue with a missionary's zeal. One week after taking his seat in the Senate, he called on the secretary of state to ask whether a proposal had been brought forward for an amendment of the Constitution to carry into effect the Louisiana Treaty. If any such arrangement was made, he should wait quietly until it should be produced, but if not, he thought it his duty to move for such an amendment. James Madison answered that he did not know that it was universally agreed that an amendment was required. For his own part, had he been on the floor of Congress, he saw no difficulty in acknowledging that the Constitution had not provided for such a case as this, but that it was "the magnitude of the object" that mattered. John Quincy agreed but still urged the necessity of removing, as speedily as possible, all questions on the subject. He departed with a most vague agreement to further meetings on the issue.[19]

Pursuit of an amendment had seemed an entirely logical step after precise, lawyerly scrutiny of Article III of the Louisiana Purchase: "The inhabitants of the ceded territory shall be incorporated in the Union of the United States and admitted as soon as possible according to the principles of the federal Constitution to the enjoyment of all these rights, advantages and immunities of citizens of the United States, and in the mean time they shall be maintained and protected in the free enjoyment of their liberty, property and the religion which they profess."

And to John Quincy it was a logical conclusion that the recent document took liberties with the Constitution's express statement (Article IV, section 3):

New States may be admitted by the Congress into this Union; but no new State shall be formed or erected within the jurisdiction of any other State; nor any State formed by the junction of two or more States, or parts of States, without the consent of the legislatures of the States concerned as well as of the Congress.

The Congress shall have power to dispose of and make all needful rules and regulations respecting the Territory or other property belonging to the United States; and nothing in this Constitution shall be so construed as to prejudice any claims of the United States, or of any particular State.

But by November 1, after numerous debates and hollow exchanges, John Quincy had heard enough to realize that no amendments he proposed would ever be made, a fact of his present situation that seemed only to inspire him to press onward. "The qualities of mind most peculiarly called for were firmness, perseverance, patience, coolness, and forbearance." Though he admitted the prospect was not promising, "yet the part to act," he vowed, "may be as honorably performed as if success could attend it."[20]

And persevere he did. On November 3, during the long debate in Congress over payment due France, he was "free to confess" to his colleagues that he saw no possible way of extricating themselves but by an amendment, or rather an addition, to the Constitution. And if proposed, "as I think it ought," it would be adopted by the legislature of every state in the Union.[21]

The speech on the third was merely a draft for the one he gave on November 25 when he reviewed with James Madison the measures he intended to propose. One was an amendment to the Constitution permitting Congress "the power to admit into the Union the inhabitants of any territory which has been or may be hereafter ceded to or acquired by the United States." The second was a bill enabling the inhabitants of Louisiana "to declare their assent to their admission into the Union of the United States." In response, Madison had not thought the bill necessary; it was too comprehensive, might endanger the ratification, and it was best to say simply: "Louisiana is hereby admitted into this Union."[22]

But John Quincy was indomitable. The whole transaction might be accomplished in time to enable Congress to pass during that same session subsequent laws for the government of the Territory of Louisiana.

Yet what had seemed moral, reasonable, logical and ethical to John Quincy was met with silence. Though ignored by the Senate, which almost unanimously refused him even the benefit of a committee of inquiry, the same was not true of the press and colleagues.

They questioned his disaffection from the Essex Junto formed that winter by members of the Federalist party who insisted that the annexation of Louisiana made for a new confederacy to which the States were not bound to adhere.

His begrudging nemesis, the *Aurora* reported on December 1:

> The speech of Mr. John Q. Adams, son of the late President, is pecu-
> liarly gratifying; he is an eastern man, as may be supposed not much
> in love with Mr. Jefferson, yet he tells us the acquisition of Louisiana
> is an event of such great importance that to be able to fulfill the treaty
> an amendment of the Constitution ought to be made, if necessary;
> and he declared his belief *"that every state in the union would be in
> favor of it."* This cannot be called democratic cant or such like, it is
> the language of the son of Mr. Adams, and probably such as our late
> President himself would express.[23]

In a private exchange between colleagues, Thomas Lyman wrote Timothy Pickering: "I hope Mr. Adams will learn by the treatment he receives from the dominant party that any attempt to accommodate himself to their views must end in disappointment as it regards him, as well as to cause regret to his friends." As far as he had been able to observe, John Quincy "inclines to be peremptory. Those who have known the father will readily, I conceive, observe as one has done before, 'Curse on the stripling, how he apes his sire.'"[24]

Not surprisingly, his mother, angered by the "stabbing in the dark," was quick and eloquent in her support. Though she expressed the thought, almost wistfully so, that his vote might have been different on some occasions, she was certain that John Quincy would as much as possible keep his mind free from party influence and vote as his conscience aided by his judgment should dictate—however impossible it was, she added, to judge accurately because "we see not the causes which have operated towards the decision."[25]

While his father offered his unqualified support, he too was concerned: "I do not disapprove of your conduct in the business of Louisiana. I think you have been right," he wrote on February

25, 1804, "though I know it will become a very unpopular subject in the northern States, especially when they see an account of expenses which must be occasioned by it."[26]

John Quincy was mindful of his precarious, tightrope position, his endless and fruitless pursuit "of another feather against a whirlwind"; of a desperate and fearful cause which he felt compelled to pursue or "feel myself either a coward or a traitor." "Yet for what?" he asked himself one rainy, snowy December day, knowing full well the answer: "For the Constitution I have sworn to support—for the Treaty that binds our national faith—for the principles of Justice—and for opposing to the utmost of my power those who in this measure will violate them all."[27]

Again, pondering his future, he wondered that his ideas were so different from those of his colleagues and questioned the danger of clinging to his own principles when

> The country is so totally given up to the spirit of party that not to follow blindfold the one or the other is an inexpiable offence. . . . Between both, I see the impossibility of pursuing the dictates of my own conscience without sacrificing every prospect not merely of advancement, but even of retaining that character and reputation I have enjoyed. Yet my choice is made, and, if I cannot hope to give satisfaction to my country, I am at least determined to have the approbation of my own reflections.[28]

He had voted against two bills, one on the appointment of a committee to form a government for Louisiana, and the second, the motion on taxation of the newly acquired territory.

The first, he explained, was premature. They could not wield with too prudent and wary hand the rod of empire and dominion that they had assumed over a foreign people. In his opinion, "It was nothing less than a total revolution, not only of government, laws, and principles over a people consisting of an hundred thousand souls (largely French and Spanish) whose language we did not understand, whose manners, opinions and prejudices were totally variant from our own, over a people whose subjection to our authority had been established without their previous consent, and whose liberty, property and religion, we are bound by solemn obligation to protect."[29]

As to the second bill, he could not prevail upon himself to vote for a law to tax the people of Louisiana "until in some shape or other their formal assent to our authority and acquiescence to our jurisdiction should have been obtained."[30]

Ultimately, John Quincy felt he had opposed the bills as long and as far as his opposition could prevail. By January 31, though he hadn't made his peace, he had at least made his choice. In the belief that "A senator should not sacrifice the interests of the whole Union to those of a section," he thought "it was the duty of good citizens to acquiesce in Mr. Jefferson's Louisiana Purchase."[31]

With obvious reluctance and a measure of steely defiance, he had reported to his mother a week earlier: "We have been engaged for several days in debating upon a question for prohibiting the slave trade in our new _____ of Louisiana (I leave the designation in blank for want of a name to call it by)—We have just decided by a large majority, in favor of the prohibition—I voted against this upon the principle that we have no right to make *anything* for that country at present."[32]

In regard to the matter of slavery, though John Quincy declared flat-out that he was opposed to the dread issue, his remarks in the Senate as he voted against the Louisiana territorial bill were disturbingly ambiguous: "Slavery in a moral sense is an evil but as connected with commerce it has its uses." Besides which, "The regulations added to prevent slavery are insufficient. I shall vote against them." Possibly, it was either or both of these statements that incited the remarkably inaccurate observation by historian Samuel Flagg Bemis that "at this stage of his political career, Adams took no opportunity to record himself unequivocally against either of these evils and to vote against them."[33]

By the following autumn, he was ardently backing a "Proposed amendment to the Constitution on Representation" first introduced by the Yale graduate and lawyer William Ely and printed in the *Columbian Centinel* the past June 16 and 20, "for the purpose of correcting that humiliating inequality which gives a representation to the slave-holding southern planters nearly double to that of the Massachusetts farmer" based on counting each slave as $\frac{3}{5}$ of a person when determining a state's population.[34]

It was, John Quincy said, "a measure of the deepest moment to the welfare of the people," Ely's reasoning "so clear, so strong, so indisputable." The number of those "miserable beings already existing in some States was such as to occasion the most serious alarm in all humane and thinking minds. The rule of representation prescribed by the Constitution of the United States was universally admitted to be unequal and by allowing representation for slaves, we encourage and reward the infamous traffic of human flesh. . . ."[35]

Furthermore, it would not be necessary at this day to prove that in the eye of morality this purchase and sale of man was criminal. "Can anything," he asked, "be more inhuman? Can anything be more absurd? Thus, in whatever point of view we contemplate this provision in the Constitution, whether as moralists, as politicians, or as citizens, it called aloud for amendment."[36]

John Quincy's eight-page manifesto, the fifth in a series signed with the name of the Roman General Publius Valerius, was published with *The Repertory* on November 6. The following month John Quincy planned to deliver before the Senate the expanded version (13 pages this time) of his proposed amendment on representation; the magnitude and importance of his message had only heightened. "Such a mode of representation is therefore unjust, inasmuch as it is unequal. It is unjust, because it establishes inequality of rights, and of the rights the most precious in the sight of freemen between fellow citizens of the same community. It is also an inequality in the highest degree immoral and impolitic. Its immorality is derived from its conferring the first of political privileges upon the basis of the greatest outrage on the rights of mankind."[37]

And then, seemingly to clarify an earlier remark, he asked: "Upon what principle, can all this tempest of indignation against a most profitable commerce be founded, in a nation so essentially commercial as ours, but upon the consideration that the trade itself is, and ever must be, a heinous crime in the sight of God, and therefore ought to be in the sight of man?"[38]

"Let us," he continued, "to set this argument in a clearer light," consider the inconsistency between this part of the Constitution and the laws of the country. By rewarding slaveholding states for every additional slave they imported—five thousand negroes introduced from Africa promised three thousand and more votes—they were empowered in the election of members of Congress, a president and vice president of the United States.[39]

It was also on this point that John Quincy more than hinted at his reason for voting against the prohibition of slavery. Basically, it was a lack of trust in the motives of those who had favored the bill. It was here that he thought the language of the Constitution tended to favor the interests of the slave owner. "As if to say: 'We, the slave owners, will suffer nothing to impede our purchase of slaves to the full extent of our purses and our credit. And in order to have the market exclusively to ourselves, we will seize, confiscate, fine and imprison without mercy, every attempt to carry or sell slaves elsewhere.' And surely, if this was the spirit of their laws, it was one of injustice and inequality in the extreme."[40]

Toward the last of December, John Quincy reported to his father that the proposition for an amendment to the Constitution regarding slavery had not yet been taken up, and indeed probably would no longer be discussed that session. So many of the state legislators had already declared against it, "without one instant of adoption or approbation, not even by Connecticut, that it would be absurd to spend time in haranguing upon it in Massachusetts." But he held out some hope, foreshadowing his own heroic role in the defense nearly 40 years later of "the unfortunate men," the slaves who sailed on the schooner *The Amistad*. "The time will come," he predicted, "when its real merits will meet proper investigation." But at present, the people of that state appeared to have disavowed the act of their own legislature supporting their rights and interests. What they did not choose to ask, they may rest assured, he surmised, their neighbors will not be anxious to grant.[41]

On March 17, 1804, with the first session of the Eighth Congress about to close, John Quincy hoped to be back in Quincy at the end of the month to tend to his farm on Penn's Hill. But even as members were dropping off, he found himself involved, as he told his mother, "in the extraordinary business of trying an impeachment." He wished, he wrote in his diary, to remember and practice the advice of the Reverend Mr. Parkinson—"to forget and forgive the resentments and injuries which have been excited and occasioned during the session of Congress."[42]

But that March had been a particularly fretful month, not only in Congress but personally. Fear of whooping cough had threatened the entire family; Louisa and the children were often ill. One evening their maid Martha Stokes, called Patty, suffered a violent fit of hysterics which proved impervious to Dr. Weems's heavy dosage of 200 drops of laudanum and nearly a pint of pure brandy, John Quincy wrote. Though her health had improved, she would not return home in the company of John Quincy on his journey from Washington to Quincy.[43]

Louisa Catherine had decided to remain in Washington with her family. But well before John Quincy reached Boston, while visiting in New York City with his sister's family, he had the pleasure of reading Louisa's letter containing information of the children's health and "sorrow by that of your own disposition," the beginning of a correspondence that was to be "equally painful and unexpected."[44]

Chapter 28

"LIKE A FISH OUT OF WATER"

*O*f the years her husband served in the Senate in Washington and commuted homeward to Quincy between sessions, Louisa said that her life was "unsettled and divided," and the loss of his company so great, she never would acquire a sufficient degree of philosophy to overcome the challenge. Lavish with ornate professions of devotion, she assured John Quincy that there was "No human being who loves you half as well as your faithful and affectionate wife."[1]

In the glare, however, of their five-month correspondence that sadly reopened the wounded temperament of her bridal days, there was no wife more bitterly unhappy. Brimming with complaints about their finances—he had little property in Boston, she was in such want of linen, the children were all in rags—she was ever mournful over her vanished dowry, pitiable in her pregnancies, quixotically moody, and feverish with "spasms." She was above all, and this admittedly so, the victim of her own towering and enduring aspiration to nurture John Quincy's candidacy for president of the United States, whatever her deprivation.[2]

As though she must remain true to an earlier pact with him, she did not mean to complain nor to *"make conditions,"* but merely to act solely for his future as he thought fit. But one August day in 1804, lonely beyond consolation, her vows gave way and with rare insight she acknowledged for fleeting seconds that she did not have the emotional or physical stamina to make the sacrifice. As she told John Quincy, "This separation life is not worth having," and she "would cheerfully relinquish it." "Formed for domestic life, my whole soul devoted to you and my children, yet ambitious to excess, my heart and head are constantly at war, my affection is the most powerful, and at this moment when every fear is roused I would willingly give up every future hope of your attaining the highest honors your country admits to be assured we never part more."[3]

But the mood was momentary and some months later it grieved her, she confided to her mother-in-law Abigail as though to a co-conspirator, to see her husband forfeit "the best years of his life in so painful and unprofitable a way."[4]

While he was in New York City, John Quincy read Louisa's first doleful, if not scorching, letter that not only questioned their separation, but shook the tenets of their marriage. In tender apology he had explained, "Of coldness or unkindness to you, at any time, I am not conscious. The first wish of my heart is to make you happy as far as it is in my power, and it is a subject of deep affliction to me that my means of accomplishing this wish are not more adequate to it in ardor and sincerity."[5]

He never, he continued, could be happy distant from her and never would be if he could avoid doing so. Patiently he reminded her that it was her own choice. And that it had been his "unvaried principle and hoped it will always be so," to leave the place of her own residence entirely to her own election. But thinking as he did that his home was the *proper* and only proper home of his wife and children, it was best that he remain silent with respect to some of the observations in her letter. "The duties of filial, of conjugal and of paternal tenderness are all equally sacred," and he wished to discharge them all with equal fidelity.[6]

He reached Boston on April 14, 1804, in all an eight-day journey from Washington. "I feel already to use a vulgar phrase 'like a fish out of water,' without you and my children," he wrote Louisa the next day, and hoped to hear from her that she was very well.[7]

On the contrary, already finding their separation "insupport-able," she was also feeling guilty. Conjuring up the forlorn image of herself as the penniless daughter of a bankrupt though beloved parent, she was apologetic. As a "wretched correspondent with a sincere desire to please," she was now ready and willing to return to Quincy immediately and to do everything in her power to lessen the heavy burden she had become. After all, she wrote in May, "I brought you nothing and therefore have no claim on you. . . ."[8]

As for the house in Quincy, his birthplace—any house was good enough for her. She did not believe she had made any objection to it. Only that she never ceased to regret the house in Franklin Place and most sorely their poor old house in Hanover Street—much as it wanted repair, she doubted she would ever be mistress of one so comfortable again. Then too, given the calamitous state of his affairs that had required the sale of these two favorite dwellings in Boston, she had thought it would be both improvident and inconsistent to build on to the Quincy house. But she judged differently now; he ought to make what alterations he pleased as soon as possible. After all, she added, if her mother-in-law Mrs. Adams could live there with four children, she could certainly live there with hers.[9]

John Quincy thanked Louisa for her offer to come to Quincy, and assured her that she would be able to accomplish it. But the summer was already running so fast that by the time she reached Quincy, it would be necessary to think of returning, and two journeys in so short a time with two infant children were more than he should be willing to hazard. Besides, in point of economy, it would be a considerable increase instead of a diminution of expense. Next spring, however, he hoped she could come home with him, though the final decision "shall be altogether as you choose."[10]

He added one parting thought about her unceasingly ravaged health—with sympathy and tact: "Your excessive tenderness overpowers the delicacy of your constitution and brings on such violent attacks." He continued in healing tones: While it was "perhaps impossible to square our conduct in such cases to the dictates of cool reason," he would suggest her making the effort "to moderate those emotions which we cannot suppress" and to be prepared with

resignation for those which Providence "through mysterious purpose, chastises us, for our own good." In plainer words, she might
heal her disorders with discipline, philosophy and prayer, the pillars
of his salvation which would remain forever beyond her reach.[11]

On his arrival in Boston, stopping off at Whitcomb's Tavern, he
had met up with his father and was home in Quincy before dark
the Saturday evening of April 14. Just weeks later, with spring beginning to show her face, the fields changing from gray to green,
and peach trees bursting into blossom, he thought himself "growing a farmer." He bought 55 apple trees in the process of planning
an orchard for his own house, pruned and trimmed a number of
trees on his father's lower garden, and planted some forsythia. He
also read passages of Spenser's *Fairie Queen* to his father, Smith's
translation of Thucydides, Juvenal's *Satires,* and an analysis of the
laws of the United States in chronological order. Having time for
a little farming, for much more plodding in the library, and for
business—"an abundance of turnpikes and bridges and banks"—
and for preparation for the next winter in Washington, except for
missing his family, he thought he should enjoy a greater tranquility
of mind than he had known for some years.[12]

On July 26—Alexander Hamilton had died on July 12, 1804
after a duel with Aaron Burr—a funeral procession in Boston
honored the former secretary of the treasury whose dreadful fate
seemed to spread a general gloom. Louisa was concerned about
John Quincy's failure to attend the service. "The opinion of the
world must be favorable," she said.[13]

John Quincy was obliged to her for her advice, often useful to
him he allowed. But he could not attend any outward demonstra-
tion of regret that he could not feel at heart for the person who had
slandered his father in a "lying pamphlet," *The Public Conduct
and Character of John Adams Esq., President of the United States.*
To do otherwise would be a "species of hypocrisy" to which he
could not descend.[14]

Louisa also passed on news of reports that Bonaparte was declared emperor of France, which meant, if true, and John Quincy
would agree, writing "that the French would plunge into [titles]

with all the fondness of children for a new rattle. Imperial Majesty Josephine, Imperial Highnesses Joseph and Louis, Grand Elector, and High-Constable, Serene Highness Arch Chancellor Cambaceres, and Arch Treasurer Lebrun, etc. etc.—was there" he asked, "ever so horrible a tragedy concluded with so ridiculous a farce?"[15]

Horticulture and gossip aside, in August, in want of exercise, John Quincy went swimming off the dock with his brother Thomas, his most frequent companion in his wanderings through the marshes, shotgun in hand hunting robins, pigeons and other small birds. He had looked forward to a reunion with Thomas. The past years had been a trial for his brother.

Thomas, at 32, on his return from abroad had settled in Philadelphia and was practicing law when he joined his Harvard classmate, Joseph Dennie, in 1801 in the publication of the "politico literary miscellany" named *Port Folio*. John Quincy had loyally, and also as a deeply partisan American, heartily endorsed his brother's new venture to which he would contribute eagerly and generously. Offended that the English still possessed exclusively "the carrying trade of all our literature and science," he regarded the new publication, he said, as a means of upgrading American literature, of removing "that foul state of literary barbarism, which has so long exposed our country to the reproach of strangers and to the derision of her enemies." As promised, John Quincy sent along—with the caveat of anonymity—his translation of myriad German and French works; his own "Letters from Silesia" had filled the initial publication on January 3, 1801.[16]

Dennie, "a man of strong prejudices and . . . rash conclusions," lawyer, writer and former editor of the *Farmer's Weekly Museum*, had by the third issue offered proof of his aspirations, to such an alarming degree, in fact, that John Quincy asked Thomas to urge the firebrand Federalist to coolness, even moderation, on political topics.[17]

Unfortunately, other problems festered. They included the matter of *Port Folio*'s irregular publication and unpaid bills, and Dennie's indictment on charges of sedition on July 4, 1803 (he would be acquitted two years later), at which time John Quincy most earnestly wished his brother would "shake the dust" from his feet. If he could exchange the bustle of the great city for rural retirement, he thought Thomas could make a more comfortable and agreeable life in his native state.[18]

By chance, early in the year after Thomas's departure, the January 7, 1805 edition of *Port Folio* carried John Quincy's eloquent tribute to his "much loved friend" William Vans Murray, who had died, age 42, on December 11, 1802. "While indulging the private tear," he remembered him for his original humor, his wit, his enlivening fancy of a poet, his taste for literature, fondness for the pursuits of science. "He was one of the brightest characters which had arisen in the American union, since the establishment of its independence."[19]

Some weeks after his return to Washington, on November 19, 1804, John Quincy sent a quasi-thank-you note to his father for his hospitality during that summer's residence under his roof. He also apologized for his "stiffness of temper," which he hoped his father had not mistaken for a lack of affection. He hoped next summer, however, he might at last occupy his own house and enjoy frequently the pleasure of his company.[20]

In cordial response, his father said that the stiffness of temper he mentioned never appeared to him more than was "honest and justifiable." He also hoped politics would not be so dark as to destroy all comfort. Of still greater concern, he did grieve, he admitted, over John Quincy's health and feared that his clothes weren't sufficiently warm as "flannels and thick cloaks were not more necessary in Holland than in America." Personally, he never could travel without getting sick till he learned to encase himself in wool flannels within, and cloak or greatcoat or both without.[21]

Clearly, his father had shared his correspondence with his mother who had smiled, she told John Quincy, at his claim to an apparent stiffness of temper. If he said that he had contracted a reserve and a coldness of address upon entering company which was unnatural to him, she would agree and rejoice that he had made that discovery. Further, she knew the reasons for his change in personality and appearance: the austere, even foreboding figure that proved invaluable in foreign service but was regarded unfavorably in the parlors of Quincy and Boston. For one, "having resided abroad during such critical periods as you witnessed both in Holland and England, you were obliged in your public capacity to be constantly upon your guard, that nothing improper escaped you either in words or looks." For another, "The constant state of anxiety for your family served to fix a weight of care upon your brow incompatible with that ease and freedom for which you [were] once noted."[22]

And another thing: he needed to upgrade his personal appearance. As this was an especially sensitive subject, she hesitated to bring it up, fearful that he would be callous to her admonitions. Nevertheless, it was her conviction that "A good coat is tantamount to a good character; and if the world be a stage, it's as necessary to dress as to act your part well. . . ."[23]

All of this maternal wisdom had masked her heartfelt concern. "There are some maladies so deep noted that the most delicate hand dare not probe," though the attempt might fix an incurable wound. "A depression of spirits," she was certain had been "the chief cause of his low state of health." In this instance, his father, who unquestionably shared Abigail's distress and frustration, was both supportive and candid in his attempt to analyze and help John Quincy cope with his darker moods.[24]

John Quincy did admit that, with respect to his work in Congress, he might be "too anxious for my personal and political situation." He felt, for example, it was his indispensable duty to comb through a dazzling amount of papers, although most of his colleagues were far less concerned about the work as they felt nothing they could say or do would have any impact. But then, he argued, if little or no good could be done by the most assiduous efforts, experience might prove "that much mischief may be prevented."[25]

Now he also fretted about taking positions no one else did and feared "pride of opinion and paltry vanity" mingled itself with his judgment. Also, as an extemporaneous speaker, he was critical of his comprehension, his inability to furnish the words to finish a thought (which "results in the use of a substitute which threw the whole into a burlesque") and concluded that he "must never flatter himself with the hope of oratorical distinction."[26]

Thankfully, John Quincy did allow that it was possible that by continual exertions, part of the ill effects of these infirmities might be remedied. Eventually, as he was to be commemorated as "Old Man Eloquence," he would obviously prove himself to have been a brilliant student.

The Eighth Congress met on February 15, 1805, for the second time in three years for the "extraordinary business of trying an impeachment." The first case had involved Judge John S. Pickering of the District Court of the United States for New Hampshire; the present one focused on Samuel Chase, associate justice of the Supreme Court. Both Federalists, one was confessedly and notoriously insane and therefore helpless, the other was horrifically unpopular for his rabid partisanship. John Quincy acutely questioned whether either of the men was justly subject to removal from office on charges of "treason, bribery, or other high crimes and misdemeanors" according to the terms stated in the Constitution, Article II, Section 4.[27]

Severely at loggerheads with Thomas Jefferson, John Quincy had protested the president's "attack by *impeachment*" upon the judicial department of their national government, "conducted with great address as well as with preserving violence" for the past two years. He had sympathized with Pickering's son Timothy who said that the president was making a "mockery of a trial, where not justice, but the demon of party, determined the proceedings."[28]

But Judge Pickering's fate was foreordained, or so it had seemed. As the senator from New Hampshire, the historian William Plumer, had noted: "The removal of the judges and the destruction of the independence of the judicial department had been an object on which Mr. Jefferson had been long resolved." Under his predecessor John Adams and the Judiciary Act of 1801, both district and circuit courts had multiplied; the night before President Adams's departure from office, he had appointed 16 Federalist circuit judges and 42 Federalist justices of the peace. Immediately after taking office, the Republican Congress set to work on its replacement with the Judiciary Act of 1802. Obviously, if Adams could pack the courts with "midnight judges," Jefferson had every intention of unpacking them, ousting them en masse as quickly as possible.[29]

Proceedings for John Pickering's impeachment had begun on February 4, 1803, grounded on four articles of complaints against him, the fourth most damaging: contrary to his trust and duty, "said Judge at said Court was intoxicated, used profane and incoherent language," and had become "a scandal and was unfit to perform his duties."[30]

Actually resolved one year later, on January 3, it was, John Quincy said, his misfortune to sit as one of Pickering's judges, and he thought it one of the most cruel of prosecutions, that of "convicting, of high crimes and misdemeanors, a person of integrity and intelligence laboring under the heaviest calamity that almighty power could inflict upon man."[31]

On March 2, the House of Representatives voted 19 to 7 to impeach Pickering on charges of drunkenness and unlawful rulings; on March 12 the Senate, 20 to 6, resolved that he be removed from office. As for John Quincy: "If proceedings like ours were had in a court of law, I have no hesitation in saying, it would be considered as a mere mock-trial."[32]

The day after the Senate passed sentence on Pickering, the House of Representatives appointed a committee to draft impeachment articles against Maryland-born Samuel Chase, a judge of the Supreme Court of the United States. John Quincy considered Chase a strong-minded man of ardent passions and of boisterous temper that "knew no laws of caution," but nevertheless a worthy man.[33]

In his "tirade" in Baltimore on May 2, 1803, Chase had warned a grand jury, owing to the repeal of the Judiciary Act of 1801, that the Democratic-Republicans had gravely compromised the independence of the judiciary already shaken to its foundation by the abolition of the 16 circuit judges and that their republic "will sink into a mobocracy—the worst of all possible governments."[34]

In response, President Jefferson questioned whether "this seditious and official act on the principles of our Constitution and on the proceedings of a State," ought to go unpunished. Ten months later, Chase was saddled with eight articles of impeachment. The eighth article censored Chase's "harangue" before the grand jury in Baltimore as "highly indecent, extra-judicial, and tending to prostitute the high judicial character with which he was invested to the low purpose of an electioneering partisan."[35]

In the anxious days that followed the impeachment trial begun early in 1805, both Congress and the public had "swallowed up" every step of the proceedings. On March 3, 1805, in "a scene of total confusion and factiousness," in the most remarkable transaction of the second session of the Eighth Congress, Samuel Chase was acquitted on all the charges.[36]

Mid-March John Quincy reported to his father that President Jefferson was said to have told a member of the Senate that impeachments were "but a clumsy engine to get rid of judges." And weighing the result, John Quincy did not imagine Jefferson would very soon attempt to ply it again, though he anticipated that other efforts would be initiated.[37]

Congress adjourned on May 3, and this time Louisa with their two sons and her sister Eliza accompanied John Quincy to Quincy. Having left on March 30 by stage, ferry, packet and carriage—the cold and stormy weather would turn warm shortly—they arrived at the senior Adams's home on April 5. A few days later John Quincy was up at his own house, inspecting it as he would daily for weeks, hiring a carpenter, moving furniture from storage in Boston, until at last on April 25 he could actually say that he "came *home*." That is, home to the humble, classic seventeenth-century salt box, the white rough-hewn wooden farmhouse in which he had been born, but in which he had not spent a night for more than 25 years.[38]

One month later, laying out his garden, when John Quincy complained that it was "impossible to reverse the doom of idleness and mental imbecility," things took a turn for the better. On June 26 he learned that the Corporation of Harvard University had the previous day elected him professor of oratory, a chair established by the Boylston Foundation. The appointment revived his spirits. He could not think of a task more agreeable to him than planning his reading list. He would begin with Quintilian, add a chapter of Aristotle's *Rhetoric* and part of Plato's *Gorgias* (a Socratic dialogue) in Denier's translation. Learning by heart

Les Racines Grecques would prove wearisome but he would not give it up.[39]

Though he was concerned about the combination of serving in Washington and in Cambridge, he wrote to the chairman of the corporation and overseer of Harvard, Samuel Dexter, that he "felt a warm and anxious desire to justify as far as I was able their confidence in me." But he did take exception to one of the rules: With the most perfect deference and respect for the legislature of the college, he could not perceive in a professorship of rhetoric and oratory anything which peculiarly called for so minute a scrutiny into the details of the professor's religious opinions. To his great satisfaction, the confirmation of his appointment on November 7 noted that the corporation and overseers had voted to agree to the proposals made in his two letters respecting the professorship effective 1806; the rules and regulations would be modified accordingly.[40]

November 8 marked the time to return to Washington. Only the children would stay behind in Quincy. George would spend the winter with Abigail's sister Mary Cranch who would charge two dollars a week for board. John would stay with his grandmother Abigail. Motivation for the decision to separate themselves from their children wasn't clear, but it was one with heart-rending resonance for Louisa. Possibly they had outgrown their rooms at the Hellen home, and without the "encumbrance" (Abigail's word) of children, she thought John Quincy would do better in lodgings closer to the Capitol.[41]

But once back in Washington and settled in at the Hellens' house, Louisa admittedly brooded over her children's absence. Having been "compelled," she wrote, to leave them, she could not command her feelings and must trust to Abigail's kindness to hear from her frequently.[42]

Abigail had reassured her daughter-in-law that her children were very well taken care of, "much better off than they would have been at any boarding house in Washington where they would have been confined in some degree or have mixed with improper persons." Furthermore, there could not be anything more disagreeable than transporting young children either by water or in crowded stagecoaches at such distances. However reluctant Louisa might feel at being separated from them, she should suppose that her "own judgment, experience and good sense would have convinced you of the propriety of the measure" she had taken. Abigail herself had experienced separations of all kinds from children equally dear to her, and however great and painful the sacrifice, it was the duty of a parent to consent to do so in the interest and benefit of their children.[43]

Still, Louisa hourly felt the loss of her children. "Kiss my darling children for me over and over and remind them continually of their mother whose every wish on this earth centers in them." And should Abigail have "any apprehension of George having worms," she advised giving him "five drops of spirit of turpentine upon a lump of sugar every other morning. . . ."[44]

Actually, Abigail's immediate concern was John Quincy. He gave himself unnecessary anxiety about George, who was "round as an apple, rosy as a carnation." But what of his own health? She fretted about the two-and-a-half-mile distance from the Hellen home to the Senate; a tedious long walk with an empty stomach was very unhealthy and served to irritate the whole nervous system which wants comfort and consolation instead of plodding. "Pray assure me that you will ride in all bad weather," she had pleaded.[45]

The day after their arrival in Washington on Thursday, November 29, John Quincy paid a round of official calls at which time, in the presence of several of his colleagues, he noted in his diary, that "the President mentioned a late act of hostility committed by the French privateer near Charleston, South Carolina, and said that we ought to assume as a principle that the neutrality of our territory should extend to the Gulf Stream, which was a natural boundary and within which we ought not to suffer any hostility to be committed."[46]

In response, Senator Gaillard had observed that on a former occasion in Jefferson's correspondence with the troublesome former envoy from the French Republic, Edmond Charles Genet, and by an act of Congress at that period, the United States had seemed to claim only the usual distance of three miles. But the president replied that he had then assumed that principle because Genet's intemperance had forced them to settle on some point, and they were not then prepared to assert the claim of jurisdiction to the extent they were reasonably entitled to. Back then he had taken care expressly to reserve the subject for future consideration. "In the meantime," he added, "it was advisable to *squint at it,* and to accustom the nations of Europe to the idea that we should claim it in the future." And to conclude, "The subject was not pushed any farther."[47]

That is, not until John Quincy heard Jefferson's fifth annual message delivered on December 3. He sent a copy of it under a blank cover to his father.

> You will perceive that the message is in a style and tone which have not been fashionable of late years. . . . It speaks of our differences with *Great Britain and with Spain* in a tone of spirit which has not been usual in the late communications from the national executive and recommends measures for the protection of our seaports, of the *militia* laws and more gun boats. It hints slightly at the materials for 74 gunships on hand, but without positively recommending their employment.[48]

John Quincy was not exaggerating. The actual content was even more alarming, in particular the fifth paragraph of the message:

> Since our last meeting the aspect of our foreign relations has considerably changed. Our coasts have been infested and our harbors watched by private armed vessels, some of them without commissions, some with illegal commissions, others with those of legal form, but committing piratical acts beyond the authority of their commissions. They have captured in the very entrance of our harbors, as well as on the high seas, not only the vessels of our friends coming to trade with us, but our own also. They have carried them off under pretense of legal adjudication; but, not daring to approach a court of justice, they have plundered and sunk them by the way, or in obscure places, where no

evidence could arise against them; maltreated the crews, and abandoned them in boats in the open sea, or on desert shores, without food or covering. These enormities appearing to be unreached by any control of their sovereigns, I found it necessary to equip a force to cruise within our own seas, to arrest all vessels of these descriptions found hovering on our coasts within the limits of the Gulf Stream, and to bring the offenders in for trial as pirates.[49]

John Quincy had supposed that the president's message would naturally lead to talk about non-importation and prohibitive duties, but he believed that they would do little more than talk about them. His mother disagreed. Judging from what she had read, she told John Quincy, "Bonaparte is a comet, a blazing one. Mankind gaze and are astonished at his power which every victory increases. . . . You will have a much more busy time in Congress than was contemplated."[50]

And indeed, by January 13, 1806, he valued his father's ploughing the past December as "an occupation which I need not say to you is much more agreeable than laboring at the political plough." The season in Washington had been in all respects uncommonly mild until within these past few days, and the world of parties and legislation as moderate as the temperature of the atmosphere. "But as the new year advances the weather grows cold, and we grow warm." The possibility of an unprofitable contest with Great Britain he feared could do the most harm, "not to the other, but to ourselves."[51]

Chapter 29

"APOSTASY"

Like Louisa, John Quincy would also brood about his unsettled and divided life, but with resignation. Still, it was
his core belief that he had discharged his duty to his country and
therefore the existing administration "in every measure that my
impartial judgment could approve."[1]

And there was much to approve and also disapprove in these
early days that would lead to the War of 1812, which concluded
officially with the Treaty of Ghent. By stirring coincidence, John
Quincy as ambassador to Russia would help to forge that treaty in
1814.

"Full of sound and fury against the foreign *nations*," "unqualified submission to France and unqualified defiance of Great Britain, are indeed the two pillars upon which our measures," that is,
the country's fate, rested, John Quincy had reported to his brother
and father. In his view, his country was trapped between the trade
restrictions of Napoleon's Continental System and the British Rule
of 1756 that fostered the impressment of American seamen.[2]

Given the momentous issues at stake, John Quincy was nearly
evangelical in the cause of his nation and union. As a member of
the committee on the president's message, after dinner the evening
of February 1, John Quincy had drawn up two resolutions for consideration by the Senate committee.

> *Resolved:* That the capture and condemnation of American vessels and their cargoes under the orders of the British government on the pretext of their being engaged in a trade with the enemies of Great Britain *not permitted before the war* is an unprovoked aggression upon the citizens of these United States. . . .
>
> *Resolved,* That the President of the United States be requested to instruct the minister of the United States at the court of Great Britain to demand and insist upon the immediate restoration of the property of the citizens of the United States. . . .[3]

The first had been adopted unanimously; the second, after debate, was adopted in a vote of 23 to 7. The success of his bills, he would claim, had taught him something: "In taking a lead, a man must rely *only upon himself.*" There were lessons very decisively to be learned "when the character of a leader was to be acquired." And ones to which he would remain sensitive, sometimes in painful bewilderment, for his entire career.[4]

By mid-March 1806 John Quincy barely had time to get home and back to the Capitol, the workload was so tremendous. Agonizing over the violent outrages of the foreign nations, both houses were crammed with motion upon motion "for everything that can exhibit temper against the British."[5]

Added to all this "was opposition from *reasonable* quarters— all the *quakerish* members of both Houses" who were averse to anything that looked even by a squint like taking drastic steps, for they were only for peace the world over. Besides fear of offending Great Britain, negotiation was the only course to pursue. In addition, members from the southern states were reluctant to agree to anything that might obstruct the freedom of their trade in foreign ships and affect the exportation of their cotton.[6]

Added to all this was the burden of domestic issues, including bills on naval appropriations, roads spreading from the Atlantic to the Ohio, Georgia land claimants, an amendment favoring free navigation of Britain's St. Lawrence River, as well as the somewhat secret and extremely delicate "Two Million Dollar Act" (debated and passed in February 1806) to cover expenses of negotiations and purchase of Florida from Spain.

Still more radically contentious, what John Quincy referred to as the Slave Prohibition Bill had provoked a long debate on January 15, 1807, in which he most deliberately took no part. Nor did he comment further on its passage just ten days later, convinced as he was that the infinite discrepancies in the new law would impede its honorable execution and that, at root, the Constitution did not give Congress the power to prohibit slavery.

On further analysis John Quincy had concluded that "the bargain between freedom and slavery contained in the Constitution of the Unites States is morally and politically vicious, inconsistent with the principles of the Revolution." By considering slaves as property and thereby nearly doubling their masters' voting privileges, "this slave representation has governed the Union."[7]

Among the evils of slavery—the "great and foul stain upon the North American union"—he continued, was that "it taints the very sources of moral principle, established false ideas of virtue and vice, for what," he wondered, "can be more false and heartless than this doctrine which makes the first and holiest rights of humanity to depend upon the color of the skin?" Indeed, he wrote in his diary years later, he found the subject "a mere preamble to a title page to a great tragic volume."[8]

Obviously, John Quincy had thought long, hard and passionately on the subject and fundamentally and repeatedly questioned the judgment of anyone who kept people of color in bondage. And at the top of his list he especially included the judgment of Thomas Jefferson, who had been a slave-holder all his life, even while publishing opinions blasting the very existence of slavery.

More than a dozen years later, on March 2, 1820, the Senate admitted Maine as a free state and admitted Missouri to the Union as a slave state while outlawing slavery in the remainder of the Louisiana Purchase north of latitude 36°30'. The condition inserted by the House of Representatives that slavery should first be prohibited by the Missouri state constitution was abandoned.[9]

At the time of the 1820 debate on the Missouri Compromise, John Quincy said that he had favored this compromise, believing it to be all that could be effected under the present Constitution, and also because he was extremely unwilling to put the Union at hazard. But he allowed that perhaps it would have been a wiser as well as bolder course to have persisted in the restriction on Missouri until it concluded in a state convention to revise and amend its state constitution. Such a course would have produced a new Union of 13 or 14 states unpolluted with slavery, with a great and glorious object: that of rallying other states to accept universal emancipation of their slaves. Then again, on second thought, if the Union must be dissolved, slavery was "precisely the question upon which it ought to break."[10]

Congress broke up Monday, April 21, 1806, "under a variety of unpleasant and unpromising circumstances." John Quincy would leave Washington on April 25 and looked forward, he wrote his brother-in-law, Colonel William Smith, to seeing him in New York City on his way to Quincy. Louisa would remain in Washington for the present, probably through the summer. He did not mention that Louisa suffered violent headaches, was bled on occasion and was unable to make the trip as she was pregnant and the baby was due that summer of 1806.[11]

After he arrived at New York's City Hotel on May 1, he visited the colonel and his wife, his beloved sister Nabby. He was so distressed to find them planning to move that same day into a cottage on the prison grounds—possibly Newgate in Greenwich Village—that "I cannot dwell upon it," he wrote Louisa.[12]

Actually, he had little choice but to be critically involved: His entire family counted on his help in "the mysterious project and expedition of Miranda." The scandal made for riveting newspaper coverage, considering the celebrity of the accused, the husband of the former president's daughter, the questionable involvement of President Jefferson and Secretary of State Madison and of a Spanish general with the alias of George Martin who had "very imprudently represented" a hero in the United States for the past 20 years.[13]

William Stephens Smith, Revolutionary War hero, son-in-law of John and Abigail Adams, and recently replaced and disgraced as surveyor of the Port of New York, had been charged on April

7 with "high misdemeanor" for violating the Neutrality Act of 1794 by providing means for a military expedition against a nation with which the United States was at peace. More specifically, Colonel Smith had supported his "very intimate friend" General Francisco de Miranda's quest to liberate his native Venezuela and other Spanish colonies in the western hemisphere from Spanish rule. In the cause, the colonel had helped supply ammunition and mercenaries—among them his son William Steuben Smith whom he had secretly encouraged to leave Columbia College—and chartered the merchant vessel *Leander* from Samuel Ogden, along with several other vessels to set sail the past February 22, 1806.[14]

Shortly, two of the schooners met with disaster and William was mistakenly reported to be imprisoned in Caracas and threatened with a death sentence unless his father would reveal to the Spanish Minister Carolos Martinez de Yrugo everything he knew of Miranda's plans, including the names of the Spaniards with him. The Spanish minister wanted to discover everything that could be confessed by a criminal under sentence of death to save himself. The colonel's trial was scheduled for mid-July 1806. If convicted, he faced three years in prison. Defending himself, supported by a team of prominent lawyers, Colonel Smith had testified that Miranda's expedition "was set on foot with the knowledge and approbation of the President."[15]

To the family's immense relief, the colonel would be acquitted in July, but obviously the involvement of the president and secretary of state remained suspect in John Quincy's thoughts. He had personally lost trust in Jefferson, scorned his "itch for telling prodigies." And though he understood that the gloomy case of the colonel's future and that of his family was "only the natural consequence of the principles and practices which have for many years been in unceasing operation," his sympathies remained with his brother-in-law, the erratic entrepreneur of extravagant success and abysmal failure. In any case, in his opinion, having removed him from the office of surveyor, the president had already done enough. He had "ruined him as completely as his heart could wish. More is unnecessary," he told Louisa.[16]

With untold sympathy, John Quincy remained protective of his sister's family. He had hoped Nabby would leave the prison's premises to join him in Quincy, but she had preferred to stay with her husband. He had, however, with Louisa's permission, offered support for her son John Smith while he studied law after his recent graduation from Harvard.

On the whole, for John Quincy, the summer of 1806 was one of privilege but also shattering sorrow. He was in Cambridge about to be inducted professor at Harvard. Louisa was in Washington in great pain, suffering abscesses in the back of her throat and ear, swelling legs, waiting out the birth of their baby. John Quincy thought, he told Louisa, of an alternative to their separate way of life. Though resigned to filling out his term with little more than two years to go, he was tempted to resume the practice of law and renounce his "official character." But Louisa responded that, though she felt unqualified to advise him, she wholly supported his public duties, in which he would shine in real and essential service to his country, self and family. Comfort, she added, must sometimes be sacrificed for the general good, and though she was conscious of how much this sentiment might cost her, she still felt an ardent desire to see at least some men of respectability and talents adorning public stations. But ultimately, he must act as he thought proper.[17]

On Thursday, June 12, John Quincy was officially installed as Boylston Professor of Rhetoric and Oratory. The academic procession was followed by a prayer, an anthem, various addresses and culminated in John Quincy's address to the "Sons of Harvard" whose "generous thirst for useful knowledge, honorable emulation of excellence" distinguished the students of the university.[18]

While all along John Quincy had faithfully reported to Louisa on his daily ventures, he had also made sympathetic inquiries about her health and well-being. Increasingly anxious, on June 30, John Quincy read what he termed "a message of misfortune," the most tragic letter he had ever received. It was from Louisa, telling him that their child was born dead. Shattered mentally and physically—"I had given up my heart to hope, and joy in the hope of a third. It is gone"—when he was able to hold his pen steadily, he wrote to urge her most earnestly to come to Quincy. Readily accepting his invitation, Louisa, with her sister Caroline, arrived on August 10, but once again the couple faced separation as she chose to remain throughout the winter in Boston with her children while John Quincy departed for Washington in November 1806, not to return till the end of the Ninth Congress's session in March 1807.[19]

Living apart once again, their renewed correspondence was affectionate in tone and even flirtatious. Louisa longed for his return, but, she concluded, "I can neither live with or without you." In answer, though he had not fully understood the last paragraph of her letter of November 25, he would say "I can neither live with you or without you but in this cold weather I should be very glad to live with you." To which Louisa replied: "I will only say that I *think* I never will part with you."[20]

Before quitting Washington for Quincy, John Quincy predicted that the termination of Congress in March 1807 would leave public affairs in a singular situation, "threatened with war on all sides, external and internal." His prophecy was fulfilled on Tuesday, June 30. He was working on his lecture for Harvard when he heard what he described as "an occurrence of very gloomy complexion," an understatement at the least. Henry Adams would call it "a moment without a parallel in American history since the battle of Lexington." For John Quincy it was the beginning of "the really important period of my life."[21]

Eight days earlier, on June 22, the British *Leopard,* a 50-gun ship, had fired on the American frigate *Chesapeake* sailing from Norfolk for service in the Mediterranean, killing 3 seamen and wounding 18, including Commodore James Barron. The British removed four seamen alleging they were deserters from the British navy, and of the four tried at a naval court-martial in Halifax, three of them were native Americans who had been impressed into British service. One was hanged, one died after undergoing his sentence of flogging, two others were returned to the *Chesapeake* on June 13, 1812. Recounting this incident 22 years later, "will my countrymen forgive the emotion" John Quincy asked, that he could not suppress? It was the last step in a gradation of outrages his country would endure from foreign insolence and oppression.[22]

In reaction to the immediate tragedy, John Quincy had hoped to rally an all-inclusive town meeting embracing both parties, but his Federalist friends had declined. Only the Republicans saw the need of the meeting at the State House on July 10, and John Quincy was the only Federalist to work in a committee of seven to draft and report resolutions in support of the administration. According to the fourth of these resolutions:

> *Resolved* unanimously, that, though we unite with our government in wishing most ardently for peace on just and honorable terms, yet we are ready cheerfully to cooperate in any measures, however serious, which they may judge necessary for the safety and honor of our country, and will support them with our lives and fortunes.[23]

Discussed, edited, unanimously adopted, signed by all the members of the committee, including John Quincy, the meeting had "adjourned in perfect order."[24]

The backlash was immediate, ugly and widespread, but not surprising. The day before the meeting, on March 9, John Quincy had "a debate somewhat warm" (actually "painfully animated") with Federalist John Lowell who sided with the British naval officers, said they had a right to seize and carry away from an American ship-of-war any deserter from the British navy. The day after the meeting, John Phillips, an intimate friend, had told him, he noted in his diary: "I should have *my head taken off* for apostasy by the Federalists."[25]

He would pay a steep price for his refusal to conform. When the essayist and poet Ralph Waldo Emerson read John Quincy's first lectures in 1806, he wrote, "not only the students heard him with delight, but the hall was crowded by professors and by unusual visitors." A number of coaches brought his friends from Boston to hear him. On his return in the winter to the Senate in Washington, he took such grounds in the debates of the following session that he lost the sympathy of many of his constituents in Boston. When he resumed lectures in Cambridge, his class attended, but the coaches from Boston did not come and "indeed many of his political friends deserted him."[26]

Family arrangements for the fall 1807 session of Congress—meeting on October 27, six weeks earlier than usual—included plans for their sons George and John to remain in Boston while Louisa returned to Washington with John Quincy and "by the blessing of God, a third son born at half past eight o'clock in the morning" of August 18, 1807. Named Charles Francis in memory of his deceased brother and as a token of honor to his old friend and patron Judge Dana, the infant was very large—possibly weighing as much as George and John together had weighed at birth—and remarkably hearty and strong. An elated John Quincy wrote of "the first moment of self-possession," to Louisa's mother, and carried the letter himself at noon to the post.[27]

In a second letter he reported that Louisa was as well as could be expected under the circumstances, he was doing very well and "the little gentleman likely to do so too," and added presciently "he is born to be lucky." Accompanied by the maid Sarah Alexander, the foursome had arrived in Washington at dusk on October 24, and thus John Quincy noted that he had, for the third time, "accomplished a long journey and voyage with an infant less than three months old."[28]

Back in Washington only five days, John Quincy took time on October 30 to review the Senate journals from the start of his membership. Having had problems enough for having signed the Non-Importation Act of April 15, 1806, which banned the import of certain British goods in an attempt at economic sanctions to compel Great Britain to respect American neutrality on the seas, he was not insensitive to further retribution when he voted for the Embargo Act. President Jefferson had proposed this new act on December 18 in response to increasing dangers to American vessels, seamen and merchandise. "This measure will cost you and me our seats, but private interest must not be put in opposition to public good," he had cautioned his colleague Stephen Row Bradley.[29]

Yet more grievous, the last straw in his betrayal of the Federalist position, he had accepted Bradley's invitation to attend the meeting of the Republican members of both houses to consult on the next presidential election, at which he witnessed the vote of 83 for James Madison for president, three for James Monroe and three for George Clinton. From this moment his "apostasy was no longer a matter of doubt with anybody," a Federalist congressman wrote John Quincy's once amiable friend, Rufus King. "Would you suppose it possible, the scoundrel could summon impudence enough to go to their caucus? I wish to God the noble house of Braintree had been put in *a hole,* and a deep one, too, twenty years ago."[30]

But in terms of exacting punishment most dramatically and decisively, it was Massachusetts Senator Timothy Pickering who "hurled a firebrand upon the stage" already crowded with John Quincy's enemies. The maverick leader of the Essex Junto, a separatist movement, he had sent a 16-page letter to Governor James Sullivan "denouncing the president and Congress for passing the embargo," and sent his formal answer to leading Federalist Harrison Gray Otis two weeks later. New England Federalists were against these acts because they knew such embargos would damage the New England economy.[31]

The title of Pickering's letter, "exhibiting to his Constituents a View of the Imminent Danger of an unnecessary and Ruinous War" said it all, as far as John Quincy was concerned, although there was no mention of his name: "When one of the senators from a state proclaims to his constituents that a particular measure, or system of measures which has received the vote and support of his colleagues, are pernicious and destructive to those interests which both are bound by the most sacred of ties, with zeal and fidelity to promote the denunciation of the measures amounts to little less than a denunciation of the man."[32]

But it was not only the content but the timing that proved ruinous to John Quincy. On June 3 in the afternoon, the House of Representatives had chosen James Lloyd to serve starting the next March when John Quincy's term expired; the vote was 248 to 213 confirmed. In the Senate, the vote was 21 for Lloyd and 17 for John Quincy. The insult was further compounded by the Senate's adoption of the anti-embargo resolution on June 7. John Quincy submitted his resignation on June 9, "not without a painful sacrifice of feeling."[33]

Worse, his father had written, "you have too honest a heart, too independent a mind; and too brilliant talents to be sincerely and confidentially trusted by any man who is under the domination of party axioms or party feelings." Furthermore, John advised, "You ought to know and expect this and by no means to regret it. . . . Devote yourself to your profession and the education of your children."[34]

Fortunately, perhaps miraculously, John Quincy had maintained a cordial relationship with the Republican Governor James Sullivan, who wrote urgently to Jefferson on his behalf on June 3, 1808. In effect, the Federalists had chosen a senator to succeed John Quincy Adams and their principal object at present appeared to be his political and even personal destruction. It was a matter therefore of grave consequence to the interest of Mr. Adams and to that of the Jefferson administration to rescue him from their "triumph," though he did not know how this could be done "otherwise than finding him a foreign appointment of respectability."[35]

Whether Jefferson forwarded Sullivan's letter to Madison is unknown. But what is documented is the newly inaugurated President Madison's meeting with John Quincy on March 6, 1809, and his proposal to nominate him as ambassador to Russia. The commercial relations between the two countries were important, and there might be other valuable advantages. Madison was apologetic about giving him short notice, but he had to send in the nomination within the course of half an hour.

John Quincy thanked Madison for his confidence and asked for more details about his assignment and departure. On the confirmation of his nomination on June 27, he was flattered but also aware of the "stormy and dangerous career" on which he embarked. He was torn about leaving his parents and his very young children. His departure from Harvard was another wrench. He would never cease to feel, he said, the warmest attachment to the interests and welfare of that seminary. But, he reasoned, it was after all an appointment of great trust and importance confirmed by almost every voice in the Senate. It also afforded him the "vague *hope* of rendering to my country some important service." And while he painfully but truthfully acknowledged it to be an escape, "an exile from [my] native land," he and his friends agreed it was after all "an honorable exile."[36]

John Quincy gave his twenty-fourth and last lecture at Harvard on June 28. He addressed his students with unusual warmth and had privately come to think of them as his "unfailing friends" as they had never forsaken him. A poignant reflection of his bitter experience of the past two years, he advised that "In a life of action however prosperous, there would be seasons of adversity and days of trial but at no hour of your life will the love of letters ever oppress you as a burden or fail you as a resource. . . . Seek refuge, my unfailing friends . . . in the friendship of Laelius and Scipio; the patriotism of Cicero, Demosthenes, and Burke."[37]

He would also caution them that their duties as a citizen took precedence over those of the individual and that a call to public service could not be negated by personal or private considerations. And reinforcing one of his family's eternal commitments, he was confident, he said, that Harvard's students would feel the moral obligations that a liberal education imposes upon those to whom it is given, that science is only valuable as it expands the heart while it enlarges the mind.[38]

On Saturday afternoon, August 5, John Quincy left his house at the corner of Boylston and Nassau streets with Louisa, their infant Charles Francis, Louisa's sister, Catherine Johnson, his nephew and private secretary William Steuben Smith, chambermaid Martha Godfrey and a valet named Nelson. Crossing over the Charles River Bridge bound for William Gray's wharf in Charlestown, they boarded the *Horace*. At 1 p.m. precisely, to the chorus of bells ringing from Boston to Charleston, they sailed down the harbor, bidding farewell to the faithful Dr. Welsh and Thomas, who had come to see them off.

John Quincy remained on deck until he lost sight of land. It was the fourth time he had sailed from Boston for Europe. But this seemed the most painful separation of all, given his parents' ages and the uncertainty of meeting up with them again and his having left two of his children behind. He received a letter from his mother "which would have melted the heart of a Stoic." "My dear Children," Abigail had written: "I would not come to town today because I knew I should only add to yours, and my own agony. My heart is with you, my prayers and blessing attend you. The dear children you have left," a decision made by Abigail and John Quincy, "will be dearer to me from the absence of their parents."[39]

John Quincy felt no less wrenched. Writing at sea to his dearest mother, "often as it has been my fortune in the course of my life to be parted from my parents, and dearest friends, as well as from my country, upon no occasion has the separation been so painful as at the present time."[40]

Part IV

Chapter 30

"IN HONORABLE
DIPLOMATIC EXILE"

The Sunday before they embarked for Russia, John Quincy had heard his "excellent friend" and pastor William Emerson (father of Ralph Waldo Emerson) speak "on the pleasing and not improbable doctrine of a guardian angel." Louisa and her sister Caroline as well as John Quincy had taken Emerson's message personally, anticipating a daunting voyage ahead.[1]

From the day they embarked from Mr. Gray's wharf in Charlestown until they landed, "in honorable diplomatic exile," opposite the commanding statue of Peter the Great at St. Petersburg on October 23, 1809, they had found hope and consolation in the belief that a guardian angel had indeed led them safely to the end of their voyage after 75 days at sea.[2]

As it turned out, the voyage was the easiest part of John Quincy's mission to Russia. On dry land (soon to be buried under snow and ice), with war looming on two continents, he and his family would face inner struggles of mind, soul and health, deepened by financial stress, a punishing climate and the mores of a society at once familiar and deeply foreign.

"I find it necessary to make preparation for leaving the country as soon as possible." A lone sentence secreted in the privacy of his diary on November 3, ten days after landing in St. Petersburg, suggests the anguished private state of His Excellency John Quincy Adams and his fragile, proud Louisa, and the sweeping breadth of their profound personal discontent.[3]

On arrival, weary and ill, they had moved promptly to meet their diplomatic obligations. The matter of dress took precedence. Having spent one day with tailors, hatters, wigmakers, shoemakers and milliners, the new minister was, much to his discomfort, in full dress, ready the next day to meet with the High Chancellor of the Empire Count Nikolay Petrovich Rumyantsev, and looking, Louisa said, "very handsome all but the wig. O horrid!"[4]

The count, a statesman and bibliophile, age 55, had welcomed John Quincy most cordially and explained the reason he could not grant his request for an immediate audience. Emperor Alexander was indisposed, his legs wounded in the breakdown of his carriage some months ago. But John Quincy's appointment was "very agreeable."[5]

John Quincy had elaborated on this meeting in his report to Secretary of State Robert Smith. Honoring his mandate, his painstaking handwriting a tidy model of clarity, he would in the ensuing months wish that he had mastered shorthand in order to fulfill President Madison's expectations of "the most exact and ample communication, for which opportunities may be found."[6]

But though his conversation with the chancellor on this occasion was short, he had touched immediately on the layover of an American ship in Christiansand, Norway, on its way to St. Petersburg, and the plight of 30 masters of American vessels and supercargoes—16 more in Jutland—captured by Danish privateers between the past months of April and August. The beleaguered seamen had notified President Jefferson of their plight; John Quincy had received a copy with a request for his intervention on their behalf.

The Russian chancellor expressed strong disapproval of the Danish aggression toward the commerce of the United States. He said that his government had some strong complaints on the same issue. He did not, however, seem poised to take action. But John Quincy persisted, and in a subsequent meeting with the chancellor, he asked that the emperor use his influence to intervene with the Danish government. To the chancellor's surprise, the emperor acceded promptly to John Quincy's wishes, resulting in the restoration of millions of dollars of American property.

In preparation for living in Russia, John Quincy had set about studying the language, purchasing a dictionary and memorizing the alphabet. He also sampled what he called the most ordinary liquors, the quas [kvas] at two kopeks the bottle and the chitslitsky at five, which had the taste of small beer, acceptable to him but much too acidic for the rest of the family. Waiting for his presentation to the emperor, John Quincy walked for hours in search of the touchstones of his youth. At age 14, he had served as secretary and interpreter to Francis Dana, America's first appointed ambassador to Russia.

Things had improved, but nostalgia was inevitable. Chancellor Rumyantsev's invitation on October 28 evoked a memory of dining at the same house in 1782 in much the same high splendor.

After dinner Chancellor Rumyantsev showed John Quincy two superb large vases of Sèvres china, and splendid editions of Virgil and Racine, presents received from Emperor Napoleon. Later, though John Quincy said the evening was "magnificent in every particular," and the company covered with "stars and ribbons beyond anything" that he had ever seen, the past took precedence. "The house—the company—the exhibitions," which he had witnessed on the same spot as a 14-year-old, "had led my mind so forcibly to the mutability of human fortunes that it shared but little in the gorgeous scene around me."[7]

Revisiting the Hermitage of the imperial Winter Palace with his family members, John Quincy saw a number of objects that had escaped him in the past. Though accompanied by the director, he sounded like a museum curator himself. He took little notice of anything but the pictures, and with these he often lingered behind, and after three hours of inspection, wished for three hours more. Voicing the frustration of several centuries of tourists, he wrote that the collection was so vast it left him confused.

For an entirely new experience in St. Petersburg he visited the Alexandrofsk manufacturer for spinning cotton, located five miles from the city on the banks of the Neva. In the factory equipped with 400 or 500 carding, spinning, and winding machines operated by three steam engines, the labor force was composed of 500 foundling children, from the foundling hospitals of St. Petersburg and of Moscow, males to remain on the premises until 21, girls until 25, marriages permitted. John Quincy was fascinated by the machinery, but appalled by the extreme poverty, the want of cleanliness, and the dinner served at the end of a 12-hour work day, which consisted of a thin turnip soup and a dish of boiled buckwheat.

Revisiting the Church of St. Isaac the following April, noting "the multitude of self-crossings, the profound and constantly repeated bows, the prostrations on the earth and kissing of the floor," he felt he had witnessed "the depth of superstition in which this people is plunged perhaps more forcibly than ever before."[8]

Easter day at St. Petersburg had some familiar aspects, John Quincy would report to his mother, ushered in as it was with an expanse of gunpowder and a volume of sound equal to their Independence Day "in the good town of Boston." The celebration lasted the week in two magnificent squares.[9]

The emperor reviewed his troops of 30,000 men, but the scene also included rope dancers, puppet shows, mechanical and optical displays and swings. And eggs were exchanged: Servants gave them to their masters, friends interchanged them with one another; common people gave hard-boiled eggs with the shells dyed red, wealthier people gave artificial eggs of pasteboard, wood, glass, marble, porcelain—almost every material that could be fashioned into an egg shape.

Alongside the entertainment, John Quincy also observed gluttony and drunkenness—the natural vice of the poor who had no other outlets, he supposed. Yet among those he met staggering and sprawling about the streets, there seemed to be a singular character of harmlessness, partly due to the rigorous vigilance of the numerous police who were authorized to use their cudgels at discretion. The regular and absolute power of the police was equally visible in the tranquility with which the crowds of people dispersed immediately after sunset.

With one day's warning, John Quincy was presented to the emperor. He found the subject of protocol—the required rounds of visits in full court dress, the leaving of calling cards at every house without getting out of the carriage—embarrassing to an American. Yet, for all his annoyance, he had concluded that it was not safe or prudent to reject these customs.

On November 5, he had gone to the imperial palace. John Quincy was 42, five feet seven inches, portly and balding; Emperor Alexander, ten years younger, red-haired, like his empress grandmother, stood six feet one inch and svelte in his bemedalled uniform.[10]

They conversed easily in French, with John Quincy conveying the respect of the president of the United States. The emperor then spoke about England's "maritime pretentions," and, "in an easy and familiar manner," posed a number of more personal questions: whether he had ever been in Russia before, what were America's principal cities, and the number of inhabitants.[11]

In turn, John Quincy told him he had passed a winter at St. Petersburg during the reign of the Empress Catherine, that he had then admired the city as the most magnificent he had ever seen but that he scarcely knew it again now. As for his own country, he cited New York and Philadelphia as the principal and most populated cities, but in point of splendor and magnificence they could not vie with St. Petersburg, which to the eye of a stranger appeared like a city for princes. Inquiring after John Quincy's home state, the emperor asked how long its winters lasted and whether it had good sledding. The emperor dismissed John Quincy with the assurance of his pleasure at receiving a minister from the United States.

The interview lasted about 15 or 20 minutes, and John Quincy was charmed by the emperor. He found him gracious, frank, animated, thoughtful and attentive. John Quincy was certain of the emperor's valor—more so with each passing encounter in the years ahead—and their storied relationship was among the intriguing curiosities of John Quincy's diary and letters home.

Louisa was presented at court on November 12. Though she admitted frequently copying notations from John Quincy's diary, her irreverent account in this instance was inimitably her own.

"Off I went with a fluttered pulse . . . among people whom I had never seen . . . dressed in a hoop under a silver tissue skirt with a train, a heavy crimson velvet robe with a long train trimmed with sleeves with a quantity of blond lace. My hair was amply arranged and ornamented with a diamond arrow. White satin shoes, gloves, fan, etc. and over all this *luggage* my fur cloak." Attended by two footmen, "thus accoutred I appeared before the gentlemen of our party who could not refrain from laughter at my appearance."[12]

About the presentation to the emperor and empress, Louisa commented only on the latter's "extreme affability." Moving on, she was bemused by the empress mother, who had evidently expected, she said, to quiz her on her ignorance of the wonders of St. Petersburg. Instead, Louisa had expressed in strong language her admiration of everything and mentioned that she had seen London, Paris, Berlin and Dresden, but was certain that no city equaled St. Petersburg in beauty. According to Louisa, "The savage had been expected!" and instead, "the American had known everything and had seen everything."[13]

The audience had lasted 20 minutes. After presentation to a Madame Lieven, a fine old lady, and to the 14-year-old Duchess Ann—an elegant presence with a most distinguished manner but not very handsome—Louisa had returned home "with an additional budget of new ideas almost as oppressive and unsuitable" as her robes. Very fatigued with "all this variety of agitation," at least she had been gratified at hearing from a courtier that she had "done very well."[14]

Just three weeks after their arrival, when ice already blocked the ports and filled the Neva River, John Quincy had explained to family, colleagues, and the secretary of state, that from now until June they would be unable to reach one another except by occasional and indirect conveyance, which could take four months or longer in each direction. This was one of the more punishing aspects of their life at this juncture. John Quincy spoke of "the greediness of appetite which we have for letters from America." He readily admitted that he had spent two or three hours reading a November file of the *Boston Patriot* that arrived in March. And he spoke of the joy with which he always recognized his mother's handwriting, that even a letter of six months in passage "was as welcome and almost as grateful as if it had come with the speed of a telegraphic dispatch."[15]

Not all communications were joyful. Louisa's first letter to reach Abigail from St. Petersburg was a disheartening preview of others to come. Apologetic about her delay in writing, Louisa cited "the tumultuous agitation" of their lives. "At length, my dear Madam, we have arrived in this splendid city and find ourselves lunged into the midst of difficulties and expenses from which nothing but a return to our own country can extricate us, unless the American government will double the present appointments."[16]

They were all well, she continued, but miserably lodged, with no prospect of finding an appropriate house at an affordable price. Moreover, Abigail could have no idea of the morals and manners of the Russian people, and she foresaw nothing but perpetual mortification heaped on them during their stay. Louisa had concluded with a few requests for fabric, including "anything light and gauzy, pink and blue ginghams, some knit drawers."[17]

Three months later, Louisa informed her mother-in-law that she had suggested returning home in the spring to lighten her husband's expenses. But he had told her he could not support her in America even in the small house at Quincy. On this dread subject of finances, Louisa, wary that that every bill she brought her husband "made pain stare in his face," assured Abigail that she was intent "to make my expenses as light as possible." To Mary Cranch, Abigail's sister, Louisa regretted that "but for a lost fortune" she might have offered "trifling gifts of affection to her darling boys."[18]

It snowed in June and Louisa was grateful for letters that cheered their "painful exile" for, she told Abigail, without them her spirits would have sunk "into such a state of apathy" that she would have "lost even the blessing of hope."[19]

John Quincy's letter home confirmed their difficulties. He apologized to his mother who was "the most constant and most frequent correspondent that he had beyond the seas." She knew of the challenges of forming a suitable domestic establishment for an American minister. The single floor of a house cost several thousand rubles a year and five times that for furnishings. He required a whole new wardrobe for the indispensable obligation to attend at court twice a day. And ladies' dress was even more expensive—besides, the climate required clothing unknown in more southern regions.[20]

Given this dire situation, he thought his mother would readily understand his desire to get out of it. Nevertheless, with obvious reluctance, he had rented part of a house and would be obliged to take on debt, drawing on his little property in America. The family moved to Novy Pereuloik or New Place near the Moika Canal in June.

John Quincy was in charge of the household budget, paying close attention to minute details. Living together under one roof, his staff included a cook with two scullions, a Swiss porter, two footmen, a mujik to make the fires, a coachman and postilion, a house maid and a laundry maid as well as their two servants brought from America, his Trinidad-born valet, Nelson, and Louisa's personal maid, Martha Godfrey. Bills were to be paid from the baker, milkman, butcher, grocer, poulterer and fishmonger, along with those for supplies of tea, coffee, sugar, wax and tallow candles. The firewood luckily was included as part of the rent.

By December 17, noting that expenses had doubled since they first moved in, John Quincy decided to fire the cook and engage a local hotel to cater their dinners at 20 rubles a day. Still, John Quincy was under no illusion about the extent of his savings, for it seemed to him "that the servant shall spoil or plunder the master." In Russia at least, it was the "universal image."[21]

John Quincy assured his father he wasn't alone in these complaints. Two colleagues shared the opinion that ambassadors should be selected with large fortunes of their own, willing to spend them as well as their salaries on behalf of their countries. He intended to pass on this idea to the president of the United States.[22]

Meanwhile, John Quincy had to endure sniping by American newspapers about his putting the nation to the enormous expense of a frigate to transport his "precious carcass" across the ocean. He acidly noted, "among other obliging notices," the editor of the *Boston Centinel* had informed the world "'how ill calculated our townsman is for the splendid and intriguing court of Ste. Petersburg.'"[23]

In self-defense, John Quincy pointed to the exorbitant cost of living—and to the competition. For instance, the French ambassador's palace and equipage furnished by Napoleon was only exceeded by that of the imperial palace: His allowance was $350,000; America's allotment was $9,000. As a result, on his limited allowance, he assured his brother Thomas that he shone as much as he could among those whose splendor he could not match, and spent as much time as possible with his family. "This you may say is not very diplomatic," but it was absolutely necessary in order "to steer clear" of the debt collectors.[24]

Abigail understood completely. Persuaded that "Giving the same salary to every foreign minister is like a tailor making a coat and requiring it to fit all sizes," she set out on her rescue mission. On August 1, 1810, she fired off a letter to President James Madison, to which he responded two weeks later. Although he had not learned that Mr. Adams had yet signified to the Department of State of his wish to return from the mission to St. Petersburg, it was sufficiently understood by her communication and accordingly he had asked the secretary of state to assure him that it was not the purpose of the executive branch to subject him to the personal sacrifices which he found unavoidable.[25]

Letters proliferated. President Madison informed the tsar that John Quincy "influenced by private considerations of an urgent value" would be returning to America. Next, Madison sent a personal message affirming his unabated friendship for John Quincy while reassuring him, in reference to a letter received from his "highly respectable mother," that he was not to suffer unreasonable sacrifices. John Quincy would be receiving a letter of leave.[26]

With a shrewd sense of John Quincy's devotion to duty, Madison went on to hope that, having not heard directly of any problems, the "peculiar urgency manifested in the letter of Mrs. Adams," was hers rather than his. Apart from the confidence in John Quincy's abilities leading to his appointment in the first place, the president feared that the ambassador's abrupt departure would lead to "unfavorable conjections" on the tsar's part. While not wishing to place unreasonable demands on him, the president was persuaded that John Quincy's patriotism "will cheerfully make the sacrifice."[27]

Although communication was halting and uncertain, Abigail tried to encourage Louisa in the hope that a remedy to their difficulties would present itself. As if by a miracle, her vision was fulfilled. In March, John Quincy was named associate justice of the Supreme Court of the United States, "An appointment so honorably made, so unanimously concurred in, and so universally approved," Abigail wrote Louisa on March 4, 1811.[28]

In June, John Quincy turned down the appointment. Mindful of his desire for a more southern climate and his ardent wish to see his parents and his boys, he acknowledged strongly conflicting emotions. He admitted feeling inept in judicial tribunals, then noted "a duty of still more commanding nature" that required him to decline. Louisa was pregnant, expecting a baby in August. It was not possible to put her through the ordeal of a transatlantic voyage that could endanger her health. Bravely, he assured Abigail that he had adjusted to life in St. Petersburg and had managed to buckle down expenses to the very edges of his means.[29]

There were signs of autumn, John Quincy noted on August 10, leaves turning yellow and rains settling in. On August 11, Mrs. Reinke, "a wise woman" John Quincy called her, came to pass the night with Louisa, whose frequent pregnancies were complex and painful. Just a year ago, July 19, so weak she could hardly guide her pen, she had suffered from "another severe indisposition" which had deprived her of the pleasure, she had written Abigail, of presenting her with another little relation. But this time, after months of anxiety, their luck had changed. John Quincy told his mother that at seven o'clock, the evening of August 12, his dear wife "had had the wisdom to produce a charming daughter, to you a granddaughter, and to my sons George and John a sister whom I trust they will love as much as if she had been born in Quincy. I think this will convince you," he added, "that the climate of St. Petersburg is not too cold to produce an American."[30]

A month later, their daughter's christening on September 10 was performed according to the ritual of the Church of England by the Reverend Dr. Pitt, chaplain to the English church in St. Petersburg. John Quincy would have preferred an American officiant, but he considered the ceremony itself so essential, he would sooner have his child, he said, baptized by the terms of the Greek or the Roman Catholic church than omit it altogether. The witnesses included Leavitt Harris, a Quaker, and Madame Bezerra, the Roman Catholic wife of the Portuguese minister. That a Quaker and a Portuguese Roman Catholic should join with a Church of England clergyman to baptize the child of a New England Congregationalist in St. Petersburg, the capital of Russia, was a unique diplomatic occasion. The child was named for her mother, Louisa Catherine. "I beg leave to recommend this incident to my honored father," John Quincy said, "as a good theme of meditations upon government. If Mr. West or Mr. Copley had been in the party, he should have proposed to them "to make a picture of it."[31]

Days earlier in his diary, on their fourteenth anniversary on July 26, he had paid Louisa an eloquent tribute, the more memorable for his candor as well as his loving appreciation. He acknowledged her suffering due to ill health, and noted many differences between them of taste and opinions in regard to domestic economy and the education of their children. But he also expressed profound gratitude to Louisa for being a faithful and affectionate wife, and a careful, tender and watchful mother to their children, all of whom she nursed herself. Accordingly, he noted "the superior happiness of the marriage state over that of celibacy," and his conviction that his lot in marriage had been highly favored.[32]

The celebration of the birth of their daughter and the pleasure of their wedding anniversary were soon subordinated to news of a tragic clash on May 15 between the American frigate *President* and the British sloop *Little Belt*. The English insisted that the Americans had fired the first shot. While John Quincy hoped that was not the case, he warned that with relations between the two nations rapidly deteriorating, war seemed inevitable.

As for Russia, awaiting "the threatened thunderbolt of the Emperor Napoleon," John Quincy had thought for months that a war with France was highly probable. There was some speculation that it might even blaze up by the end of the summer. But then France yielded on certain points, and the possibility of immediate rupture was postponed. "Peace," he told his brother Thomas, "will be some time longer preferred."[33]

Chapter 31

"WHETHER OF PEACE OR WAR"

Almost from the moment he arrived in Russia, John Quincy recognized the geopolitical truth that in "the present state of the world . . . two great powers," France and England, held sway. Since he and his brother Thomas had last served together in Europe less than a decade ago it was "scarcely conceivable what a change in this respect had taken place."[1]

There was not a republic left in Europe. In England there was passionate concentration on intrigues and cabals of princes and ministers to supplant one another and on prices of seats at the play-house. In France and all the rest of Europe, the focus was on king-making and king-breaking, orders of chivalry and dissolutions of marriages, with laundresses and Jacobin grubs bursting into but-terfly princes, dukes and counts. Famine was grinding the people into soldiers, and soldiers were sprouting into sultans.[2]

By contrast, Russia had undergone the least change of any country in Europe and, John Quincy assured his brother, that change had been for the better. The Emperor Alexander was "a powerful and absolute prince," so strong and so universally recog-nized that the only criticism of him was to imply he lacked energy. John Quincy could not judge the accuracy of this alleged flaw, but was convinced that firmness and perseverance were central to Alexander's character.[3]

As for peace with France, Alexander had very decisively pursued the treaty signed at Tilsit on July 7, 1806. As for relations with the United States, Alexander's aid to the Americans detained by the Danish in the Holstein harbors indicated a man of vision, "capable of appreciating distant objects and remote consequences, one of the rarest and most valuable" assets a statesman could possess.[4]

They made an improbable twosome, the Russian emperor and the American patriot, one the scion of princes, the other of revolutionaries. But a genuine rapport developed over repeated chance encounters, free of any official formalities, along the Nevsky Prospect, the Fontanka River, and the mall opposite the Admiralty.

Most often John Quincy met Alexander walking—the healthiest exercise John Quincy's physician had told him—or on a sled with a single attendant or on a horse-drawn droshky. In one of their earliest encounters, he asked whether John Quincy planned to take a house in the country in the summer, guessing that the cost of doing so was the cause of his hesitation. Alexander's advice, delivered with a smile: One must always spend in proportion to one's revenues. "A maxim worthy of an emperor," John Quincy concluded, "though few emperors practice upon it."[5]

On a March morning John Quincy had noticed that one of the palace windows was open and wondered, he told the emperor, if the emperor didn't suffer from the cold. But no, the emperor made it a rule to rise in the morning and dress with his windows open, and he added that in the time of Empress Catherine it had been very much the practice to be confined in very hot apartments. He had then worn a flannel waistcoat that irritated his skin and, on a physician's advice, had left it off; since then he was wholly free from rheumatic complaints. In response, John Quincy said he was so accustomed to wearing flannel in winter that he believed he should die if he left it off.[6]

John Quincy found the emperor highly observant in matters of appearance, extremely quick and particular in observing slight peculiarities in dress. One December day in 1810, the emperor told John Quincy that he had passed by him on several occasions without recognizing him because of his headdress, ranging as it did from bald to wig to fur cap. Wasn't he afraid of heating his head too much by the use of fur? Alexander had asked. He wore it only in very cold weather, and then, John Quincy replied, as his head "was so much uncovered by nature, the fur was not too much for it." At a ball the following December, Alexander spoke to John Quincy about how different he looked without a wig, that "it was not so showy, but more convenient to go without it."[7]

John Quincy's admiration and respect for the emperor only deepened with time and exposure nurtured by his personal good will, his exceedingly cordial acknowledgment of the American government, and his avowed determination to favor commerce between the two nations. John Quincy's success in helping release American ships at Archangel, Kronstadt, Riga and other Russian ports in time for spring navigation was pointedly noted. "It seems you are great favorite here," France's Ambassador Caulaincourt, the Duc de Vicence, had told him.[8]

Louisa was equally charmed, writing home to Abigail that she "had the honor of dancing with the emperor a short time ago at a splendid ball given by the French ambassador in honor of the late Great Marriage" of Napoleon to Marie Louise of Austria. Also, she reported, she found the emperor "remarkably unaffected in his manners and dislikes very much the forms and etiquette of his court. He is remarkably handsome and very mild and amiable."[9]

Royal attention to Charles, now four and large for his age, was very gratifying. Starting to spell in French and fluent in German, "he had been the admiration of Petersburg." The boy was presented to their imperial majesties who played with him for almost an hour, the empress on her knees looking at some prints with Charles. The emperor told Louisa he was a most charming child.[10]

Altogether, John Quincy appreciated, but did not take for granted, this productive and tranquil period in Russian-American relations, and he hoped to strengthen and celebrate it. Undoubtedly recalling America's first failed mission by Francis Dana, he sensed the fragility of the moment: "If we suffer it to pass away, a century may not give us such another" opportunity.[11]

The alliance would likely come at a time of momentous change. The fraught subject, "whether of peace or war, between France and Russia" was known to depend on "the will of the French Emperor," as John Quincy alerted James Monroe on July 6, 1811. The outlook was dire. Some months later Emperor Alexander told John Quincy "that war is coming which I have done so much to avoid . . . but thus it ends." He said he would not begin the war and would continue trying to prevent it, but expected to be attacked: everything pointed to war.[12]

Count Rumyantsev, the Russian high chancellor, was far more voluble and alarming. He described the forces massing on the frontiers as immense on both sides. "There was in history scarcely anything like it. . . . That perpetual restlessness and agitation of the emperor Napoleon was such that it was impossible to say how it would end; and most extraordinary of all there was no cause of war." France's takeover of the Duchy of Gottenburg was hardly a reason for renouncing the alliance at Tilsit. And terminating all commerce between the countries was impossible. "You might as well set up a total exclusion of all air to breathe, or all food to subsist on."[13]

The utter lack of motive for war deeply troubled John Quincy. It was strange that such a drastic action, "lightly, wantonly, unjustly undertaken," should begin while both parties were protesting there was no cause of war between them. The French ambassador, M. de Caulaincourt, questioned by John Quincy during their walk on the morning of April 23, answered that he had not abandoned all hope that some resolution might be found. By June, however, all optimism disappeared. Caulaincourt's departure was followed by almost all the diplomatic corps—Austrian, Spanish, Neopolitan, Saxon, Bavarian, Wurtembergian and Westphalian. As he was virtually the lone diplomat to remain in Russia, numerous colleagues had entrusted their countries' archives to John Quincy, who warned James Monroe on June 11, 1812: "the political drama in the north of Europe is drawing towards its catastrophe."[14]

Soon after, John Quincy would report on "the wars which broke out in the course of one week last summer." With regard to the war between America and Great Britain in his own country, the cause on America's side was personal liberty; on the British side it was oppression.[15]

Beyond anxious concern for his countrymen, he had little to offer. But of the war taking place where he was posted, he understood both the responsibility and opportunity of providing credible reports on events of global concern. Sources of information, he warned, were exceedingly varied, not always reliable and almost never timely. (Tolstoy's masterful *War and Peace* would be published 30 years later.) Private correspondence from the armies could not vary much from official battlefield reports: "*Discretion* is one of the most universal virtues in government organized like [Russia's]." People were sentenced to sweeping streets for want of it.[16]

Despite these challenges, there was great advantage to witnessing the course of war in St. Petersburg, only three days away from Moscow, especially so for John Quincy, with fluent pen (though fingers stiff with cold), the courage of his curiosity and access to powerful colleagues and informative couriers. Steeped in the latest facts, figures and urgent rumors, his intensely personal letters home, his diary and his merciless "sketch" of "Napoleon the Great" document the "fire and the sword that are ravaging the country."[17]

He also recorded the impact of war on St. Petersburg. He noted the peasants working noble lands; they came from the country in their one-horse wagons, having taken leave of their families. Or the government sending away the valuables of the Hermitage in broad daylight. The Russian nobility, too, in expectation of Napoleon's domination, fleeing with crates of their famous art. The Duc de Laval and his wife, for instance, fugitives from one of the most magnificent establishments in St. Petersburg, consigning one especially valuable painting to its own carriage to travel with them through Finland and Sweden.[18]

John Quincy's most trenchant accounts follow Napoleon's invasion, providing unique perspective on a pivotal moment in history:

> [Napoleon] entered Russia at the head of three hundred thousand men on the 24th of last June [1812]. On the 15th of September he took possession of Moscow, the Russian armies having retreated before him

almost as fast as he could advance, not, however, without attempting to stop him by two battles. . . .[19]

Then, as the northern climate took hold, Napoleon's stunning success evaporated. John Quincy wrote his mother on November 30 that within six weeks of taking Moscow, Napoleon

found himself with a starving and almost naked army eight hundred miles from his frontier, exposed to all the rigors of a Russian winter, with an army before him superior to his own, and a country behind him already ravaged by himself, and where he had left scarcely a possibility of any other sentiment than that of execration and vengeance upon himself and his followers. He began his retreat on the 28th of October . . . [with] scarcely the ruins of an army remaining with him. He has been pursued with all the eagerness that could be felt by an exasperated and triumphant enemy. Thousands of his men have perished by famine, thousands by the extremity of the season, and in the course of the last ten days we have heard of more than 30,000 who had laid down their arms almost without resistance.

It may well be doubted whether in the compass of human history since the creation of the world, a greater, more sudden and more total reverse of fortune was ever experienced by a man . . . whom fortune for a previous course of nearly twenty years had favored with a steadiness and a prodigality equally unexampled in the annals of mankind.[20]

But according to his next report to Abigail, on December, 31, 1813, Napoleon had apparently saved himself not only by the "swiftness of his flight," but at least on one occasion in disguise:

Of the immense host with which six months since he invaded Russia, nine-tenths at least are prisoners or food for worms. They have been surrendering by ten thousands at a time, and at this moment there are at least one hundred and fifty thousand of them in the power of Emperor Alexander.

From Moscow to Prussia, eight hundred miles of road have been strewed with his artillery, baggage, wagons, ammunition chests, dead

and dying men, whom he has been forced to abandon to their fate—
pursued all the time by three large regular armies of a most embittered and exasperated enemy, and by an almost numberless militia of
peasants, stung by the destruction of their harvests and cottages . . .
and spurred to revenge at once themselves, their country, and their
religion. To complete his disasters the season itself during the greatest
part of his retreat has been unusually rigorous, even for this northern
climate; so that it has become a sort of by-word among the common
people here that the two Russian generals who have conquered Napoleon and all his Marshals are *General Famine* and *General Frost*.[21]

But then again, the pendulum took a most unpredictable turn.
"To the astonishment of the world," John Quincy wrote on June
5, 1813, "Napoleon instead of sinking under his calamities has
already returned to the field, less powerful but perhaps not less
formidable." Fortified surprisingly by a large army, he had eluded
capture by the Russians.[22]

If there were any lessons to be learned from "the great and
decisive events of the past year," John Quincy said he clung "more
fondly than ever to the principles of peace." So he was optimistic
and grateful upon hearing of Emperor Alexander's proposal for
bringing a pacific end to America's war with England.[23]

Given the various indications that neither side was anxious to
pursue this war, it had occurred to the emperor that perhaps an indirect approach via a third party would be most effective. Emperor
Alexander had therefore directed Count Rumyantsev to inquire
whether John Quincy was aware of any difficulty America might
have in accepting this offer. In relating this inquiry to Secretary
of State James Monroe, John Quincy wrote that as he "deeply lamented the very existence of the war," he would welcome "any
facility for bringing it to a just and honorable termination."[24]

The count had concluded this conversation with a highly personal diplomatic gesture, John Quincy recalled, "his enquiries and
condolence upon my domestic misfortune." This was an especially
meaningful but discreet reference to the devastating loss he and
Louisa had suffered this past summer of 1812: the death of their
beloved little daughter, her mother's namesake Louisa Catherine.[25]

Just the past June all had been well, and Louisa wrote adoringly of "a good-natured little madcap" who "looks like Grandmama Adams, she is very handsome and has the finest pair of black eyes you ever saw." By a stormy August 21, the child was suffering a violent fever and convulsions from dysentery, and a frantic John Quincy roused the doctor in the middle of the night. Every remedy was tried: renewed breastfeeding, warm baths, injections of laudanum and digitalis, even a haircut. "Language," John Quincy wrote on September 12, "cannot express the feeling of a parent beholding the long continued agonies of a lovely infant." After a vigil of three days and nights in which Louisa scarcely left the side of the cradle, on the morning of September 15, John Quincy wrote, "The Lord gave and the Lord hath taken away."[26]

On returning home from his daughter's funeral on September 17, John Quincy took a walk with Charles, read and tried to collect his scattered spirits and to seek consolation, as he wrote, for the "heavy calamity." Stung by the memory of their infant's "beaming intelligence and angelic temper," he prayed for "improvement in piety and virtue" to cope with an affliction which was "inexpressibly grievous." He also realized that for Louisa, having been more constantly at their infant's side, "the loss was most severe if not irremediable."[27]

John Quincy had the unwelcome task of informing his mother of the death of the infant Louisa, who he had hoped would "contribute much to the happiness of their lives as she did to the charm" of his. To her mother-in-law, Louisa confided her unbearable grief. Altogether, she felt her existence "was a calamity to all who surrounded her," and she often questioned her sanity. In an April letter, she variously wrote of wishing to remain in Russia and be buried with her child and wanting to reunite with her older children.[28]

Abigail's response was heartrendingly sympathetic. She urged her daughter-in-law to be "cheerful, submissive and resigned"—but she also mentioned, perhaps for the first time, her own grief over the long-ago death of her infant Susanna, confiding that "forty years has not obliterated from my mind the anguish."[29]

She also told Louisa of a more recent tragedy. Mrs. Smith, her daughter Nabby, who had suffered surgery for breast cancer nearly two years past, had arrived in Quincy on July 26, 1813. "You see my dear daughter," she wrote, "I have my sorrows and my trials— may I be equal to them." Nabby died three weeks later at the age of 48.[30]

The anguish proved unrelenting. John Quincy would write his mother on June 30, 1814, "Two years have nearly gone by since *my* only daughter was taken from me and to this hour I cannot meet in the street an infant of her age in its mother's arms, but it cuts me to the heart. If such are my feelings for a child cut off before the dawn of reason in the soul; what must be those of a *mother*."[31]

The season was turning mild and the ice of the River Neva was not more than three feet thick. In one month's time the river itself would be open. "Oh! that I could take, not the wings of the morning and fly to the uttermost parts of the East, but the wings of a fast sailing ship and swim to the nearest parts of the West," John Quincy had written his mother in March 1813. He still hoped, he said, to see his parents, his brother and his boys before the end of the year. But his plans depended on the proposal by Emperor Alexander to serve as mediator between the United States and England. If accepted, John Quincy would have to postpone his return home for another season.[32]

In any case, he could still serve as his children's schoolmaster. Charles already spoke three languages (French, German and English) and was being tutored twice a week in Russian. Father and son spent the first two hours after breakfast together, reading chapters in the English New Testament followed by a short lesson in arithmetic. Charles was not yet firmly the master of decimal numeration nor reading numbers to the hundreds of millions, but John Quincy refrained, he said, from pressing too hard on the young boy's mind. His approach was the product of much thought. "The most essential part of education after all," he wrote his brother, "is to teach a child to think. Perhaps, too, it is the most difficult."[33]

During the first year of their separation he had assured George and John of his tender affection, and that "the greatest pleasure that you can give to your parents is to pursue your studies with diligence, and improve yourselves as fast as you can." As gifts, meant to be "amusing and at the same time instructive," George received three packs of cards in French containing ancient history, Roman history, and the history of France. His father assumed John would not know enough French to understand the cards and so sent him a picture book.[34]

There were also the "Letters of John Quincy Adams to His Son on the Bible and Its Teaching," the first written in September 1811, advising George of his father's strong belief that it was books that contributed most to make men good, wise and happy, as well as "useful citizens to their country, respectable members of society, and a real blessing to their parents."[35]

The boys were boarding with their aunt and uncle, Abigail's sister and schoolmaster husband, and John Quincy had not heard from his sons in more than a year; on April 3, 1813, he begged Thomas to remind George to write to him. He trusted George would be seriously preparing himself for college and would not change schools again before matriculating. It was one of the inconveniences of John Quincy's own education and, though it afforded him other advantages, it accounted for always having "small Latin and less Greek," though the little he had contributed so much to the "uses, the comforts and the pleasures" of his life. He also hoped that his sons would be much more accomplished scholars than he was or ever could be.[36]

Thinking of his children reminded him of his own boyhood, much of it fraught with wartime dangers. All this had passed away like a troubled dream, and he hoped that their country's current struggle for her rights might serve to rivet their affections to their nation and her cause.[37]

Their mother chimed in with her vision of the family's destiny. Louisa wrote George, urging him to "use the utmost exertion to emulate the talents and merits of your father, and grandfather. Much is expected of you my darling boy . . . equally meant for [John]."[38]

On July 14, 1813, having learned of Secretary of State Monroe's acceptance of Emperor Alexander's proposal of mediation, John Quincy wrote to say that he had received a letter from Albert

Gallatin and James A. Bayard, regarding their appointment to serve with him as envoys to negotiate a peace with Great Britain under the mediation of the Russian emperor. Though he remained ever hopeful of a good outcome, no information from England encouraged the belief that the British would ultimately accept the mediation of the emperor.[39]

John Quincy's sense of history only magnified his frustration. On September 3, he noted that 30 years earlier his father had signed a definitive treaty of peace between the United States of America and Great Britain and "here am I, authorized together with two other of our fellow citizens to perform the same service, but with little prospect of a like successful issue."[40]

By November, the British had positively refused the emperor's offer, claiming that it was sort of a family quarrel of no concern to other nations. By March, however, when letters again reached him after frozen harbors thawed, John Quincy received word of his appointment with Mr. Bayard, Henry Clay and Jonathan Russell to negotiate with the British government on the invitation of Lord Castlereagh at Gothenburg.[41]

Other auspicious news was forthcoming on the afternoon of April 20, 1814, when one of the palace couriers hurried to John Quincy's house to tell him that Paris had been seized. Napoleon had been constitutionally deposed, and he had formally abdicated and renounced all pretensions to the thrones of France and Italy. "The Bourbons are to receive France and France is to receive the Bourbons, as presents from the allies; and the allies must necessarily dictate the terms upon which these generous donations are to be granted." The arch tone of this summary suggested skepticism regarding the ultimate satisfaction of all concerned; nevertheless, the war in Europe was terminated. It was "a good, a great, and a happy piece of news," John Quincy wrote in his diary.[42]

In the course of winding up his affairs in Russia, John Quincy would have liked to have paid his respects to Emperor Alexander who, off with his troops, was "commander-in-chief, quartermaster, and, in short, superintended everything." As president, 12 years later, John Quincy would pay tribute to Alexander on learning of his death in Crimea at age 48. His heroic defeat of Napoleon made the emperor "the man whose life was most important to the rest of mankind," in John Quincy's assessment. Alexander had "rendered essential good offices to my country;" in addition, "his influence upon the history of my own life has been great and auspicious."[43]

In this combination of professional and personal significance, Alexander embodied a pivotal time in John Quincy's career. For the American, shaped by his father's ardent, arduous devotion to nation-building, establishing a connection at once deeply human and strategically essential with a scion of Russia's royal family was a transformative success. Driven by infinite conviction and passion to fight for his causes, ever mindful that his native country did not value his services, at home John Quincy often felt "like a fish out of water." Yet his ability to provide deeply informed accounts of Napoleon's wartime machinations and to interest a world power in America's struggle with Great Britain were of undeniable value, even to those who initially regarded John Quincy's posting to Russia as an honorable way of ridding the government of an inconveniently independent voice.[44]

Far from home as ambassador to Russia the vilified apostate was reinvented as "his excellency," the consummate diplomat. Russia provided him with a starring role in a monumental theater that earned him his prize-winning career. Both Secretary of State James Monroe and President Madison showered John Quincy with approval of his knowledge and judgment in managing America's concerns.

He left St. Petersburg with soaring recognition of his unique talents, with honors and even greater challenges to follow. In March 1815, Madison appointed him ambassador to Great Britain. Two years later, on March 6, 1817, James Monroe, now president, asked him to serve as secretary of state.[45]

John Quincy gratefully accepted this "distinguished mark of . . . confidence" with a characteristic blend of understatement—he knew quite a lot about "moving smoothly along with associates, equal in trust" and had an implacable sense of duty. His role would be "to *support,* and not to counteract or oppose, the president's administration . . . and never be unmindful of the respect for his character, the deference to his sentiments, and the attachment to his person."[46]

John Quincy's education would continue, and his responsibilities would broaden and change. While the probabilities of ultimate reward were unpredictable, his zeal for public service was unwavering. Literally to his last breath, dying as he did in the Capitol, after a collapse on the House floor, he pursued his passionate desire to "become a useful member of society, a friend to [his] country and a guardian of her laws and liberties."[47]

AFTERWORD

The extraordinary breadth of John Quincy's presidential ambitions reflect the unique scope of his upbringing and experiences. He envisioned a "great magnificent government" that would end slavery and wars, and create a national university, an astronomical observatory, a naval academy, a new Department of the Interior and another for research and exploration. Thwarted by Congress, whose contrary ghosts have continued to stalk subsequent presidents to the present day, John Quincy's advice rings true almost 200 years later: "Nothing was ever lost by kind treatment. Nothing can be gained by sullen repulses and aspiring pretention."[1]

The challenges John Quincy faced in shaping his public persona as a presidential candidate also seem primal reactions to his upbringing. His determination to shrink from any manifestation of public feeling led to misunderstandings of his motives and character. His wife Louisa was deeply worried that his "natural coldness and reserve of manners" were attributed to pride when she knew better—they stemmed "from modesty and a desire to avoid display." She urged him to meet the demands of a campaign "with ease and grace, than to be thought to shun it with disdain."[2]

In response, he complimented her: she reasoned "exceedingly well," both on his real character and on his unfortunate reputation. But he well knew that he would never be judged a popular man, "being as little qualified by nature, education, or habit, for the arts of a courtier" as he was desirous of being courted. Although he was not intentionally "repulsive" in his manners, he had no "powers of fascination; none of the honey which the profligate proverb says is the true fly-catcher." While it would be utterly out of character to alter his deportment, he did not envy others who made a more popular impression, he assured Louisa on August 1, 1821, more than three years before he took office as the nation's sixth president on March 4, 1825.[3]

Louisa's astute assessment of her husband's merits and vulnerabilities as a public figure exemplify her considerable insight. She was certainly capable of great charm and spirit. On an impressive adventure of her own, traveling with Charles from St. Petersburg to Paris to join John Quincy in the early spring of 1815, she wrote Abigail that she had performed her journey with "little uneasiness and as few misfortunes as could possibly have been anticipated" and "really acquired the reputation of a heroine at a very cheap rate." Twenty years later, regretting that she had not kept a journal, she decided to formally recreate her "Narrative of a Journey from Russia to France," an account of her trip overland. Already intrigued by the feminist sisters Angelina and Sarah Grimke, Quaker abolitionists from South Carolina, she wished now to "show that many undertakings which appear very difficult and arduous to my sex, are by no means as trying as imagination forever depicts them— And that energy and discretion . . . protect the fancied weaknesses of feminine imbecility."[4]

Louisa has her admirers. "She wasn't Abigail," the historian C. James Taylor has said, "but in the 1820s and beyond she was better suited to navigate the political scene than her mother-in-law would have been." But Louisa was also frequently weary, ill and depressed over the years; she was both her husband's great supporter and his bitter critic. Her memoirs are vivid, but they are often serious distortions of fact, shaping generations of overly negative opinions about John Quincy and his family.[5]

Their children met with very mixed fates. Charles Francis served as ambassador to Great Britain during Abraham Lincoln's administration, with his son Henry serving as his secretary. He and his wife Abigail Brown Brooks named their daughter Louisa Catherine Adams. In April 1829, George Washington Adams, who had fathered an illegitimate child, died after he jumped or fell from the *Benjamin Franklin* in Long Island Sound. John Adams II died an alcoholic on October 24, 1824.

John Quincy's grandson characterizes with great empathy his family's complex legacy, at once crushing and priceless, in his haunting autobiography, *The Education of Henry Adams.* "One had to pay for Revolutionary patriots; grandfathers and grand-mothers; presidents; diplomats; Queen Anne mahogany and Louis Seize chairs, as well as for Stuart portraits. Such things warp young life," he wrote. And yet he noted with profound pride that his family was "anti-slavery by birth, as their name was Adams and their home was Quincy." Ultimately embracing the tenuous balance for which his grandparents struggled so hard, he affirmed that "running order through chaos, direction though space, discipline through freedom . . . must always be the task of education."[6]

ACKNOWLEDGMENTS

$\mathcal{T}$he Adams Papers, in breadth and depth, are astonishing, inspiring and best of all, thanks to John Quincy, wondrously available to any researcher who comes their way. Back in January 18, 1847, along with his bequest of books, manuscripts, documents and papers, and those of his father, he made two recommendations to his son Charles Francis. First he hoped that he would create a fireproof building in which to keep them safe; second, it was his wish that he keep them together as far as it was in his power as one library, to remain in the family and not to be sold or dispersed "as long as may be practicable."

Honoring John Quincy's vision, if not his name, and designed by the Boston architect Edward Cabot in brick, stone and slate, the one-room Stone Library, built on family property, opened in September 1780 and housed the collection accordingly until April 4, 1956 when, for want of space, the Adams family "gave custody of the personal and public papers (all but the books) written over a span of three centuries" to the safekeeping of the Massachusetts Historical Society, which remains a treasury not only for its contents but also for the staff, whose successive editions of Adams Family Correspondence and other related works are masterful works of impeccable scholarship.

On my first encounter at the MHS, writing about Abigail Adams, the esteemed Lyman H. Butterfield was editor in chief of the Adams Papers, and Len (Louis Leonard) Tucker was the Society's president. Fortunately for me, Len's generosity of spirit prevails. Dennis A. Fiori now presides as energetic president. C. James

Taylor, whose thoughtful reading improved my book immeasurably in matters of both fact and content, is now editor in chief of the Adams Papers. Members of his staff who have graciously come to my rescue include Judith Graham, Sara Georgini, Elaine Grublin, Hobson Woodward, Caitlin Christian-Lamb (former research associate) and especially Amanda Mathews. And none more faithfully or crucially over the years than Sara Sikes, who reached out to sources in St. Petersburg while assembling the images reproduced in this book.

Fortunately, a microfilm copy of the Adams Papers exists at Columbia University, to which affable David Adams, then a student at Marymount Manhattan College, made innumerable trips in order to photocopy John Quincy Adams's diary as well as much of his then unprinted correspondence, prior to its recent digital renderings. I am also grateful to Kelly McMaster who, as a Hertog fellow at Columbia University, rounded up information on John Quincy's many colorful, if often obscure, colleagues.

Frustration over the skimpy trove of Louisa Catherine Adams's letters, thought to be lost or destroyed, provoked the stubborn search of relevant libraries in locations where members of her family had lived in the hope that one or more might have preserved the stray remnants of her correspondence. In this cause, I was enormously aided by Candace Wainwright, who once and bravely owned a unique travel bookstore that stocked guide books together with corresponding literature. In this quest on behalf of Louisa Catherine, Candy contacted the Maryland Historical Society; the Wisconsin Historical Society, which holds the Boyd and Tanner Family Papers; the Hamilton College Library; the Bryn Mawr College Library; the Library of Congress; the Houghton and Widener Libraries at Harvard University; the New-York Historical Society and the Haverhill Public Library. Though the "dig" did not unearth a single early treasure, what was surprising was the number of letters Louisa Catherine wrote in old age that were heartbreaking in recollection of the frailties of her youth.

When it came to general research and access to streams of scholarly papers and for their spontaneous all-around assistance at the New York Public Library, I am indebted to Wayne Furman and

David Smith, and to Laura Ruffin for her gentle guidance in the Manuscripts and Archives Division.

In the initial stages of the book, it seemed as though Geraldine Sheehan's homecoming was perfect. After early years at *The New York Times* in Paris and New York, she served the State Department on both coasts of Africa, in Liberia and Somalia, and returned to Washington in time to encourage me to brave a biography of John Quincy Adams and to plan the scope of the book I would write. Her untimely death deprived me not only of an admirable friend but, if prior experience counts, a blunt yet inspiring critic.

When it came down to editing the book, as John Quincy was a man of infinite words and sensibilities and I in his thrall, it was my greatest luck that Michael Leahy offered to discipline both of us as chapter after chapter slipped out of my printer. Michael was, in the course of his years at *The New York Times,* a superb editor of several sections of the paper, including Arts & Leisure and Travel, and my book is infinitely improved by his discreetly penned "fly specks" and his probing questions about content, form and grammar. Heartened by his thoughtful judgment and taste, my appreciation of his friendship on behalf of John Quincy Adams is boundless.

My great good fortune has held with Deborah C. Gaisford's valiant role as a kind of managing editor, a coordinator in chief on all issues. Gifted as she is able and with a miraculous respect for detail, Deb, who writes and consults on the subject of health care, came to help with footnotes and to my enormous pleasure and relief stayed steadfast from introduction to bibliography.

Ultimately, I am indebted to my nephew, William Schwalbe, author and editor who introduced me to Elisabeth Dyssegaard. As executive editor at Palgrave Macmillan, Elizabeth's interest in John Quincy Adams and her appreciation of his talents and challenges has been extremely heartening. I also thank Donna Cherry, senior production manager, for her cordial guidance in routing the book to publication. Also, I happily share with Will his admiration of Lisa Queen, my wise and ever supportive agent.

Over the years, while John Quincy has seemed unfairly demanding, he has also been surprisingly rewarding. In the cause I have made and cherish new and deepened friendships, thankful for Jean Angell, Mardee Stone, Barbara Miller, Zoneida Felix, Elizabeth Niedbala, Karen Wilcox, Dr. Andrew Winneg, Blitz (Harriet) Leahy, Dr. Alvin Tierstein, Tony Downer and my office moving team of four, including Chris Yockey, Nate Diana, Will Levin and Rawle Deland. It is with great pleasure that I remember Catherine Hull, acclaimed horticulturist and a direct descendant of Louisa Catherine, who twice invited me to the fall family gathering at the Stone Library. For the solution and treatment of a unique health issue, I am ever in Dr. Anne Liebling's debt. And I will not forget Shirley Hazzard's deep smile and nod of certainty on learning that the book had come to pass.

Long in researching, rereading and rewriting, in the end it takes my entire family to actually produce any book that I write. I once likened the process to a kind of cottage industry, and so it remains. For translations from the French, for interpretation of Adams family finances and health issues, for literary, technological, philosophical and spiritual support, I am thankful for my sons John and Peter; my sons-in-law, Jonathan Deland and Mark di Suvero; my daughter-in-law Anna; my daughter Emme. In the past I noted that my daughter Kate, once a favorite filer, had turned into a thoughtful, witty and decisive editor. And so she has proven, indispensable this time around to the fate of John Quincy Adams. My grandson William Hayes Levin is the most recent recruit, as competent as he is inventive.

Usually, I could depend on my husband Wilbur Arthur Levin to read every word I put on paper. I counted on his help as stern grammarian, rigorous statistician and patient philosopher. When he suddenly became ill, I promised him I would keep at my work. I have done so, remembering him as my "Dearest Friend" every word of the way.

NOTES

INTRODUCTION

1. *Memoirs* 1:32.
2. The spelling JQA used is de la Fayette.
3. Anne Newport Royall, *Sketches of History, Life, and Manners in the United States* (New Haven: Johnson Reprint Corporation, 1826), 166.
4. Royall, *Sketches of History, Life, and Manners in the United States*, 166; AA to JQA, Jun. 23, 1797, Adams Papers; Andrew Oliver, *Portraits of JQA and His Wife* (Harvard Univ. Press, 1970), 38; AA2 to JQA, Sep. 5, 1785, *AFC* 6:307.
5. RC to JA, Nov. 3, 1781, *AFC* 4:242.
6. JQA to AA2, Sep. 27, 1778, *AFC* 3:93–4.
7. AA to Mary Cranch, Oct. 11, 1789, *New Letters of Abigail Adams*, 30.
8. George Washington to JA, Feb. 20, 1797, Jared Sparks, ed., *Writings of George Washington* (New York: Harper & Brothers, 1847) 11:188.
9. John F. Kennedy, *Profiles in Courage* (New York: Harper & Brothers, 1955), 35.
10. *Memoirs* 9:14.
11. Kennedy, *Profiles in Courage*, 35.
12. Ibid., 36.
13. *Memoirs* 1:28; AA to John Thaxter, Feb. 15, 1778, *AFC* 2:390; Oct. 4, 1785, *JQA Diary*. The last line is a reference to Hamlet, Act 1, scene iii, line 63: "Grapple them unto thy soul with hoops of steel."
14. L. H Butterfield, *DAJA* 1: xvi; May 20, 1840, *JQA Diary*; Apr. 1, 1791, *JQA Diary*.
15. Joseph Allan Nevins, ed. *The Diary of John Quincy Adams, 1794–1845* (New York, 1951), introduction.
16. *Memoirs* 1: viii.
17. *Writings* 1: vi; *AFC* 1, introduction.
18. Henry Adams, *The Education of Henry Adams* (Boston and New York: Houghton Mifflin, 1918), 17; *Diary of CFA*, xxiv.
19. Jul. 30, 1826, *JQA Diary*; Massachusetts Historical Society, "Miscellany," Fall 2009.

CHAPTER 1: "A LEGACY MORE VALUABLE THAN GOLD OR SILVER"

1. *DAJA,* 1:80; *JQA Diary,* Jun. 3, 1794.
2. *Memoirs* 1:28.
3. JA to JQA, May 26, 1794, *Writings* 1:190, n. 2.
4. Ibid.
5. JA to JQA, May 29, 1794, *Writings* 1:190, n. 2.
6. JA to JQA, May 30, 1794, *AFC* 10:199.
7. Henry Adams, *The Education of Henry Adams,* 8–9.
8. Charles F. Adams, *Three Episodes of Massachusetts History,* 2:872; Henry Adams, *The Birthplaces of Presidents John and John Quincy Adams,* 3.
9. JA to the Hon. Cotton Tufts, Esq., Aug. 27, 1787, *Proceedings of the Massachusetts Historical Society,* 1882–1883, 20:360.
10. JA to JQA, Dec. 2, 1794, *AFC* 10:285.
11. John T. Morse, *John Quincy Adams* (Cambridge: Riverside Press, Houghton Mifflin, 1899), 1; JQA to Skelton Jones, Apr. 17, 1809, *Writings* 3:252–96.
12. There is some conflict about the extent of the family: "in all eight sons and one daughter lived to grow up" states James Truslow Adams, *The Adams Family,* 4. According to J. Gardner Bartlett, *Henry Adams of Somersetshire, England, and Braintree, Mass.* (1927), Henry Adams did indeed have eight sons, but it was son # 3, Jonathan, who remained in England when the family came over in 1638 and only later came to America. JQA writes in a letter, August 25, 1840, to Josiah Adams, and Bartlett concurs, that the land grant Henry Adams had was for ten persons: himself, his wife, his daughter and seven sons. So, "if there were eight sons, did one son simply come here later or did he travel back to England and return to America at a later date? That remains unclear." Courtesy of Amanda A. Mathews, Assistant Editor, The Adams Papers, Massachusetts Historical Society.
13. JQA to Skelton Jones, Apr. 17, 1809, *Writings* 3:294–95.
14. Ibid.
15. Ibid.
16. Ibid.
17. *DAJA* 1:265.
18. AA to JA, Sep. 14, 1767, *AFC* 1:62.
19. Richard Frothingham, *Life and Times of Joseph Warren* (Boston: Little, Brown, 1865), 101.
20. *DAJA* 3:293.
21. *DAJA* 1:13.
22. JA to James Warren, Dec. 17, 1773, *Works of John Adams,* 9:333.
23. AA to JA, Aug. 19, 1774, *AFC* 1:143.
24. Eliza S. M. Quincy, *Memoir of Eliza S. M. Quincy* (Boston: J. Wilson & Son, 1861), 209.
25. *Memoirs* 8:325; AA to JA, Mar. 2–10, 1776, *AFC* 1:354.
26. JQA to Joseph Sturge, Mar. 1846, *AFC* 1:223, n. 3, (also original AA to JA, Jun. 20, 1776); *Memoirs* 1:5–6.
27. Jun. 17, 1786, *JQA Diary.*
28. AA to JA, Sep. 29, 1776, *AFC* 2:136; JA to AA, Oct. 8, 1776, *AFC* 2:141.

29. JA to AA, Jul. 3, 1776, *AFC* 2:27–8.

CHAPTER 2: "A GREAT DEAL OF ROOM
FOR ME TO GROW BETTER"

1. JA to AA, Jun. 30, 1774, *AFC* 1:117; JA to JQA, Aug. 11, 1777, *AFC* 2:308.
2. *DAJA* 3:256.
3. JA to AA, Jun. 23, 1774, *AFC* 1:109; JA to AA, Jul. 1, 1774, *AFC* 1:118.
4. *DAJA* 6:37–8.
5. AA to John Thaxter, Feb. 15, 1778, *AFC* 2:391; AA to Mercy Otis Warren, Jul. 16, 1773, *AFC* 1:85.
6. *Memoirs* 1:12.
7. JA to AA, Oct. 29, 1775, *AFC* 2:317–18.
8. Ibid.
9. JA to TBA, Mar. 16, 1777, *AFC* 2:178.
10. JA to CA, Mar. 17, 1777, *AFC* 2:179–80.
11. JA to AA2, Mar. 17, 1777, *AFC* 2:179.
12. JA to AA2, Apr. 18, 1776, *AFC* 1:388.
13. JA to AA, Sep. 26, 1775, *AFC* 1:285–86.
14. JA to AA, Apr. 15, 1776, *AFC* 1:384; AA to JQA, Jan. 19, 1780, *AFC* 3:268.
15. JA to JQA, Mar. 16, 1777, *AFC* 2:178.
16. JA to JQA, Aug. 11, 1777, *AFC* 2:307; JA to JQA, May 14, 1783, *AFC* 5:160.
17. JA to JQA, Jul. 27, 1777, *AFC* 2:290–91.
18. JA to JQA, May 14, 1781, *AFC* 4:114.
19. JA to JQA, May 14, 1783, *AFC* 5:161.
20. JQA to Elizabeth Cranch, 1773(?), *AFC* 1:91. This letter is undated but is assumed to be 1773 based on JQA's handwriting. See note 1.
21. JQA to JA, Oct. 13, 1774, *AFC* 1:167.
22. JQA to JA, Jun. 2, 1777, *AFC* 2:254.
23. JQA to JA, Mar. 23, 1777, *AFC* 2:186.
24. JA to AA, Jun. 29, 1777, *AFC* 2:271; JA to JQA, Apr. 18, 1776, *AFC* 1:388.
25. JA to AA, Jul. 7, 1776, *AFC* 2:39–40.
26. *DAJA* 4:5.
27. AA to John Thaxter, Feb. 15, 1778, *AFC* 2:390–92.
28. Ibid.
29. AA to JQA, Jun. 10(?), 1778, *AFC* 3:37.
30. Ibid.
31. AA to John Thaxter, Feb. 15, 1778, *AFC* 2:390.
32. Ibid.; AA to Hannah Quincy Lincoln Storer, Mar. 1, 1778, *AFC* 2:397.

CHAPTER 3: "SOME COMPENSATION FOR MY NOT
BEING WITH MY FRIENDS AT BRAINTREE"

1. *Life in a New England Town: Diary of JQA*, 7.
2. *DAJA* 2:286.
3. *DAJA* 2:282; *DAJA* 2:276–77.
4. *DAJA* 4:36.

5. *DAJA* 4:38–41.
6. *DAJA* 4:42–43.
7. JA to AA, Apr. 19, 1778, *AFC* 3:14 and n. 3.
8. JQA to AA, Apr. 20, 1778, *AFC* 3:16.
9. Ibid.
10. JQA to AA, May 25, 1778, *AFC* 3:29.
11. JQA to William Cranch, May 31, 1778, *AFC* 3:30.
12. JQA to TBA, May 29, 1778, *AFC* 3:29.
13. JQA to CA, Jun. 6, 1778, *AFC* 3:33.
14. JA to AA, Sep. 9, 1778, *AFC* 3:88.
15. JQA to CA, Oct. 3, 1778, *AFC* 3:102.
16. JQA to CA and TBA, Oct. 3, 1778, *AFC* 3:103–5.
17. Ibid.
18. *DAJA* 2:304; *DAJA* 4:120.
19. *DAJA* 2:347; *DAJA* 3:186; *DAJA* 2:302.
20. JA to AA, Nov. 27, 1778, *AFC* 3:122–23.
21. JA to AA, Dec. 3, 1778, *AFC* 3:128; JA to AA, Feb. 26, 1779, *AFC* 3:179; JA to AA, Feb. 28, 1779, *AFC* 3:183.
22. JQA to AA, Feb. 20, 1779, *AFC* 3:175–76.
23. *DAJA* 2:352.
24. *DAJA* 2:377; *DAJA* 2:354; JQA to AA, Feb. 20, 1779, *AFC* 3:176.
25. JA to AA, May 14, 1779, *AFC* 3:195.
26. *DAJA* 2:359, n. 3.
27. *DAJA* 2:375.
28. *DAJA* 2:385.
29. *DAJA* 4:179.
30. *DAJA* 4:174.
31. JQA Diary 1:xxxvii (editor's introduction); JQA to Rev. Henry Coleman, Aug. 25, 1826, Adams Papers.
32. AA to CA, Jan. 19, 1780, *AFC* 3:270.
33. AA to JQA, Jan. 19, 1780, *AFC* 3:267–69.
34. Ibid.

CHAPTER 4: A JOURNAL

1. JA to JQA, Jun. 1784, *AFC* 5:353.
2. Nov. 12, 1779, *JQA Diary*.
3. *Memoirs* 3:408; *Memoirs* 9:159.
4. Samuel F. Bemis, *John Quincy Adams and the Foundations of American Foreign Policy* (Westport: Greenwood Press, 1981), 258.
5. Nov. 14, 1779, *JQA Diary*.
6. JQA to AA, Nov. 20, 1779, *AFC* 3:238–39.
7. Nov. 24, 1779, *JQA Diary*.
8. Nov. 27, 1779, *JQA Diary*; Francis Dana's Journal of 1779–1780 quoted in JQA to AA, Nov. 20, 1779, AFC 3:238, n. 3.
9. Nov. 29, 1779, *JQA Diary*.
10. Dec. 7, 1779, *JQA Diary*.
11. Dec. 9, 1779, *JQA Diary*.
12. Dec. 8, 1779, *JQA Diary*.
13. *DAJA* 2:403–4.
14. *DAJA* 2:201.

15. Dec. 26, 1779, *JQA Diary*.
16. Dec. 14, 1779, *JQA Diary*.
17. The knight Hudibras and his squire Ralpho are the principal characters in Samuel Butler's mock-heroic poem *Hudibra*s. Dec. 15, 1779, n. 1, *JQA Diary*.
18. Dec. 18, 1779, *JQA Diary*.
19. Dec. 25, 1779, *JQA Diary*.
20. Dec. 26, 1779, *JQA Diary*.
21. Jan. 3, 1780, *JQA Diary*.
22. Jan. 4 & 6, 1780, *JQA Diary*.
23. JA to AA, Feb. 12, 1780, *AFC* 3:271–2; JA to AA, Jan.16, 1780, *AFC* 3:259; JQA to AA, Jan. 16, 1780, *AFC* 3:260.
24. JQA to AA, Feb. 17, 1780, *AFC* 3:279.
25. JQA to JA, Mar. 16, 1780, *AFC* 3:307.
26. JA to JQA, Mar. 17, 1780, *AFC* 3:307.
27. John A. Garraty, *The American Nation* (New York: Harper & Row, 1971), 174–45; Richard B. Morris, ed., *Encyclopedia of American History* (New York: Harper & Row, 1976), 105, 107.
28. Morris, ed., *Encyclopedia of American History,* 116, 118; Garraty, *The American Nation,* 175; Samuel F. Bemis, *The Diplomacy of the American Revolution: the Foundation of American Diplomacy* (New York, London: D. Appleton-Century, 1935), 184, 186–87.
29. *AFC* 3:391, n. 5; *DAJA* 2:442; *AFC* 3:394, n. 5.
30. Rector Verheyk to JA, Nov. 10, 1780, *AFC* 4:11–12.
31. JA to Rector Verheyk, Nov. 10, 1780, *AFC* 4:12.
32. Sep. 6, 1780, *JQA Diary*.
33. JA to AA, Dec. 18, 1780, *AFC* 4:34.
34. JA to AA, Jul. 11, 1781, *AFC* 4:170.
35. Ibid.

CHAPTER 5: "ALMOST AT THE WORLD'S END"

1. JQA to AA, Oct. 12 [23], 1781, *AFC* 4:233; instructions to Francis Dana from the President of Congress, Dec. 19, 1780, in Francis Wharton, ed., *The Revolutionary Diplomatic Correspondence of the United States* (Washington: Government Printing Office, 1888), 4:201.
2. *Francis Dana Letterbook, Official, 1781–1784,* Dana Family Papers, Massachusetts Historical Society, Series VI, Vol. 24–25.
3. JA to AA, Jul. 2, 1781, *AFC* 4:171, n. 3. See also *Correspondence of the Late President Adams originally published in the Boston Patriot in a series of letters,* (Boston: Everett and Munroe, 1809), 570–71.
4. Benjamin Franklin to the President of Congress, Aug. 9, 1780, in Wharton, ed., *The Revolutionary Diplomatic Correspondence of the United States,* 4:24; JA to Francis Dana, Apr. 18, 1781, *JA Papers,* 11:269.
5. Francis Dana to JA, *Francis Dana Letterbook, Official, 1781–1784,* Dana Family Papers, Massachusetts Historical Society, Series VI, Vol. 24–25. Francis Dana to Arthur Lee, May 17, 1781, *Francis Dana Letterbook,* 1780–1781, 182, Dana Family Papers, Massachusetts Historical Society; Albert S. Cosby, *America, Russia, Hemp, and Napoleon: American Trade with Russia and the Baltic, 1783–1812* (Columbus: Ohio State University Press, 1965).

6. Jul. 9, 1781, *JQA Diary.*
7. Jul. 10–11, 1781, *JQA Diary.*
8. Jul. 12, 1781, *JQA Diary; Francis Dana Journals, 1781–1783,* Dana Family Papers, Massachusetts Historical Society, Series VI, Vol. 26–27.
9. Jul. 16, 1781, *JQA Diary.*
10. JQA to JA, Aug. 21, 1781, *AFC* 4:206–7.
11. Ibid.
12. AA to JA, Sep. 22, 1774, *AFC* 1:162; Henry Adams, *The Education of Henry Adams,* 25.
13. JQA to JA, Aug. 21 [Sep. 1], 1781, *AFC* 4:206–7; JQA to John Thaxter, Sep. 8/19, 1781, *AFC* 4:214; *Memoirs* 2:53.
14. JQA to AA, Oct. 12, 1781, *AFC* 4:233–34.
15. Ibid.
16. W. P. Cresson, *Francis Dana, A Puritan Diplomat at the Court of Catherine the Great,* (New York: Dial Press, 1930), 183, 196.
17. Francis Dana to JA, Aug. 28, 1781. *JA Papers* 11:478; Cresson, *Francis Dana, A Puritan Diplomat,* 177.
18. JQA to JA, Oct. 12, 1781, *AFC* 4:234–35.
19. JA to JQA, Dec. 15, 1781, *AFC* 4:264.
20. Ibid.
21. JQA to JA, Jan. 1 [12], 1782, *AFC* 4:275–77.
22. Ibid.
23. Francis Dana to JA, Jan. 11, 1782, *AFC* 4:277 n. 1.
24. Jan. 27. 1782, *JQA Diary.*
25. JQA, 15 years later, as United States minister to Berlin, became proficient in the language and was considered an American pioneer in the study of German culture, the "father of German studies" in America. (See Francis Dana to JA, Mar. 28 [Apr. 8], 1782, in *JA Papers* 12:397; Walter J. Morris, "John Quincy Adams's German Library," in *Proceedings of the American Philosophical Society,* v. 118, no. 4, August 1974, Penn State, diss.1963, microfilm, 1965.)
26. JQA to John Thaxter, Jan. 2, 1782, *AFC* 4:278–79.
27. Ibid.
28. Jul. 11, 1782, *JQA Diary.*
29. JQA to Elizabeth Cranch, Mar. 17, 1782, *AFC* 4:297.
30. Ibid.
31. JQA to John Thaxter, Jul. 11, 1782, *AFC* 4:352.
32. John Thaxter to JQA, Aug. 14, 1782, *AFC* 4:359.
33. Mar. 10, 1787, *JQA Diary;* Charles F. Adams, "Memoir of Charles Francis Adams, by his son," in *Proceedings of the Massachusetts Historical Society, 1899–1900,* 199.
34. JA to JQA, May 13, 1782, *AFC* 4:323.
35. JQA to AA, Jul. 23, 1783, *AFC* 5:214–16.
36. Ibid.
37. AA2 to JQA, Nov. 27, [1785], *AFC* 6:469; JQA to Alexander H. Everett, Aug. 19, 1811, *Everett-Peabody Papers,* Massachusetts Historical Society.
38. AA to JQA, Nov. 13, 1782, *AFC* 5:38.
39. JQA to AA, Jul. 30, 1783, *AFC* 5:220–21.
40. JQA to AA, Sep. 10, 1783, *AFC* 5:242–44.
41. Ibid.
42. AA to JQA, Dec. 26, 1783, *AFC* 5:283–84.

43. Ibid.

44. Ibid.

45. AA to JQA, Mar. 15, 1784, *AFC* 5:310.

CHAPTER 6: "PROMISE TO PRODUCE A WORTHY CHARACTER"

1. Quote from *The Studio,* New York, new series 2:154 (March 1887) in Andrew Oliver, *Portraits of John Quincy Adams and His Wife* (Harvard Univ. Press, 1970), 19.

2. Oliver, *Portraits of John Quincy Adams and His Wife,* 17.

3. *Memoirs,* 2:650.

4. JA to Sigourney, Ingraham & Bromfield, Apr. 13, 1781, *JA Papers,* 11:257; JA to Francis Dana, Mar. 15, 1782. *JA Papers,* 12:323.

5. JA to JQA, May 14, 1783, *AFC* 5:161; John Thaxter to AA, Jul. 27, 1782, *AFC* 4:355.

6. Samuel Flagg Bemis, *Diplomacy of the American Revolution* (New York and London: D. Appleton-Century, 1935), 126; JA to JQA, May 14, 1783, *AFC* 5:161.

7. JQA to JA, May 24, 1783, *AFC* 5:165; Oliver, *Portraits of John Quincy Adams and His Wife,* 17.

8. JA to JQA, May 14, 1783, *AFC* 5:160.

9. JA to JQA, May 19, 1783, *AFC* 5:162–3.

10. JA to JQA, May 29, 1783, *AFC* 5:166.

11. Jul. 22, 1783, *JQA Diary;* Oliver, *Portraits of John Quincy Adams and His Wife,* 17.

12. JA to AA, Mar. 22, 1782, *AFC* 4:300.

13. *JA Papers* 12:420; *DAJA* 3:9, n. 1.

14. *DAJA* 3:106.

15. JA to AA, Jul. 17, 1783, *AFC* 5:202; *DAJA* 3:141, n. 1.

16. Aug. 7, 1783, *JQA Diary.*

17. JA to AA, Aug. 14, 1783, *AFC* 5:221.

18. JA to AA2, Aug. 13, 1783, *AFC* 5:223.

19. Aug. 12, 1783, *JQA Diary.*

20. Aug. 16, 1783, *JQA Diary.*

21. Aug. 27, 1783, *JQA Diary.*

22. Aug. 28, 1783, *JQA Diary,* n. 3; Sep. 20, 1783, *JQA Diary.*

23. Aug. 27 and Sep. 22, 1783, JQA *Diary.*

24. Sep. 3, 1783, *JQA Diary.*

25. Sep. 7, 1783, *JQA Diary;* Jared Sparks, ed. *The Diplomatic Correspondence of the American Revolution* (Boston: Nathan Hale and Gray & Bowen, 1830) 7:156, note.

26. JA to AA, Sep. 7, 1783, *AFC* 5:236.

27. Ibid.

28. Sep. 22, 1783, *JQA Diary; DAJA* 3:144, n. 4; *DAJA* 3:146.

29. JA to AA, Sep. 1, 1783, *AFC* 5:231.

30. *DAJA* 3:147; *Boston Patriot,* May 6, 1812, reprinted in *DAJA* 3:149, n. 1.

CHAPTER 7: "A SON WHO IS THE
GREATEST TRAVELLER OF HIS AGE"

1. *Boston Patriot,* Feb. 17, 1812, reprinted in *DAJA* 3:153, n. 3.

2. JQA to Elizabeth Cranch, Apr. 18, 1784, *AFC* 5:322–24.
3. Ibid.
4. Ibid.
5. Ibid.
6. Ibid.
7. Ibid.
8. Ibid.
9. Ibid.
10. Oct. 28, 1783, *JQA Diary.*
11. JQA to Peter Jay Munro, Nov. 4, 1783, in Landa M. Freeman et al., eds., *Selected Letters of John Jay and Sarah Livingston Jay: Correspondence by or to the First Chief Justice of the United States and His Wife,* (Jefferson, N.C., 2005), 145–46.
12. *Boston Patriot,* Feb. 17, 1812, reprinted in *DAJA* 3:153, n. 3.
13. Ibid.
14. JA to AA, Jan. 25, 1784, *AFC* 5:302.
15. AA to JQA, Mar. 15, 1784, *AFC* 5:310.
16. JA to JQA, May 28, 1784, *AFC* 5:334.
17. JQA to JA, Jun. 1, 1784, *AFC* 5:335.
18. JA to JQA, Jun. 11, 1784, *AFC* 4:342–43.
19. JQA to JA, Jun. 6, 1784, *AFC* 5:339–40.
20. JQA to JA, Jun. 18, 1784, *AFC* 5:347–48.
21. Ibid.
22. JQA to Elizabeth Cranch, Apr. 18, 1784, *AFC* 5:324.
23. JA to JQA, Jun. 21, 1784, *AFC* 5:351.
24. AA to JA, Jul. 23, 1784, *AFC* 5:397.
25. JA to AA, Jul. 26, 1784, *AFC* 5:399.
26. AA2 to Elizabeth Cranch, Jul. 30, 1784, *AFC* 5:411–12.
27. Ibid., *AFC* 5:412.
28. AA to Mary Smith Cranch, Jul. 30, 1784, *AFC* 5:382.
29. AA to Elizabeth Cranch, Aug. 1, 1784, *AFC* 5:414.
30. JQA to JA, Jul. 30, 1784, *AFC* 5:412.
31. AA2 Diary, Aug. 7, 1784, in L.H. Butterfield et al., eds., *The Book of Abigail and John: Selected Letters of the Adams Family, 1762–1784,* (Cambridge, MA, 1975), 397–98.
32. AA to Mary Cranch, Jul. 30, 1784, *AFC* 5:382.

CHAPTER 8: "A SISTER WHO FULFILLS MY MOST SANGUINE EXPECTATIONS"

1. AA to Mary Smith Cranch, Dec. 12, 1784, *Letters of Mrs. Adams* 2:64.
2. Phyllis Lee Levin, *Abigail Adams* (New York: St. Martin's Press, 2001), 174–75; *DAJA* 3:171.
3. AA to Elizabeth Cranch, Sep. 5, 1784, *AFC* 5:434.
4. AA2 to Elizabeth Cranch, Sep. 4, 1784, *AFC* 5:428.
5. Ibid.
6. AA2 to Lucy Cranch, Sep. 4, 1784, *AFC* 5:431.
7. *AFC* 3:xxxv. It's possible that JQA's response may have been lost when AA2's papers were destroyed by fire in 1862. *AFC* 4:127, n. 1.
8. AA to JA, Jun. 8, 1777, *AFC* 2:258; AA to JA, Dec. 30, 1782, *AFC* 5:62; JA to AA, Dec. 2, 1778, *AFC* 3:125.

9. Jonathan Mason to AA, Sep. 18, 1776, *AFC* 2:127; AA to Mercy Otis Warren, Dec. 10, 1778, *AFC* 3:133; JA to AA2, Dec. 12, 1779, *AFC* 3:248.
10. AA2 to JQA, May 24, 1781, *AFC* 4:127.
11. AA2 to JQA, May 3, 1782, *AFC* 4:319–20.
12. Ibid.
13. Ibid.
14. AA to JA, Jul. 17, 1782, *AFC* 4:344.
15. JA to AA2, Sep. 26, 1782, *AFC* 4:383.
16. AA2 to JA, May 10, 1783, *AFC* 5:156.
17. Ibid.
18. AA to JA, Dec. 23, 1782, *AFC* 5:56.
19. AA to JA, Dec. 23, 1782, L. Butterfield, ed., *The Book of Abigail and John* (Cambridge: Harvard University Press, 1975), 334.
20. Ibid.
21. Dec. 23, 1782, *The Earliest Diary of John Adams,* ed. L.H. Butterfield, 4 vols. (Cambridge: Harvard University Press, Belknap Press), 23.
22. *The Book of Abigail and John,* 334–36.
23. Ibid.
24. AA to JA, Dec. 23, 1782, *AFC* 5:55.
25. Ibid., 334–35.
26. JA to AA, Jan. 22, 1783, *The Book of Abigail and John,* 338.
27. Ibid. The remark about his own ability to support a family is a direct reference to his recent concern: the protracted final negotiations to achieve agreement on fishing rights in the Treaty of Paris.
28. JA to AA, Jan. 29, 1783, *AFC* 5:83.
29. JA to AA, Jan. 25, 1784, *AFC* 5:301.
30. JA to AA, Jul. 26, 1784, *AFC* 5:400.
31. AA in *DAJA* 3:161, Jul. 1, 1784.
32. Royall Tyler to JA, Aug. 27, 178, *AFC* 5:425–26.
33. AA2 to Elizabeth Cranch, Sep. 30, 1784, *AFC* 5:464–65.
34. AA2 to Mercy Otis Warren, Sep. 5, 1784, *AFC* 5:454.
35. AA2 to Elizabeth Cranch, Dec. 10, 1784, *AFC* 6:23–6; AA to Royall Tyler, Jan. 4, 1785; *AFC* 6:45–50.
36. AA2 to Elizabeth Cranch, Dec. 10, 1784, *AFC* 6:25.
37. AA to Royall Tyler, Jan. 4, 1785, *AFC* 6:47.
38. Ibid.
39. Jan. 29, 1785, *JQA Diary;* Mar. 11, 1785, *JQA Diary.*
40. May 4, 1785, *JQA Diary.*
41. Feb. 26, 1785, *JQA Diary.*
42. Jan. 10, 1785, *JQA Diary.*
43. Mar. 12, 1785, *JQA Diary.*
44. Ibid. Mar. 15, 1785, *JQA Diary.*
45. Mar. 25, 1785, *JQA Diary;* Mar. 24, 1785, *JQA Diary.*
46. Mar. 27, 1785, *JQA Diary.*
47. Mar. 28, 1785, *JQA Diary,* n. 2.
48. Feb. 21, 1785, *JQA Diary.*
49. Apr. 1, 1785, *JQA Diary* 1:243.
50. Ibid.
51. Ibid.
52. Apr. 9, 1785, *JQA Diary.*

53. Ibid.
54. Ibid.
55. Apr. 26, 1785, *JQA Diary.*
56. *DAJA* 2:177, n. 1; Apr. 26, 1785, *JQA Diary.*
57. Ibid.
58. Ibid. Quote is from Shakespeare's *Henry VIII.*
59. *Memoirs,* 1:20.
60. Charles Thomson to Benjamin Franklin, Mar. 7, 1785, Resolution from the Continental Congress in *The Papers of Benjamin Franklin* (New Haven: Yale University Press).
61. JQA to William Cranch, Dec. 14, 1784, *AFC* 6:32–33.
62. AA to Mary Cranch, Dec. 12, 1784, *Letters,* 2:66.
63. Worthington C. Ford, ed., *Statesman and Friend: Correspondence of John Adams with Benjamin Waterhouse, 1784–1822,* (Boston: Little, Brown, 1927), 46.
64. Corres. in the *Boston Patriot,* 572 in AFC 4:332–33.
65. Ford, ed. *Statesman and Friend,* 5–9.
66. AA to Mary Cranch, Apr. 15, 1785, *AFC* 6:83; AA to JQA, Jun. 26, 1785, *AFC* 6:194–97.
67. AA to Elizabeth Smith Shaw, Jan. 11, 1785, *AFC* 6:56.
68. Ibid.
69. AA2 to Lucy Cranch, Jun. 23, 1785, *AFC* 6:183.
70. AA2 to Lucy Cranch, May 6, 1785, *AFC* 6:127: AA2 to Elizabeth Cranch, May 6, 1785, *AFC* 6:124–26.
71. Ibid.
72. Ibid.
73. Ibid.
74. AA2 to Lucy Cranch, May 6, 1785, *AFC* 6:127.
75. May 11, 1785, *JQA Diary.*
76. May 12, 1785, *JQA Diary;* JQA to AA2, May 11[12], 1785, *AFC* 6:144.

CHAPTER 9: "YOUR EVER AFFECTIONATE BROTHER"

1. AA2 to JQA, Aug. 3, 1785, *AFC* 6:218; JQA to AA2, May 29, 1785, *AFC* 6:155; AA2 to JQA, Aug. 3, 1785, *AFC* 6:218.
2. AA2 to JQA, Jul. 26, 1785, *AFC* 6:212.
3. JQA to AA2, May 17, 1785, *AFC* 6:149.
4. JQA to AA2, May 18, 1785, *AFC* 6:149–50.
5. JQA to AA2, May 20, 1785. *AFC* 6:150.
6. AA2 to JQA, Jul. 4, 1785; letter, Friday, undated, possibly Jul. 11, 1785, *AFC* 6:208.
7. JQA to AA2, Aug. 26, 1785, *AFC* 6:289.
8. JQA to AA2, Aug. 31, 1785. *AFC* 6:319.
9. AA2 to JQA, Jul. 4, 1785, *AFC* 6:204–5.
10. Ibid.
11. Ibid.
12. AA2 to JQA, Aug. 11, 1785, *AFC* 6:220.
13. Ibid.
14. *AFC* 6:181, n. 8.
15. AA2 to JQA, Jul. 26, 1785, *AFC* 6:212–16 and n. 24.
16. Ibid.

17. Ibid.
18. Ibid.
19. AA2 to JQA, Jul. 31, 1785, *AFC* 6:216.
20. AA2 to Mary Cranch, Jun. 22, 1785, *AFC* 6:181.
21. AA2 to JQA, Sep. 13, 1785, *AFC* 6:310.
22. AA2 to JQA, Sep. 22, 1785, *AFC* 6:380.
23. AA2 to JQA, Aug. 11, 1785, *AFC* 6:219.
24. AA to JQA, Aug. 11, 1785, *AFC* 6:261.
25. AA2 to JQA, Jul. 7, 1785, *AFC* 6:207.
26. AA to JQA, Feb. 16, 1786, *AFC* 7:63–65.
27. AA to JQA, Sep. 6, 1785, *AFC* 6:343–44.
28. AA to JQA, Sep. 6, 1785, *AFC* 6:343, n. 6.
29. AA2 to JQA, Thursday (probably Sep. 29, 1785), *AFC* 6:385.
30. AA to JQA, Sep. 6, 1785, *AFC* 6:343.
31. AA to JQA, Feb. 16, 1786, *AFC* 7:62.
32. AA2 to JQA, Sep. 5, 1785, *AFC* 6:306–7.
33. AA2 to JQA, Sep. 5, 1785, *AFC* 6:306–7; JQA to AA2, May 25 & 29, 1785, *AFC* 6:155.
34. JQA to AA2, Jun. 14, 1785, *AFC* 6:157–58.
35. JQA to AA2, Jul. 17, 1785, *AFC* 6:161; Robert East, *John Quincy Adams: The Critical Years (1785–1794)* (New York: Bookman Associates, 1962), 15.

CHAPTER 10: "THE SENTIMENTS OF MY HEART AS THEY RISE"

1. JQA to AA2, Jul. 19, 1785, *AFC* 6:226.
2. JQA to AA2, Aug. 5, 1785, *AFC* 6:244.
3. JQA to JA, Aug. 3, 1785, *AFC* 6:250–51 and n. 3.
4. Aug. 14, 1785, *JQA Diary;* JQA to AA2, Aug. 14, 1785, *AFC* 6:253.
5. JQA to AA2, Aug. 19, 1785, *AFC* 6:255.
6. JQA to AA2, Aug. 25, 1785, *AFC* 6:289; Aug. 26, 1785, *JQA Diary*.
7. Ibid.
8. JQA to AA2, Aug. 26, 1785, *AFC* 6:289–90.
9. JQA to AA2, Aug. 28, 1785, *AFC* 6:291; Aug. 28, 1785, *JQA Diary;* JQA to AA2, Sep. 26, 1785, *AFC* 6:375 and n.17; Aug. 28, 1785, *JQA Diary*.
10. Aug. 31, 1785, *JQA Diary*.
11. The population of Haverhill, Massachusetts, in the first U.S. Census of 1790 was 2,408. George W. Chase, ed. *Abstract of the Census of Massachusetts, 1860* (Boston: Wright & Potter, 1863), 26; JQA to AA2, Sep. 7, 1785, *AFC* 6:325.
12. Elizabeth Smith Shaw to AA, Sep. 7, 1785, *AFC* 6:347–8.
13. Ibid.
14. Dec. 12, 1785, *JQA Diary*.
15. Dec. 25, 1785, Oct. 4, 1785, *JQA Diary*.
16. Dec. 25, 1785, *JQA Diary*.
17. Elizabeth Smith Shaw to AA, Jan. 8, 1786, *AFC* 7:3; Mary Cranch to AA, Feb. 9, 1786, *AFC* 7:47.
18. Feb. 22, 1786, *JQA Diary*.
19. Jan. 14, 1786, *JQA Diary*.
20. JQA to William Cranch, Nov. 1, 1785, *AFC* 6:448; Nov. 23, 1785, *JQA Diary*.

21. Jan. 17, 1786, *JQA Diary.*
22. Dec. 21, 1785, *JQA Diary;* Jan. 6, 1786, *JQA Diary.*
23. Jan. 13, 1786, *JQA Diary;* JQA to AA2, Oct. 5, 1785, *AFC* 6:399–400.
24. Ibid.
25. Ibid.
26. JQA to AA2, Oct. 19, 1785, *AFC* 6:402.
27. Ibid.
28. Oct. 10, 1785, *JQA Diary;* Oct. 16, 1785, *JQA Diary.*
29. JQA to AA2, Oct. 27, 1785, *AFC* 6:443; JQA to AA2, Oct. 29, 1785, *AFC* 6:444.
30. Nov. 3, 1785, *JQA Diary.*
31. Nov. 12, 1785, *JQA Diary.*
32. Jan. 9, 1786, *JQA Diary.*
33. Feb. 9, 1786, *JQA Diary.*
34. JQA to AA2, Sep. 27, 1785, *AFC* 6:374–75.
35. Elizabeth Smith Shaw to AA2, Jun. 4, 1786, *AFC* 7:213–14.
36. Ibid.
37. Jan. 31, 1786, *JQA Diary;* Nov. 14, 1785, *JQA Diary.*
38. Jan. 7, 1786, *JQA Diary.*
39. Elizabeth Smith Shaw to AA2, Feb. 14, 1786, *AFC* 7:58.
40. Matthew Prior, "An English Padlock," lines 78–79, only JQA has reversed the lines. *JQA Diary,* Jan. 13, 1786, n. 1; Elizabeth Smith Shaw to AA2, Feb. 14, 1786, *AFC* 7:58–59.
41. Elizabeth Smith Shaw to AA2, Feb. 14, 1786, *AFC* 7:58–59; Elizabeth Smith Shaw to AA, Mar. 18, 1786, *AFC* 7:93–94.
42. Elizabeth Smith Shaw to AA, Mar. 18, 1786, *AFC* 7:93–94.
43. Feb. 4, 1786, *JQA Diary.*
44. Ibid.
45. Mar. 15, 1786, *JQA Diary:* "The first book was Horace, where Mr. [Eleazar] James, the Latin tutor told me to turn to the Carmen saeculare where I construed 3 stanza's, and parsed the word *sylvarum,* but called *potens* a substantive. Mr. [Timothy Lindall] Jennison, the Greek tutor then put me to the beginning of the fourth Book of Homer; I construed Lines, but parsed wrong [Greek word]. I had then [Greek word] given me. I was then asked a few questions in Watts's Logic by Mr. [John] Hale, and a considerable number in Locke, on the *Understanding,* very few of which I was able to answer. The next thing was Geography, where Mr. [Nathan] Read ask'd me what was the figure of the Earth, and several other questions, some of which I answered; and others not. Mr. Williams asked me if I had studied Euclid, and arithmetic, after which the president conducted me to another room, and gave me the following piece of English to turn into Latin—from *The World* [which John Quincy copied into his diary from memory], No. 171, 8 April, 1756:

> There cannot certainly be an higher ridicule, than to give an air of importance, to amusements, if they are in themselves contemptible and voice of taste, but if they are the object and care of the judicious and polite and really deserve that distinction, the conduct of them is certainly of consequence. I made it thus: *Nihil profecto risu dignior, potest esse, quam magni aestimare delectamenta, si per se despicienda sunt, atque sine sapore. At si rest oblatae atque cura sunt sagtacibus et*

*artibus excultis, et revera hanc distinctionem merent, administration
eorum haud dubie utilitatis est.*

46. JQA to AA2, Mar. 15, 1786, *AFC* 7:90.
47. JQA to AA2, Mar. 22, 1786, *AFC* 7:91.
48. Ibid.; JQA to Elizabeth Smith Shaw, Mar. 29, 1786, *AFC* 7:118.
49. JA to JQA, May 26, 1786, *AFC* 7:205.
50. Mar. 15, 1786, *JQA Diary.*
51. JQA to JA, Apr. 2, 1786, *AFC* 7:131.

CHAPTER 11: "STUDY IS MY MISTRESS"

1. Henry Adams, "Harvard College 1786–87," *North American Review* (Boston: James Osgood, vol. 114, Jan. 1872), 115–18.
2. Dec. 22, 1787, *JQA Diary.*
3. JQA to AA2, Mar. 22, 1786, *AFC* 7:92.
4. Mar. 23, 1786, *JQA Diary.*
5. JQA to Elizabeth Smith Shaw, Mar. 29, 1786, *AFC* 7:118; Mar. 24, 1786, *JQA Diary.*
6. Mar. 28, 1786, *JQA Diary.*
7. JQA to AA2, Apr. 1, 1786, *AFC* 7:118–19.
8. Ibid.
9. JQA to AA, May 15, 1786, *AFC* 7:163–64.
10. Elizabeth Cranch to AA, Jul. 1, 1786, *AFC* 7:229.
11. Lucy Cranch to AA, Jun. 24, 1786, *AFC* 7:227.
12. May 16, 1786, Sep. 12, 1786, Sep. 9, 1786, Sep. 26, 1786, *JQA Diary.*
13. Jun. 26, 1786, *JQA Diary.*
14. Jun. 21, 1786, *JQA Diary.*
15. Jul. 6, 1786, *JQA Diary.*
16. Ibid.
17. Ibid.
18. Bemis, *John Quincy Adams and the Foundations of American Foreign Policy* (Westport: Greenwood Press, 1981), 21.
19. Sep. 7, 1786, *JQA Diary.*
20. Ibid.
21. Ibid.
22. Nov. 20, 1786, *JQA Diary.*
23. Sep. 14, 1787, *JQA Diary.*
24. AA to Thomas Jefferson, Jan. 29, 1787, *AFC* 7:455; Charles F. Adams, *History of Braintree, Massachusetts (1639–1708)* (Cambridge: Riverside Press, 1891), 265.
25. JQA to AA, Dec. 30, 1786, *AFC* 7:418.
26. Ibid.
27. Ibid.
28. Sep. 26, 1786, *JQA Diary.*
29. Ibid.
30. Sep. 29, 1786, *JQA Diary.* Quote is from *King Henry V,* Act IV, sc.3.
31. Ibid.
32. Ibid.
33. JQA to AA2, Apr. 15, 1786, *AFC* 7:157; paraphrase of Alexander Pope, "Ode for Music on St Cecilia's Day."

34. Mar. 28, 1787, *JQA Diary;* JQA to AA2, Jan. 14, 1787, *AFC* 7:434.
35. *Memoirs* 1:99.
36. JQA to AA2, Apr. 11, 1786, *AFC* 7:121; Mar. 26, 1786, *JQA Diary;* May 15, 1786, *JQA Diary;* Oct. 27, 1786, *JQA Diary.*
37. Feb. 15, 1787, *JQA Diary.*
38. AA2 to JQA, Sep. 1, 1786, *AFC* 7:328.
39. Oct. 19, 1786, *JQA Diary.*
40. JQA to AA, Dec. 30, 1786, *AFC* 7:419; JQA to AA2, Jan. 14, 1787, *AFC* 7:433.
41. Ibid., 7:434–37.
42. Ibid.
43. Ibid.
44. Ibid.
45. Ibid.
46. JQA to AA, May 19, 1786, *AFC* 7:165: JQA to AA2, Jun. 10, 1786, *AFC* 7:169.
47. JQA to AA2, Jan. 14, 1787, *AFC* 7:434; AA to JQA, Feb. 16, 1786, *AFC* 7:63.
48. Ibid.
49. JQA to AA, May 19, 1786, AFC 7:164.
50. AA2 to JQA, Jul. 22, 1786, *AFC* 7:282–83.
51. Mar. 2, 1787, *JQA Diary.*
52. Jun. 20, 1787, *JQA Diary;* JQA to AA, Aug. 1, 1787, *Writings* 1:33–34, n. 3.
53. Lucy Cranch to AA, Aug. 18, 1787, *AFC* 8:142; Elizabeth Smith Shaw to AA, Jul. 22, 1787, *AFC* 8:135.
54. *Writings* 1:34.
55. Jul. 18, 1787, *JQA Diary.*
56. JQA to JA, Aug. 30, 1786, *AFC* 7:326.
57. AA to JQA, Nov. 22, 1786, *AFC* 7:394; JQA to JA, Sep. 21, 1790, *AFC* 7:118; JA to JQA, Jan. 10, 1787, *AFC* 7:429.
58. Jul. 11, 1787, *JQA Diary.*
59. Aug 14, 1787, *JQA Diary.*
60. Aug. 16, 1787, n. 1, *JQA Diary.*
61. Mary Cranch to AA, Sep. 1, 1787, *AFC* 8:146.
62. Aug. 30, 1877, *JQA Diary.*

CHAPTER 12: "A STUDENT IN THE OFFICE OF THEOPHILUS PARSONS"

1. *Memoirs* 1:23; Charles F. Adams, ed., *Life in a New England Town* (Newburyport: Little, Brown, 1903), 6.
2. C. F. Adams, ed., *Life in a New England Town,* 6–7.
3. Ibid., 8–9.
4. Ibid., 8.
5. Sep. 9, 1787, *JQA Diary;* Sep. 19, 1787, *JQA Diary.*
6. Sep. 29, 1787, *JQA Diary.*
7. Sep. 30, 1787, *JQA Diary.*
8. Oct. 3, 1787, *JQA Diary.*
9. Mar. 8, 1788, *JQA Diary.*

10. Oct. 20, 1787, *JQA Diary.*
11. Oct. 22, 1787, *JQA Diary.*
12. Nov. 23, 1787, *JQA Diary.*
13. Ibid.
14. Nov. 24, 1787, *JQA Diary.*
15. Dec. 6, 1787, *JQA Diary.*
16. Ibid.
17. Dec. 18, 1787, *JQA Diary;* Dec. 25, 1787, *JQA Diary.*
18. JQA to AA, Dec. 23, 1787, *Writings* 1:37.
19. Jan. 1, 1788, *JQA Diary.*
20. Samuel F. Bemis, *John Quincy Adams and the Foundations of American Foreign Policy* (Westport, CT: Greenwood Press, 1981), x.
21. Jan. 4, 1788, *JQA Diary.*
22. Jan. 2, 1788, *JQA Diary;* JQA to Dr. Benjamin Waterhouse, Dec. 15, 1832 in Bemis, *Foundations,* 24, n. 51.
23. Jan. 12, 1788, *JQA Diary.*
24. Jan. 16, 1788, *JQA Diary.*
25. Jan. 24, 1788, *JQA Diary;* JQA to AA, May 19, 1786, *AFC* 7:165; AA2 to JQA, Jul. 22, 1786, *AFC* 7:284; Elizabeth Smith Shaw to AA, May 20, 1787, *AFC* 8:55, n. 8.
26. Mar. 28, 1788, *JQA Diary;* Apr. 8, 1788, *JQA Diary.*
27. Dec. 28, 1839, *Memoirs* 10:175.
28. Oct. 12, 1787, *JQA Diary.*
29. Ibid.
30. Feb. 8, 1788, *JQA Diary.*
31. Feb. 7, 1788, and Mar. 5, 1788, *JQA Diary.*
32. Jul. 9, 1827, *Memoirs* 7:307.
33. Jan. 26, 1788, *JQA Diary.*
34. May 13, 1788, *JQA Diary.*
35. Ibid.; JA to JQA, Sep. 9, 1785, *AFC* 7:356.
36. Aug. 2, 1787, *JQA Diary.*
37. Mercy Otis Warren to AA, Jul. 30, 1788, *AFC* 8:283–84.
38. Jun. 18, 1788, *JQA Diary.*
39. Jun. 20, 1788, *JQA Diary.*
40. Jul. 17, 1788, *JQA Diary.*
41. Jul. 11, 1788, *JQA Diary.*
42. Jan. 2 and May 16, 1788, *JQA Diary.*
43. Aug. 13, 1788, *JQA Diary.*
44. Sep. 13–20, 1788, *JQA Diary;* Elizabeth Smith Shaw to AA, Sep. 21, 1788, *AFC* 8:297.
45. Ibid.
46. Elizabeth Smith Shaw to AA, Oct. 3, 1788, *AFC* 8:301.
47. Oct. 1, 1788, *JQA Diary,* from *Henry IV,* pt. 2, Act 3, sc. 1.
48. Oct. 14, 1788, *JQA Diary.*
49. Oct.-Dec., 1788, *JQA Diary;* Dec. 10, 1788, *JQA Diary;* Dec. 11, 1788, *JQA Diary.*

CHAPTER 13: "EXPOSED TO THE PERILS OF SENTIMENT"

1. JQA to JA, Jun. 28, 1789, *AFC* 8:380.

2. JQA to JA Jun. 28, 1789, *AFC* 8:384, n. 2, 3 and 7: Parsons never held any federal positions; he was named chief justice of the Mass. Supreme Judicial Court in 1806.
3. JA to JQA, Jul. 9, 1789, *AFC* 8:386.
4. AA to JQA, Nov. 22, 1789, *AFC* 8:442.
5. Oct. 18, 1789, *JQA Diary*; C. F. Adams, ed., *Life in a New England Town* (Newburyport: Little, Brown, 1903), 177.
6. AA to JQA, Nov. 22, 1789, *AFC* 8:442.
7. JQA to AA, Dec. 5, 1789, *AFC* 8:445–46.
8. Ibid.
9. JA to JQA, Feb. 9, 1790, *AFC* 9:14.
10. JA to JQA, Feb. 19, 1790, *AFC* 9:16.
11. JQA to JA, Mar. 19, 1790, *AFC* 9:29–32.
12. Ibid.
13. JA to JQA, Apr. 1, 1790, *AFC* 9:36–37.
14. JQA to JA, Apr. 5, 1790, *Writings* 1:49–50.
15. Ibid.
16. JQA to JA, Oct. 19, 1790, *AFC* 9:136.
17. JQA to William Cranch, Apr. 7, 1790, *AFC* 9:41–44.
18. Ibid., n.1.
19. Ibid.
20. Ibid.
21. Ibid., n. 7. Quoted from *The Rape of the Lock*, Canto 1, l. 76.
22. Ibid.
23. James Bridge to JQA, Sep. 28, 1790, Adams Papers.
24. Ibid.
25. Ibid.
26. Ibid.
27. Ibid.
28. AA2 to JQA, Apr. 18, 1790, *AFC* 9:47.
29. Ibid.
30. AA2 to JQA, Jun. 6, 1790, *AFC* 9:68. JQA letter is lost.
31. Ibid.
32. Shakespeare, *Hamlet,* Act II, sc. 2.
33. William Cranch to JQA, Jun. 10, 1790, *AFC* 9:70.
34. Ibid.
35. Jul. 11, 1790, *JQA Diary*.
36. Jul. 15, 1790, *JQA Diary*; AA to Mary Cranch, Mar. 12, 1791, *New Letters,* 70.
37. JQA to JA, Aug. 9, 1790, Adams Papers.
38. JQA to AA, Aug. 14, 1790, *AFC* 9:90.
39. AA to JQA, Aug. 20, 1790, *AFC* 9:92.
40. JA to JQA, Oct. 4, 1790, *AFC* 9:129.
41. Ibid.
42. AA to JQA, Sep. 12, 1790, *AFC* 9:110.
43. Ibid.
44. Jun.-Dec. 1790, *JQA Diary*.
45. Elizabeth Shaw to AA, Sep. 28, 1790. *AFC* 9:123; AA to JQA, Nov. 7, 1790, *AFC* 9:142.
46. Ibid.
47. AA to JQA, Aug. 20, 1790. *AFC* 9:92.

48. JQA to AA, Aug. 29, 1790, *AFC* 9:96.
49. JQA to AA2, Nov. 20, 1790, *AFC* 9:147.
50. JQA to AA, Oct. 17, 1790, *AFC* 9:133.
51. CA to JQA, Oct. 21, 1790, *AFC* 9:137.
52. JQA to AA, Oct. 17, 1790, *AFC* 9:132.
53. JA to JQA, Dec. 8, 1790, *Writings* 1:64.
54. Charles F. Adams, *The Works of John Adams, Second President of the United States* (Boston: Little & Brown, 1850), 2:29; JQA to JA, Jun. 30, 1787, *AFC* 8:96; JQA to AA, Aug. 14, 1790, *AFC* 9:89–90.
55. JQA to AA, Nov. 20, 1790, *AFC* 9:146.
56. JQA to TBA, Apr. 20, 1791, *AFC* 9:209.
57. Ibid., 212.
58. AA to JQA, Apr. 18, 1791, *AFC* 9:210; JA to JQA, Jun. 1791, Adams Papers.
59. JQA to CFA, Mar. 15, 1828, Samuel Flagg Bemis, *John Quincy Adams and the Foundations of American Foreign Policy* (Greenwood Press, 1981), 24, n. 55.
60. JQA probably to Thomas Woodbridge Hooper, Aug. 29, 1794, *AFC* 9:43, n. 5.
61. Nov. 18, 1838, *JQA Diary*.
62. Ibid.
63. AA2 to JQA, Jun. 6, 1790, *AFC* 9:68; AA to TBA, Mar. 20, 1803, *AFC* 9:xxx, n. 22.
64. Elizabeth Smith Shaw to JQA, Jun. 9, 1794, *AFC* 10:202–203.
65. Ibid.

CHAPTER 14: "ON THE BRIDGE BETWEEN WISDOM AND FOLLY"

1. Address to the bar of Cincinnati, 1843 in Josiah Quincy, *Memoir of the Life of John Quincy Adams* (Boston: Crosby, Nichols, Lee, 1860), 7; Nov. 15, 1790, *JQA Diary*.
2. Apr. 1, 1791, *JQA Diary*.
3. James Bridge to JQA, Jun. 1791, *Adams Papers*.
4. May 4, 1785, *JQA Diary*.
5. "Extract from a Sermon by Dr. Price," *The Parliamentary Magazine,* 89.
6. Edmund Burke, *Reflections on the Revolution in France* (New York: Penguin, 2004), 25, 13.
7. Ibid., 25, 90, 93–94.
8. AA to William Stephens Smith, Mar. 16, 1791, *AFC* 9:204.
9. Ibid.
10. JQA to TBA, Apr. 2, 1791, *AFC* 9:209.
11. Thomas Paine, *The Rights of Man* (London: J.M. Dent & Sons, 1969), 4, 33.
12. Ibid.
13. *The Selected Writings of John and John Quincy Adams,* ed. Adrienne Koch and William Peden (New York: Alfred A. Knopf, 1946), 226.
14. JA to Benjamin Rush, Apr. 18, 1790, *JA Works,* 9:565.
15. Ibid.
16. *Selected Writings of JA and JQA,* 226.
17. Ibid.

18. *Writings of James Madison,* vol. 8, quoted in *Writings* 1:66.
19. *Writings* 1:107.
20. John Quincy Adams and Charles Francis Adams, *The Life of John Adams, 2 vols.* (New York: Haskell House, 1968), 2:150–51.
21. Thomas Jefferson to JA, Jul. 17, 1791, *The Adams-Jefferson Letters* 1:245.
22. Ibid.
23. Ibid.
24. Thomas Jefferson to George Washington, May 8, 1791, Thomas Jefferson to James Madison, May 9, 1791, Thomas Jefferson to Thomas Mann Randolph Jr., Jul. 3, 1791, *The Papers of Thomas Jefferson, Princeton University,* ed. Julian Boyd, (Princeton: Princeton University Press, 1950), 20:291–96.
25. JA to Thomas Jefferson, Jul. 29, 1791, *The Adams-Jefferson Letters* 1:247–48; JA to JQA, Aug. 25, 1795, *Writings* 1:66.
26. JA to Thomas Jefferson, Jul. 29, 1791, *The Adams-Jefferson Letters* 1:247–48.
27. Thomas Jefferson to JA, Aug. 30, 1791, *The Adams-Jefferson Letters* 1:251–52.
28. *Memoirs* 8:270.
29. Oct. 20, 1791, *JQA Diary;* JQA to TBA, Oct. 28, 1791, *AFC* 9:235.
30. JQA to TBA, Feb. 1, 1792, *AFC* 9:254.
31. Ibid.
32. Ibid.
33. Apr. 13, 1792, *JQA Diary.*
34. Apr. 17, 1792, *JQA Diary.*
35. Apr. 14, 1792, *JQA Diary.*
36. May 4, 1792, *JQA Diary.*
37. May 16, 1792, *JQA Diary.*
38. Sep. 1, 1792, *JQA Diary.*
39. Jan. 6, 1792, Mar. 1, 1792, Feb. 23, 1793, *JQA Diary.*
40. David McCullough, *1776* (New York: Simon & Schuster, 2005), 27.
41. Sep. 3, Jun. 20, Jul. 12, Sep. 7, Dec. 31 1793, *JQA Diary.*
42. JQA to JA, Dec. 16, 1792, *AFC* 9:350, n. 1; JQA to JA, Dec. 8, 1792, *AFC* 9:341.
43. Alden Bradford, *History of Massachusetts* (Boston: Richardson and Lord, 1822), 116.
44. George O. Seilhamer, *History of the American Theater: New Foundations 1792–1797* (Philadelphia: Globe Printing House, 1891), 17–19.
45. JQA to JA, Dec. 16, 1792, *AFC* 9:349, n.3.
46. JQA to JA, Dec. 16, 1792, *AFC* 9:349.
47. Oct. 8, 1792, *JQA Diary.*
48. JQA to JA, Feb. 10, 1793, *Writings,* v. 1. John Quincy Adams was one of the original stockholders in the Boston Theater, which opened on February 3, 1794, went bankrupt after one season, and burned down in 1798, noted in JQA to John Gardner, The Hague, May 28, 1795, Adams Papers; Justin Winsor, ed., *Memorial History of Boston,* v. IV, 362–64; quoted in Bemis, *Foundations,* 28, n. 68.
49. Dec. 24, 1792, *JQA Diary;* JA to JQA, Dec. 26, 1792, *AFC* 9:358; Elizabeth Smith Shaw to AA, Dec. 31, 1792, *AFC* 9:363.

50. AA to JA, Jan. 7, 1793, *AFC* 9:374; JA to JQA, Jan. 27, 1793, *AFC* 9:383.
51. *Columbian Centinel,* Jan. 26, 1793, *AFC* 9:388–89, n. 1; JQA to JA, Feb. 10, 1793, *AFC* 9:403.
52. JA to CA, Mar. 18, 1793, *AFC* 9:411; JQA to JA, Feb. 10, 1793, *AFC* 9:403.
53. *Memoirs* 1:27.
54. Samuel Flagg Bemis, *John Quincy Adams and the Foundations of American Foreign Policy* (Westport, CT: Greenwood Press, 1981), 29.

CHAPTER 15: "I, TOO, AM A SCRIBBLER"

1. JA to AA, Dec. 4, 1796, Adams Papers.
2. AA2 to AA, Sep. 13, 1792, *AFC* 9:304–5.
3. TBA to JA, Apr. 7, 1793, *AFC* 9:421.
4. Ibid.
5. Jared Sparks, *Writings of George Washington,* v. 10 (Boston: Russell, Shattuck, and Hilliard & Hilliard, Gray, 1836), 533–34.
6. Ibid.
7. Ibid.
8. CA to JA, May 29, 1793, *AFC* 9:430–31.
9. *Writings* 1:135–46.
10. Ibid.
11. Ibid. Marcellus appeared in the Boston *Columbian Centinel,* April 24, May 4, 11, 1793. The third installment was reprinted in the Philadelphia *Gazette of the United States* on May 25.
12. JA to CA, Jun. 5, 1793, *AFC* 9:434.
13. JQA to TBA, Jun. 23, 1793, *AFC* 9:438.
14. An Oration pronounced Jul. 4, 1793, at the Request of the Inhabitants of the Town of Boston in Commemoration of the Anniversary of American Independence, by John Quincy Adams, (Boston: Benjamin Edes & Sons, 1793). Also see Jul. 4, 1793, *JQA Diary:* "Independence Day. Delivered the Oration at the request of The Town, the performance well received for which I feel grateful."
15. CA to JQA, Jul. 29, 1793, *AFC* 9:440.
16. Nov. 25, 1793, *JQA Diary.*
17. *Writings* 1:148–76.
18. *Writings* 1:148–76.
19. Ibid.
20. Ibid.
21. Ibid.
22. Ibid.
23. JQA and his thoughts on abstention from European political conditions would be reflected in George Washington's Farewell Address, and still later, in the Monroe Doctrine. Samuel Flagg Bemis, "John Quincy Adams and George Washington," Proceedings of the Massachusetts Historical Society, vol. LXVII, Oct. 1941–1944, (Boston, 1945), 365–85.
24. Sparks, *Writings of George Washington,* 12:96.
25. JQA to JA, Jan. 5, 1794, *AFC* 10:11.
26. CA to JA, Dec. 30, 1793, *AFC* 9:491; JA to AA, Dec. 30, 1793, *AFC* 9:492.

27. JA to JQA, Dec. 14, 1793, AFC 9:469; JA to AA. Dec. 19, 1793, *AFC* 9:477.
28. JQA to JA, Jan. 5, 1794, *AFC* 10:11–13; also in *Writings* 1:176–79.
29. Ibid.
30. JQA to TBA, Feb. 13, 1794, *AFC* 10:77.
31. Feb. 13, 1794, *JQA Diary;* JQA to TBA, Feb. 13, 1794, *AFC* 10:78.
32. Ibid. John Quincy Adams in 1793 collected 222 pounds 4 shillings from 94 fees; for January to Jun. 1794, 170 pounds 11 shillings from 77 fees. By year four year of his law practice, Adams finally began to reap the rewards of his patience. As he recalled in 1843, he found his practice "swelling to such an extent that I felt no longer any concern as to my future destiny as a member of that profession." Comparisons are difficult to make but "Adams's income in 1793 was roughly the equivalent of approximately $60,000 in today's money . . . although because he had to pay overhead expenses his income was not sheer profit." William G. Ross, "The Legal Career of John Quincy Adams," *Akron Law Review,* v. 23:3, 415–53, spring, 1990; Joseph Quincy, *Memoir of the Life of John Quincy,* 7–8.
33. JQA to JA, Mar. 2, 1794, *AFC* 10:98; JA to AA Mar. 8, 1794, *AFC* 10:104.
34. JQA to JA, Mar. 2, 1794, *AFC* 10:97; JQA to JA, Mar. 24, 1794, *AFC* 10:125; JQA to TBA, Mar. 27, 1794, *AFC* 10:129.
35. JA to JQA, Apr. 3, 1794, *AFC* 10:134.
36. Ibid.
37. JQA to JA, Apr. 12, 1794, *AFC* 10:142.
38. Ibid.
39. JA to JQA, Apr. 23, 1794, *AFC* 10:151.
40. JA to AA, May 19, 1794, *AFC* 10:184.
41. AA to JA, May 27, 1794, *AFC* 10:196.
42. Jun. 3, 1794, *JQA Diary.*
43. JA to AA, May 27, 1794, *AFC* 10:197.
44. JA to JQA, May 29, 1794, *AFC* 10:198.
45. AA to Martha Washington, Jun. 20, 1794, *AFC* 10:206.
46. Ibid.
47. Martha Washington to AA, Jul. 19, 1794, *AFC* 10:214–15.
48. JA to JQA, May 30, 1794, *AFC* 10:200.
49. Jun. 10, 1794, *JQA Diary.*
50. Jun. 4, 6, 7, 14, 15, *JQA Diary.*
51. Jun. 18, 1794, *JQA Diary;* Jun. 29, 1794, *JQA Diary.*

CHAPTER 16: "THE TIMES CHANGE AND WE CHANGE WITH THEM"

1. Jun. 30–Jul. 7, 1794, *JQA Diary;* JA to AA, May 3, 1794, *AFC* 10:163.
2. Jul. 7, 1794, *JQA Diary.*
3. JQA to AA, Jul. 8, 1794, *AFC* 10:207.
4. Jul. 7, 1794, *JQA Diary.*
5. Katherine Metcalf Roof, *Colonel William Smith and Lady* (Boston: Houghton Mifflin, 1929), 38, 90–95.
6. JA to AA, Mar. 2, 1793, *AFC* 9:415; AA to JQA, Sep. 12, 1790, *AFC* 9:109.
7. JA to AA, Mar. 2, 1793, *AFC* 9:416.

8. *Memoirs* 1:34–36.
9. Jul. 11, 1794, *JQA Diary*.
10. Ibid.
11. Ibid.
12. Ibid.
13. JQA to JA, Jul. 18, 1794, *AFC* 10:211.
14. JQA to AA, Jul. 12, 1794, *AFC* 10:209; AA to JQA, Jul. 20, 1794, *AFC* 10:215; JQA to JA, Jul. 18, 1794, *AFC* 10:213.
15. JQA to JA, Jul. 27, 1794, *Writings* 1:193–97.
16. Ibid.
17. JA to JQA, Aug. 24, 1794, *AFC* 10:227–28.
18. Ibid.
19. Ibid.
20. Instructions from Edmund Randolph to JQA, Jul. 29, 1794, *Writings* 1:198–200.
21. JQA to AA, Jul. 29, 1794, *AFC* 10:223.
22. *Writings* 1:201, n. 1; JQA to AA, Jul. 27, 1794 and n. 2, *AFC* 10:222, 224.
23. *Memoirs* 1:39.
24. Ibid.

CHAPTER 17: "THE MAGNITUDE OF THE TRUST AND MY OWN INCOMPETENCY"

1. AA to JQA, Sep. 12, 1790, *AFC* 9:109; JA to AA, Jan. 16, 1795, *AFC* 10:350; JA to TBA, Dec. 3, 1794, *AFC* 10:286; AA to TBA, Jan. 10, 1795, *AFC* 10:346.
2. *Memoirs* 1:43.
3. *Memoirs* 1:13.
4. Samuel F. Bemis, "The London Mission of Thomas Pinckney, 1792–1796," *American Historical Review,* 28:229–31 (Jan. 1923).
5. JQA to AA, Jan. 6, 1796, *AFC* 11:125.
6. JQA to JA, Oct. 31, 1795, *Writings* 1:424; JQA to JA, Oct. 23, 1794, *Writings* 1:203.
7. Philadelphia *Aurora General Advertiser,* May 13 and 22, 1797, 2–3.
8. JQA to AA, Nov. 11, 1794, *AFC* 10:254; JQA to AA, Oct. 25, 1794, *AFC* 10:240.
9. Oct. 27, 1794, *Memoirs* 1:54–55; JQA to AA, Nov. 11, 1794, *AFC* 10:254.
10. Simon Schama, *Patriots and Liberators* (New York: Knopf, 1977), 3; JA to JQA, Aug. 24, 1794, *AFC* 10:227.
11. JQA to JA, Oct. 23, 1794, *Writings* 1:205–9.
12. Ibid.
13. Instructions from Edmund Randolph to JQA, Jul. 29, 1794, *Writings* 1:198–200; JQA to JA, Nov. 9, 1794, Adams Papers.
14. Schama, *Patriots and Liberators,* 2; Samuel F. Bemis, *John Quincy Adams and the Foundations of American Foreign Policy* (Westport, CT: Greenwood Press, 1981), 31.
15. JQA to JA, Nov. 9, 1794, *Writings* 1:224–25.
16. Ibid.
17. JQA to JA, Dec. 3, 1794, *Writings* 1:246; JQA to AA, Nov. 11, 1794, *AFC* 10:255.
18. Ibid.

19. Ibid.
20. JQA to JA, Dec. 3, 1794, *Writings* 1:247.
21. Nov. 14, 1794, *JQA Diary*; Feb. 2, 1795, *Memoirs* 1:66.
22. Ibid.
23. His wife, the Princess of Orange, Frederica Sophia Wilhelmina (1747–1802), niece of Frederick the Great and daughter of Prince August of Prussia.
24. Feb. 2, 1795, *Memoirs* 1:66.
25. Jan. 18, 1795, *JQA Diary*.
26. JQA to Edmund Randolph, Jan. 22, 1795, *Writings* 1:264.
27. Jan. 22, 1795, *JQA Diary*.
28. Ibid.
29. JQA to AA, Feb. 12, 1795, *AFC* 10:384–85.
30. Ibid.
31. JQA to JA, Apr. 1, 1795, *Writings* 1:312.
32. JQA to Thomas Welsh, Apr. 26, 1795, *Writings* 1:339, n. 1.
33. JQA to JA, May 4, 1795, *Writings* 1:343.
34. May 1–2, 1795, *Memoirs* 1:115.
35. Ibid.
36. JQA to JA, May 22, 1795, *Writings* 1:353–55.
37. Ibid.
38. Ibid.
39. Ibid.
40. JQA to JA, Jun. 27, 1795, *Writings* 1:375.
41. JQA to AA, May 16, 1795, *AFC* 10:434; JQA to JA, Jun. 27, 1795, *Writings* 1:378.
42. JQA to JA, Jun. 27, 1795, *Writings* 1:388.
43. JA and AA to JQA, Apr. 26, 1795, *AFC* 10:423.
44. George Washington to JA, Aug. 20, 1795, *The Writings of George Washington from the Original Manuscript Sources, 1745–1799*, ed. John C. Fitzpatrick, 39 vols., Washington, D.C., 1931–1944, 13:91.
45. *Writings* 1:397.
46. *Memoirs* 1:121.
47. Oct. 14, 1795, *JQA Diary*.
48. *Writings* 1:418; JQA to JA, Oct. 31, 1795, *Writings* 1:423–24; Oct. 21, 1795, *Memoirs* 1:126.
49. JQA to AA, Nov. 7, 1795, *AFC* 11:60–62.
50. Ibid.
51. Ibid.
52. Ibid.
53. Nov. 11, 1795, *JQA Diary*.
54. Nov. 12, 1795, *Memoirs* 1:133.

CHAPTER 18: "THE USUAL MIXTURE BETWEEN SWEET AND BITTER"

1. Nov. 11, 1795, *JQA Diary*.
2. LCA, *Diary and Autobiographical Writings of Louisa Catherine Adams*, ed. Judith S. Graham and others, 2 vols. (Cambridge: Harvard University Press, 2013), 1:33.
3. LCA, *D&A* 1:33–34.

4. JQA to Sylvanus Bourne, Dec. 24, 1795, *Writings* 1:466.
5. JQA to JA, Nov. 17, 1795, *Writings* 1:433.
6. JQA to Sylvanus Bourne, Dec. 24, 1795, *Writings* 1:466–67.
7. Ibid.
8. Nov. 22, 1795, *JQA Diary*.
9. Nov. 27, 1795, *Memoirs* 1:140–41.
10. Ibid.
11. Dec. 1, 1795, *Memoirs* 1:143–46.
12. Ibid.
13. Ibid.
14. Dec. 2, 1795, *Memoirs* 1:148–49.
15. Dec. 8, 1795, *Memoirs* 1:161; Dec. 11, 1795, *Memoirs* 1:164.
16. JQA to Secretary of State Timothy Pickering, Jan. 20, 1796, *Writings* 1:472, n. 1.
17. JQA to Lord Grenville, Dec. 9, 1795, *Writings* 1:450.
18. Dec. 11, 1795, *Memoirs* 1:164.
19. JQA to JA, Dec. 29, 1795, *Writings* 1:473; Dec. 12, 1795, *JQA Diary*.
20. JQA to JA, Dec. 29, 1795, *Writings* 1:471–72.
21. Dec. 9, 1795, *Memoirs* 1:162–63.
22. Jan. 13, 1796, *Memoirs* 1:167.
23. JQA to JA, Feb. 10, 1796, Adams Papers.
24. *Memoirs* 1:167.
25. *Memoirs* 1:viii.
26. Dec. 28, 31, 1795, *Memoirs* 1:165–66.
27. Apr. 4, 1796, *JQA Diary*.
28. Apr. 22, 1796, *JQA Diary*; Dec. 22, 1795, *JQA Diary*; Jan. 27, 1796, *JQA Diary*.
29. Jan. 17, 1796, *JQA Diary*.
30. Mar. 28, 1796, *JQA Diary*; Feb. 25, 1796, *JQA Diary*; Feb. 29, 1796, *JQA Diary*.
31. JQA to AA, Feb. 20, 1796, *AFC* 11:181–82.
32. JQA to AA, Feb. 28, 1796, *AFC* 11:190.
33. LCA, *D&A* 1:41; Mar. 2, 1796, *JQA Diary*.
34. Mar. 11–14, 1796, *JQA Diary*.
35. Apr. 10 & 13, 1796, *JQA Diary*.
36. Apr. 18, 1796, *JQA Diary*.
37. Apr. 26, 1796, *JQA Diary*.
38. May 24, 1796, *JQA Diary*; May 2, 1796, *JQA Diary*.
39. May 1, 1796, *JQA Diary*.
40. May 10–11, 1796, *JQA Diary*; May 18, 1796, *JQA Diary*.
41. Apr. 26, 1796, *JQA Diary*.
42. May 27, 1796, *JQA Diary*.
43. May 28–31, 1796, *JQA Diary*.
44. AA to JQA, May 20, 1796, *AFC* 11:296–97; AA to JQA, May 25, 1796, *AFC* 11:299.
45. AA to TBA, Jun. 10, 1796, *AFC* 11:316.
46. LCA, *D&A* 1:65, 21.
47. LCA to Abigail Brooks Adams, Mar. 2, 1834, Adams Papers.
48. Henry Adams, *The Education of Henry Adams, An Autobiography* (Boston and New York: Houghton Mifflin, 1918), 15.

CHAPTER 19: "THE AGE OF INNOCENCE
AND THOUGHTLESSNESS"

1. LCA, *Diary and Autobiographical Writings of Louisa Catherine Adams,* ed. Judith S. Graham and others, 2 vols. (Cambridge: Harvard University Press, 2013), 2:612, 1:1–2.
2. LCA, *D&A* 1:64.
3. LCA to Abigail Brooks Adams, Mar. 2, 1834, Adams Papers.
4. LCA, *D&A* 1:64; LCA to CFA, Aug. 19, 1827, Adams Papers.
5. LCA, *D&A* 1:64.
6. LCA, D&A 1:64, 24–25; Tobias George Smollett, *The Adventures of Peregrine Pickle* (London: George Routledge and Sons Ltd, 1890), 2:38; LCA, *D&A* 1:21; Lars E. Troide, ed., *The Early Journals and Letters of Fanny Burney, Volume I: 1768–1773,* London: McGill-Queens's Press, 1988.
7. LCA, *D&A* 1:21, 2–3, 7.
8. LCA, *D&A* 1:7.
9. LCA, *D&A* 1:8.
10. LCA, *D&A* 1:2.
11. LCA, *D&A* 1:3.
12. LCA, *D&A* 1:2–3.
13. Joshua Johnson to John Davidson, Jul. 22, 1771, *Joshua Johnson's Letterbook, 1771–1774: Letters from a Merchant in London to His Partners in Maryland,* ed. Jacob M. Price (London, 1979), 1–4.
14. Ibid.
15. Joshua Johnson, Feb. 1772, *Letterbook,* 27.
16. Joshua Johnson, Mar. 25, 1772 and Jun. 4, 1772, *Letterbook,* 31, 36.
17. Joshua Johnson, *Letterbook,* 50–59.
18. Johnson, *Letterbook,* 109; Joshua Johnson to Denton Jacques, Jul. 20, 1771, quoted in Joan R. Challinor, "'A quarter taint of Maryland blood': An Inquiry into the Anglo/Maryland Background of Mrs. John Quincy Adams," *Maryland Historical Magazine,* 80:412 (Winter 1985). Regarding "quanturns," Challinor writes in a footnote to the text that Johnson meant "quartern . . . which in the eighteenth century meant either one-fourth or four of something."
19. Joshua Johnson to Denton Jacques, Mar. 18, 1773, quoted in Challinor, "Quarter taint," *MHM,* 80:412; Joshua Johnson, Sep. 4, 1773, *Letterbook,* 98.
20. LCA, *D&A* 1:7; Henry Adams to Maria Louisa Crane, May 27, 1893, quoted in Challinor, "Quarter taint," *MHM,* 80:410.
21. Henry Adams to Charles Francis Adams Jr., Jul. 12, 1800 quoted in Challinor, "Quarter taint," *MHM,* 80:412.
22. Undated genealogical note on the Johnson family in LCA's handwriting, quoted in Challinor, "Quarter taint," *MHM,* 80:411.
23. Challinor, "Quarter taint," *MHM,* 80:411–13.
24. Henry Adams, *The Education of Henry Adams* (Boston & New York: Houghton Mifflin, 1918), 17–18.
25. Quoted in Edward C. Papenfuse, *In Pursuit of Profit: The Annapolis Merchants in the Era of the American Revolution, 1763–1805* (Baltimore: Johns Hopkins University Press, 1975), 72; Challinor, "Quarter taint," *MHM,* 80:415.

26. LCA to Abigail Brooks Adams, Mar. 2 1834, Adams Papers.
27. LCA, *D&A* 1:3–4.
28. LCA, *D&A* 1:7, 9–10.
29. LCA, *D&A* 1:3, 10.
30. LCA, *D&A* 1:6.
31. *The Papers of Thomas Jefferson*, ed. Julian P. Boyd, Charles T. Cullen, John Catanzariti, Barbara B. Oberg, and others (Princeton, 1950), 17:119.
32. LCA, *D&A* 1:19–20.
33. LCA, *D&A* 1:37.
34. LCA, *D&A* 1:43.
35. Ibid.

CHAPTER 20: "ALBEIT UNUSED TO THE MELTING MOOD"

1. JQA to LCA, Jun. 2, 1796, *AFC* 11:304.
2. JQA to LCA, Jun. 17, 1796, *AFC* 11:318.
3. JQA to LCA, Jun. 2, 1796, *AFC* 11:305–6.
4. Ibid.
5. Jul. 11, 1796, *JQA Diary.*
6. JQA to LCA, Jun. 2, 1796, *AFC* 11:306.
7. JQA to Joshua Johnson, Jun. 2, 1796, *AFC* 11:300–1.
8. JQA to AA, Jun. 30, 1796, *AFC* 11:328.
9. Ibid.
10. JQA to JA, Jun. 6, 1796, Adams Papers; Jun. 2–15, 1796, *JQA Diary.*
11. Jun. 30, 1796, *JQA Diary.*
12. Ibid.
13. JQA to JA, Jul. 21, 1796, *Writings* 2:3–13.
14. Ibid.
15. Ibid.
16. JQA to AA, Jul. 25, 1797, *AFC* 11:338–41.
17. Ibid.
18. Ibid.
19. Ibid.
20. AA to JQA, May 20, 1796, *AFC* 11:298; JQA to AA, Jul. 25, 1796, *AFC* 11:338–41.

CHAPTER 21: "OH MY LOUISA!"

1. LCA, *D&A* 1:84, 65.
2. JQA to LCA, Apr. 13, 1797, Adams Papers.
3. Henry Adams, *Education of Henry Adams,* 19.
4. JQA to LCA, Aug. 13, 1796, *AFC* 11:358; Bemis, Samuel Flagg. *John Quincy Adams and the Foundations of American Foreign Policy,* 82.
5. LCA, *D&A* 1:46.
6. LCA to JQA, Jul. 4, 1796, *AFC* 11:329–30.
7. LCA, *D&A* 1:44.
8. JQA to LCA, Jul. 9, 1796, *AFC* 11:331–33.
9. Ibid.
10. LCA to JQA, Jul. 4, 1796, *AFC* 11:330.
11. JQA to LCA, Jul. 9, 1796, *AFC* 11:333–34.
12. Ibid.

13. LCA to JQA, Jul. 24, 1796, *AFC* 11:337–38; JQA to LCA, Aug. 6, 1796, *AFC* 11:344.
14. LCA to JQA, Jul. 25, 1796, *AFC* 11:342.
15. Timothy Pickering to JQA, Jun. 11, 1796, Adams Papers; Aug. 7, 1796, *JQA Diary.*
16. JQA to LCA, Aug. 13, 1796, *AFC* 11:359–60.
17. Ibid.
18. Ibid.
19. LCA to JQA, Aug. 28, 1796, *AFC* 11:371–72.
20. Ibid.
21. AA to JQA, May 20, 1796, *AFC* 11:296.
22. JA to JQA, Aug. 7, 1796, *AFC* 11:354–55.
23. JQA to AA, Aug. 16, 1796, *AFC* 11:364.
24. AA to JQA, Aug. 10, 1796, *AFC* 11:356–57.
25. Ibid.
26. JQA to AA, Nov. 14, 1796, *AFC* 11:405.
27. JQA to Joshua Adams, Nov. 9, 1796, Adams Papers; JQA to LCA, Nov. 15, 1796, Adams Papers.
28. LCA to JQA, Nov. 29, 1796, *AFC* 11:426–27.
29. Ibid.
30. Ibid.
31. JQA to LCA, Dec. 20, 1796, *AFC* 11:452–53.
32. Ibid.
33. Dec. 31, 1796, *JQA Diary.*
34. Jan. 31, Mar. 4, 1797, *JQA Diary.*
35. JQA to AA, Jul. 25, 1796, *AFC* 11:340.
36. JQA to LCA, Jan. 7, 1797, Adams Papers.
37. Ibid.
38. Ibid.
39. JQA to LCA, Jan. 10, 1797, *AFC* 11:490.
40. Joshua Johnson to JQA, Sep. 30, 1796, *AFC* 11:383–84.
41. Joshua Johnson to JQA, Dec. 16, 1797, Adams Papers; JQA to LCA, Jan. 10, 1797, *AFC* 11:490–91.
42. LCA to JQA, Jan. 17, 1797, *AFC* 11:503–4.
43. Ibid.
44. Ibid.
45. Ibid.
46. Ibid.
47. LCA to JQA, Jan. 31, 1797, *AFC* 11:534–35.
48. JQA to LCA, Feb. 12, 1797, *AFC* 11:557–59.
49. Ibid.
50. Ibid.
51. Ibid.
52. Ibid.
53. Feb. 13, 1797, *JQA Diary.*
54. JQA to LCA, Feb. 12, 1797, *AFC* 11:559.
55. JQA to LCA, Feb. 20, 1797, *AFC* 11:569.
56. LCA to JQA, Feb. 28, 1797, *AFC* 11:577.
57. JQA to LCA, Apr. 13, 1797, Adams Papers.
58. JQA to LCA, Feb. 7, 1797, *AFC* 11:543.
59. LCA to JQA, Feb. 28, 1797, *AFC* 11:577–78.

CHAPTER 22: "FOR THE FRIEND OF YOUR LIFE"

1. JQA to LCA, Apr. 13, 1797, Adams Papers.
2. JQA to LCA, May 12, 1797, Adams Papers.
3. Ibid.
4. LCA to JQA, May 26, 1797, Adams Papers; JQA to LCA, Jun. 6, 1797, Adams Papers.
5. JQA to AA, Jun. 26, 1797, Adams Papers.
6. Jul. 1, 2, 7, 1797, JQA Diary; William Vans Murray to JQA, Jul. 6, 1797, *Letters of WVM to JQA 1797–1803*, 354.
7. William Vans Murray to JQA, Jul. 6–7, 1797, *Letters of WVM to JQA 1797–1803*, 356–7.
8. Uriah Tracy to Oliver Wolcott, Sr., May 27, 1797 in *Writings* 2:191, n. 1.
9. JQA to AA, Nov. 14, 1796, *Memoirs* 1:194.
10. AA to JQA, Nov. 3, 1797, Adams Papers; (Excerpt in *Writings* 2:253) JA to JQA, Oct. 25, 1797, Adams Papers.
11. JA to JQA, Nov. 3, 1797, *Writings* 2:173–4, n. 1.
12. AA to MC, Jun. 3, 1797, *New Letters of Abigail Adams*, 95.
13. Jul. 13, 1797, *JQA Diary*.
14. Joshua Johnson to JQA, Jul. 19, 1797, Adams Papers.
15. Ibid.
16. Jul. 26, 1797, *JQA Diary*.
17. JQA and LCA to JA and AA, Jul. 28, 1797, Adams Papers.
18. Aug. 30 and Sep. 8, 1797, *JQA Diary*.
19. Joshua Johnson to JQA, Sep. 12, 1797, Adams Papers.
20. Catherine Nuth Johnson to JQA, Sep. 18, 1797, Adams Papers.
21. LCA, *D&A* 1:86; Frederick Delius to JQA, Sep. 29, 1797, Adams Papers; *Joshua Johnson Letterbook*, xxvi.
22. TBA to AA, Sep. 10, 1797, Adams Papers; AA to Mary Cranch, Oct. 31, 1797, *New Letters of Abigail Adams*, 110.
23. AA to Mary Cranch, Oct. 22, 1797, *New Letters of Abigail Adams*, 109; AA to Mary Cranch, Nov. 28, 1797, *New Letters of Abigail Adams*, 113; AA to Mary Cranch, Feb. 6, 1798, *New Letters of Abigail Adams*, 131.
24. Boston *Independent Chronicle*, Sep. 14–18, 1797, 3; Boston *Columbian Centinel*, Sep. 20, 1797, 3.

CHAPTER 23: "WISE AND IN THE BEST INTERESTS OF THE COUNTRY"

1. AA to MC, Apr. 21, 1798, *New Letters of Abigail Adams*, 157. (From JQA to AA, Dec. 28, 1797.)
2. Nov. 8, 1797, *Memoirs* 1:203.
3. Dec. 5, 1797, *Memoirs* 1:207.
4. Nov. 16, 1797, *JQA Diary*.
5. LCA, *D&A* 1:69–70.
6. Nov. 17–19, 25, 30, 1797, *JQA Diary*.
7. TBA Diary, Jun. 11, 1798 in Victor Hugo Paltsits, ed., *Berlin and the Prussian Court in 1798: Journal of Thomas Boylston Adams, Secretary to the United States Legation at Berlin,* (The New York Public Library, 1916), 19.
8. Dec. 8, 1797, *Memoirs* 1:210.

9. Jan. 6, 1798, *Memoirs* 1:215

10. AA to Mary Cranch, Jun. 13, 1798 via Catherine Johnson, *New Letters of Abigail Adams,* 190–91.

11. JQA to Catherine Johnson, Feb. 7, 1798, Adams Papers. JQA's letter goes into greater detail: "Three days after our arrival, on the 10th Mrs. Adams was taken ill, and from that time until the 20th I could scarcely for a moment leave her bedside. I shall not attempt to describe what she suffered nor the deep distress of my own feelings in considering that she was remote from her beloved mother and sisters from all her friends, at a public Inn in a foreign land with a strange language, and without the benefit of a single female, who could give her assistance or relief. Amidst these numerous afflictions we had however the consolation of meeting an able English physician who attended her not only with professional skill but with that kindness and interest which is more efficacious in sickness than medicine. She recovered slowly, but I hope effectually, and notwithstanding some remains of weakness, I think her health and appearance for this month past has been a good as I have known it, at any period. Since her recovery she has been presented at court. . . ."

12. Feb. 16, Mar. 21, Jul. 18, 1798, *JQA Diary.*

13. TBA Diary, Jul. 17, 1798, in *Berlin and the Prussian Court,* 21.

14. Jul. 15, 1798, *JQA Diary.*

15. Jul. 31, 1798, *JQA Diary.*

16. JQA to AA, Feb. 5, 1797, Adams Papers; JQA to AA2, Feb. 7, 1797, Reel 130, Adams Papers; JQA to John Gardner, Oct. 10, 1798, Reel 133, Adams Papers; Jul. 26, 1798, *JQA Diary.*

17. JA to JQA, Jun. 2, 1797, Adams Papers.

18. Timothy Pickering to JQA, Jul. 15, 1797, *Writings* 2:188–91.

19. Ibid.

20. JQA to JA, Dec. 16, 1797, *Writings* 2:234.

21. Ibid.

22. JQA to Elbridge Gerry, Feb. 20, 1798, *Writings* 2:260; JQA to JA, Sep. 21, 1797, *Writings* 2:214–16.

23. JQA to TBA, Jul. 11, 1800, *Writings* 2:467.

24. JQA to the Secretary of State Timothy Pickering, Jan. 15, 1798, *Writings* 2:239.

25. Inaugural Address of John Adams, Mar. 4, 1797. Regarding their "long-tried and affectionate friendship," John Quincy praised Murray for his pleasing manners, amusing and instructive conversation, good nature, original humor, wit and keen observation, all united with the enlivening fancy of a poet. He also spoke of his strong and genuine relish of the fine arts, his refined and delicate taste for literature, his fondness for the pursuits of science: JQA in *Port Folio,* Jan. 7, 1804 in *Letters of WVM to JQA 1797–1803,* 351.

26. William Vans Murray to JQA, Nov. 4, Aug. 23, Oct. 1, 1797 and Apr. 13, 1798, *Letters of WVM to JQA 1797–1803,* 360–69, 393.

27. AA to Mary Cranch, Jun. 3, 1797, *New Letters of Abigail Adams,* 94; AA to Mary Cranch, Jun. 23, 1797, *New Letters of Abigail Adams,* 99; William Vans Murray to JQA, May 18, 1798, *Letters of WVM to JQA 1797–1803,* 407.

28. JQA to Rufus King, Jul. 11, 1798 in *Writings* 2:329, n. 2; Mar. 19, 1798, *Annals of Congress,* 5th Congress, 2d session, 1217.

29. William Vans Murray to JQA, Apr. 3, 1798, *Letters of WVM to JQA 1797–1803,* 391 and *Writings* 2:274, n. 2.
30. William Vans Murray to JQA, Apr. 13, 1798, *Letters of WVM to JQA 1797–1803,* 393.
31. JQA to William Vans Murray, Apr. 27, 1798, *Writings* 2:280–81.
32. Ibid.
33. JQA to William Vans Murray, Jun. 7, 1798, *Writings* 2:301.
34. JQA to William Vans Murray, May 25, 1798, *Writings* 2:295–96.
35. JQA to William Vans Murray, Jun. 7, 1798, *Writings* 2:299.
36. AA to William Smith, Apr. 8, 1798, Smith-Townsend Collection, Massachusetts Historical Society.
37. AA to Mary Cranch, May 26, 1798, *New Letters of Abigail Adams,* 179.
38. Alexander Hamilton to Jonathan Dayton, *The Papers of Alexander Hamilton,* ed. Harold C. Syrett, 26 vols. (New York: Columbia University Press, 1961–), 23:604; Jun. 16, 1798, *Annals of Congress,* 5th Congress, 2nd Session, 1961.
39. The Sedition Act, Jul. 14, 1798, U.S. Statutes at Large, 1:596–7; reprinted in Henry Steele Commager, ed. *Documents of American History.* 9th ed., in 2 vols. (Englewood Cliffs, New Jersey: Prentice-Hall, 1973) 177–78.
40. Nov. 16, 1798, "Kentucky Resolutions" and Dec. 24, 1798, "Virginia Resolutions" in Commager, *Documents of American History,* 178–80.
41. Thomas Jefferson to Elbridge Gerry, Jan. 26, 1799, *The Life and Selected Writings of Thomas Jefferson,* ed. Adrienne Koch and William Peden (New York: The Modern Library, 1972), 545.
42. Aug. 29, 1836, *Memoirs* 9:306.
43. Aug. 30, 1836, *Memoirs* 9:306–7.
44. JQA and CFA, *The Life of John Adams* (Philadelphia: J. B. Lippincott & Co., 1871), 2:241; Sep. 2, 1836, *Memoirs* 9:307.
45. William Vans Murray to JQA, Aug. 2, 1798, *Letters of WVM to JQA 1797–1803,* 443; JQA to AA, Sep. 14, 1798, *Writings* 2:360; William Vans Murray to JQA, Apr. 17, 1798, *Letters of WVM to JQA 1797–1803,* 395.
46. "Du Pont and Talleyrand, 1798," *Proceedings of the Massachusetts Historical Society,* 49:75.
47. "Du Pont and Talleyrand, 1798," *Proceedings of the Massachusetts Historical Society,* 49:76, n. 3; *Writings* 2:360–61.
48. William Vans Murray to JQA, Aug. 2, 1798, *Letters of WVM to JQA 1797–1803,* 444.
49. William Vans Murray to JQA, Aug. 6, 1798, *Letters of WVM to JQA 1797–1803,* 448.
50. Dec. 11–12, 1798, *Annals of Congress,* Senate, 5th Congress, 3rd Session, 2192–93. The next day John Adams took the question of whether "individuals affecting to interfere in public affairs between France and the United States, whether by their secret correspondence or otherwise, and intended to impose upon the people and separate them from their government, ought not to be inquired into and corrected."
51. Jan. 30, 1799, *Annals of Congress,* Statutes at Large, 5th Congress, 3rd Session, 613.
52. JQA to AA, May 7, 1799, *Writings* 2:416.
53. Feb. 18, 1799, *Annals of Congress,* Senate, 5th Congress, 3rd Session, 2223–24.

54. Stanley Elkins and Eric McKitrick, *The Age of Federalism* (Oxford University Press, 1995), 622.
55. JQA to AA, Jul. 3, 1799, *Writings* 2:431.
56. JQA to AA, May 7, 1799, *Writings* 2:417–18.
57. Ibid.
58. William Vans Murray to JQA, Aug. 6, 1799, *Letters of WVM to JQA 1797–1803,* 581.
59. Jan. 1800, *JQA Diary.*
60. Apr. 9, 1799, *JQA Diary;* JQA to Joshua Johnson, Dec. 10, 1800, Adams Papers.
61. Dec. 31, 1799, *JQA Diary.*

CHAPTER 24: "TO TURN WEARINESS ITSELF INTO PLEASURE"

1. Jan. 2, 8–9, 1800, *JQA Diary.*
2. JQA to William Vans Murray, Feb. 11, 1800, *Writings* 2:453.
3. JQA to the Secretary of State Timothy Pickering, Mar. 8, 1800, *Writings* 2:454.
4. William Vans Murray to JQA, Aug. 20, Feb. 17 and Nov. 7, 1800, *Letters of WVM to JQA 1797–1803,* 643, 651, 658–59.
5. William Vans Murray to JQA, Oct. 5, 1800, *Letters of WVM to JQA 1797–1803,* 654.
6. JQA to Joshua Johnson, Dec. 10, 1800, Adams Papers.
7. JQA to William Vans Murray, Oct. 30, 1800, *Writings* 2:472.
8. Linda K. Kerber and Walter John Morris, "Politics and Literature: The Adams Family and the Port Folio," *The William and Mary Quarterly* Third Series, Vol. 23, No. 3 (Jul. 1966), 450–476; JQA to TBA, Mar. 21, 1801, Adams Papers. This section is also printed in *Writings* 2:521.
9. JQA, *Letters on Silesia* (London: J. Budd, at the Crown and Mitre, Pall Mall, 1804), 2.
10. Oct. 17, 1833, *Memoirs* 9:22.
11. JQA to TBA, Sep. 24, 1800, Reel 134, Adams Papers.
12. Sep. 20, 1800, *JQA Diary.*
13. Sep. 27–29, 1800, *JQA Diary.*
14. JQA to Joshua Johnson, Dec. 10, 1800, Adams Papers.
15. Ibid.
16. Ibid.
17. JQA to William Vans Murray, Oct. 30, 1800, *Writings* 2:473.
18. Alexander Hamilton, *The Public Conduct and Character of John Adams, Esq., President of the United States* (New York: John Lang / George Hopkins, 1800), 2.
19. JQA to TBA, Dec. 3, 1800, *Writings* 2:485.
20. Jan. 31, 1801, *JQA Diary.*
21. Feb. 2, 1801, *JQA Diary.*
22. AA2 to JQA, Oct. 26, 1795, *AFC* 10:43; AA to MC, Dec. 8, 1800, *New Letters of Abigail Adams,* 262; AA to JQA, Dec. 2, 1800, Adams Papers (AA quotes to JQA a letter, not extant, that she received from CA on the subject); AA to William Smith, Dec. 28, 1798, Massachusetts Historical Society: Smith-Townsend Collection.
23. AA to MC, Dec. 8, 1800, *New Letters,* 262; JQA to AA, Apr. 14, 1801, Adams Papers.

24. JQA to AA, Mar. 10, 1801, *Writings* 2:510.

25. JQA to JA, Mar. 24, 1801, *Writings* 2:527, n. 1.

26. JQA to AA, Mar. 10, 1801, *Writings* 2:511.

27. Ibid.; JQA to JA, Nov. 25, 1800, *Writings* 2:480.

28. JQA to TBA, Dec. 27, 1800, *Writings* 2:489–500.

29. JQA to AA, Mar. 10, 1801, *Writings* 2:512.

30. Joseph Pitcairn to JQA, Mar. 31, 1801, *Writings* 2:513, n. 1.

31. JA to John Marshall, Jan. 31, 1801, Adams Papers.

32. JQA to AA, Apr. 14, 1801, Adams Papers.

33. Dec. 31, 1800, Jan. 9, 1801, *JQA Diary.*

34. Feb. 28, May 4, 1801, *JQA Diary.*

35. AA to TBA, Jul. 12, 1801, Adams Papers.

36. May 5, 1801, *JQA Diary.*

37. May 18, 1801, *JQA Diary.*

38. In JQA's youth there was controversy over the choice of having smallpox the "natural" way, as opposed to the "artificial" way, by inoculation. A census after the epidemic of 1764 proved to the dubious that in 4,977 cases of inoculation only 45 had died. Of the 619 who endured smallpox without inoculation, 124 had died. Dr. Zabdiel Boylston, John Adams's great-uncle, experimented with inoculation against smallpox on Jun. 26, 1721, on his own child and two servants. He published in London in 1730 an "Historical Account of the Small Pox inoculation in New England upon all sorts of persons, whites, blacks, and of all ages and constitutions," including some "Short directions to the unexperienced in this method of practice," with a dedication to the princess of Wales. It was only after Dr. Edward Jenner's discovery of a milder vaccine, that of cow pox, that inoculation against smallpox became less hazardous. Phyllis Lee Levin, *Abigail Adams* (New York: St. Martin's Press, 1987), 497–98, n. 24; John B. Blake, *Public Health in the Town of Boston, 1630–1822* (Cambridge: Harvard University Press, 1959), chs. 4–5; "Smallpox Inoculation in Colonial Boston," *Journal of the History of Medicine* 8 (1953), 284–300. See also Jun. 3, 1801, *JQA Diary;* JQA to TBA, Jun. 9, 1801, Adams Papers; AA to JA, Jul. 21, 1776, *AFC* 2:57, n. 1.

39. JQA to TBA, May 30, 1801, Adams Papers.

40. Jul. 11, 1801, *JQA Diary.*

41. Thomas Adams describes the work his brother John Quincy "*intends* to give to the world at some future date. The first a Treatise upon Government; second, History of the American Revolution; third, a parallel between the Roman history till the reign of Augustus and the French Revolution. Fourth, a book against Voltaire. Within no less compass than this are the literary and scientific schemes of this grasping genius restrained." *TBA Diary,* Reel 282, Adams Papers.

CHAPTER 25: "PAINFUL RETROSPECTION"

1. JQA to JA, Sep. 4, 1801, Reel 401, Adams Papers.

2. JA to JQA, Sep. 12, 1801, Reel 401, Adams Papers.

3. Sep. 12, 1801, *JQA Diary.*

4. Sep. 14, 1801, *JQA Diary.*

5. JQA to Rufus King, Oct. 13, 1801, *Writings* 3:1–2.

6. Sep. 21, 1801, *JQA Diary;* Sep. 30, 1801, *JQA Diary.*

7. JA to JQA, Sep. 12, 1801, Adams Papers.
8. AA to JQA, Sep. 23, 1801; AA to TBA, Jul. 5, 1801, Adams Papers.
9. AA to JQA, Sep. 23, 1801, Adams Papers.
10. Ibid.
11. LCA to JQA, Sep. 22, 1801, Adams Papers.
12. LCA to AA, Oct. 2, 1801, Adams Papers.
13. JQA to LCA, Sep. 29, 1801, Adams Papers.
14. TBA to AA, Oct. 24, 1801, Adams Papers.
15. LCA to JQA, Sep. 22, 1801, Adams Papers.
16. JQA to LCA, Oct. 9, 1801, Adams Papers.
17. Oct. 26, 1801, *JQA Diary.*
18. Ibid.
19. Nov. 14, 1801, *JQA Diary.*
20. JQA to TBA, Nov. 28, 1801, Adams Papers; Nov. 30, 1801, *JQA Diary.*
21. AA to TBA, Dec. 27, 1801, Adams Papers.
22. LCA, *D&A* 1:162, 86.
23. Ibid., 164.
24. Ibid., 210, 86.
25. LCA to George Washington Adams, Jun. 25, 1825, Adams Papers.
26. LCA, *D&A* 1:167.
27. Sep. 17, 1801 and Jan. 8, 1802, *JQA Diary.*

CHAPTER 26: "NO SMALL DIFFICULTY"

1. Jan. 8–9, 1802, *JQA Diary.*
2. JQA to TBA, Nov. 28, 1801, Adams Papers.
3. TBA to JQA, Dec. 7, 1801, Adams Papers.
4. Ibid.
5. JQA to TBA, Sep. 27, 1801, Adams Papers.
6. Apr. 4, 1802, *JQA Diary.*
7. JA to JQA, Feb. 2, 1802, Adams Papers; JQA to JA, Mar. 2, 1802, Reel 401, Adams Papers.
8. The Society for the Study of Natural Philosophy, 1801–1813, John Collins Warren Papers, Massachusetts Historical Society; Marlana Portolano, "John Quincy Adams's Rhetorical Crusade for Astronomy," ISIS 91:3, Sep. 2000, 480–503.
9. George Adams's publications included "Lectures on Natural and Experimental Philosophy" (1784) and "An Essay on Electricity Explaining the Principles of that Useful Science, and Describing the Instruments Contrived Either to Illustrate the Theory, or Render the Practice Entertaining" (1799).
10. Henry Adams, *The Degradation of the Democratic Dogma* (New York: Macmillan, 1920), 47, 53; Jan. 31, 1802, *JQA Diary.*
11. A. Hunter Dupress, quoted in Marlana Portolano, "John Quincy Adams's Rhetorical Crusade for Astronomy," ISIS, v. 91; the speech is also quoted in Nina Burleigh, *The Stranger and the Statesman: James Smithson, John Quincy Adams and the Making of America's Greatest Museum: The Smithsonian* (New York: William Morrow, 2003).
12. JQA, State of the Union Address, Dec. 6, 1825.
13. Jan. 10, 1837, *JQA Diary.*
14. *Memoirs* 1:249.

15. Letter of Massachusetts Federalists to John Quincy Adams, Nov. 26, 1828, Henry Adams, ed., *Documents Relating To New-England Federalism, 1800–1815,* (Boston: Little, Brown, 1905), 43–45; May 27, 1802, *Memoirs* 1:252.

16. JQA to Henry Knox, Feb. 14, 1803, *Writings* 3:12; *Writings* 3:5, n. 1.

17. Feb. 4, 1803, *JQA Diary;* Fisher Ames to Christopher Gore, Feb. 24, 1803, *Writings* 3:11, n. 3.

18. JQA "Ecce Iterum" written about 1825 in *Writings* 3:10.

19. JQA, "An Address to the Members of the Massachusetts Charitable Fire Society," May 28, 1802 (Boston: 1802); JQA "Ecce Iterum" written about 1825 in *Writings* 3:10.

20. JQA, "Oration at Plymouth Massachusetts Commonwealth of the First Landing of Our Ancestors at That Place" (Boston: Russell and Cutler, 1802).

21. Jul. 31, 1802, *JQA Diary.*

22. AA to Thomas Jefferson, Oct. 25, 1804, *The Adams-Jefferson Letters,* vol. 1.

23. Dec. 31, 1802, *JQA Diary.*

24. Dec. 31, 1803, *JQA Diary.*

25. Dec. 31, 1802, Jan. 7, 1803, April 27–28, 1802, *JQA Diary.*

26. Jul. 4, 1803, *JQA Diary;* TBA to JQA, Jul. 10, 1803, Adams Papers.

27. Catherine Johnson to JQA, Jul. 1803, Adams Papers.

28. Jul. 11, 1803, *JQA Diary.*

29. Sep. 1803, *JQA Diary.*

30. Oct. 9, 1803, *JQA Diary.*

31. Oct. 20, 1803, *JQA Diary;* JQA reply to the Letter of Massachusetts Federalists, Dec. 30, 1828, Henry Adams ed., *Documents Relating To New-England Federalism, 1800–1815* (Boston: Little, Brown, 1905), 46–62.

32. Oct. 31, 1803, *JQA Diary.*

CHAPTER 27: "ANOTHER FEATHER AGAINST A WHIRLWIND"

1. Henry Adams, *History of the United States of America* (New York: Scribner, 1909), 2:49.

2. Henry Adams ed., *Documents Relating To New-England Federalism, 1800–1815* (Boston: Little, Brown, 1905), 155.

3. Thomas Jefferson to John C. Breckinridge, Aug. 12, 1803, "The Louisiana Purchase," *Jefferson Papers,* U. of Va. Library, Electronic Text Center.

4. Nov. 3, 1803, *Annals of Congress,* 8th Congress, 1st Session, 67–68.

5. JQA to JA, Apr. 25, 1801, *Writings* 2:531.

6. JQA to William Vans Murray, Apr. 7, 1801, *Writings* 2:526.

7. JQA to JA, Apr. 25, 1801, *Writings* 2:531.

8. Thomas Jefferson to Robert Livingston, Apr. 18, 1802, *The Works of Thomas Jefferson,* Paul L. Ford, ed., (New York and London: Putnam, 1904) 8:143–47.

9. Ibid.

10. Ibid.

11. Ibid.

12. Thomas Jefferson to Thomas Mann Randolph, Jan. 17, 1799, in *Correspondence Between Thomas Jefferson and Pierre Samuel Du Pont De Nemours 1789–1817,* Dumas Malone, ed. (Boston and New York:

Houghton Mifflin Company, 1930), 1, n. 1; Pierre Du Pont to Thomas Jefferson, Sep. 8, 1805, *Correspondence Between Thomas Jefferson and Pierre Du Pont 1789–1817,* 86.

13. Thomas Jefferson to Pierre Du Pont, Apr. 25, 1802, *Correspondence Between Thomas Jefferson and Pierre Du Pont 1789–1817,* 46–48.

14. Pierre Du Pont to Thomas Jefferson, Apr. 30, 1802, *Correspondence Between Thomas Jefferson and Pierre Du Pont 1789–1817,* 52–60.

15. Ibid.

16. Ibid., 2:27.

17. Ibid., 2:28.

18. Henrietta Elizabeth Marshall, *This Country of Ours: The Story of the United States* (New York: George H. Doran Company, 1917), 437.

19. Henry Adams, ed. *Documents Relating to New-England Federalism 1800–1815,* 156.

20. Nov. 1, 1803, *JQA Diary.*

21. Nov. 3, 1803, *Annals of Congress,* 8th Congress, 1st Session, 67.

22. Henry Adams, ed., *Documents Relating to New-England Federalism 1800–1815,* 157.

23. *Aurora,* Dec. 1, 1803, quoted in *Writings* 3:20, note 1.

24. Theodore Lyman to Timothy Pickering, Jan. 4, 1804 quoted in *Writings* 3:30, n. 1.

25. AA to JQA, Dec. 11, 1803, Adams Papers.

26. JA to JQA, Feb. 25, 1804, Adams Papers.

27. Dec. 8, 1803, *Memoirs* 1:285.

28. Dec. 31, 1803, *JQA Diary.*

29. *Writings* 3:27.

30. *Writings* 3:30.

31. Bemis, *JQA and the Foundations of American Foreign Policy,* 131.

32. JQA to AA, Jan. 22, 1804, Adams Papers.

33. Bemis, *JQA and the Foundations of American Foreign Policy,* 122.

34. *Writings* 3:50.

35. *Writings* 3:71.

36. *Writings* 3:72.

37. JQA, Proposed Amendment, *Writings* 3:87, 90–91 and n. 1: These remarks were to be delivered in the Senate, but it is doubtful if an opportunity offered, as they are not mentioned in the *Annals of Congress* for this session.

38. Ibid.

39. Ibid.

40. Ibid.

41. Nov. 27, 1820, *JQA Diary;* JQA, Proposed Amendment, *Writings* 3:101–02.

42. Mar. 25, 1804, *Memoirs* 1:311.

43. Mar. 4, 1804, *JQA Diary.*

44. JQA to LCA, April 9, 1804, Adams Papers. JQA says the letter is of April 4, but there is no record of it.

CHAPTER 28: "LIKE A FISH OUT OF WATER"

1. LCA to JQA, May 6, 1804, Adams Papers.

2. LCA to JQA, May 29, 1804, Adams Papers.
3. LCA to JQA, May 29, 1804, Adams Papers; LCA to JQA, Aug. 12, 1804, Adams Papers.
4. LCA to AA, Nov. 27, 1804, Adams Papers.
5. JQA to LCA, Apr. 9, 1804, Adams Papers.
6. Ibid.
7. JQA to LCA, Apr. 15, 1804, Adams Papers.
8. LCA to JQA, Jun. 26, 1804, Adams Papers; LCA to JQA, May 13, 1804, Adams Papers; LCA to JQA, May 6, 1804, Adams Papers.
9. LCA to JQA, May 6, 1804, Adams Papers.
10. JQA to LCA, May 20, 1804, Adams Papers; JQA to LCA, May 9, 1804, Adams Papers.
11. JQA to LCA, Sep. 30, 1804, Adams Papers.
12. JQA to LCA, Jun. 9, 1804, Adams Papers; JQA to LCA, May 20, 1804, Adams Papers.
13. LCA to JQA, Aug. 5, 1804, Adams Papers.
14. JQA to LCA, Sep. 2, 1804, Adams Papers.
15. LCA to JQA, Jul. 4, 1804, Adams Papers; JQA to LCA, Jul. 19, 1804, Adams Papers.
16. JQA to TBA, May 21, 1801, *Writings* 2:521.
17. William Warland Clapp, *Joseph Dennie, Editor of "The Port Folio" and Author of "The Lay Preacher"* (Cambridge: John Wilson & Son, 1880), 8; *The Port Folio,* Fourth Series, Vol. II, No. IV (October 1816), 273; JQA to TBA, Mar. 21, 1801, *Writings* 2:525.
18. JQA to TBA, Aug. 19, 1803, Adams Papers.
19. *Letters of William Vans Murray to John Quincy Adams, 1783–1803,* ed. Worthington Chauncery Ford, reprint from the Annual Report of the American Historical Association for 1912, 341–715 (Washington, DC, 1914).
20. JQA to JA, Nov. 19, 1804, Adams Papers.
21. JA to JQA, Nov. 30, 1804, Adams Papers; JA to JQA, Dec. 14, 1804, Adams Papers.
22. AA to JQA, Dec. 18, 1804, Adams Papers.
23. AA to JQA, Mar. 24, 1806, Adams Papers. This line is a quotation from Frederick Reynolds's play, *Speculation.*
24. AA to Eliza Susan Quincy, Mar. 24, 1806, Adams Papers.
25. JQA to JA, Jan. 5, 1805, *Writings* 3:105.
26. Jan. 4 & 15, 1805, *JQA Diary.*
27. JQA to AA, Mar. 15, 1804, Adams Papers.
28. JQA to JA, Mar. 8, 1805, *Writings* 3:108; quoted in JQA to Timothy Pickering, Mar. 11, 1804, *Writings* 3:35, n.1.
29. William Plumer, *Memorandum of Proceedings in the United States Senate, 1803–1807,* March 11, 1804 (Macmillan, 1923), 101.
30. Henry Adams, *History of the United States* 2:143.
31. Henry Adams, *Documents Relating to New-England Federalism, 1800–1815,* 11.
32. William Plumer, *Memorandum of Proceedings in the United States Senate, 1803–1807,* March 11, 1804 (Macmillan, 1923), 175.
33. Henry Adams, *History of the United States* 2:148.
34. Ibid., 149.

35. Ibid., 150, 229–30.
36. Ibid., 243.
37. JQA to JA, Mar. 14, 1805, *Writings* 3:117.
38. Apr. 25, 1805, *JQA Diary.*
39. May 29, 1805, *JQA Diary;* Jul. 31, 1805, *JQA Diary.*
40. JQA to Samuel Dexter, Aug. 6, 1805, *Writings* 3:123–25; JQA to Corporation of Harvard College, Oct. 11, 1805 and Jun. 26, 1806, *Writings* 3:126–29, 148–49.
41. AA to JQA, Dec. 17, 1805, Adams Papers.
42. LCA to AA, Jan. 6, 1806, Adams Papers.
43. AA to LCA, Jan. 19, 1806, Adams Papers.
44. LCA to AA, May 5, 1806, Adams Papers; LCA to AA, Dec. 6, 1805, Adams Papers.
45. AA to JQA, Jan. 9, 1806, Adams Papers.
46. Nov. 30, 1805, *Memoirs* 1:375–76.
47. Ibid.
48. JQA to JA, Dec. 6, 1805, Adams Papers.
49. Thomas Jefferson, Fifth Annual Message to Congress, Dec. 3, 1805.
50. AA to JQA, Dec. 17, 1805, Adams Papers.
51. JQA to JA, Jan. 14, 1806, *Writings* 3:131–32.

CHAPTER 29: "APOSTASY"

1. JQA to Skelton Jones, Apr. 17, 1809, *Writings* 3:303.
2. JQA to TBA, Dec. 18, 1805, Adams Papers; JQA to JA, Feb. 11, 1806, *Writings,* 3:134.
3. JQA, Resolutions, Feb. 1806, *Writings* 3:133–34.
4. *Memoirs* 1:397.
5. JQA to JA, Feb. 11, 1806, *Writings* 3:136.
6. Ibid.
7. Mar. 3, 1820, *Memoirs* 5:11.
8. Feb. 24, 1820, *Memoirs* 4:531; Mar. 3, 1820, *Memoirs* 5:11; Jan. 8, 1820, *Memoirs* 4:502.
9. Annals of Congress, Senate, 16th Congress, 1st Session, 367–428, 1571–1588.
10. Mar. 3, 1820, *Memoirs* 5:12.
11. JQA to William Stephens Smith, Apr. 16, 1806, *Writings* 3:140.
12. JQA to LCA, May 1, 1806, Adams Papers.
13. JQA to TBA, Mar. 19, 1806, Reel 404, Adams Papers; JA to Daniel E. Updike, Aug. 7, 1806, Adams Papers.
14. Katherine Metcalf Roof, *Colonel William Smith and Lady* (Boston: Houghton Mifflin Company, 1929), 268–70.
15. Ibid.
16. Jan. 11, 1805, *JQA Diary;* JQA to LCA, May 4, 1806, Adams Papers; JQA to LCA, Jul. 13, 1806, *Writings* 3:153.
17. JQA to LCA, Jun. 8, 1806, Adams Papers; LCA to JQA, Jun. 15, 1806, Adams Papers.
18. John Quincy Adams, *Lectures on Rhetoric and Oratory,* (Cambridge: Hilliard and Metcalf, 1810), 1:29.
19. Jun. 30, 1806, *JQA Diary.*

20. LCA to JQA, Nov. 25, 1806, Adams Papers; JQA to LCA, Dec. 8, 1806, Adams Papers; LCA to JQA, Dec. 14, 1806, Adams Papers.
21. JQA to AA, Feb. 13, 1807, Adams Papers; Henry Adams, *History of the United States* (New York: Scribner, 1890), 4:38; Jun. 30, 1820, *Memoirs* 5:136.
22. Henry Adams, ed. *Documents Relating to New-England Federalism 1800–1815* (Boston: Little, Brown, 1905), 180.
23. Ibid., 183.
24. Jul. 10, 1807, *JQA Diary*.
25. Henry Adams, ed., *Documents Relating to New-England Federalism*, 181; Jul. 9, 1807, *JQA Diary*; Jul. 11, 1807, *JQA Diary*.
26. Ralph Waldo Emerson, *Eloquence, Letters and Social Aims* (Boston, 1888), 120.
27. Aug. 18, 1807, *JQA Diary*; JQA to Catherine Nuth Johnson, Aug. 18, 1807, Adams Papers.
28. JQA to Catherine Nuth Johnson, Aug. 20, 1807, Adams Papers; Oct. 24, 1807, *JQA Diary*.
29. Letter of Stephen Row Bradley, Sep. 21, 1824 in *Writings* 3:169, n. 2 (continued from page 168).
30. Barent Gardenier to Rufus King, Jan. 26, 1808, *Life and Correspondence of Rufus King*, vol. 68 in *Writings* 3:232–33, n. 2.
31. Henry Adams, ed., *Documents Relating to New-England Federalism, 1800–1815*, 194.
32. Timothy Pickering, "A letter from the Hon. Timothy Pickering, a Senator of the United States from the United States, exhibiting to his Constituents a View of the Imminent Danger of an unnecessary and Ruinous War, Addressed to his Excellency James Sullivan, Governor of the said State," Boston, published by Greenough & Stebbins, 1898; JQA to Harrison Gray Otis, Mar. 31, 1808, Adams Papers.
33. JQA to Skelton Jones, Apr. 17, 1809, *Writings* 3:303.
34. JA to JQA, Jan. 8, 1808, *Writings* 3:189, n. 1.
35. James Sullivan to Thomas Jefferson, Jun. 3, 1808, *Writings* 3:236–37, n. 1.
36. Jul. 5, 1809, *Memoirs* 1:549; JQA to William Plumer, Aug. 16, 1809, *Writings* 3:338; "A mission to the Court of St. Petersburg is, to a man of active talents, somewhat like an honorable exile." Ezekiel Bacon to JQA, Jun. 29, 1809, *Writings* 3:321, n. 1.
37. John Quincy Adams, *Lectures on Rhetoric and Oratory*, 2:396.
38. Ibid.
39. Aug. 6, 1809, *Memoirs* 2:5; AA to JQA and LCA, Aug. 5, 1809, Reel 408, Adams Papers.
40. JQA to AA, Aug. 9, 1809, Reel 408, Adams Papers.

CHAPTER 30: "IN HONORABLE DIPLOMATIC EXILE"

1. JQA to AA, Feb. 8, 1810, *Writings* 3:393.
2. Ibid.; JQA to Charles W. Upham, Feb. 2, 1837, Samuel F. Bemis, *John Quincy Adams and the Foundations of American Foreign Policy* (Westport, CT: Greenwood Press, 1981), 152, n. 68.
3. Nov. 3, 1809, *JQA Diary*.

4. LCA, *D&A* 1:293.
5. Nov. 25, 1809, *JQA Diary*.
6. Secretary of State Robert Smith to William Short, Sep. 8, 1808, *Writings* 3:327. This letter was sent to JQA in lieu of particular instructions.
7. Oct. 28, 1809, *JQA Diary*.
8. Apr. 15, 1810, *JQA Diary*.
9. JQA to AA, May 2, 1811, Adams Papers.
10. Several sources, including Scribner's article from 1872, say Alexander I was more than six feet tall. Nov. 5, 1809, *JQA Diary*.
11. Ibid.
12. LCA, *D&A* 1:297–99.
13. Ibid.
14. Ibid.
15. JQA to AA, Oct. 14, 1810, Adams Papers; JQA to TBA, Mar. 29, 1811, Adams Papers.
16. LCA to AA, Oct. 28, 1809, Reel 408, Adams Papers.
17. Ibid.
18. LCA to AA, May 13, 1810, Reel 409, Adams Papers; LCA to MC, Jun. 5, 1810, Reel 409, Adams Papers.
19. LCA to AA, Jun. 2, 1810, Reel 409, Adams Papers.
20. JQA to AA, Feb. 7, 1810, Reel 409, Adams Papers.
21. Dec. 17, 1810, *JQA Diary*.
22. JQA to JA, Sep. 2, 1810, Adams Papers.
23. JQA to TBA, Oct. 23, 1810, *Writings* 3:521; JQA to AA, Oct. 14, 1810, *Writings* 3:517. The last sentence is a direct quotation from the newspaper.
24. JQA to TBA, Oct. 23, 1810, *Writings* 3:522.
25. AA to LCA, May 15, 1810, Adams Papers.
26. James Madison to His Imperial Majesty, Oct. 10, 1810, Adams Papers; James Madison to JQA, Oct. 16, 1810, Adams Papers.
27. Ibid.
28. AA to LCA, Mar. 4, 1811, Adams Papers.
29. JQA to AA, Jun. 11, 1811, Adams Papers.
30. Aug. 11, 1811, *JQA Diary*; LCA to AA, Jul. 19, 1810, Adams Papers; JQA to AA, Aug. 12, 1811, Reel 412, Adams Papers.
31. JQA to AA, Sep. 10, 1811, Adams Papers.
32. Jul. 26, 1811, *JQA Diary*.
33. JQA to Secretary of State James Monroe, Jul. 22, 1811, *Writings* 4:151; JQA to TBA, May 13, 1811, *Writings* 4:67.

CHAPTER 31: "WHETHER OF PEACE OR WAR"

1. JQA to TBA, Feb. 14, 1810, *Writings* 3:397–99.
2. Ibid.
3. Ibid.
4. Ibid.
5. "Il faut toujours proportionner la dépense à la recette." May 31, 1811, *Memoirs* 2:268.
6. Mar. 3, 1812, *Memoirs* 2:345.
7. Dec. 22, 1810 and Dec. 24, 1811, *JQA Diary*.
8. Feb. 15, 1811, *Memoirs* 2:226.

9. LCA to AA, Jun. 2, 1810, Reel 409, Adams Papers.
10. Ibid.
11. JQA to William Eustis, Feb. 28, 1810, *Writings* 3:404.
12. JQA to James Monroe, Jul. 6, 1811, *Writings* 4:131; Mar. 19, 1812, *Memoirs* 2:352.
13. Apr. 20, 1812, *Memoirs* 2:363–64.
14. JQA to James Monroe, Feb. 2, 1813, *Writings* 4:431; April 23, 1812, *Memoirs* 2:365; JQA to James Monroe, Jun. 11, 1812, *Writings* 4:347.
15. JQA to JA, Feb. 15. 1813, *Writings* 4:437; JQA to TBA, Jan. 31, 1813, *Writings* 4:427.
16. JQA to JA, Oct. 4, 1812, *Writings* 4:394.
17. JQA to AA, Dec. 31, 1812, *Writings* 4:420; JQA to AA, Oct. 24, 1813, Reel 414, Adams Papers.
18. Sep. 30, 1812, *Memoirs* 2:408–9.
19. JQA to AA, Nov. 30, 1812, *Writings* 4:411–13 and Adams Papers.
20. Ibid.
21. JQA to AA, Dec. 31, 1812, *Writings* 4:421–22.
22. JQA to AA, Jun. 5, 1813, *Writings* 4:488.
23. JQA to AA, Dec. 31, 1812, *Writings* 4:423.
24. Sep. 21, 1812, *Memoirs* 2:401–4.
25. Ibid.
26. LCA to GWA, Jun. 14, 1812, Adams Papers; Aug. 21, 1812–Sep. 15, 1812, *JQA Diary*.
27. Sep. 31, 1812, *JQA Diary*.
28. JQA to AA, Sep. 21, 1812, Adams Papers; LCA to AA, Apr. 4, 1813, Adams Papers.
29. AA to LCA, Jul. 24, 1813, Adams Papers; AA to LCA, Jan. 30, 1813, Reel 415, Adams Papers.
30. AA to LCA, Jul. 24, 1813, Adams Papers.
31. JQA to AA, Jun. 30, 1813, Adams Papers.
32. JQA to AA, Mar. 25, 1813, *Writings* 4:459.
33. JQA to TBA, Apr. 10, 1811, *Writings* 4:43–45.
34. JQA to GWA and JA2, May 1810, Adams Papers.
35. JQA to GWA, Sep. 1 and 8, 1811, *Writings* 4:211–17.
36. JQA to TBA, Apr. 3, 1813, *Writings* 4:460–61.
37. Ibid.
38. LCA to GWA, Jun. 14, 1812, Adams Papers.
39. JQA to James Monroe, Jul. 14, 1813, *Writings* 4:493–94.
40. JQA to JA, Sep. 3, 1813, *Writings* 4:512.
41. Mar. 20, 1814, *Memoirs* 2:583–84.
42. JQA to JA, May 8, 1814, *Writings* 5:41–42, n. 1; Apr. 23, 1814, *Memoirs* 2:600.
43. Jun. 22, 1813, *Memoirs* 2:480; Feb. 5, 1826, *Memoirs* 7:112.
44. JQA to LCA, Apr. 15, 1804, Adams Papers.
45. James Monroe to JQA, Mar. 6, 1817, *Writings* 6:165–66.
46. JQA to James Monroe, Apr. 17, 1817, *Writings* 6:177; JQA to AA, May 16, 1817, *Writings* 6:181–82.
47. AA to JQA, Nov. 13, 1782, *AFC* 5:38. Abraham Lincoln, a freshman Congressman from Illinois, was an honorary pall bearer at JQA's funeral, two days after his collapse.

AFTERWORD

1. JQA, Message to the United States House of Representatives, House Journal, 19th Congress, Mar. 17, 1826, 351.
2. LCA to JQA, Aug. 3, 1821, Reel 452, Adams Papers.
3. JQA to LCA, Aug. 11, 1821, *Writings* 7:170–71.
4. LCA to AA, Jun. 12, 1815, Adams Papers. The 48-page manuscript is dated Jun. 27, 1836. LCA, *D&A* 1:375 and n. 1.
5. C. James Taylor, Editor in Chief of the Adams Papers, to Phyllis Lee Levin, Sep. 22, 2014.
6. Henry Adams, *The Education of Henry Adams* (Boston and New York: Houghton Mifflin, 1918), 20, 25, 12.

BIBLIOGRAPHY

MANUSCRIPT SOURCES

Adams Papers, Microfilms, 1639–1889, The Massachusetts Historical Society, Boston, 1954–1959, 609 Reels.

Challinor, Joan R. "Louisa Catherine Johnson Adams: The Price of Ambition." American University, 1982.

Everett-Peabody Papers, The Massachusetts Historical Society, Boston.

Francis Dana Letterbooks and Journals, Dana Family Papers, The Massachusetts Historical Society, Boston.

John Collins Warren Papers, The Massachusetts Historical Society: The Society for the Study of Natural Philosophy, 1801–1813, Boston.

The Smith-Townsend Collection, The Massachusetts Historical Society: Letters from Abigail Adams to Her Cousin, William Smith of Boston, and to Her Niece Betsy Cranch of Haverill.

PUBLISHED SOURCES

"Mrs. John Quincy Adams' Ball, 1824." *Harper's Bazaar,* March 18 1871.

Proceedings of the Massachusetts Historical Society, 1882–1883. Vol. XX. Boston: Massachusetts Historical Society, 1884.

"Du Pont and Talleyrand." *Proceedings of the Massachusetts Historical Society* 49 (November 1915).

"American Ties with All Hallows Church, London." *Maryland Historical Magazine* XLII.3 (1947).

"JQA, Twitter Celebrity." *Massachusetts Historical Society Miscellany.*97 (2009).

Adams, Abigail. *Letters of Mrs. Adams, the Wife of John Adams.* 3rd ed. 2 vols. Boston: C. C. Little and J. Brown, 1841.

———. *New Letters of Abigail Adams, 1788–1801.* Boston: Houghton Mifflin, 1947.

Adams, Abigail, and John Adams. *The Book of Abigail and John: Selected Letters of the Adams Family, 1762–1784.* Cambridge, Mass.: Harvard University Press, 1975.

Adams, Charles Francis. *Diary.* The Adams Papers Series I, Diaries. Ed. Donald, Aïda DiPace. Cambridge, Mass.: Belknap Press of Harvard University Press, 1964.

———. *History of Braintree, Massachusetts (1639–1708) the North Precinct of Braintree (1708–1792) and the Town of Quincy (1792–1889)*. Cambridge, Mass.: Riverside Press, 1891.

———. "Memoir of Charles Francis Adams, by His Son." *Proceedings of the Massachusetts Historical Society, 1899–1900.*

———. *Three Episodes of Massachusetts History: The Settlement of Boston Bay; the Antinomian Controversy; a Study of Church and Town Government*. 2 vols. Boston: Houghton, Mifflin, 1892.

Adams, Charles Francis, and Henry Adams. *A Cycle of Adams Letters, 1861–1865*. 2 vols. Boston: Houghton Mifflin Co., 1920.

Adams, Charles Francis, and John Quincy Adams. *The Life of John Adams (1871)*. Rev. and corr. ed. 2 vols. New York: Haskell House, 1968.

Adams, Henry. "Harvard College 1786–87." *North American Review* 114. Jan. (1872): 115–18.

———. *Historical Essays*. New York: C. Scribner's Sons, 1891.

———, ed. *Documents Relating to New-England Federalism, 1800–1815*. Boston: Little, Brown, 1905.

———. *History of the United States of America*. 9 vols. New York: C. Scribner & Sons, 1909.

———. *The Education of Henry Adams; an Autobiography*. Boston: Houghton Mifflin Co., 1918.

———. *The Degradation of the Democratic Dogma*. New York: Macmillan, 1920.

———, ed. *John Adams's Book, Being Notes on a Record of the Births, Marriages & Deaths of Three Generations of the Adams Family, 1734–1807*. Boston: Boston Athenæum, 1934.

———. *A Catalogue of the Books of John Quincy Adams Deposited in the Boston Athenæum, with Notes on Books, Adams Seals and Book-Plates*. Boston: Boston Athenæum, 1938.

———. *The Letters of Henry Adams*. Ed. Levenson, J. C. 6 vols. Cambridge, Mass.: Belknap Press of Harvard University Press, 1982.

———. *History of the United States of America During the Administrations of Thomas Jefferson*. Library of America. New York: Literary Classics of the United States: distributed by Viking Press, 1986.

———. *The War of 1812*. New York: Cooper Square Press, 1999.

Adams, Henry, and John Quincy Adams. *Documents Relating to New-England Federalism, 1800–1815*. New York: B. Franklin, 1965.

Adams, Henry, and Mabel La Farge. *Letters to a Niece and Prayer to the Virgin of Chartres*. Boston, New York: Houghton Mifflin Company, 1920.

Adams, John. *The Works of John Adams*. Ed. Adams, Charles Francis. 2 vols. Boston: Freeman and Bolles, 1841.

———. *Diary and Autobiography of John Adams*. Ed. Butterfield, L. H. 4 vols. Cambridge, Mass.: Harvard University Press, 1964.

———. *The Earliest Diary of John Adams; June 1753–April 1754, September 1758–January 1759*. The Adams Papers Series I: Diaries. Ed. Butterfield, L. H. Cambridge, Mass.: Belknap Press of Harvard University Press, 1966.

———. *My Dearest Friend: Letters of Abigail and John Adams*. Cambridge, Mass.: Belknap Press of Harvard University Press, 2007.

———. *John Adams: Revolutionary Writings 1775–1783*. The Library of America. New York: Library of America, 2011.

Adams, John, Abigail Adams, and Thomas Jefferson. *The Adams-Jefferson Letters*. Chapel Hill: Published for the Institute of Early American History and Culture at Williamsburg Va., 1959.

Adams, John, and Charles Francis Adams. *The Works of John Adams, Second President of the United States*. 10 vols. Boston: Little & Brown, 1850.

Adams, John, and John Quincy Adams. *The Selected Writings of John and John Quincy Adams*. Eds. Koch, Adrienne and William Peden. New York: A.A. Knopf, 1946.

Adams, John, Thomas Jefferson, and Abigail Adams. *The Adams-Jefferson Letters: The Complete Correspondence between Thomas Jefferson and Abigail and John Adams*. Chapel Hill: Published for the Institute of Early American History and Culture at Williamsburg, Virginia by the University of North Carolina Press, 1988.

Adams, John, and Benjamin Waterhouse. *Statesman and Friend; Correspondence of John Adams with Benjamin Waterhouse, 1784–1822*. Ed. Ford, Worthington Chauncey. Boston: Little, Brown, 1927.

Adams, John Quincy. *Lectures on Rhetoric and Oratory: Delivered to the Classes of Senior and Junior Sophisters in Harvard University*. 2 vols. Cambridge, Mass.: Hilliard and Metcalf, 1810.

———. *Memoirs of John Quincy Adams, Comprising Portions of His Diary from 1795 to 1848*. Ed. Adams, Charles Francis. 12 vols. Philadelphia: J.B. Lippincott & Co., 1874.

———. *Life in a New England Town: 1787,1788. Diary of John Quincy Adams, While a Student in the Office of Theophilus Parsons at Newburyport*. Boston: Little, Brown, 1903.

———. *Letters of John Quincy Adams to Alexander Hill Everett, 1811–1837*. New York:1906.

———. *Writings of John Quincy Adams*. Ed. Ford, Worthington Chauncey. 7 vols. New York: Macmillan, 1913.

———. *The Diary of John Quincy Adams, 1794–1845*. Ed. Nevins, Allan. New York: Longmans, Green, 1928.

———. *John Quincy Adams in Russia, Comprising Portions of the Diary of John Quincy Adams from 1809 to 1814*. Praeger Scholarly Reprints Source Books and Studies in Russian and Soviet History. New York: Praeger, 1970.

———. *Diary of John Quincy Adams*. The Adams Papers Series I, Diaries. Vol. 1. 2 vols. Cambridge, Mass.: Belknap Press of Harvard University Press, 1981.

Adams, John Quincy, and Allan Nevins. *Diary, 1794–1845; American Diplomacy and Political, Social, and Intellectual Life from Washington to Polk*. New York: Charles Scribner & Sons, 1951.

Adams, James Truslow. *The Adams Family*. Boston: Little, Brown, 1930.

———. *The Epic of America*. Boston: Little, Brown, 1931.

Adams, Louisa Catherine. "Mrs. John Quincy Adams's Narrative of a Journey from St. Petersburg to Paris." *Scribner's Magazine,* July-December 1903.

———. *Diary and Autobiographical Writings of Louisa Catherine Adams*. The Adams Papers, Series 1 Diaries. 2 vols. Cambridge, Mass.: Belknap Press of Harvard University Press, 2013.

Adams, Thomas. *Berlin and the Prussian Court in 1798; Journal of Thomas Boylston Adams, Secretary to the United States Legation at Berlin*. New York: The New York Public Library, 1916.

Agar, Herbert. *The Price of Union*. Boston: Houghton Mifflin, 1950.

Allgor, Catherine. "'A Republican in a Monarchy': Louisa Catherine Adams in Russia." *Diplomatic History* 21.1 (1997): 15–44.

———. *Parlor Politics: In Which the Ladies of Washington Help Build a City and a Government*. Jeffersonian America. Charlottesville: University Press of Virginia, 2000.

Amar, Akhil Reed. *America's Constitution: A Biography*. 1st ed. New York: Random House, 2005.

American Council of Learned Societies. *Concise Dictionary of American Biography*. 5th ed. 2 vols. New York: Scribner; Simon & Schuster and Prentice Hall International, 1997.

Anthony, Carl Sferrazza. *First Ladies: The Saga of the Presidents' Wives and Their Power*. 2 vols. New York: W. Morrow, 1990.

Bartlett, Joseph Gardner. *Henry Adams of Somersetshire, England, and Braintree, Mass.* New York: Priv. print., 1927.

Bemis, Samuel Flagg. "The London Mission of Thomas Pinckney, 1792–1796." *The American Historical Review* 28.2 (1923): 228–47.

———. *The Diplomacy of the American Revolution*. New York: D. Appleton-Century, 1935.

———. "John Quincy Adams and George Washington." *Proceedings of the Massachusetts Historical Society* LXVII. Oct. 1941–1944 (1945): 365–85.

———. "The Scuffle in the Rotunda: A Footnote to the Presidency of John Quincy Adams and to the History of Dueling." *Proceedings of the Massachusetts Historical Society* 71 (1953): 156–66.

———. *John Quincy Adams and the Union*. New York: Knopf, 1956.

———. *John Quincy Adams and the Foundations of American Foreign Policy*. Westport, Conn.: Greenwood Press, 1981.

Benardo, Leonard, and Jennifer Weiss. *Citizen-in-Chief: The Second Lives of the American Presidents*. New York: William Morrow, 2009.

Berridge, Virginia, and Griffith Edwards. *Opium and the People : Opiate Use in Nineteenth-Century England*. New Haven: Yale University Press, 1987.

Blake, John B. "Smallpox Inoculation in Colonial Boston." *Journal of the History of Medicine and Allied Sciences* VIII. July (1953): 284–300.

Blake, John Ballard. *Public Health in the Town of Boston, 1630–1822*. Harvard Historical Studies. Cambridge: Harvard University Press, 1959.

Bobbé, Dorothie De Bear. *Mr. & Mrs. John Quincy Adams, an Adventure in Patriotism*. New York: Minton, Balch, 1930.

Bowen, Catherine Drinker. *John Adams and the American Revolution*. Grosset's Universal Library. New York: Grosset & Dunlap, 1950.

Bowers, Claude Gernade. *The Young Jefferson, 1743–1789*. Boston: Houghton Mifflin, 1945.

Bradford, Alden. *History of Massachusetts*. 3 vols. Boston: Richardson and Lord Research Reprint, 1822.

Brookhiser, Richard. *America's First Dynasty: The Adamses, 1735–1918*. New York: Free Press, 2002.

Buck, Howard Swazey. *A Study in Smollett, Chiefly "Peregrine Pickle," with a Complete Collation of the First and Second Editions*. New Haven: Yale University Press, 1925.

Burke, Edmund. *Reflections on the Revolution in France*. New York: Penguin, 2004.

Burleigh, Nina. *The Stranger and the Statesman: James Smithson, John Quincy Adams, and the Making of America's Greatest Museum: The Smithsonian.* New York: Morrow, 2003.

Burney, Fanny. *The Early Journals and Letters of Fanny Burney.* Kingston; Montreal: McGill-Queen's University Press, 1988.

Butterfield, L. H., ed. *Adams Family Correspondence.* Cambridge, Mass.: Belknap Press of Harvard University Press, 1963.

———. "Tending a Dragon-Killer: Notes for the Biographer of Mrs. John Quincy Adams." *Proceedings of the American Philosophical Society* 118.2 (1974): 165–78.

Caroli, Betty Boyd. *First Ladies.* New York: Oxford University Press, 1987.

———. *Inside the White House: America's Most Famous Home, the First 200 Years.* Guild America Books. New York: Canopy Books, 1992.

Chalfant, Edward. *Both Sides of the Ocean: A Biography of Henry Adams, His First Life, 1838–1862.* Hamden, Conn.: Archon Books, 1982.

Challinor, Joan R. "An English Idyll: John Quincy Adams and Louisa Catherine Johnson Adams in England, 1815–1817." Ed. National Museum of American History, Smithsonian Institution. Washington, D.C.

———. "'A Quarter Taint of Maryland Blood': An Inquiry into the Anglo/ Maryland Background of Mrs. John Quincy Adams." *Maryland Historical Magazine* 80.4 (1985).

———. "The Mis-Education of Louisa Catherine Johnson." *Proceedings of the Massachusetts Historical Society* 98.(1986): 21–48.

Chase, George W., ed. *Abstract of the Census of Massachusetts, 1860.* Boston: Wright & Potter, 1863.

Chernow, Ron. *Alexander Hamilton.* New York: Penguin Press, 2004.

———. *Washington: A Life.* New York: Penguin Press, 2010.

Clapp, William Warland. *Joseph Dennie: Editor of "the Port Folio" and Author of "the Lay Preacher."* Cambridge: J. Wilson and son, 1880.

Commager, Henry Steele, ed. *Documents of American History.* 9th ed. 2 vols. New York: Appleton-Century-Crofts, 1973.

Cresson, W. P. *Diplomatic Portraits.* Boston and New York: Houghton Mifflin, 1923.

———. *Francis Dana, a Puritan Diplomat at the Court of Catherine the Great.* New York, Toronto: L. MacVeagh Longmans, Green, 1930.

Crosby, Alfred W. *America, Russia, Hemp, and Napoleon: American Trade with Russia and the Baltic, 1783–1812.* Columbus: Ohio State University Press, 1965.

Crowley, John E. *The Privileges of Independence: Neomercantilism and the American Revolution.* Early America. Baltimore: Johns Hopkins University Press, 1993.

Dangerfield, George. *The Awakening of American Nationalism, 1815–1828.* The New American Nation Series. New York: Harper & Row, 1965.

De Madariaga, Isabel. *Catherine the Great: A Short History.* Yale Nota Bene. 2nd ed. New Haven: Yale University Press, 2002.

Duberman, Martin B. *Charles Francis Adams, 1807–1886.* Boston: Houghton Mifflin, 1961.

East, Robert Abraham. *John Quincy Adams; the Critical Years: 1785–1794.* New York: Bookman Associates, 1962.

Elkins, Stanley M., and Eric L. McKitrick. *The Age of Federalism.* New York: Oxford University Press, 1993.

Ellis, Joseph J. *Passionate Sage: The Character and Legacy of John Adams*. New York: W. W. Norton, 1993.

———. *American Sphinx: The Character of Thomas Jefferson*. New York: Alfred A. Knopf, 1997.

———. *American Creation: Triumphs and Tragedies at the Founding of the Republic*. 1st ed. New York: A. A. Knopf, 2007.

Emerson, Ralph Waldo. *Letters and Social Aims*. Boston: J. R. Osgood, 1876.

Franklin, Benjamin. *The Papers of Benjamin Franklin*. Eds. Labaree, Leonard Woods, William Bradford Willcox and Barbara Oberg. New Haven: Yale University Press, 1959.

French, Allen. *The Day of Concord and Lexington, the Nineteenth of April, 1775*. Boston: Little, Brown, and Company, 1925.

Frothingham, Richard. *Life and Times of Joseph Warren*. Boston: Little, Brown, 1865.

Garraty, John A. *The American Nation; a History of the United States*. A Harper-American Heritage Textbook. 2d ed. New York: Harper & Row, 1971.

Good, HG. "To the Future Biographers of John Quincy Adams." *The Scientific Monthly* 39.3 (1934): 247–51.

Griffiths, David M. "American Commercial Diplomacy in Russia, 1780 to 1783." *The William and Mary Quarterly* 27.3 (1970): 379–410.

Grimsted, Patricia Kennedy. *The Foreign Ministers of Alexander I; Political Attitudes and the Conduct of Russian Diplomacy, 1801–1825*. Russian and East European Studies. Berkeley: University of California Press, 1969.

Hamilton, Alexander. *Letter from Alexander Hamilton, Concerning the Public Conduct and Character of John Adams, Esq., President of the United States*. New York: Printed for John Lang by George F. Hopkins, 1800.

———. *The Papers of Alexander Hamilton*. 27 vols. New York: Columbia University Press, 1961.

Hecht, Marie B. *John Quincy Adams; a Personal History of an Independent Man*. New York: Macmillan, 1972.

Heffron, Margery M., and David L. Michelmore. *Louisa Catherine: The Other Mrs. Adams*. New Haven: Yale University Press, 2014.

Homans, Abigail Adams. *Education by Uncles*. Boston: Houghton Mifflin, 1966.

Hunt, John Gabriel, ed. *The Inaugural Addresses of the Presidents: From George Washington to George W. Bush*. New York: Gramercy Books, 2003.

Jay, John. *John Jay: Unpublished Papers, 1743–1780*. New York: Harper & Row, 1976.

Jay, John, and Sarah Livingston Jay. *Selected Letters of John Jay and Sarah Livingston Jay: Correspondence by or to the First Chief Justice of the United States and His Wife*. Ed. Freeman, Landa M. Jefferson N.C.: McFarland & Co., 2005.

Jefferson, Thomas. *Papers*. Princeton: Princeton University Press, 1950.

———. *Writings*. The Library of America. New York: Literary Classics of the United States, distributed by Viking Press, 1984.

Jefferson, Thomas, and Pierre Samuel Du Pont. *Correspondence between Thomas Jefferson and Pierre Samuel Du Pont De Nemours, 1798–1817*. Boston and New York: Houghton Mifflin, 1930.

Jenkins, Paul, and United States. *We the People: The Declaration of Independence, 1776, the Constitution of the United States, 1787, the Bill of Rights, 1791*. Paris: Ann Reeves and Edouard Weiss, 1987.

Johnson, Joshua. *Joshua Johnson's Letterbook 1771–1774: Letters from a Merchant in London to His Partners in Maryland*. Publications–London Record Society V 15. London: London Record Society, 1979.

Kennedy, John F. *Profiles in Courage*. New York: Harper, 1956.

Kerber, Linda K. "Science in the Early Republic: The Society for the Study of Natural Philosophy." *The William and Mary Quarterly* 29.2 (1972): 263–80.

Kerber, Linda K., and Walter John Morris. "Politics and Literature: The Adams Family and the Port Folio." *The William and Mary Quarterly* 23.3 (1966): 450–76.

Kerr, Laura. *Louisa: The Life of Mrs. John Quincy Adams*. New York: Funk & Wagnalls Co., 1964.

Kirker, Harold, and James Kirker. *Bulfinch's Boston, 1787–1817*. New York: Oxford University Press, 1964.

Kurtz, Stephen G. *The Presidency of John Adams; the Collapse of Federalism, 1795–1800*. Philadelphia: University of Pennsylvania Press, 1957.

Leish, Kenneth W. *The American Heritage Pictorial History of the Presidents of the United States*. New York: American Heritage Pub. Co.; distributed by Simon and Schuster, 1968.

Levin, Phyllis Lee. *Abigail Adams: A Biography*. New York: St. Martin's Press, 1987.

Lipsky, George A. *John Quincy Adams, His Theory and Ideas*. New York: Crowell, 1950.

Madison, James. *Writings*. Library of America. New York: Library of America, 1999.

Malone, Duman ed. *Correspondence Between Thomas Jefferson and Pierre Samuel du Pont de Nemours, 1789–1817*. Boston: Houghton Mifflin, 1930.

Maier, Pauline. *Ratification: The People Debate the Constitution, 1787–1788*. New York: Simon & Schuster, 2010.

Marshall, H. E. *This Country of Ours; the Story of the United States*. New York: George H. Doran, 1917.

Massachusetts Historical Society. *John Adams & a "Signal Tryumph": The Beginning of 200 Years of American-Dutch Friendship*. Boston: Massachusetts Historical Society, 1982.

Meacham, Jon. *Thomas Jefferson: The Art of Power*. New York: Random House, 2012.

Meyer, Sheldon. *American Places: Encounters with History: A Celebration of Sheldon Meyer*. Oxford: Oxford University Press, 2000.

Miles, Edwin A. "President Adams' Billiard Table." *The New England Quarterly* 45.1 (1972): 31–43.

Minnigerode, Meade. *Some American Ladies; Seven Informal Biographies*. New York: G.P. Putnam's Sons, 1926.

Morgan, Edmund S., and Helen M. Morgan. *The Stamp Act Crisis; Prologue to Revolution*. Rev. ed. New York: Collier Books, 1963.

Morris, Richard Brandon, and Jeffrey Brandon Morris, eds. *Encyclopedia of American History*. New York: Harper & Row, 1976.

Morris, Walter J. "John Quincy Adams's German Library, with a Catalog of His German Books." *Proceedings of the American Philosophical Society* 118.4 (1974): 321–33.

Morse, John Torrey, Jr. *John Quincy Adams.* American Statesmen. Standard Library ed. Boston, MA: Houghton Mifflin, 1899.

Murray, William Vans, and John Quincy Adams. *Letters of William Vans Murray to John Quincy Adams, 1797–1803.* Washington D.C.: Reprint from the Annual Report of the American Historical Association for 1912, 1914.

Nagel, Paul C. *Descent from Glory: Four Generations of the John Adams Family.* New York: Oxford University Press, 1983.

———. *The Adams Women: Abigail and Louisa Adams, Their Sisters and Daughters.* New York: Oxford University Press, 1987.

———. *John Quincy Adams: A Public Life, a Private Life.* New York: Knopf, 1997.

O'Brien, Michael. *Henry Adams and the Southern Question.* Mercer University Lamar Memorial Lectures. Athens: University of Georgia Press, 2005.

———. *Mrs. Adams in Winter: A Journey in the Last Days of Napoleon.* New York: Farrar, Straus and Giroux, 2010.

Oliver, Andrew. *Portraits of John Quincy Adams and His Wife.* The Adams Papers Series IV: Portraits. Cambridge, Mass.: Belknap Press of Harvard University Press, 1970.

Paine, Thomas. *Rights of Man.* London: J.M Dent & Sons, 1969.

Papenfuse, Edward C. *In Pursuit of Profit: The Annapolis Merchants in the Era of the American Revolution, 1763–1805.* Maryland Bicentennial Studies. Baltimore: Johns Hopkins University Press, 1975.

Parini, Jay. *Promised Land: Thirteen Books That Changed America.* New York: Doubleday, 2008.

———. *The Last Station: A Novel of Tolstoy's Final Year.* New York: Anchor Books, 2009.

Parsons, Lynn H. *John Quincy Adams.* American Profiles. Madison, Wis.: Madison House, 1998.

Plumer, William. *William Plumer's Memorandum of Proceedings in the United States Senate, 1803–1807.* University of Michigan Publications Humanistic Papers. New York: The Macmillan Company, 1923.

Portolano, Marlana. "John Quincy Adams's Rhetorical Crusade for Astronomy." *Isis* 91.3 (2000): 480–503.

Quincy, Eliza Susan. *Memoir of the Life of Eliza S. M. Quincy.* Boston: J. Wilson & Son, 1861.

Quincy, Josiah. *Memoir of the Life of John Quincy Adams.* Boston: Crosby, Nichols, Lee, 1860.

Richards, Leonard L. *The Life and Times of Congressman John Quincy Adams.* New York: Oxford University Press, 1986.

Roof, Katharine Metcalf. *Colonel William Smith and Lady.* Boston: Houghton Mifflin, 1929.

Rorabaugh, W. J. *The Alcoholic Republic, an American Tradition.* New York: Oxford University Press, 1979.

Ross, William G. "The Legal Career of John Quincy Adams." *Akron Law Review* 23 Spring (1990): 415–53.

Royall, Anne Newport. *Sketches of History, Life, and Manners, in the United States.* New Haven, 1826.

Russell, Francis. *Adams, an American Dynasty*. New York: American Heritage: distributed by McGraw-Hill, 1976.

Samuels, Ernest. *The Young Henry Adams*. Cambridge: Harvard Univ. Press, 1948.

Schama, Simon. *Patriots and Liberators: Revolution in the Netherlands, 1780–1813*. New York: Knopf, 1977.

———. *Citizens: A Chronicle of the French Revolution*. New York: Knopf, 1989.

Schiff, Stacy. *A Great Improvisation: Franklin, France, and the Birth of America*. New York: Henry Holt, 2005.

Seilhamer, George O. *History of the American Theater: New Foundations 1792–1797*. Philadelphia: Globe Printing House, 1891.

Sharp, Allen. "Presidents as Supreme Court Advocates: Before and after the White House." *Journal of Supreme Court History* 28.2 (2003): 116–44.

Shepherd, Jack. *Cannibals of the Heart: A Personal Biography of Louisa Catherine and John Quincy Adams*. New York: McGraw-Hill, 1980.

———. "Seeds of the Presidency: The Capitol Schemes of John Quincy Adams." *Horticulture* January 1983: 38–47.

Skolnik, Richard. *1803; Jefferson's Decision; the United States Purchases Louisiana*. N.Y.: Chelsea House, 1969.

Smollett, Tobias George. *The Adventures of Peregrine Pickle*. London: George Routledge & Sons Ltd., 1890.

Sparks, Jared, ed. *The Diplomatic Correspondence of the American Revolution*. 12 vols. Boston: N. Hale and Gray & Bowen, 1829.

Stevenson, Elizabeth. *Henry Adams, a Biography*. New York: Macmillan, 1955.

Thompson, Robert R. "John Quincy Adams, Apostate: From "Outrageous Federalist" to "Republican Exile," 1801–1809." *Journal of the Early Republic* 11.2 (1991): 161–83.

Tucker, Louis Leonard. *Worthington Chauncey Ford: Scholar and Adventurer*. Boston: Northeastern University Press, 2001.

Unger, Harlow G. *Lafayette*. New York: John Wiley & Sons, 2002.

Wagner, Vern. *The Suspension of Henry Adams; a Study of Manner and Matter*. Detroit: Wayne State University Press, 1969.

Washington, George. *The Writings of George Washington; Being His Correspondence, Addresses, Messages, and Other Papers, Official and Private*. Ed. Sparks, Jared. 12 vols. New York Harper & Brothers, 1847.

———. *The Writings of George Washington from the Original Manuscript Sources, 1745–1799*. Ed. Fitzpatrick, John Clement. 39 vols. Washington D.C.: U.S. Government Printing Office, 1931.

Wharton, Francis, ed. *The Revolutionary Diplomatic Correspondence of the United States*. 6 vols. Washington: Government Printing Office, 1889.

Wilentz, Sean. *The Rise of American Democracy: Jefferson to Lincoln*. 1st ed. New York: Norton, 2005.

Wills, Garry. *Henry Adams and the Making of America*. Boston: Houghton Mifflin, 2005.

Wood, Gordon S. *The Radicalism of the American Revolution*. New York: A.A. Knopf, 1992.

INDEX